Plays from
The New York
Shakespeare Festival

357 W 20th St., NY NY 10011
212 627-1055

Plays from The New York Shakespeare Festival

First printing: September 1986

ISBN: 0–88145–036–7

Design by Marie Donovan
Set in Aster by Rainsford Type, Inc., Ridgefield, CT
Printed and bound by BookCrafters, Chelsea, MI

Contents

Introduction

To say that art reflects life may seem to smack of cliché; it is, however, undeniable that we are the product of our personal and collective environment, and in the artistic expression of writers of any given generation there exists a symbiotic relationship between what is lived and what is perceived.

Each of the six plays in this volume came to my attention in a different way and in different years. They did not appear in a file labeled "political", "avant-garde", or "socially relevant". Indeed they are a mixed bag in style and in content.

The ultimate test of a script, for me, is the singular vision of the writer and my own instinct as a producer and theatergoer. Without exception, all six of these plays were produced by the New York Shakespeare Festival because the writing was exemplary; that is to say, these playwrights shot straight from the hip. I felt that if they could touch a nerve in me then I should take them on and allow their voices to reach the ears of the public. This is the natural movement from the subjective to the objective, from the mind to the stage.

The chronology of the plays as they were produced is: *Short Eyes* (1974), *The Leaf People* (1975), *The Time Trial* (1975), *for colored girls who have considered suicide/when the rainbow is enuf* (1976), *Streamers* (1976), and *Necessary Ends* (1983). So then, chronologically speaking—

Short Eyes was written by Miguel Piñero, a writer of considerable talent and the first Puerto Rican to win the coveted Drama Critic's Circle Award for this piercing drama that dealt with the realities of the prison system. Piñero, having been an inmate himself, wrote from his personal experiences, and it was this honesty as well as his cleanness of style that first struck me. After a successful run at the Public Theater, I moved the play to Lincoln Center's Beaumont stage. The institutional nature of the Beaumont seemed to contradict the terse street writing of Piñero; this is a man who pulls no punches either in ideas or language. Some of the economically and socially upscale audience, unwilling or unable to admit to the play's authenticity, walked out during the performance. But *Short Eyes* was acknowledged as one of the strongest statements of the 1974 theater season, on or Off-Broadway.

I became aware of Dennis Reardon when he sent a play to me in the early 70's titled *The Happiness Cage*, a powerful drama about psychological and medical experimentation carried out by the Army on American soldiers, none of whom were aware that they were being tested. It was beautifully and extraordinarily written. At the time, Dennis still had six more months of required service in the US Army in Korea. I wrote his commanding officer requesting an early release in order that we could properly do this play; surprisingly, he agreed. After this play, Dennis presented me with *The Leaf People*, a play about an Amazon tribe thriving for centuries outside the mainstream of Euro-American culture, and now suddenly threatened by extinction with the encroachment of the "Coca-Cola culture."

Dennis created an actual "artificial" language for these people and made it accessible to the audience via "interpreters" suspended in glass booths above the stage. Not a commerical success, *The Leaf People* was a very strange, exotic, and powerful play whose validity, unfortunately, is still an issue. I regard this work as one of the finest I've produced.

In *The Time Trial*, Jack Gilhooey, another exceptional talent, presented us with a cultural experience quite different from that of the average civilized theatergoer. Yet the predicament of a gang of smalltown, Southern outcasts struck me as profoundly human. Speaking in a language as brutal and quick-witted as any New York street person's, they spend the day drinking and watching cars circle a race track. In many ways the play became a powerful account of lives going in circles; of drugs, sex, and "speech" going nowhere. For these people, small-town America has become a raw, bloody place with no way of fitting in or getting out; a kind of destructive maze containing nothing of lasting value. It's a mordant and unsparing work written without apology and, in an odd way, aimed directly at us.

When I first encountered ntozake shange I saw a very nervous young black woman with a ring through her nose and I thought, "I'll *never* be able to communicate with her!" I was wrong. *for colored girls...* was first produced by Woodie King, Jr. at the New Federal Theater under the direction of Oz Scott. ntozake insisted that it should not be called a play or a musical but a "choreopoem", probably the least commercially viable term I could imagine. The language was most certainly poetry and also drama of the highest poignancy. It was set to minimal music, song, and dance. Her poems were about black women who spoke of their relationships with black men and their struggles to maintain their identity in the midst of cultural and personal turmoil. When I brought *colored girls* to the Public, it was enthusiastically received by both critics and audiences. While obviously a black theater piece, its wide appeal compelled me to take the chance and move it to Broadway, where I gambled that it could reach a larger and more racially mixed audience. The gamble paid off and the "choreopoem" played to sold-out houses at the Booth Theatre for over two years.

ntozake's perceptions are matched by her beautifully poetic sensibilities which made what could have been simply dramatic soliloquies into vibrant theatrical life.

In *Streamers*, David Rabe shares the gut-level veracity of Miguel Piñero and the poetic insight of ntozake shange. Where Piñero wrote of his own prison experience, Rabe wrote of his wartime experiences in Vietnam. His language ranged from the gutter to the farthest edge of poetry. This odd hybrid of playwriting created such extraordinary fireworks on stage that on a dozen or so occasions when I watched the play, I had to turn my eyes away at the payoff—it was truly one of the most agonizing dramas ever written in the language. I believe that *Streamers*, beautifully directed by Mike Nichols, was successful because although it dealt with Vietnam, it didn't address itself to the frontline battles in Vietnam, but rather to a training camp where there was no "them", only "us". *Streamers* was a hurricane of a play delivered with credibility and veracity.

The term "character" was coined with Marvin Cohen in mind. A gentle observer of the unpredictable and slightly absurd, Marvin has a fondness for mankind that is unmistakably his own. Sometimes I think of him as a comedian-chronicler standing at the center, his head turned slightly toward your line of speaking to accommodate his hearing aid. *Necessary Ends* is the sum of these parts, as Marvin positions and repositions people within relationships, that ever-aimed ear to the pun and odd bits of conversation, as though he's walking slowly through a cocktail party. The strength of his writing stems from his baroque sense of humor and his ability to see both the world and himself as wonderfully delightful miscreants.

I've shared just a few of my opinions on the six plays you are about to read. Each of these writers has a very special place in my memory. There will always be writers with incredible philosophies or writers whose styles and expressions reinterpret the world anew. It is rare, however, when these two qualities reside in the same person. Please enjoy, as I have, these remarkable plays that follow with the knowledge that in each play, these two qualities remain and thrive, side by side.

New York   JOSEPH PAPP
September 1986

A Note from the Publisher

Joseph Papp correctly points out that this is a "mixed bag" of plays. Our first step in choosing these six was to think about the type of work for which the New York Shakespeare Festival is best known. The most accurate term we could come up with to describe the NYSF's collective creative persona was "exciting eclecticism", which is how we arrived at our "mixed bag."

Obvious choices were *Short Eyes*, *for colored girls . . .*, and *Streamers*. (*A Chorus Line* would have been a natural, but obtaining the rights could have taken years.) Miguel Piñero, ntozake shange, and David Rabe are all writers with powerful artistic visions. In addition, we believe that *Streamers* shows David Rabe to be one of America's major playwrights.

Our one provisio for the other three plays was that they have no prior publication history. It makes no sense to print a book of already available plays; as publisher we have the responsibility to expose the public to works that otherwise might be lost forever. There is no question that Dennis Reardon, Jack Gilhooley, and Marvin Cohen are all extremely talented. This is demonstrated not only by their plays in this volume, but by the formidable body of work each has accumulated. Naturally, we hope producers will think they are as interesting as we do, and that these plays will enjoy a long life.

CHRISTOPHER GOULD

Marvin Cohen

Necessary Ends

An Unnecessary Autobiographical
Pre-beginning to *Necessary Ends*

Necessary Ends was a collaboration with the director James Milton. He suggested many wholesale elaborate changes, scene by scene, from my original shorter version, with the result as published here.

Necessary Ends was privately auditioned to Mr. Papp and his brain staff, with Wallace Shawn, Andre Gregory, Angela Pietropinto, and Gretchen Van Riper in the four roles.

Necessary Ends is still a "virgin" (in case some theater company wants to premiere it), because its run at the Public Theater was a workshop production, with no official "opening" and no invited press reviewers.

Earlier, James Milton had adapted, from two unpublished novels by me, a play, *The Don Juan and the Non-Don Juan*. It was produced in London, but is still a *U.S.* "virgin" (in case some theater company wants to U.S.-premiere it). It had staged readings at the Public Theater, N.Y.U.'s Loeb Student Center, and Los Angeles' Groundlings Theater. Appearing in it at one time or another were Richard Dreyfuss, Keith Carradine, Wallace Shawn, Jill Eikenberry, Lewis J. Stadlen, Mimi Kennedy, Larry Pine, Gretchen Van Riper, and Alma Cuervo.

The newest "virgin" (in case, etc.) is *Topsy-Turvy*, a recent collaboration with the playwright and director Tom Riccio. It's about to be workshopped at the Cleveland Playhouse.

Speaking of Cleveland, I was born and grew up in Brooklyn, the Bensonhurst part. For the last many years, I've been living in Manhattan's Lower East Side. I worked in an odd assortment of different jobs in occupational miscellany. I only got about halfway through college, so no degree. But by being a "published author," I was able to conduct writing workshops, first for college undergraduates at City College (C.C.N.Y.), and then for adult- or continuing-education programs at Queens College, Hofstra, Adelphi, C.W. Post (currently), and the New School (currently).

For a while in the sixties I lived in London. A sort of episodic novel, *The Self-Devoted Friend*, had been rejected by New Directions in New York, but in London a publisher got New Directions to share the production (thus reducing expenses for both houses). The same two ocean-divided houses also published *The Monday Rhetoric of the Love Club, and Other Parables*. Books by other publishers: *Fables at Life's Expense*; *The Inconvenience of Living* (collection of short fictions); *Baseball the Beautiful* (eulogistic essays on philosophy/baseball); *Others, Including Morstive Sternbump* (a novel); and a collection of fictions by Gull Books, *Aesthetics in Life and Art. Existence in Function and Essence. And Whatever Else is Important, too*.

One book, *The Hard Life of a Stone*, has been rejected by publishers on the grounds that the title would render it unsuitable for a paperback edition. My offer to change the title did not soften the publishers' hearts. (Even cardiologists, who call spades spades, wouldn't call those hearts hearts.)

That last paragraph was the only fib of this self-autobiography—I swear on a stack of pancakes.

Currently, I'm being guided by two literary friends in putting together a miscellany cross-section selection sampler of (from a small pile) my book-published pieces, as well as (from a larger pile) my periodical- and anthology-published pieces, and (from the overwhelmingly largest pile) my unpublished pieces: all com-*piled* into a sort of *Marvin Cohen Omnibus*, of unknown route. If any publisher....

Currently, I'm trying to collaborate with a composer (former oboe-ist) in a musical play/opera: My words to his music. Problem is, I can't read music. So he pianos his song music onto a cassette, including abstracting the melody; so then from dummy-lyrics and repeated re-hearings, I arrive at lyrics, from which he criticizes and I revise accordingly. If any impressario would like to risk an adventurous sum of money....

After, as a result of, living in London for a while in the sixties, I've been staying there for a spell of practically every summer since, as an annual visit, mainly extensively social.

I also have a nice social life in New York, flavored and peppered by a helpful sprinkle of parties.

My favorite thing in life is to hit a thrown ball with a bat. I've been doing a little of that in London (cricket), and more in New York/Brooklyn (baseball bat on softball; and broomstick bat on tennis balls in schoolyards).

The dread of no longer being able to connect bat to ball (even in old-age imagination) is behind the play printed in this book, *Necessary Ends*, which is based on the dread of that notoriously bad old life-ender, Death. Death deservedly has been given a bad press, and no wonder.

Other passions of which death is an ugly enemy-in-the-wings are Gilbert and Sullivan, and the human voice in general, especially to Mozart. Also, watching professional football on T.V. My happiest pride of triumph is when the Yankees end a season by winning pennant, League Championship Series, and World Series. Since I identify with them in indissoluble oneness, it's as if I've been elected King of the World.

If I *were* King of the World, I'd aim to alleviate as many human woes and miseries as possible, wherever people live: to lift as many prospects as possible, with the least long-term or short-term cost and damage to others.

I've been trying to figure out life philosophically, meaning what makes people psychologically tick. It has to do with what people want and then their *learning not to want* when such wanting is shown to be of no avail, or no longer of any avail; and their developing new wants that do have more probable hopeful possibilities of getting themselves, by the outside world of mainly people but including one's body itself, co-operated with.

(No piece of writing should ever end with "with." Such an effect of undignified irregularity may well be dispensed with.)

(In order, therefore, not to end this car-biography—I mean auto-biography—with "with," I'll go on:)

Life seems very strange, in that so many people are, and were, living it. As only one of its current practitioners, I'm modestly put in place. I'm numbered, among those numerous current practioners, until my number is up.

Any number can play. But my playing declines, as I get numb-er.

Necessary Ends ran at the Public's Lu Esther Hall from December 12–26, 1982, for a total of 20 performances, under the direction of James Milton, with the following cast:

Georgia	Alma Cuervo
Burt	Larry Pine
Jasper	Bill Sadler
Ginger	Gretchen Van Ryper

The Scenery was constructed by Jim Clayburgh, the Costumes by Amanda J. Klein, the Lighting by John Gisondi, and the Music by Robert Dennis.

Characters

BURT (boyfriend of GEORGIA, friend of JASPER)
GEORGIA (girlfriend of BURT)
JASPER (boyfriend of GINGER, friend of BURT)
GINGER (girlfriend of JASPER)

Time: Now

Place: Optional

> "Of all the wonders that I yet have heard,
> It seems to me most strange that men should fear;
> Seeing that death, a necessary end,
> Will come when it will come."
>   (*Julius Caesar*, Act II, Scene II)

Scene One

(The getting-into-bed ritual of BURT *and* GEORGIA. *This could include (but not necessarily) brushing of teeth, listening to radio, undressing and getting into night clothes, reading, eating, playing cards or a game, etc. Action should establish the practicality and precision of* BURT *and* GEORGIA *(though hers is inorganic, hence she might have a lapse or two). Couple then turn off lamp light (beside bed), for lovemaking interlude, which audience can hear. Something is wrong, however, and light is switched back on.* GEORGIA *puts on nightgown,* BURT *puts on pajamas. Both are sitting up in their one bed.)*

GEORGIA: What's the matter?

BURT: I'm worried about Jasper.

GEORGIA: But Burt—why?

BURT: He appears to be crazy.

GEORGIA: On what evidence?

BURT: He wants to end death.

GEORGIA: In that event, we're *all* crazy.

BURT: You mistake me. I mean, Jasper thinks he can pull it off!

GEORGIA: Pull *what* off?

BURT: The trick of eliminating death.

GEORGIA: You mean he's *serious*!?

BURT: Yes, he's as serious as . . .

GEORGIA: Death?

BURT: I'm afraid so. He's also mad at me.

GEORGIA: What did you do to him?

BURT: I was skeptical. I doubted he could do it.

GEORGIA: Do what—end death?

BURT: Precisely.

GEORGIA: *(Enthusiastically, hopefully)* But Burt—what if he's right!?

BURT: Right? About what?

GEORGIA: That he *can* end death! Oh, Burt—what that could mean! Just think! *(Takes* BURT*'s hand in hers)* We'd be alive, always!

BURT: *(Skeptically)* How lovely, Georgia. It's just *too* romantic—to be true.

GEORGIA: *(Hurt)* Burt! Don't you love me?!

BURT: Of course!

GEORGIA: Forever?

BURT: Naturally.

GEORGIA: *Not* so naturally. Jasper must succeed, first.

BURT: You have a point there. Rather, *two* points. Or rather, *three*.

GEORGIA: Three? *What* three?

BURT: There's *you*.

GEORGIA: *(Counting on her fingers.)* That's one.

BURT: There's *me*.

GEORGIA: *(Counting on her fingers.)* That's two.

BURT: There's our *love*: undying.

GEORGIA: *(Awed)* Love undying! Do you think he can do it?

BURT: Do what? End death?

GEORGIA: Yes, of life and love!

BURT: Not a chance!

GEORGIA: *(Disappointed)* You mean he can't?

BURT: Be realistic.

GEORGIA: *(Weeping)* Goodbye, love.

BURT: *(Clutching her closely)* But not yet!

GEORGIA: *(Weeping)* But *one* day. *(Sobs violently.)*

BURT: Calm yourself. It's Jasper's fault.

GEORGIA: For what?

BURT: For falsely getting your hopes up. You accepted—or were resigned to—our death before. Now, you're all upset.

GEORGIA: I'm sorry. *(She composes herself.)* He's crazy, then?

BURT: Not only that, but vindictively so. Listen to this: He's expelled us from inclusion in his immortality-for-all feast: You and I to be the sole exceptions to an otherwise democratically unexclusive eternal-life gift for every human universally alive enough to be a perpetually grateful recipient of Jasper's landmark endowment: a vital revolution to liven up man's long evolution.

GEORGIA: But Burt—in such largesse, why are *we alone* to be dreadfully cursed as exceptions?

BURT: To punish me, for it was my sin to doubt.

GEORGIA: Doubt that he could...?

BURT: Yes, end...

GEORGIA: ...finally for ever...

BURT: ...Death.

GEORGIA: But that's cruel—he's your friend!

BURT: No longer. I'm guilty of a high crime: actively sabotaging his proposed abolishment of Death, by virtue of treacherous skepticism, in not lending my moral support. *(Ironically)* But if his invention works out in spite of my "sabotage," then his revenge shall take effect: to deprive you, me, our love—all three—of the everlasting bounty of that impossible invention's humane worldwide munificence in miraculous salvation of all souls physically entire, save ours.

GEORGIA: So we'd be out in the cold?

BURT: Such is Jasper's threat—or, rather, pronouncement. *(Apprehensively looks at her.)* Georgia—*please* don't credit it!

GEORGIA: *(With a glazed look of determined faith)* Jasper passes your understanding. You did wrong, withholding your support. At such great cost!

BURT: At *no* cost, since he won't do what's so strictly impossible.

GEORGIA: *(Poignant, tragic)* But what if it's not!? Our love leaps high with life's blessing. To lose those irreplaceable prizes of love and lives— *(Accusingly)* merely because you doubt! *(Desperately pleading)* Burt, Burt, retract that doubt! Go back to Jasper, and beg his forgiveness! For all our eternal sakes!

BURT: Georgia—you're no more sane or rational than poor Jasper! Surely you can't believe—

GEORGIA: *(Fervently)* But he *might* do it! Impossible or not, he *could* do it!

BURT: *(Defiantly)* Are you on *his* side—or *mine*?

GEORGIA: How can I tell? Yours is reason's side—cold, stoical resignation, with Death waiting surely at the end. *His (Glowingly, fervently, in a leap of piety)* is magic's side, that defies reason by leaping past scientific barriers of realism: the reward for such belief is *(Ecstatically)* Eternity! *(Suddenly switching to worldly suavity.) That* appeal surely is not without a certain undeniable charm?

BURT: Hedging, you want your cake and yet must eat it. How does this dilemma resolve itself?

GEORGIA: Bring before me the discussion you had with Jasper. Set back alive that scene, re-enact its dialogue, as I sit in judgment, choosing between an eternal soul— *(Wistfully ecstatic)* if possible!—or *(Sternly, bravely)* the damnation of cold reason's consoling resignation.

BURT: *(As lights fade)* Well, it was like this. Earlier this very evening itself, I ate out with Jasper. So agitated was he, that—most untypically— he even left some food on his plate. I forget what denomination of food it was, but that's irrelevant to my impression that poor Jasper did seem off his feed. This impression was confirmed when, later, walking along matching strides with me to our club for an after-dinner drink, he would occasionally pause to question the night's air with some pathetic up- ward glance, looking, for all the world, like a man distracted by the inner disorder of trouble. On arrival at our club, he took familiar bear- ings there, then proceeded to unravel, bit by bit, what his agitation state strangely owed itself to.

(During this last speech, BURT changes into the clothes he wore to dinner with JASPER. Then he walks to the set of JASPER's living room, even as GEORGIA watches from their bed. She remains as witness to BURT's enactment of flashback, the trans- ition to which may be accompanied by effects and/or music.)

Scene Two

(This scene is told through BURT's point of view; hence, he makes himself appear to be brilliant, realistic, rational: a logician/scientist of humanity and vision. He portrays JASPER as a fanatic, a religious nut completely out of touch with reality.)

(Some time shortly before Scene One. JASPER and BURT, sitting (at conversational distance from each other) in living room of former's apartment. JASPER looks in- nocent, unworldly. Burt seems more self-possessed and prepared with "all the an- swers"; low-keyed, often cynical, tastefully negative.)

JASPER: The world is in dreadful shape. What's it coming to?

BURT: Who knows? But once it gets to where it's coming to, it won't stop *there*—it'll plunge right on: right into another generation. You and I, meanwhile, by that time, will be dead.

JASPER: That's what I really hate about life—*mortality*!

BURT: Your hating it is a good sign—shows your values are in the right place.

JASPER: I'm serious, Burt. Now, listen. *(Pause. Recites following two paragraphs with deliberateness and elocution.)*

Something must really be done about death. It's been going much too far, with outrageous consumptive audacity, these very many years! The lives it's claimed! Snatched by so many snares, gobbled up by all matter, manner, and ruse of catastrophe by nature, internal disease, or man-devised means.

Before it's too late, it'll take us all! This scandal is escalating, by outlandish degrees. If we don't soon arrest it—oh!

BURT: *(Reciting dramatically)*
Eventually, you will die.
Not to pop into the sky,
but down in the ground to lie,
with not the slightest hint of "why."

JASPER: Mock me if you like, Burt. But Death darkly undergoes its concealment: stealthy, patient. Though instantaneously everywhere, Death lurks hidden within and resists all subtle onslaughts to free human life of . . . its secret undoer.

BURT: Secret?! Death is out in the open. By now, it's hardly a secret. Otherwise, why all those long faces you see in the streets and on the buses? They've all caught on, about this death business.

JASPER: Yes, people are dearly fond of life; in time they've learned to hold life as their dearest prize. Nothing's so valuable as each new moment, so fleeting—

BURT: *(Interrupting)* Oh, not so fleeting. Sometimes life lags and flags so slow, as dull monotony endures to tedious boredom. Even *with* our mortal awareness.

(BURT yawns, illustrating his last point; and he might stretch, get up, move about, do something or other, before sitting down again.)

JASPER: But Burt—there's something I must tell you.

BURT: *(Urbanely)* What on Earth can it be? Please, spare me any further suspense. Life is tricky enough, without the upset of unnecessary palpitations. What's on your sleeve—or up your mind? Spill it!

JASPER: Attend: bend your ear: I do intend to outdo Death, at his own game, cut him off, and purge life of its own worst enemy.

Such precisely is the mission I was brought into the world for: my calling I've only just discovered: my ordained task *(Enunciating with deliberateness to emphasize inner rhyme repetition of four "term" sounds.)*, by divine determination: I'm granted a term to terminate our termination.

BURT: Old friend, forgive me: I completely fail to understand.

JASPER: Take me seriously, now. Come under my spell.

BURT: I'd have to be under your spell, to take you seriously.

JASPER: Then let me spell it out for you! It's only too simple. The worst thing about life is that it must end. Why "must" it end? I declare an end to that ending. Death has been in business so long, it must by now have outlived its original purpose—whatever that might have been.

BURT: *(Making JASPER's last phrase into a query and answering it.)* Death's purpose? Shall I tell you? To unclutter the stage and unblock the sun, and clean the halls, and clear the decks, for the free access of newborn generations that come to inherit the works that get passed on to them by those who conveniently leave the stage tidy for the next lot to use.

Be reasonable, dear Jasper. Were death to be abolished (as though it could!), life then would immediately cease to be that dear, lovely, transient, precious, movingly cherished spark of invaluable commodity, unbearably tragic, prized infinitely for its very draining away, beat by beat, as slowly we witness our increasing failure to be a match for a world that gradually fails us, the world we slowly lose as it loses us. Were you to deprive life of its own gradual loss (as though you could!), life would become a contemptuously cheap, banal, wretched, common, tawdry enterprise, open to anyone's ambitious hustle and shoddy self-seeking. Lacking its highest asset—mortality—life would lose value and self-respect; would desire to discard itself: the irony being, that without death, life would find its own shedding difficult to the damning edge of impossibility.

JASPER: Is it possible—what I've heard? Is this the support of a long friendship? Of the whole unwillingly mortal world, are you alone—my old friend—to openly oppose my inspired defiance of death?

BURT: Not I alone. What about our poor undertakers and gravediggers? They have families to support, mouths to feed. Are they to praise you while you deprive them of livelihoods and increase the dismally staggering figures of mass unemployment, thus swelling our swollen economy by increasing the involuntary recruits in the vast, useless army of the out-of-work?

JASPER: *(Impatiently)* Oh, fooey! Cut out the sophistry of your skeptical rhetoric and sour, negative arguments. I appeal to your practical nature, in down-to-earth terms. The main thing is first to do the deed—end death.

BURT: Just like that? How simple! End death? Oh, my! This subject, since time immemorial, has already been thoroughly covered, picked through, and worn out by discussion, fretful worry, and intermittent anxiety. Yet no clueful hint, to date, has been yielded even to patient genius, to saintly brilliance. Then *you* come along, with tonight's agitation that hindered your dinner appetite. You spout a brain-*r*ave: "Do the deed—end death." Historically, the loftiest aim. But *how*, dear boy? Just how?

JASPER: *(Pompously)* Mundane matters of method are but irrelevant vulgarities, when set beside the sublime glory of my pure goal itself. The blazing zeal of faith shall, in its own sweet time, reveal the pedestrian practical matter of mere means. Nor shall I demean, by meanly telling of means, the dear divinity of my faith.

BURT: Let me skeptically persist in asking: What's your method? Alchemistry? Black witchcraft? Mumbo jumbo? Astrological revelation? Revealed truth, by divine visitation?

I know you, Jasper. You're smart in some things, but dumb in science. To dust Death off the human map without resorting to magic of a supernatural kind, you'd have to be up on biology, anatomy, physics, chemistry, organic molecular structure, medicine, right up to the borderline of mystery itself.

JASPER: *(Admitting)* I *am* scientifically ignorant, that's true.

BURT: True? Not merely true! It's a handicap, considering what you propose to do.

JASPER: Handicaps *can* be overcome. They're not all insurmountable.

BURT: *(With heated emphasis)* But in *this* case, your optimism would be the very height of certifiable folly! You've hatched an unworkable scheme. It's unutterably implausible.

JASPER: How do *you* know? Are you an expert?

BURT: *I*'m not. But others are, or were. There've been plenty. Genius has been in no short supply: Population and time, on our rotund global sphere charged with history, have abundantly seen to that. Great minds have abounded. They've tackled many problems, plowed into the thickets of mystery on pioneering tractors that cultivated wilderness into hygienic sophistication and refined our primitive fear. Longevity has inched ahead; yet Death itself, with its borders mildly retracted, slightly retrenched, remains ever grimly, monstrously, mythically, in an ironbound control over the fragile, swaying destiny of each proud mortal.

JASPER: But Burt—that was before *I* was reckoned on.

BURT: Are you, then, of Christlike proportion, to historically create a new tide on our astronomical surface?

JASPER: I'm a major figure. My advent is nigh. I've arrived.

BURT: And with you—the era of the immortals?

JASPER: *(Darkly)* We'll see.

BURT: As you're not getting any younger, you'd better get to work.

JASPER: Don't harass me. I only conceived my plan this evening. Why the rush? What's to be, comes on apace. It's in the works. We're swooped down on. And you can help.

BURT: *(Incredulous)* Now really! *I*?! How?

JASPER: By having faith.

BURT: Jasper, you're being exceedingly silly.

JASPER: Don't bully me. Have faith.

BURT: Death is not a person to be conquered. It's a built-in condition—

JASPER: *(Cutting in; violently)* Shut up! Have faith!

BURT: Tempered by pity and loyalty, I patiently refrain from exploding at the driven pathos of your drivel. I contend that faith—in which you put your hope—does *not*, contrary to that hope, conquer all.

JASPER: *Prove* that blasphemy, you sacrilegious cur!

BURT: *(Lightheartedly, despite* JASPER'*s outbursts of violent insult.)* A world-famous example is Joan of Arc, whose burning zeal led to her own burning squeal. Her saint-like faith didn't keep her goose from being cooked and done to a turn, giving her a fatal burn, when more than her faith was at stake. Her heroic faith led to her making an ash of herself. From a *member* of the devout, she became an *ember*. We'll go to Islam for our next example. The more Mohammed prayed, the more the mountain remained just where it was, in stony stubbornness.

The Crusades—all that human effort fueled by holy hope—ended the day of many a dazed knight with the bleak blight of an endless night.

JASPER: Are you troubling yourself to inform me that faith cannot conquer all? Don't bother dredging more examples from the teeming archives of the past. You may cite failure after failure from legend and history, the sorry lot that befell the stubborn strife of high endeavor. Argue endlessly that faith cannot conquer all. The point is: Mine *will*! *(He's been reaching a stage of turbulent frenzy and fanatical mayhem.)*

BURT: You're a holy fake.

JASPER: *(Piously)* I forgive you. You know not what you say. But you're too ignorant not to say it.

BURT: *(Still lighthearted, but generous-mindedly concerned, worried, solicitous.)* You're not even in your own control, but you're a man possessed of "a faith worse than death." Or perhaps you're stubbornly sticking to your guns in order to "save faith." You exceed your own sane boundary, and rove wildly outside the old Jasper I've known as a friend: the mock pretender of the "you" known and loved by me for years.

JASPER: *(In mounting wrath)* For your flippant attempt to misguide me, using the name of friendship unfriendily, using trust untrustworthily, to slip me evil advice to renege on my divine inspired calling—I call you my enemy, my worm in friend's guise; and I call on you to backtrack and apologize with humiliating humility.

BURT: If I don't?

JASPER: Then, I'll exclude you and your Georgia from the Eternity feast to which everyone else is warmly only too welcome. You and your love shall be the sole poor exemptions from my Universal Liberation and Salvation Program. You'll go uninvited! *(In vindictive wrath)* How I relish this pronouncement!

BURT: Jasper, please! Don't give way—

JASPER: *(Interrupting)* You dare prevent me from achieving my mission by withholding your moral support? That's sabotage—traitor! With the authority entrusted in me—from sources I prefer at this time not to divulge—I pronounce, on you and Georgia—Death!

BURT: You'd murder us?

JASPER: No: you'd live out your "normal" lifetimes—without entitlement to my New Dispensation.

BURT: Your insane delusions border on the frenzy and mayhem of a pseudo-semblance of mock violence.

JASPER: *(Amused, undaunted, superior)* What a quaint accusation! Let me remind you, my former friend, that the material deaths of you and Georgia will be automatically fatal to the spiritual *Love* that binds you two together in an enduring blaze of passion.

BURT: Whereas, the love between you and your Ginger will partake of your joint personal immortalities?

JASPER: *(His megalomania showing)* Quite! *Our* love survives, in glorious plenitude, outlasting the obsolete datedness of mere former mechanical time.

You scoff—all *you're* capable of is to be *against*. Well, *I'm* against our hitherto unbeatable adversary. Death so far has proved inevitable on the field of combat, and has gone undefeated, taking on all comers. There's where *I* come in, as history's special agent, and evolution's hidden spy. I'm Life's secret weapon, in a surprise attack. I'm on my mark, ripe and hot and raring to go—ready for the kill. I'm roused to my task, divinely guided to a firm girding of living loins placed stupendously to the test. *(Spews out)* May my great scheme survive your horrid little opposition, and greatly prevail: your death-loving venom notwithstanding!

BURT: No scheme—ineffectual dream.

JASPER: *(Livid with demonic, furious rage)* Then *die, die, die,* you—

BURT: *(Calmly interrupting)* You have strange ideas. You theorize without foundation, then accuse me of disloyalty in friendship just because I honestly proclaim my misgivings as to just how tenable your life-per-petuation proposition sincerely seems to me. As of now, your craziness has impaired our friendship. I will now leave you, to return to a happier prospect—my dear Georgia. *(Begins to start to leave. Firmly, solemnly, in grim warning.)* Alone, perhaps, you'll reconsider just what's in your power and what's not. The potent "magic" of your wish, however passionately felt, is only an unseen mental thought. Its manifestation *would* be Death's end. But that thought's *actual* manifestation is—simply put— your temporary leaving of your senses; or rather, your senses' leaving of you. Sensibly, I do too. Good-bye.

(BURT comes over to JASPER; he tries to restrain, comfort, or calm JASPER by putting his former familiar friendly arm around JASPER; but JASPER squirms out and abruptly flings the proffered embrace-arm away.)

JASPER: *(Hatefully, spiteful, loathing)* Get away!

BURT: Jasper, I fear that you're mad.

JASPER: I am—at *you!* *(While BURT leaves.)* Die, you faithless former friend turned foe: die, die, die, die: most emphatically die . . . *(In strident raucousness, obsessedly incoherent)*

(BURT has left.)

JASPER: *(Alone now; standing, shifting about, restless, resolute, determined, offended, smarting.)* He'll rue that speech: he'll eat it. May my venture succeed. On it hangs so much. Going to the moon was once a miracle: Now, it's only history.

(Upon exiting, BURT has re-entered his own bedroom, changed back to pajamas, and re-joined GEORGIA in bed in time for Scene Three. Blackout on JASPER.)

Scene Three

(BURT, in pajamas, and GEORGIA, in nightgown, both sitting up in one bed as before, at end of Scene One.)

BURT: There: that's what took place between us. I'm able to include in my thorough report his final soliloquy, having eavesdropped on it after walking out to conclude our dialogue. Scientific curiosity, and concern for a deranged old friend, justify my sneaky snooping: which also helps to round out this report I file, to completely inform you; as I abide, I hope, your verdict kind to me.

(Kisses GEORGIA, who receives it passively, or obliviously.)

GEORGIA: God!—all these years I've known Jasper—who would have expected it of him!?

(GEORGIA *means that she never would have guessed* JASPER *could ever be such a nobly brilliant visionary of courage;* BURT *mistakes her meaning: he thinks she means she never thought that* JASPER *would ever lose his mind and go crazy.*)

BURT: *(Charitably)* He's not dangerous—to himself or to anyone else. Alone, he grapples in the grip of a grandiose idea—his back turned on the collective commonplace shallow sanity of his fellow men. Let him wrestle with what has taken full possession of his deranged senses. He'll lose, and then—bowed, subdued, humble, modest, he'll return to us his friends and partake of our plain and simple aspirations, the bounty of our doomed and mortal kind.

(*Turns off bedside lamp on his side.*) Enough about *him*—it's too pathetic to think about. Let's return to each other, where it's healthier. Switch your light off, now. *(Suggestively)* Let me grope for you—and you for me—by amorous touch and feel. *(Makes advance and pass.)*

GEORGIA: *(Keeping the table lamp on her side on; totally ignoring* BURT'*s innuendo and advances.*) Oh Burt—what a sublime, supreme, noble, glorious goal Jasper is consumed by. It's too anguishing—it's wrenchingly poignant—to think that he must fail. *(Pause. In dreamlike quavering.)* But should his salvation-for-everyone scheme succeed in the face of your disbelief, Jasper has condemned us to unique deaths. Infidelity and treachery deserve no less than the death penalty. Why should my innocent life share your awful fate? I terminate, then my alliance with your coldly reasoning, irreverently rational cause; and switch to him, however fanatical or futile his storming the fortress that guards the dark secret of Death's final word over human life.

BURT: Be plain—is it him or me?

GEORGIA: Let your grief flow.

BURT: But Georgia—we're in love—remember?

GEORGIA: Our love is surely doomed if I remain with you. It's finite: We're condemned to death, without mercy, by our lord Jasper. He's my salvation—you're my damnation. I transfer affection convert to the winning side. I'm now Jasper's devotee.

BURT: You're like Jasper—out of control. Let me caution you—as in vain I cautioned him—to level down your passionate peaks from that heady atmosphere where fulfillment frantically follows and tumbles in an agonized reeling to keep up with the spiral of inflated dreams, the balloon voyage from which fulfillment must bail out and plunge—parachuteless—to its absolute wreckage on the plains of hard sense.

GEORGIA: Burt—our love is dead!

BURT: *(Alarmed)* No!—not that!

GEORGIA: *Jasper* shares my soul—you *never* can.

BURT: Georgia, you're abandoning me? Our love was developed over a long time, in organic stress and trial. Now, in a wayward perversion and superstitious dread of Death, you toss aside our sacred love, to share the faith of Jasper's folly, in your protective dash of maternal pity for so vulnerably insane a self-proclaimed Saviour of scientific ineptitude.

GEORGIA: *(During following section, she's gradually changing into street clothes and packing her small bag.)* I follow my heart! Is that clear enough? He's the better man, Burt. By far. He looks far. You accept the mean near. By your own recounting, he came to life—at your expense. Your reason paled to brittleness, while my heart went out to his soul that flowed free from the man-made manacles of petty reason that shackles itself to the miserable confines of reality.

BURT: But Jasper isn't free—he's possessed! He's chained! He's deluded!

GEORGIA: He fights Death. Cravenly, you accept it.

BURT: He's *against* Death, but how can he fight it? It's unopposable.

GEORGIA: *(In finality and loathing)* Burt, you're a physical materialist. I hate to think that a body belonging to such a mind ever made love to mine. I'll purge your body from mine, in the violated shrine of my memory, by alliance with noble Jasper!

BURT: You forget: he already loves and is loved—by Ginger.

GEORGIA: I'll easily relieve her of him.

BURT: *(Anguished)* No! Say you're joking! Put out this sudden nightmare, and let sensible light illumine our resumed sanity!

GEORGIA: Though Ginger's been with Jasper for years in living love, I'll supplant her and take over. Nothing—but nothing!—will stand in the way of my deathless newfound passion: joining missions with humanity's crusading Saviour in his vast, miraculous campaign to conquer that bane of life—the worm of death. *(Carried away)* Death: the fly in humanity's ointment. The rotten apple in mankind's contentedness barrel. The black lining on an otherwise spotless horizon. Our ancient, and still-going-strong, nemesis: Death, the dread of which has given rise to religion, metaphysics, the occult, magic, superstition, astral speculation, tragedy, drama, art, philosophy, music, literature, romance, and idealism. Death: the eternal worm slowly trickling through the core of our pathetic, body-based egoes.

(BURT tries to keep her from packing.)

GEORGIA: Out of my way, scum. You're far behind my life, already.

BURT: So Georgia—we're done?

GEORGIA: Goodbye, you defective man. I leave you to the lonely solace of your reason. Our love is now a warm corpse. In breath and beat of heart, our love has gone still. From this burial, a new love leaps for me: for Jasper, and his noble crusade to wage war in a holy match against Death, a mortal combat with me racing to be his ally or nurse or lieutenant or assistant, ministering to his distress or to his glory, in his unarmed fight to the very finish.

BURT: "Unarmed" is right. He'll prove a pushover for Death. *You'll* topple, alongside: the foolish warrior, and his silly bride.

GEORGIA: We'll see!

(In a burst of determination, GEORGIA finally bolts past BURT's physical barrier-like resistance, and exits. BURT is left standing there, sharply outlined in the shock of sudden loneliness, unloved.)

BURT: Has the world caved in and gone mad? Logic has bolted, rationality fled, leaving only me to piece together broken remnants and shattered debris. Are things totally out of hand, beyond repair? Maybe normality and order can reclaim themselves, through me alone, as their abandoned agent. Resolutely, I'll follow Georgia, trace her fugitive flight to Jasper's house; there she'll make a scene, joining nonsenses with her model in madness. I'll enter and make my own scene, to undo, forestall, or curb their compounded foolish danger. I must avert their double doom, and repair my desperate loss of Georgia: who, in her *right* mind, is my life's fit companion, my love's double—if only I can patch the leak and unleak the flood from the violent crack of her stability.

(Exits, in desperate resolve, in same direction as GEORGIA's recent flight.)

Scene Four

(Very dim lights at top, just to distinguish from blackout. Sounds of attempted lovemaking, which stop prematurely because lovemaking is unsuccessful. Pause. Lamp is switched on by JASPER: revealing bedroom of JASPER and GINGER. This bedroom is seen in typical state of disarray, giving very different feeling from BURT's bedroom.)

(Time is shortly earlier than time of preceding scene. JASPER is not as BURT had portrayed him, being far calmer, though still a visionary type. JASPER, having put on pajamas, and GINGER, having put on nightgown, are now sitting up in their bed.)

GINGER: What's the matter?

JASPER: I'm worried about Burt.

GINGER: But Jasper—why?

JASPER: He appears to be crazy.

GINGER: On what evidence?

JASPER: He won't oppose that worst of all evils—Death. In addition to which, moreover, he betrayed me by cutting off the usual loyal support I've always expected from him.

GINGER: But what does that first point have to do with the second? Really, Jasper, I'm still quite in the dark, despite your just having turned on the light.

JASPER: *(Putting his arm around* GINGER.*)* Oh, let's drop the whole complicated, confounded matter. It's beneath our tired consideration, and besides, is rather unsavory.

GINGER: Let's *not* drop this whole matter. I'm getting fascinated, if not yet intrigued. Now, what's this business between you and Burt?

JASPER: He has a phony mask of slick, level-headed confidence, on a plane of superficial materiality. His spiritual void is thinly layered over by a veneer of shallow cynicism.

GINGER: How can you so slight him—an old friend?

JASPER: He just refuses to go along with me on this new scheme I've concocted—an immensely practical, desperately needed scheme.

GINGER: *What* scheme?

JASPER: I intend to free all people from their own very worst enemy, which spoils their happiness and ruins their lives.

GINGER: And what may *that* be?

JASPER: Life's arch-rival: Death itself.

GINGER: You can't be serious?

JASPER: I *am*—as serious as . . .

GINGER: Death?

JASPER: You named that dread word!

GINGER: Be sensible—how on Earth, *how*?

JASPER: Ginger—that's exactly what I objected to in Burt; and you're sounding just like him.

GINGER: It's a reasonable question—from him *or* from me.

JASPER: Please, Ginger—one Burt is enough. In fact, *too* much. Don't *you* go imitating what I already find too intolerable in *him*. Losing him is bad enough. Losing you—I couldn't recover from it. So take care. *(He turns out his bedside lamp light.)* Just go on loving me, and extend your love to my new idea as well, without the interference of a questioning and doubting attitude. *(Turns off light and kisses* GINGER *passionately.)*

GINGER: *(Breaking the embrace.)* Curiosity now intrigues me confoundingly. I'd like to hear the whole story. How did your bitter dispute start, which ended in such upset, with dear old allies so at odds apart?

JASPER: Since you insist, I'll now illuminate you. *(Turns on his lamp light.)* But recounting what happened seems pointlessly not worth the trouble, in view of Burt's dastardly, knavish, cutthroat defiance of an idea too beautifully humane even to contest.

GINGER: *Please* indulge me—it's a whim, but I must hear all.

JASPER: Then prepare yourself, dear Ginger. You'll end up agreeing how hateful Burt is, and how lovable I. And you'll embrace my marvelous scheme.

GINGER: Divulge! Hold back no longer.

JASPER: *(As lights fade)* Well, it was like this. Earlier this very evening itself, I ate out with Burt. So inspired was I, that—most untypically— I even left some food on my plate. I forget what denomination of food it was, but that's irrelevant to my sublime conviction that I really had something great up here *(Points to his own head.)* to chew on. This conviction was confirmed when, later, walking along matching strides with Burt to our club for an after-dinner drink, I would occasionally pause to question the night's air with some ecstatic upward glance, detecting ample signs favorably prophetic to my divinely ordained mission. On arrival at our club, I took familiar bearings there, then proceeded to unravel, but by bit, what my inspiration state so elatedly owed itself to.

(During this last speech, JASPER changes into the clothes he wore to dinner with BURT. Then he walks to the living room set, even as GINGER watches from their bed. She remains as witness to JASPER's re-enactment of flashback, the transition to which may be accompanied by effects and/or music.)

Scene Five

(BURT and JASPER at latter's apartment, sitting at conventional distance from each other in living room. Identical setting to that of Scene Two. This scene, however, is told through JASPER's eyes. Hence JASPER appears to be a far-sighted visionary: the ultimate, passionate visionary; a benevolent philanthropist willing to dedicate all his energy in a self-sacrificing effort to free mankind from bondage to death. BURT, on the other hand, is made to appear petty, cynical, bitchy, negative.)

JASPER: The world is in dreadful shape. What's it coming to?

BURT: Who knows? But once it gets to where it's coming to, it won't stop *there*—it'll plunge right on: right into another generation. You and I, meanwhile, by that time, will be dead.

JASPER: That's what I really hate about life—*mortality!*

BURT: Your hating it is a good sign—shows your values are in the right place.

JASPER: I'm serious, Burt. Now, listen. *(Pause. Recites following two paragraphs with deliberateness and elocution.)*

Something must really be done about death. It's been going much too far, with outrageous consumptive audacity, these very many years! The lives it's claimed! Snatched by so many snares, gobbled up by all matter, manner, and ruse of catastrophe by nature, internal disease, or man-devised means.

Before it's too late, it'll take us all! This scandal is escalating, by outlandish degrees. If we don't soon arrest it—oh!

BURT: *(Reciting in a sing-song)*
Eventually, you will die.
Not to pop into the sky,
but down in the ground to lie,
with not the slightest hint of "why."

JASPER: Mock me if you like, Burt. But Death darkly undergoes its concealment: stealthy, patient. Though instantaneously everywhere, Death lurks hidden within and resists all subtle onslaughts to free human life of...its secret undoer.

BURT: Secret?! Death is out in the open. By now, it's hardly a secret. Otherwise, why all those long faces you see in the streets and on the buses? They've all caught on, about this death business.

JASPER: Yes, people are dearly fond of life; in time they've learned to hold life as their dearest prize. Nothing's so valuable as each new moment, so fleeting—

BURT: *(Interrupting)* Oh, not so fleeting. Sometimes life lags and flags so slow, as dull monotony endures to tedious boredom. Even *with* our mortal awareness.

(BURT yawns, illustrating his last point; and he might stretch, get up, move about, do something or other, before sitting down again.)

JASPER: But Burt—there's something I must tell you.

BURT: *(Sarcastically)* What on Earth can it be? Please, spare me any further suspense. Life is tricky enough, without the upset of unnecessary palpitations. What's on your sleeve—or up your mind? Spill it!

JASPER: Attend: bend your ear: I do intend to outdo Death, at his own game, cut him off, and purge life of its own worst enemy.

Such precisely is the mission I was brought into the world for: my calling I've only just discovered: my ordained task *(Enunciating with deliberateness to emphasize inner rhyme repetition of four "term" sounds.)*

by divine determination: I'm granted a term to terminate our termination.

BURT: If this is a joke, what's the punch line?

JASPER: I've never been this serious before.

BURT: Then, justify yourself. It's late, I want to go home. Georgia's waiting.

JASPER: So has everyone so far been: for their mortal end. But I'm putting an end to that wait. *(Pause)* I don't intend idly to stand by like all our other doomed sheep, to watch Death gradually unfold its malice with decomposing cells, physical decay, bodily rot, working insidiously from within like a Trojan Horse of classical treachery or deception.

BURT: *(With arch cynicism)* So *you* are to be history's very first circumventer, forestaller, arrester, outwitter, and ultimate undoer of our prolific devastator, Death?

JASPER: I confess to that purpose.

BURT: With what means, at hand?

JASPER: My goal will find its instrument, my aim its tool, my crusade its revelation.

BURT: That sounds evasive.

JASPER: I evade nothing. Open-eyed, I take deliberate aim. Like an antiquated monster of pestilence that should have been shuffled off in prehistoric obsolescence, Death has been around too long for our own good as a species. It should long ago have been dispatched, in a merciless act of enlightened mercy. By my ready hands I'll do now what the rusty hands of the human race have been overdue to do. To outdo Death— our deliverance so dormant, so latent. Better dormant, than a doormat. Better latent than never. By my ready hand and deadly eye—

BURT: *(Cutting in)* Your stalking Death as a prey is an act of foolish idiocy. Low on sense, you resort to a senseless profusion of *words*, that reproduce like rabbits drugged with aphrodisiacs and deprived of birth control methods—just like *you're* deprived of *death*-control methods, you hare-brain! You're comic, not cosmic.

JASPER: *(Visionarily)* I behold it: a secular Last Judgment, with blessings of paradisical enormity on literally a global scale. Life in its own absolute magnitude: Life of incontestable virtue in itself. To compound Life by infinity, to unstop it of mortal limits, to eternalize its stupendous essence in a riot of abundance to the superlative excess of an extremely good thing, would be to place our happiness, our dignity, on a scale of imperishability, in a daily delight of an endless treasure. The world shall be a stage for lovers—sweet lovers, in spring's tide; and lovers will dally forever.

BURT: *(Bluntly, annihilatingly practical; thus negatingly)* Frankly, I doubt it. It's late, Georgia is waiting.

JASPER: *(Still glowing, full-blast, in spite of* BURT'*s negative tone.)* Everyone, you and your Georgia included, is warmly ever so welcome to my lavishly programmed Eternity Feast. The loves you and your Georgia feel for each other, the loves that link Ginger and me, all true bonds, shall now, with the magnitude of a new bounty, partake of our joint personal immortalities. Should my scheme's grand potential succeed as planned, its humane strategy is devised to prolong indefinitely each marvelous illustration of the human condition.

Numbly, our society in all its customs has succumbed to tragedy—chronicling it but barely opposing it. Death is the invisible breeder of tragedy, working with all its cunning maggots to secretly separate our cells from the wholesome healthy radiance that sings the vibrant song of life. Let life now celebrate its liberation from what undermines its fiery self! Let the world throb with its genius, Life! Let life finally command its continuity! Let it build a pedestal to the purity and praise of an indwelling permanence!

BURT: *(Sarcastically)* How lovely it sounds, my dear Jasper! How I'd dearly love to be in your debt—to join all other no-longer-mortals in a rejoicing, jubilant cry of endless gratitude. Alas, I fear that being obligated to you will not be my great fortune—nor my Georgia's, nor your Ginger's, nor anyone's—due to your not coming through on your vaunted promise.

JASPER: I give you my supreme Word! To the old Creation I'll affix an amendment—a royal addition, a crucial editorial revision!

Whatever extraordinary or divine means this entails, I'll make it my uncanny business—if I haven't already done so—to find; and somehow put to work, so as to take effect: *(Apocalyptically)* Then— *(Pause for suspense)* soon Behold! *(Raises his arms and circles slowly)* Oh, how can you decline into a wet-blanket whining killjoy, in the face of the immense challenge I've undertaken? My friend—

*(*JASPER *tries to put his arm around* BURT *in a gesture of friendliness and an attempt to include* BURT *in* JASPER'*s messianic glow and ardent fervor—but* BURT *angrily thrusts the proffered arm—and* JASPER*—away, with violent, scornful rejection.)*

JASPER: Burt—you thrust me aside? As my best friend, in my hour of crucial need, you should be dishing out love and support unstintingly.

BURT: As your best friend, I'm only telling you some dreary truths. Your phoniness is betrayed verbally. Your choice of words is abominable. Your rhetoric abounds with shameless patches of purple. Not only don't people think like you—they don't even talk like you. You're out of touch—you're remote from the fabric and fiber of others, their pulse and gristle, their beat and thump. So as a friend, I should be supporting you? In defying what's sacred to you, I deny all of you? In your time of need, do I prove a false friend? Can I be so petty or spiteful, to despise your ultimate mission to rescue humanity and redeem our universe?

How too true! It's my confessed crime. Gaily, I exempt my conscience from the stain of any guilt. I don't even deign to care!

JASPER: *(In calm holiness)* Notwithstanding those words, I confer on you, your Georgia, and every living other person, a lifetime of permanence in the beautiful universe of existence. There, love and life both grow ever endless.

BURT: Cut out that dopey bribery. Georgia and I will die. So will, therefore, that third entity: the love that binds Georgia and me. The three of us—Georgia, I, and the love between us—are bound, despite you and your drippy benevolence, to die—die—die!

JASPER: Mock me all you wish—on *your* account. But, gallantly, for your dear Georgia's sake, shouldn't you shelter her, protect her, from joining your doom down the gloomy river of a death-wish?

BURT: Even to the River Styx she sticks with me—quite nonexempt, in reasonable resignation to the most inevitable force of existence: life's sure demise.

JASPER: Joined in love, she shares equally the folly of your blunder?

BURT: Yes. Heartless, aren't I? I've signed her death-warrant. A suicidal pact between lovers!

JASPER: *(In noble compassion)* Poor Georgia! I'd never treat her that way if she were *mine*! Ginger's luckier, by far!

BURT: I really must go. Georgia's been expecting me. My death-acceptance speech must, like life itself and love itself, end. Dying, I'll go join my dying love—while we're still young enough to be sexy and vital.

JASPER: Dear would-be betrayer! How you'll come to realize your error, once you live to see that what you call my "dream" has come to be performed on the real, real stage! Only the true drama shall convince you. How ripe the theatre readies, to rehearse its never-ending climax! O bold scheme! Turn my perfect faith to joy and triumph. Turn spectators into actors, to perform everlastingly. Let life realize deathlessness, to perfection! Then doubt is ousted, along with its dire source, Death. For then, all blessings shall excel. Farewell!

(He exits.)

BURT: To contradict your bloated dream's futility, in blunt finality:

Georgia and I will die, and so will you. And love will die as we do. Let me repeat. "Die, die, die!"

Not only will we and love all die, but before all that, our friendship precedes those deaths, and is the first to die. Let our friendship's death be your rehearsal for *stronger* stuff! It will harden you, yet!

(As he's concluding this speech, JASPER *is changing back into his pajamas and rejoining* GINGER *in their bed for Scene Six.)*

Scene Six

(Same setting as for Scene Four: JASPER, *in pajamas, and* GINGER, *in nightgown, both sitting up in same bed.)*

JASPER: That, alas, is what took place, my darling Ginger.

GINGER: I'm so glad you told me. Now I know.

JASPER: Know what, my dear?

GINGER: *(Springing her surprise)* That you and I, you jerk, are through!

JASPER: *(Incredulous)* What have I heard?!

GINGER: In your strongly biased version that purported to report your rather polarized conversation with Burt, I could see through your glaring effort at self-glorification. You maligned a sensibly respectable man, unjustly portraying him as a nit-picking, negative ingrate. You contemptibly failed to render him contemptible. Your scheme to strip our mortal world of mortality is precisely what Burt criticized it to be: the sheerest hokum, an out-and-out work of nonsensical fraudulence. I'm ashamed to have been associated with you in so-called love.

JASPER: Our love was patiently built up over years...

GINGER: Now an issue has come on which to sever our bond by driving home a basic incompatibility. Let us now agree on only one thing: to part. To that extent, our love harmoniously ends.

JASPER: *(Desperately)* But my darling!—

GINGER: *(As though waking up)* I'm a realist. It's unreasonable to try to end death. What was I doing, loving *(Contemptuously) you* all this time? It was crazy of me. By getting rid of you, I'm happily rational now. Next man, I'll know better.

JASPER: *(Urgently)* I beg you!

GINGER: *(As though to herself)* Burt and I are realists: passively resigned, fortified by stoical reasoning, to death's ultimate, conclusively unconquerable eventuality. That paragon of worldly reasonableness, the coolly level-headed, calmly down-to-earth Burt, is now the only possible man for me. After years of you, he's the surest antidote. I hold you in a total abhorrence. Make way. *(During this speech, she'd been getting out of bed and dressing.)*

JASPER: *(Alarmed, miserably upset)* Don't desert me! I need you!

GINGER: However, *I* need *you not.*

JASPER: That was the accurate Burt I took the pains to depict. His shallow narrowness of spirit—if you throw yourself away on *him*—you'd be shrunk to his size!

(Unheeding JASPER's passionately desperate protest, GINGER has meanwhile been dressing decisively.)

JASPER: *(Hysterical)* Reconsider! At stake—

(GEORGIA suddenly bursts into the room, interrupting JASPER in mid-apoplectic outburst. She shows a different kind of agitation than JASPER's, being passionately positively in the thrall of his (now hers as well) death-conquering vision mania.)

GEORGIA: *(Puffing, gloriously out of breath)* I see, Ginger, that you've been dressing to go out. Don't go just yet. I have a most vital announcement to make—of direct bearing on the core of our changing lives.

GINGER: *(With deliberate calmness and chilling composure, putting the finishing touches on her going-out dressing-grooming.)* "On the core of our changing lives." Dear me. Whatever can it be? *(Ironically)* Please spare me further suspense. I wait with all the breathlessness of death.

GEORGIA: *(Looking at, motioning ardently to, JASPER.)* Ginger, that man I'm pointing to is kindred to my very soul. Nothing—least of all you— shall stand in our holy union's way. I'm now divine Jasper's devoted apprentice, in deathless support of his undying devastation of that old devastater, dire Death.

GINGER: In other words, you're a fool. It's a case of a fool being attracted to another. As though two fools together would undo each one's foolishness. Ah, if mathematics were only that simple!

GEORGIA: You insult us both!

GINGER: You're already so possessive and joined with him. As though *two* quests to kill death would turn the trick, in the stead of merely one.

Let me personally invite you to get the hell out of here. One of you is bad enough: Two quite tops my very limit.

GEORGIA: What you mean with that rude invective, which you put so indirectly, is simply that you refuse to give up Jasper to me—isn't that it? But by ordinance of God (or His equivalent in these unpious times), Jasper's now mine. If to win him I'll have to fight, then fight I will. So purely purposed is my desperate might to take what's mine, I'll resort to force—like this— *(GEORGIA has swung her large, heavy bag, in violence, at GINGER's head.)*

GINGER: *(Ducking) (Gloating)* Missed! You cracked idealist! You lousy hunk of death-fright!

(GEORGIA swings her bag, with violence, a second time at GINGER.)

GINGER: *(Again ducking)* Again missed, you whore to insanity! You camp-following groupie to the magnetic irrational!

(Seething, with murderous intent, GEORGIA swings her bag for the third time, in vicious violence—harder than ever. Just at that moment, BURT has entered.)

GINGER: *(Distracted by her affectionate discovery on seeing her new love, BURT, thus forgetting to duck.)* Burt! Burt!

BURT: *(In complete surprise)* Why, Ginger!

(Just as BURT replies "Why, GINGER!", the violently swung-directed bag lands with a hard thud on GINGER's head. Collapsing, she remains motionless on floor where fallen. BURT and JASPER are stunned. BURT frantically attempts to revive GINGER, but fails. Hurriedly, GEORGIA extracts a mirror from her purse and holds it under GINGER's nose.)

BURT: *(Anxiously, to GEORGIA)* Well?

GEORGIA: *(In tense disappointment)* Not the slightest fog of cloud on this mirror!

BURT: *(Alarmed)* Then her nose isn't giving any breath?

JASPER: *(Anguished at encountering premature mundane banal situational example of his lofty abstract chosen opponent.)* Is she—O dreadful, unthinkable—"dead"?!

GEORGIA: *(In horror)* Damn it, it looks like it! No breathing is indicated on this slick, slick, smooth mirror surface!

(GEORGIA and the two men now start to panic.)

BURT: What can we do!?

JASPER: Just what *I* was wondering.

GEORGIA: Here's your brilliant chance, my divine new-found Jasper, to give an advance sample of your greater later full-scale campaign.

JASPER: But how, my sudden Georgia?

GEORGIA: Vindicate by an early example the courageous soundness of your daring mission against *all* of death, by making a raid in particular against the precisely specific possible danger that *Ginger* is here now, thanks to me, dead.

JASPER: But Georgia—I may not be ready! My plan was projected—

GEORGIA: *(Urgently interrupting)* Come down prematurely to Earth, from your vast onslaught of your projections. Here lies Ginger. Apply the earliest advance of your grand and wholesale remedy, in her concrete case, at once!

JASPER: *(Sputtering with alarm)* Too soon! My calculations—

GEORGIA: *(Interrupting; supplicates, genuflects, worshipfully embraces her new idol.)* Save universal humanity; but before you do, make a swift trial practice run, against the hastily roused mortality of poor endangered Ginger, there in her morbid state. I vow my love in support. Show a hint of what's to come. *(Seeing* JASPER *display obvious fright-stagger.)* Pluck at the talent source of your magic gift, humbly now to perform!

JASPER: *(Pathetically inadequate to* GEORGIA's *strong plea.)(Whining, petulant)* Whatever miracle you expect, I'm not up to, at present.

BURT: *(To* GEORGIA*)* You see, Georgia: I told you, but you wouldn't believe me; he's showing his flying colors as a craven phony. It was all wind—he can't do a thing! Phoning for an emergency hospital ambulance would be infinitely wiser than to place, in the hysterical impotence of our panic, reliance on a charlatan's homeopathic self-proclaimed spiritualist hocum.

GEORGIA: *(Dismissingly)* Much too late, by now, to resort to so prosaic an expediency as to phone for emergency hospital ambulance service. Either Jasper comes through by divine miracle's merciful agency, or the ghost is up.

BURT: Let's face it plainly: the poor girl is dead. Being Jasper's girlfriend (or technically *former* girlfriend if she's dead, not to raise too fine a point on it), then she's *Jasper's* responsibility (although with the airs he puts on, do you call that responsibility?). Anyway, incompetent though he may be, it's *his* affair—not ours. But you and I, Georgia, quick!, let's leave this sticky mess before we get too involved! Let's get out of here!

GEORGIA: But we already *are* involved! Or, rather, it's *me* who's involved; after all, damn it, aren't I the one who killed her? For that, I must face, however onerous or unpleasant, the key responsibility for the abominable atrocity of poor lifeless Ginger's lying there *(Gesturing toward* GINGER*)*, pathetically translated to a precocious corpsehood from the customary lively quickness that characterizes normal city life.

BURT: Let's run away, Georgia! There's the devil to pay!

GEORGIA: *(Derisively)* Theology from *you*, Burt? I'm surprised! As the one who killed her, poor dear, she's *my* responsibility: which, imploringly, I pass on now to a man built in a hero mold—Jasper: Perform heroism, O brave one!

JASPER: *(Hangdog)* As I said before—I'm just not up to that line of work tonight; I'm off my game; the mood just isn't on me.

GEORGIA: Not inspired? Waiting to work up enthusiasm? Brooding on your Muse?

JASPER: Must I confess to fear?

The chips are down, but I choke up in the clutch. When it comes down to the crunch, I'm asked to perform a simple resurrection by retroactive resuscitation. That's all I need do. And yet— *(In pathetic futile impotence; confessing)* I simply can't!

GEORGIA: *(With reluctance, mocking)* "I simply can't!" You say that looking woefully constipated. If this weren't a life-or-death matter, there would be comical overtones—

JASPER: *(Admitting)* All abject, my true colors cowardly come crawling through. *(Covers his face with his hands in classical posture of shame, theatrically overdone.)* Oh, my ignominy!

GEORGIA: *(Furious, impassioned)* In the person—lying there—of poor Ginger, your girlfriend till now: Death—your chosen nemesis—turns, for once, real. Your abstractly humanitarian antideath posture, so bravely declared and proclaimed by yourself that I too have fallen for it, is now exposed and debunked in clear view.

My love, so new, dissolves in a shame of tears and disgust, beholding craven weakness where strength promised brazen in your bold show of old words. Oh, phew!

JASPER: *(Who, except for his brief attempt with GEORGIA and BURT to revive GINGER, has remained sitting up in bed all this time since scene's beginning. Now reduced to a terrified hiding under the sheets. In muffled but nevertheless clearly audible voice.)* No, I just can't! Oh, the horror of death!

BURT: Jasper, try, I beg you! Just try, at least!

JASPER: What?!

GEORGIA: You?!

(JASPER and GEORGIA staring in surprise at this unexpected source.)

BURT: I now retract everything I said, in belittling your powers of miracle. I was being glibly negative by prejudice: for such flippancy, please forgive. Now Ginger is in a state of moribund emergency; do *attempt* her resurrection, Jasper: give it your all. Should you restore her languid cadaver to the shining health of life and fortune, I shall then declare my personally permanent allegiance, and join your League and Legion of lively stalwarts that will deal a long-overdue mortal wound to this Beast we call Death.

JASPER: *(Still from bed, but no longer hiding under sheets.)* Why, Burt, is that *you* talking?! Are those words the altered creatures of your own tongue?

BURT: I implore you, exert your talent, in which now I place pure belief. Animate, by one act, both Ginger's life and my own boundless faith.

JASPER: I'd counted on you as a reliably disloyal detractor; now you switch roles on me. I'm confused, amazed, surprised, and—I fear—still unequal to the task that you, and Georgia before you, set for me to do.

BURT: *(Whimpering, supplicating, forsaking all pride.)* Only *try*, O miracle maker!

GEORGIA: *(To* JASPER, *like a fiery Joan of Arc.)* Try, damn you! I order you to try!

BURT: *(Like a wheedling puppy dog)* O glorious Might, try, I beg of you!

JASPER: *(Finally getting down from bed; but plainly terrified, a far cry from his calm saintlike serene confidence of before.)* All right, Burt, I'll do—or try to—what you mocked me for daring to think I could ever pull off before, though now *I* have the doubts about it that *you* once did. And you as well, Georgia, in your touching faith, or stern command, you prevail on me—to only try. Now in the crunch of my test, impotence devours me; and far from mastering Death, I feel my inadequacy before that fell master. In futility of faith and trembling void of grace, I'll go alas through my feeble motions. Weakly bending over Death's fresh new captive, I'll try to wrest her from the august dread of his awesome power.

(Kneeling, JASPER *extends his arms over* GINGER's *lifeless form. In absurd pantomime, he makes a pathetic, ridiculously half-hearted invocation, then pauses to test effect and result. In backfired melodrama turned flat, nothing whatever happens—* GINGER *remains still and lifeless. In a parody of grotesquely anguished failure,* JASPER *collapses in tears: witnessed by* GEORGIA *and* BURT, *who stand looking on, sagging in depression and despair.)*

(Cameo frozen tableau of above, all paused.)

(A moment later, GINGER's *eyes open. She stirs, then slowly comes to her feet. The three stare at her with amazement—and awe. It appears as though—after all— Jasper has miraculously derived powers from a majestic divine mystery.)*

GEORGIA: *(Elated and vindicated; to* BURT.*)* You see, you old Doubting Thomas—didn't I make a perfect choice in dropping you, on a wise spiritual impulse, in favor of my newer, truer love, the immaculate Saint of Death-Negation? He's done it!

BURT: But not till I, at the last minute, recanted my persistent skepticism, and prodded him with my belated faith, becoming most likely the critical key contributing factor in boosting him to the breakthrough marvel we have just witnessed: in all of history probably the one greatest single event to date; and I *(Pointing to himself in gloating pride.)* helped make it happen! Give me, then, a major credit!

GEORGIA: As though that would reverse my decision to make the switch of you for my noble Jasper! But aren't we being petty, in the wake of Death's glorious defeat? Let's lift up our acclaiming voice, as apostles in attendance to attest to this stirring occasion, this pure miracle. Simply to stand back in awe—not to quibble, but to quiver to cosmic vibrations—

GINGER: *(Dramatically cutting in on* GEORGIA; *suddenly beginning a harsh, mocking laugh.)* Ha! You fools! *(Pause, for stunned effect on other three.)* Merely playing possum, I was never the least bit dead whatever—just stunned somewhat. When Georgia held her mirror to my mouth, I made a quick decision: to hold my breath in under suspension, in order to discover, if each of you and all together thought me dead, what foolishness you'd be capable of. Thanks to my little impromptu ruse, this scientific deception of mine has revealed each of you most strangely. *(Pause. Turning to—on—*JASPER, *upbraidingly.)* As for you: When the chips were down, when under fire, when the call for courage was stressed squarely on the line, you let down your ideals ignobly, as your high principles cracked at the bend of the breaking point. Such weakness shows you even more despicable than when you earlier put on a holy mission and a saintly pretense. How vindicated I am for deciding to leave your bed and love, and break up with you after years I now regret! *(Contemptuously)* Enough, though, for you: why waste further words, in empty fury's lost song of bitterness, showing only how well I can scold and scorn? *(Turning now, abruptly, to* BURT.) As for *you*, weird turncoat of a Burt: I made the mistake of weaving a fancy full of love for you while Jasper described your reasonable realistic rejection of his request for faith in his abortive messiah crusade. Resolving on the spot to dispose of that deluded visionary, to replace him with sensible-seeming you on my love's aching throne, I was just about to leave this stale old bedroom and go seek you out and claim your rational aid in starting life and love all over, under an authentic sanctity of sanity. So then, by playing possum and feigning the ominous chill and lull of death, what have I discovered in *you*, the paragon of the down-to-earth, on which trait I placed love's value? Losing nerve in the test and crisis of crucial artificial stress, you beg like a dog, like a broken-down dog, for the very Miracle I'd credited you to discredit in the strong light of your skepticism. My admiration, love, respect for you have quickly, in the light of my springing this test on you, soured. My contempt for my outrageous discarded former love Jasper has now been shifted for even better reason to *you*. Thus, my opinion races to these unsound events, acutely critical of two loves in uncanny succession. The trick showed that, of all three of you, Georgia alone kept faith with her proclaimed point of view, sticking in crisis to her recently declared stance; though I deem her professed vision ill-conceived, glaringly defective, at least, in my mock contrived emergency, she forged decisive courage to uphold it, and alone acted out her misguided assumed role.

GEORGIA: *(To* GINGER*)* Thank you for your somewhat qualified compliment, and longwinded assurance that such a slimy thing as yourself dares compete with us to draw air again. *(Angrily)* How *dare* you scare us all to death by feigning a ploy of death, which drove me to such heights of unnecessary guilt!? Too cruel to be a practical joke—or scientific experiment, as you slyly justify it.

GINGER: *(Angrily)* It was a *fair* ruse, to call your bluff! How dare you—who nearly almost killed me—get on your high horse and scorn me so critical! What hardskinned nerve you have!

GEORGIA: *(Angrily)* The nerve you have, to say that *I* have nerve! *You* caused Jasper to act a mockery of his capabilities, to the undermining of his heroic credibility. In further unkindness, you even forced Burt into self-betrayal of his shallow, cool, skeptical creed! You deserve him! It was a detestably cynical thing to do!

GINGER: *(Angrily)* Was it, you violent ass? You nearly killed me—in earnest!

GEORGIA: *(Angrily)* Your death-feigning deception was even more earnest. Had you actually been completely and sincerely dead, Jasper would very well have performed the old Lazarus stunt on you, and raised you back to life's plateau from death's abysmal valley level. To resurrect Justice from the crooked, untrue test you rigged, I strike from the record what invalidly you brought to be. *(With threatening gesture)* And you yourself, I'd strike from the record—most willingly.

GINGER: *(With fury)* You nearly did—already. Let *me*, in kind, pay you back, to quite requite your nasty deed, by my bitter aping of your violence upon me! *(While saying that, she's swung her bag at* GEORGIA, *in vicious roundhouse, and clunked her full-blast on head, knocking* GEORGIA *instantly down, in her turn, into a death-resembling heap—but (audience is made to wonder) in earnest this time?)*

GINGER: *(To* JASPER, *vindictively)* There! You wanted somebody to resurrect; well, then, I *give* you somebody to resurrect!

JASPER: *(Appalled)* Could you have done that?! Why didn't you turn the other cheek?!

GINGER: *(Unrepentently)* I only repaid what I *owed* to Georgia; there, I've now discharged my one outstanding debt! *(Viciously)* Tauntingly, Jasper, I challenge you to prove yourself. You had your one chance before, which you proceeded comically or pathetically to bungle. I took matters into my own hands, to afford you another opportunity. Let's see what you can do *now*! Put your faith to action. I've tossed up the perfect test for it!

JASPER: Yes, but...but...

BURT: *(To* GINGER, *with admiration)* Oh Ginger, you're devastatingly superrational, after having proved yourself a woman of immense practical action. In swift succession, you've annihilated both of those sad and sloppy romantics, besides restoring me to my wholesome former state. I admire you almost to idol-worship, for what you've done, for what you've said! How well we go together, you and I! We're each other's logical mates by obviously natural selection from the jungle warfare of all these preceding events; we alone survive as sane! We're the superior lords of those *(Indicating* JASPER *and fallen* GEORGIA) fallen to the stupidity of their absurd faiths!

GINGER: *(Snuggling close to* BURT) Oh Burt, how wisely you analyze! Your love completes my queenly violence.

BURT: *(Snuggling close to* GINGER) Do let's sit side by side, spectators to the next sporting event: Jasper's attempt to revive his fallen new love. What shall we wager, on his success or otherwise? I offer you odds of ten to one he won't.

JASPER: *(Indicating* GEORGIA's *"corpse".)* Are you playful at a time like this!? How can you ...

GINGER: *(To* BURT) A mere ten to one you offer me?! My dear Burt, the weakness and benevolence of your generosity, in the soft compassion of your mercy, still tarnish somewhat the staunch sanity of your cynicism. *(Viciously)* If realism were the true pure goal of yours, you'd offer me a *million* to one!

BURT: *(Converted into* GINGER's *spirit of things.)* Would I be *more* realistic, by offering a *zillion* to one?

GINGER: Not even! Just give me infinity-to-nothing! Those are the *likeliest* odds, in the weighed estimate of the plausible.

JASPER: *(His resolve returning)* Halt! you callously inhuman, viciously heartless pair of brain machines! Mock me together! But I'm your one hope, and one alone, to save you *(Glaring at* GINGER), venomous Ginger, from the murderous consequences of your chilling violence, your "rational" retribution. *(To them both)* Set your playful odds at the grim mathematical wager to an absurd ratio: Bet your mightiest against me, you pair of calculating computers that ill conceal your insect souls: Offend me at your worst—heaping insult on insolence—the more will my success utterly upset your joint contempt!

BURT: *(Smugly, to* GINGER) Is he serious?—or crazed?

GINGER: He's both!

JASPER: I'll outreason you both, at your own idle game! *(To* GINGER, *in concession)* In *your* case, my former Ginger, you're right, it's true, I proved pathetically inadequate to my self-imposed task of wresting you from Death—though, in my defense, you were, of course, quite alive all the time; nevertheless, my performance stunk out the joint—it was awful, it was a bomb. Now, to redeem and vindicate that miserable, appalling fiasco, I'm determined, this time *(Looking down at* GEORGIA'S *lifeless-looking form)*, to challenge, head-on, one on one, my grim nemesis Death, in direct man-to-man (if Death is a man) strife and clash—to the finish! May the better man (if he's a man) win! To the victor belongs—now that Georgia has thrown her lot on *my* side, having left Burt for me—the spoils! I fling down my gauntlet *(Mimes this)* and issue mortal defiance to the Grim One!

(As BURT *and* GINGER *watch,* JASPER *goes through his magic-invoking ritual again, but in complete contrast to the ineffectual, bungling effort before over* GINGER'S *fallen body. This time, his incantation is mightily, majestically acted out—so much so, that* BURT *and* GINGER, *as audience, applaud enthusiastically, like wild, delirious spectators.)*

(In spite of this, the fallen GEORGIA *remains inert, unstirring.)*

BURT: *(Cuttingly)* Up to your old tricks, Jasper? You looked great, *this* time. You were magnificent! What a performance! It brought down the house—but it didn't bring up Georgia. But perhaps I quibble, over a mere technical detail.

GINGER: *(Beaming on* BURT*)* Burt, how exquisitely cynical of you! You're reconstituted now! An urbane model of supremely deft, cutting realism, annihilating those caught up in cloudy poetic magic! You show how disbelief stands higher than the puffery of faith! I'm won over! You're adorable!

*(*JASPER *is devastated, stung, by* BURT'S *remark.)*

*(*GINGER, *overcome once again with attraction to her new preferred man, kisses* BURT *impulsively.* BURT *seizes the occasion to join in on the impulsive kiss—which lingers, on and on, as they both, having thrown themselves into it, find it an invigorating diversion—as* JASPER'S *rousing magic ritual performance was—from* GEORGIA'S *fallen state, from which they seek the blessings of amorous oblivion.)*

(Ignoring the twittering love-birds, and overcoming his having been stung and devastated by BURT'S *crack,* JASPER *goes back to work, with redoubled determination and impressive, masterful-seeming concentration, over* GEORGIA'S *lifeless form, trying still another method of magical incantation.)*

(However, that doesn't have any effect, either. GEORGIA *is still unstirring. But this time,* JASPER'S *effort, though definitely authoritative and impressive, was greeted with no applause by* BURT *and* GINGER. *Nor is there another cutting, sarcastic remark by* BURT.*)*

*(*BURT *and* GINGER'S *attention is mainly on each other, as they go on lying on the bed, necking and petting, as though discovering each other as the right types for each other through fleshly exploration, amorous touch and feel.)*

(JASPER *pauses momentarily before resuming his enormous task, as though wondering what other method to try.* BURT *and* GINGER *take time out from their hugging, embracing, kissing, to notice that* JASPER—*though maintaining his dignity—is at a loss.*)

BURT: *(To* JASPER, *in spirit of helpful cooperation rather than skeptical sarcasm.)* Jasper, may I suggest something? Since Ginger and I *(They keep fondling each other, etc., in illustration)* find kissing so very *invigorating,* perhaps *Georgia* might find it enough so to stir and revive from her dull, death-twinned stupor: were you to try that natural old formula, that homeopathic remedy of nature's simple erotics, that amorous resuscitation device—the kiss.

JASPER: If it invigorates you two *(Indicating* BURT *and* GINGER'*s resuming, or rekindling, or redoubling, their panting embrace.)* to such shameless abandon and a display to delight even the most demanding voyeur, then perhaps the kiss technique might— *(Hopefully)* it just might—invigorate Georgia *(Looking down at her.)* here, to life's minimum display of breath. Just *breathing,* is all *I* exact. *(Primly, puritanically)* Not the *panting* condition of *you* shameless two *(Looking disapprovingly at them.)* but only, in Georgia's case, the modest, prim, unromantic little functioning of her lungs—physical yes, passionate no. That's all I require.

BURT: *(Losing patience)* Go ahead then—you can only try.

JASPER: *(Ignoring* BURT; *grandly, but ponderingly; theoretical, head in clouds.)* A kiss is the gateway to love. Perhaps love has the power to ignite, stir up, quicken, the momentarily inactive life. *(Looking at* GEORGIA'*s fallen, lifeless form; rousing himself to the task.)* There she lies. I must try it. She's locked inside Death's grim house. Surely, Love must be the ultimate key—perhaps the skeleton key—to Life's lock, tampered with by Death's locksmith. With the kissful key of my lips, I'll pry open the misfunctioning difficulty—this deadlock of Death's lock.

(Getting on his hands and knees, JASPER *demonstratively, flamboyantly, theatrically, but devoutly, plants a profound, prolonged kiss on* GEORGIA'*s lifeless face.* BURT *and* GINGER *suspend their mutual fondlings to look on, rapt, while suspense builds up.* JASPER *persists—kissing with all his heart and soul.)*

(At length—slowly—it works!)

JASPER: *(Still on hands and knees, leaning over the reviving* GEORGIA.*)* Were you in *Death*? Did I bring you back from it?

GEORGIA: Having been unconscious and oblivious at the time, I can't tell. If I *was* in Death—maybe I was—I bring back no report, nor finding, nor information, as to that dread state.

As to whether *you* brought me back from it: Not knowing whether I was dead or not, I don't know whether *you* brought me back—*if* I was *there.*

One thing, though: Waking up to your kiss was terribly nice. Even though I'm revived, can you repeat the dose?

JASPER: Most gladly. Not only did it do *you* good—*I* didn't mind it, either. Here goes.

(Still on hands and knees, JASPER leans over the still reclining GEORGIA, to repeat his long-drawn-out kiss ministration. From bed where they've been necking, BURT and GINGER also close-to in a kiss-clinch. Thus, the two new couples are seen simultaneously overlapping in full-blown new amorous discovering, dead set on roads to new intimacies through gradual stages that audience can observe.)

(Finally, the two couples end this phase of their kissings.)

GEORGIA: Jasper, I've regained enough strength to tell you that I'm determined to join and help your crusade to rid our old Earth—finally, forever—of that thing you may or may not have just brought me back from.

JASPER: Welcome aboard, my new love. Love is fun, while Death isn't. We sure know our priorities.

GEORGIA: Yes, we know what to value—and what's rotten, thus to be eliminated.

JASPER: We're a spiritual pair—together!

GEORGIA: By your side I take unflinching, steadfast stand, to help ready not *one* person's (such as, perhaps, my own) recovery, but the universal barrier-hurdling of our total species, the race itself.

JASPER: *(Relieved, then gradually taking charge.)* Finally, I have an ally! Burt and Ginger both refused, but Georgia's my true champion to step forth and rally me from self-doubt. *(To BURT)* To join me, Burt, she's left you: it's a just step. *(To GEORGIA)* We've unlumbered ourselves—or been unlumbered—of loves abruptly grown incompatible. As for those two *(Indicating BURT and GINGER)*, they deserve each other—it's a fitting match of two cold over-reasonings who'll take tepid comfort in each other.

(BURT and GINGER kiss passionately.)

JASPER: *(To GEORGIA)* As for *us*, we're a pair of passionates that blazingly merge to the same spiritual core. *(JASPER and GEORGIA kiss primly.)*

(To all three) Love has suffered today, but grown improved, in the radical surgery of the switches.

BURT: I wholeheartedly agree.

GEORGIA: I agree with all my heart.

GINGER: With my whole heart, I agree.

JASPER: Are we then all agreed?

BURT: Yes!

GEORGIA: Absolutely!

GINGER: Emphatically!

BURT: Then we seem at last to be positively in accord—all four of us, without exception. Might I safely make bold to venture such conclusion in the fullness of your endorsement?

GEORGIA: Yes!

GINGER: Absolutely!

JASPER: Emphatically!

GEORGIA: Our enthusiasm, then, seems to be positive, as well as unanimous. In that, are we in full accord?

GINGER: Yes!

JASPER: Absolutely!

BURT: Emphatically!

GINGER: *(Matter of factly)* Your affirmations are most reassuring. Well, I guess *that* settles *that*. Would you, perhaps, agree?

JASPER: Yes!

BURT: Absolutely!

GEORGIA: Emphatically!

JASPER: Well, that's that.
     From pain to joy, we've exchanged our way into new-fledged hearts. *(To GEORGIA)* Darling—finally I realize—it should *always* have been you! *(Pause. Reconsiders; changes mind. Now addresses all three.)* But maybe it's better *this* way—to be "born again," or to be "twice-born," or to be "reborn." *(To BURT)* Wouldn't you say so, Burt?

BURT: Yes it is! There's a new surge of energy, a new charge of excitement, by belated conversion! *(To JASPER)* No hard feelings, I hope, about my absconding with your recently phony-dead but genuinely self-resurrected Ginger, who's ditched your love most wisely to favor me instead?

JASPER: No hard feelings whatever, old man. You're entirely welcome to my former Ginger: make yourself free with her, to your double hearts' content. *(To GINGER)* But Ginger: if, perchance, you manage to retain luxury to sentimental emotions in your new regime of rational practicality, I do hope, in reflecting back occasionally on me in nostalgic remnants of your heart, you'll spot the ever-warm embers to set you missing me somewhat slightly a bit?

GINGER: Perhaps undoubtedly I surely might. How long ago already it seems! Yet we ended just tonight!

JASPER: Strangely, so it did.

GINGER: We'll feel just a wee bit contrite. For old times' sake. We'll rake a few regretful coals, stirring embers of remembrance in being members of the remnants of each other. But *you* weep—not I.

BURT: *(To* GEORGIA*)* You've left me. May you not regret it!

GEORGIA: *(In deliberateness, emphasizing sentence-ending rhymes)* We're both better off, my old dear. For old times' sake, we'll shed perhaps a tear. Tonight ended our many-a-year. A farewell kiss, old dear. *(They kiss.)*

GINGER: *(To* GEORGIA*)* We've traded *men*: For the better: *Amen.*

GEORGIA: I echo your very words. We've chosen fates more suited to our souls' respective bents. In choosing those fates for *ourselves*, we've been the active instruments for our men's accepting new fates which *we*, by pleasing *ourselves*, have bestowed on them. They've been controlled, by us!

GINGER: Shake, partner. *(They shake hands.)*

GEORGIA: And I have a promise to make.

GINGER: What?

GEORGIA: I'll never murder you again.

GINGER: I'll hold you to that. And *you* hold me to *this*: I vow never again to murder, even in retaliation, you as well! Embracingly, we seal this pact. *(They embrace, while* GINGER *continues.)* On this treaty of ours may well depend the stability and endurance of our freshly established love relations.

But do you suppose for an instant, that either Georgia or I—who are paragons of constancy and fidelity—have either forgotten or forgiven your unforgivable whimperings, simperings, and belief-reversals at my feigned death?

GEORGIA: How too true, my mutual understander. Will either of you survive such shame?

BURT: Ginger, may I vindicate myself? Your possum-playing test showed us two men failing in reverse ways: Jasper by lapsing from faith, and me by lapsing into faith. My embarrassed apology for my weakness goes thus: It was a momentary aberration at a time of stress, shock, alarm, fear, confusion, and concern for you, compassion for your state, longing to see you well again.

More recently, on the contrary, during my former Georgia's quite seeming death, inflicted so briskly by you—did not my reactions then atone admirably for such shortcomings and malperforming I fell prey to at earlier your own demise?

GINGER: Your critical capacity does *seem* restored, noble Burt; and the skeptic's scalpel may be sharpened to a surgical venom. *(Pause, in transition from praise to caution.)* But a word of caution: The weakness of your former lapse into flabby romantic faith still threatens dangers of recurrence. A ruthless vigilance, I now prescribe. You—demoted to a novice now in penalty of your shameful sentimental display—must take a solemn vow to undergo a disciplinary regimen of stern demands that I—in the role of trainer and coach—shall impose on you in ruthless rigor: a hardening program by which you shall regain an identity wholeness, a pure embodiment of the cynical principles of tough-minded superrational practical materialism. I'll crack the whip to enforce this reinforced development of your old self.

BURT: *(Down on his knees.)* Princess of Realism, Empress of Reason, Queen of the Worldly Realm, resigned to accept our mortal fate allowing no dream of hope: as I extol you I vow to perform and obey as your command sets forth, to rebecome fully what I was, and nevermore slip or disappoint:

GINGER: You may rise now. *(*BURT *rises)* Let's leave those two *(Indicating* JASPER *and* GEORGIA.*)* soft-minded saps. Their company sets the worst example. *(Bearing suitcase, packed with her clothes, etc. in one hand, and arm in arm with* BURT *with her other hand, she's leaving apartment with him.)* Of course, dear *(Indicating* JASPER *and* GEORGIA.*)*, we *do* wish them well.

(They exit. JASPER *and* GEORGIA *are left to each other.)*

JASPER: A touching demonstration! Now that *they*'ve outlined the plain agenda for the ideological working of their love—what about you and me, Georgia? On what contrary ideology shall be based the structure of *our* working love?

GEORGIA: *(Undressing for bed, carelessly tossing her clothes around the room, in contrast to her previous, more repressed, stiff, or formal bedroom behavior with* BURT.*)* Ginger has extracted from Burt a solemn vow. From you, Jasper, I must extract a vow similarly solemn, though of opposite nature and reverse character. Ginger's possum-playing ploy demonstrated your weakness under stress. However sterling, stirring and—bravo—well done your perhaps resuscitation of myself may just have been, you earlier displayed a vulnerability that must be corrected. To that end, I now impose on you a stiff, severe regimen, a program of disciplinary demands designed to develop you into the pure embodiment of steadfast visionary zeal tempered to the perfect pitch that burns a blazing path through Death's smooth armor, hitherto unassailable.

I'll make you the right man for a tough job: one who'll tackle it head-on, and get the job done. When you get through, you will have wiped out the very dream we dreamed, the very vision we envisioned: you will have ruthlessly destroyed them the hard way—the unprecedented way: by replacing their *dream* and *vision* stuff, by stamping it all as now— behold *(Pause for effect.)* —Real!

JASPER: *(Down on his knees, just as* BURT *had just been in taking his vow to* GINGER.*)* Princess of Idealism, Empress of Vision, Queen of the passionate dream: As I extol you I vow to perform and obey as your command sets forth, to rebecome fully what I was, and nevermore slip or disappoint.

(As JASPER *is making that vow, lights come up on other (right) side of stage, on* BURT's *and* GINGER's *bedroom, where* BURT *and* GINGER *are getting into bed.)*

(Both couples kiss and turn out their respective lights at same time. Then sounds of ardent lovemaking are heard.)

(Continued darkness. End of scene.)

Scene Seven

(Stageset: Two separate bedrooms (in two separate houses, of course), revealed on opposite sides of stage: JASPER *and* GEORGIA *sitting up on their bed on the left;* BURT *and* GINGER *sitting up on their bed on the right. The years have abundantly gone by; all four characters are shown (aided by makeup, etc.) to have perceptibly and profoundly aged.)*

(On the left, JASPER *and* GEORGIA *are staring into the space in front of their bed. On the right,* BURT *and* GINGER *are reading books in their bed.)*

(Focus is on GEORGIA's *and* JASPER's *bedroom.)*

GEORGIA: When will it be? It should be before we're too old.

JASPER: It'll come! It'll come!

(Pause)

GEORGIA: Hurry! We're getting old!

JASPER: Death's end comes of its own accord. By voluntary will, I'm powerless to hasten it.

(Pause)

GEORGIA: Our love mustn't go the dwindling way of our flesh. Spare us! *Meet* this Death, and slay him!

JASPER: *(Irritated, admonishing)* For that, grant me peace.

(Pause. From this point on, the lights grow gradually dimmer and dimmer until, by the end of this final scene, there's total and final blackness to end the play.)

GEORGIA: *(Puzzled, in growing alarm)* Jasper—what's happening?

JASPER: Although I'm not sure, it could be that this might very well be it.

GEORGIA: "It"? What "it"?

JASPER: I'm referring, my darling, to my long, long-awaited encounter with my long-sought-out, mystically hand-picked adversary.

GEORGIA: *(Anxiously)* The approaching showdown becomes momentously imminent, momentarily eminent, ferociously at hand! At last, about to take place, is that meeting so counted on, planned for, deliberated on, in studied readiness and ever-steadied nerve. Are you at your fully prepared strength to cope head-on, on this collision course? Oh Jasper, my dear belovéd!

JASPER: *(Calm, tranquil, unperturbed) (Examining* GEORGIA *closely, with concern.)* You're agitated, you tremble. Is your longstanding equanimity, ever so faithful and confident, crumbling somewhat now with the onslaught of the dread unknown darkness?

GEORGIA: So it sadly seems. Whereas you, sterling Jasper, on the other hand are now become perfect in calm anticipation of what shall be triumphantly your *un*fatal encounter. How I remember . . .

JASPER: Remember what, my dear?

GEORGIA: Your brave calm spirit and ready magic holiness show such stark, decisive contrast to a scene so many years ago that the earlier scene seems placed already in an entirely previous lifetime!

JASPER: At such a time as this, are you referring to—?

GEORGIA: *(Fallen into a momentary trance of memory.)* I am . . . I can see it in a phantom of returned presence. Subjected suddenly to Ginger's possum-playing test, how inadequate you proved!: fumbling, incompetent, pathetic, an impromptu revelation of such total, pitiful lack in the very confidence and faith which— *(Recovering from trance, looking up at* JASPER.*)* —now . . .

JASPER: —Which now, in almost excessive abundance, I do have? I owe my recovery and reformed development to you. For it was your own perhaps lifeless form on which my first perhaps struggle against Death took perhaps place. Then, on vowing knees at your recovered feet, I swore on sacred oath such firmness—

GEORGIA: *(Interrupting)* But now look at *me—I* tremble! This time it's no toy trial or mock test. It all stares at us; it's *for real!*

JASPER: My darling, I feel that too. There *is* something real; it's coming on a-nigh. It's breathing on us.

My old vow—. All my life since has been slow preparation, arduous, uphill, towards this very strangeness, this event obscured in the vastness of its own uncertainty, which now, in glorious suspension or eerie suspense, hangs pending, impending, nigh, already here—upon us—at hand—closely knotted in the tissue of our breathing, at one with us, permeable with us...

GEORGIA: *(Uneasy; somewhat whiningly)* You're honed, primed, steeled, for it; you're raised to its level (whatever "it" may be); but not *me*— I'm jittery!

JASPER: *(August, calm, imperious)* Stop gnashing about. Calm yourself.

GEORGIA: *(Shrill, uneasy)* Advice is cheap. *(Pause)* Kiss me. *(JASPER kisses her.) This* time, your kissing hasn't done the trick of when you first tried it on me. Did your first kissing revive me, save me? Where's the magic *this* time? I'm too far gone now, the tides have overtaken me, I'm past the grace of recovery, beyond the blissful benefit?

JASPER: This time, is not the past. Calm yourself. We're coming on a greater unknown.

GEORGIA: *(Shrieks)* But what's your formula?!

(Focus now shifts to other side of stage, other bedroom: GINGER *and* BURT *sitting up reading in bed.)*

GINGER: Burt, something's wrong with this light! Have you noticed it?

BURT: Indeed. I must confess that, by all appearances, it's getting more difficult to read. Please do this favor—check the light switch. The realistic, practical, down-to-earth step for us to make would be to locate the difficulty, by getting empirically to the concrete root of this mechanical illumination problem, to make simplicity of its complication, and sensibly to fix it. I recommend this simple course of action, as directly bearing on, and alleviating, our complaint that the light seems to wane.

(GINGER does as requested, checking the light switch.)

GINGER: My dear longstanding partner of domesticity, Burt: When it comes down to it (though I'm not a licensed electrician, nor even an amateur specialist), there appears nothing whatever to be wrong with the light switch, so far as what its *surface* would indicate, beyond which my normal vision can't penetrate, especially in *this* dwindling light. In short, I report: I'm in the dark.

BURT: Then, could there be something wrong with the lamp? Logically, you should examine that next. Obviously, this increasing dimness must be traced to its correct causality.

(GINGER goes to examine lamp, then reports back.)

GINGER: I've discovered nothing mechanically amiss with this lamp, within the capacity of what I'm able to determine. *(Pause)* Burt! I fear— *(Hesitates)*

BURT: Fear!? Fear what?

GINGER: *(Timid at first, then gradually more out of control in disobedience to* BURT.*)* That—I venture to conjecture—it's not electrical problems that we're facing. That there's "something else": something even too specific for words. *(Agitated)* To me, it all looks too fishy, or creepy, or ... There's something grim or gruesome going on. I dread to even *imagine* what it must come out to be. *(Now in terror.)* Burt! My terror is worried over it! I'm sick where my body can never reach!

BURT: *(Reprimandingly)* You're letting me down! Your silly phobia about some apparently engulfing darkness contrasts shockingly with that memorable occasion of long ago: Playing a brilliant pose of possum, you evinced such superior practical supremacy to the rest of us who failed in ignominy and fell apart in odd assorted heaps of imbecility.

Then, you astounded further, having in perfection of retribution ostensibly slain Georgia my former love, when above her fallen remnants you laughed at apparent death's gruesome trappings by kissing me in passionate abandon.

Then it was I took my stern vow of resolve to be your disciple, to harden myself, steel-like, to a spartan regime of realism and a bone-dry devotion to the rational.

I implore you: rally yourself! After years of dishing it out, practice those precepts that *I*, in arduous obedience to the rigors of your discipline, have now contemptuously mastered!

GINGER: I'm compelled, Burt, in my gathering fear, to disobey. I must persist, then, in insisting: The problem we both face is strictly non-electrical, in a non-appliance sense. I dread to intuit—yet intuit I must—that there's "something else" afoot. For the life of me, I can't put my imaginative finger on it; yet it stares me brazen in the face. What it can be, I wouldn't want to look in the face. *(Terrified)* Burt—hold me, I'm scared!

*(*BURT *obeys, holds her, but perfunctorily, with no passion or conviction.)*

GINGER: Kiss me! I need love!

*(*BURT *obeys, kisses her, but perfunctorily.)*

BURT: Ginger—

GINGER: *(Eagerly; starving for some love affirmation, a sign of passion.)* Yes!? Yes!?

BURT: *(Coolly)* Do reach into the side table drawer, and pull out the electrical repair manual, won't you? *(Sees her do this. Coldly.)* The next step, of course, is to hand it over to me. *(She does so. Then, with chilling formality.)* That's terribly kind.

(Squinting in the ever-dimming light to read repair manual, BURT *leaves* GINGER *alone with her mounting fear, her chilled loneliness, her love deprivation.)*

(Focus shifts back to the left, to other bedroom.)

JASPER: *(Slowly, gravely)* Across great Darkness, encountering terrors that belong only to the Unknown, double-mounted on one slow steed of Love, we travel in quest of timelessness. Suspend your breath. Stop your heart. We're not in this bedroom. We're lost, directionless, and hand in our senses, abandon them....

GEORGIA: *(Alarmed)* It should be the *other* way: brighter! more vivid!

JASPER: *(In comparison with GEORGIA—gravely, slowly, wonderingly, discoveringly.)* Hush up your interference! Ordinary expectations don't apply here. Stop preparing. Abandon habitual logic. We're in a world-lessness. It's beginning to envelop us. No more mental "meaning," now. We're coming into word-lessness.

GEORGIA: *(Half-shrieking)* I'll quit! I back out! Is there no will left?!

JASPER: *(Slow tempo, gravely)* Are we there? My final feeling is only familiar fear.

GEORGIA: Have you won? Or lost?

JASPER: It's *"we"*—in *either* case.

GEORGIA: *(Ordering)* Define our state!

JASPER: No definitions ease this complete change. It's beyond our figuring out. We're converted into sound-lessness. What *we* are ... is only what we *were. (Pause)* Something we've never been without, is stopping: It's what we knew as ... "Now."

(Focus switches back, in gradually further dwindling light, to right side of stage, to other bedroom.)

BURT: *(Straining and squinting in dim light; but calmly reading instructions out loud from repair manual.)* Detach the lampshade from its axis base. Lower the switch from its adjacent hook. Pluck out the plug from its companion socket. Check the bulb's metal filament magnet. Using plyers, carefully dismantle ...

GINGER: *(Increasingly fearful while following BURT's instructions and dismantling lamp.)* It's not working—*nothing* is working!

BURT: *(Stops squinting at repair manual; turns to squint at GINGER instead; admonishingly.)* Resist hysteria; cling to rational practical realism at all odds, at any cost. We must determine what in this world—or to be more precise, in this *room*—is so irritatingly, disturbingly wrong, that we can't put it to rights. Everything—which includes anything—is explainable.

(Squints more at GINGER) You look, in the groping scarcity of light, troubled, disturbed, agitated, bothered; so I ask, multibly: What's your

fuss or disturbance? What's bothering you, or eating you? Woman, what's up?!

GINGER: *(Jitteringly agitated, but defiant)* There's more at foot, or wherever, or at hand, or wherever, than meets, dear Burt, the apparent eye of your speculation. Shallow mechanical facts won't help us now. *(Pause; alarmed, decisive)* We're in for it!

BURT: *(Scoffing)* Nonsensically pumped-up melodrama, richly thrilling! You indulge your sweet throb of delicious terror!

GINGER: *(Vehement)* I'm not in this for fun! This is no enjoyment feast! Neither pleasure nor delight attends my conviction: Something's lurking—more than meets the fading eye.

(Focus now includes both sides of stage, both bedrooms.)

JASPER: *(Now standing on bed, peering forward, thrust into unknown, like figurehead on prow of ship. Speaking with cadence of incantation.)* What we are—is only what we *were*. Something we've never been without, is stopping: It's what we knew as—"Now." *(Pause)* Just what was that "now"? (Strange to be almost looking back!) Now by now by now; it was the familiar succession, duration, sequence, consecutiveness, of now by now by now, like the common daily air of the ever-reassuring breath of atmosphere all around about us in the air of ever-onward consciousness. Now by now by now— *(Pause. In a stroke of grave fright-realization:)* But there's no "now," now! *(Shouting)* No more "now"! We've run out of "now"s!

BURT: *(Sitting on edge of bed, squintingly and strainingly referring to electrical handbook manual. Scolding GINGER.)* Don't you stall! In the socket mechanism are those wires fastened securely? Don't go lax! Brace up!

GEORGIA: *(Clutching a leg of JASPER, who's still standing on their bed.)* Am I deceived? Are you fraud—or are you saint? Which is it, finally? Reveal a conclusion! Am I unforgiving—or grateful? I insist I be told! This loyalty I invested... What returns on our faith? *(Slight pause)* How did we come out?

GINGER: As to what's happening *(Kneeling on floor beside bed)* —there's not only more than meets the eye, but the eye, in its turn, isn't met any more, it being too dark.

From the eye's side, and from the side of what feeds and meets the eye, there's equally the falling away. There's less than meets the eye, and less the eye itself—and even the "less" runs out.

Now, there's no eye: for there's nothing to meet it! *(Weeping with terror.)*

JASPER: In conclusion, what is there to conclude? I sought immortality for every member of my club here—the Humanity Club, that doesn't exclude anyone. But it seems we four have been admitted to a club of even broader membership, to the least exclusive club of all—to the club of nonexistence.

(To audience) Join us, there's no hurry. Join us, when, in common with us, you're unmade with the same lack of clay. Time shall unite us. But don't make haste. Procrastinate. Joining us too soon would be self-destructive. Put it off.

CURTAIN

Jack Gilhooley

The Time Trial

JACK GILHOOLEY is a recent alumnus of New Dramatists and a member of ASCAP Musical Theatre Workshop. His plays have been developed at The O'Neill Theatre Center, The Aspen Playwrights Festival, The Sundance Playwrights Lab, and The Avignon Festival. As a National Endowment for the Arts and PEN grant recipient, and a Shubert Fellowship winner, his works have received five Ford Foundation production grants. Additionally, he has been commissioned twice by the Actors Theatre of Louisville, and twice by The Corporation For Public Broadcasting (*Earplay* and *American Playhouse*). His work has been produced on three continents and throughout the USA at such theatres as NYSF, the Manhattan Theatre Club, the Circle Rep, The Phoenix, Theatre for the New City, The Folger (D.C.), Theatreworks (Colorado), The Shubert (Philadelphia), Asolo State Theatre (Florida), Theatre By The Sea (New Hampshire), Indiana Rep (twice), ACT/SF, and a score of other playhouses. He recently has finished the book and lyrics to a nine-character musical, *Mummers*.

Raised in Manhattan and Philadelphia and a dual citizen of Ireland and America, Gilhooley is on The Board of Directors of The National Theatre Workshop of The Handicapped.

For stock and amateur production rights, contact: Broadway Play Publishing, Inc., 357 West 20th Street, New York, NY 10011. For all other rights, contact: Jack Gilhooley, 639 West End Avenue, New York, NY 10025.

The Time Trial opened in a workshop production on March 16, 1975, and later reopened in a rewritten workship production on April 29, 1975, with the following cast:

Slime	Tracey Walter
Candy	Diane Stilwell
Ziggie	Tom Lee Jones
Glenna Rae	Ellen Sandler
Bo Peep	Jayne Haynes
Ricky	Robert Burgos
Slick	Graham Beckel

Joseph Papp was the Producer; Peter Maloney, the Director; Bernard Gersten, the Associate Producer; the Setting by John Pitt; Costumes by Patricia McGourty; Lighting by Spencer Mosse; and Music by David Maloney, with Lyrics by Jack Gilhooley.

Cast of Characters

CARLTON "SLIME" PINE—twenties, retarded(?), slovenly. He's accepted out of pity and the need for a "go-fer".

CANDY—early twenties, her looks are her real asset.

ZIGGIE—twenties, mean, handsome/ugly. Head honcho.

GLENNA RAE—twenties, pretty but dissipated. Smart, tough.

BO PEEP—twenties, pretty. Fancies herself an artist.

RICKY—twenties, Nam vet, and wears it like a badge.

SLICK—twenties, strong, silent, Tiresias of the pack.

Time and Place

The time is the seventies, small town America (The South[?]). Act One takes place in a raceway grandstand in the morning. Act Two takes place in an automobile graveyard somewhat before sunrise the next morning.

Production Notes

The Time Trial is not intended to be staged or designed naturalistically. Rather, the director should view it in terms of "off-center" realism. How far "off-center" is a matter of choice, but it's suggested, for instance, that the automobile grave-yard needn't have as its focal point a *real* wrecked car (although that's a pos-sibility, if the theatre can manage it). Ideally, something resembling a Chamberlain auto-collage that's been brightly painted gold, with the number "7" decipherable on its mangled hood, should be a suggestion of the desired effect. Nor need the wreck be composed of real auto parts, especially since the machine should be smashed and burned beyond recognition. A designer who has worked in light sheet metal, or a similar material, should almost be able to "mold" the effect.

Hopefully, it should soon become apparent that the language is something other than documentary realism, and the staging should almost be choreo-graphed at times. When, for instance, a crash occurs, the actors should "rivet" not to the point of a stylized freeze, but enough so that there should be a sense of suspended animation. When the possibility of physical confrontation (e.g., Ziggie vs. Ricky) seems imminent, the others should "scramble" to vantage points.

In brief, despite the summer's oppressive heat, these seven are the town's "activists" for better or for worse, and their rambunctiousness and deviltry are almost practiced with a sense of pride or honor in a languid environment.

The sound track *should* be available from the author.

Act One

(The play opens on a tiny portion of the grandstand at The "Speed" Constant Raceway. The characters will sit (or romp) on raked rows. In all, they don't need much room. In fact, a sense of confinement should be sought since that's really what's at the core of their lives.)

(A three-foot wall (theoretically concrete) should separate the actors from the audience if played proscenium. It should be decorated with logos of trade products.)

(At rise, we see a single young man and hear an approaching racing car. He watches from his left and, of course, as it approaches, he will shift his gaze (and his head) further right. The car will pass him in a flash as the roar peaks. The young man pivots his gaze as fast as the car has passed. From the outset, we should have the notion that CARLTON *(affectionately nicknamed "*SLIME*") is a bit "off" in his look and in his demeanor. Perhaps a perenially slack jaw or drooping eyelids should give the impression of a semiretarded state. His clothes should reflect a certain carelessness . . . sloppiness . . . indifference, etc. (e.g., his jeans might be held-up by clothesline).)*

PUBLIC ADDRESS ANNOUNCER: *(Off)* And that was Sutter Sinclair of Tullahoma, Tennessee drivin' a Bobcat Superstreak.

*(*SLIME *stands and shouts almost as though Sutter could hear him.)*

SLIME: ATTA GO, SUTTER! THAT'S USING' YOUR LEAD FOOT! *(As he sits)* Only don't cut that turn so wide.

(He stares blankly ahead. After a moment, he spies a trash can. He crosses and starts tossing stuff out of the can until he comes to a crumpled sheet of tin foil. He removes a ball of foil from his pocket and adds the new sheet to it. He packs the new sheet down with concentrated effort. When he incorporates the new piece, he looks at the slightly expanded ball with pride.)

SLIME: Silver!

*(*ZIGGIE *and* CANDY *enter. He is a tall, lean, mean son of a bitch. She is pretty, blank, and couldn't care less about auto racing.)*

CANDY: Hiya, Slimebucket.

ZIGGIE: *(Crossing)* Whatcha got there, boy?

*(*SLIME *extends the ball of foil.)*

ZIGGIE: *(Scruffing him affectionately.)* Shoulda known. *(Indicating the can)* Now, tidy up. Cleanliness is next t'Godliness. You ever heard that, boy?

SLIME: Yeah, but I never believed it.

CANDY: Ain't that the truth. You could grow potatoes in your ears.

(SLIME *crosses and redeposits the trash.*)

CANDY: *(Angrily)* Not a sign of 'em! Hey Slime, you seen a sign of 'em?

SLIME: Don't believe so. I seen a blue car in the parkin' lot awhile back but I couldn't tell if—

CANDY: A simple "Yes" or "No" will do.

SLIME: Blue's a pretty common col—

CANDY: YES OR NO?

SLIME: *(A confused pause)* No.

CANDY: Thanks, Slime.

SLIME: Welcome, Candy.

CANDY: We shouldna listened t'that dizzy-ass bitch, Glenna Rae. Ziggie, you better inventory the goods when they get here. They're probably off gettin' stoned this very minute and laughin' up their sleeves at us.

(SLIME *raises his hand to his mouth and laughs up his sleeve.*)

CANDY: *(Ignoring him)* We oughtta go lookin' for those mothas.

ZIGGIE: Candy, will you shut your face? Just sit back an' wait for the next run.

SLIME: Hey Zig, maybe she's right. I wouldn't trust Glenna an' those—

ZIGGIE: All four a'them ding-a-lings put together don't have the guts t'cop what's mine. 'Sides, Glenna Rae ain't gonna miss ole Speed.

CANDY: Yeah, she'll never miss his time trial. All week long, time trial this an' time trial that. *(Beat)* Say, what in hell is a time trial?

ZIGGIE: You don't much care for this sport, huh?

CANDY: *(Shrugs)* Hmph! Driver drivin' in a circle till some guy waves a teensy tablecloth at him.

SLIME: You hit it, baby.

CANDY: Don't *you* call me "baby". That's Ziggie's term of endearment.

SLIME: I wasn't referrin' t'no endearment. I was referrin' ti'im-maturity.

(ZIGGIE *cuffs* SLIME, *playfully.* SLIME *smiles proudly at his own one-upsmanship.*)

P.A.: *(Off)* And Sutter Sinclair qualifies.

CANDY: Car ever go outta control in a time trial?

SLIME: Nah, hardly ever.

CANDY: Then it's not likely we'll see anyone get smithereened, today.

SLIME: *(Shakes his head)* Tomorra more likely. Durin' the race.

CANDY: Well then, I'm goin home t'get some shuteye.

(She heads off. She stops out of their sight but not out of earshot. The men pretend they think she's left.)

ZIGGIE: Good riddance t'her, huh, Slime?

(SLIME grins, nods, and ZIGGIE throws his arm over SLIME's shoulders. SLIME pats ZIGGIE on the back in a mock display of male camaraderie.)

SLIME: Don't know why they let broads inta raceways, anyway.

ZIGGIE: Who'd fetch our beer?

(They laugh as CANDY returns.)

CANDY: Changed my mind. I'll stay just t'spite you guys. *(Beat)* An' t'keep you away from one another.

(The men laugh again.)

ZIGGIE: "Smithereened"? Candy, you are a cold-hearted woman.

CANDY: Only with racin'. How can you—of all people—call me a cold-hearted woman? *(Shakes her head)* The things I do for you . . . Hey Zig, d'you think Speed's the only guy Glenna ever loved? I mean *love*, loved.

SLIME: He's just the first guy she ever screwed. First in a long, long parade.

CANDY: A parade you ain't marched in, Slimey-boy.

SLIME: I wouldn't touch 'er, 'less a doctor checked 'er out.

CANDY: You'd do more than touch 'er but she wouldn't come within reach of your cage.

SLIME: *(Thoughtlessly)* I get mine, Candy.

(ZIGGIE and CANDY react simultaneously and angrily to the remark. ZIGGIE springs at the terrified SLIME.)

CANDY: YOU FILTHY LITTLE PIG!!!

ZIGGIE:: You better watch how you talk t'my girl, you little tub a'scum. *(Beat)* You better go to the car an' fetch that bottle a'wine!

SLIME: I'm sorry . . . It slipped out . . . Honest . . . Please, Zig. Don't hurt me . . . Won't never happen again . . .

(SLIME has been shaking his head vigorously in terror. ZIGGIE releases him.)

ZIGGIE: An' don't hurry back!

(As SLIME starts to exit, ZIGGIE grabs him again. SLIME re-defenses.)

ZIGGIE: An' it ain't gonna happen again, Mr. Bigmouth! An' if you ever, *ever* tell anybody. . . .

SLIME: *(Quaking)* Lips're sealed, Zig.

ZIGGIE: You tell *anyone* an' they'll be sealed in cement! Now get a move on.

(He releases him with a kick. SLIME's off like a shot. Long pause. ZIGGIE crosses to caress the dejected CANDY.)

CANDY: *(Wry smile)* I never seen that little turd hurry anywhere.

(She starts to whimper. ZIGGIE holds her comfortingly.)

ZIGGIE: You heard me. It ain't gonna happen again.

CANDY: Once is more than enough.

ZIGGIE: Hey, it ain't like ya had sex with him.

CANDY: Of sorts, I did!

ZIGGIE: You gave 'em a bath out at the quarry was all.

CANDY: That's *not* all. I don't mind soapin' his back . . . his greasy hair, even. But . . . *(She grimaces, shakes her right hand.)* . . . disgustin'.

ZIGGIE: Look, he got excited . . . aroused . . . had an accident a'nature, that's all. Nothin' disgustin' about it.

CANDY: With him, it's disgustin'. A quarry's not a bathtub. An' he's able t'bathe himself.

ZIGGIE: Well . . . I dunno about that. Hey Candy, the boy was so dirty he was becomin' a health hazard. Look at it as civic duty. *(Beat)* Hey, it's probably as close as he'll ever get t'the real thing with a girl. *(Beat)* It was an act of compassion.

CANDY: Yeah, well, I didn't feel like any Angel of Mercy. Compassion's when ya feel somethin' for someone. I don't feel nothin' for him . . . not even contempt.

ZIGGIE: *(Diverting her)* Hey, hey, looka here.

(We hear a faint motor. ZIGGIE puts a battered pair of binoculars to his eyes.)

CANDY: Is it Speed?

ZIGGIE: *(Shakes his head)* Some West Coast punk drivin' a Panther II.

(He offers her the glasses. She declines.)

CANDY: Ya seen one, ya seen 'em all.

P.A.: *(Off)* From Fresno, California, drivin' a Panther II, Billy Harland.

ZIGGIE: *(Smiles proudly)* What'd I tell ya?

CANDY: There must be a market for a mind like yours.

(ZIGGIE stares menacingly.)

CANDY: Only kiddin', Zig.

(The car starts off with a terrific blast. They watch, as did SLIME.)

CANDY: Is Mr. Billy Harland doin' good?

ZIGGIE: He'll make it O.K. Can't touch Speed, though. He'll kick ass an' take numbers offa these diddleyshitters.

CANDY: Zig, how come if Speed's so good he come back t'this hick town and second-rate track? He usta race that big one in Europe...

ZIGGIE: The Grand Prix.

CANDY: That's how you say it? I been sayin' it like it's spelled: Prix! That's a whole other contest.

ZIGGIE: Pree! It's French

CANDY: But I'm not. *(Beat)* You dunno French.

ZIGGIE: No, but I know racin'. Anyway, it ain't a bad track. Best in the region. An' it's all we got we're known for.

CANDY: That an' the hog-callin' championships.

ZIGGIE: He came back for us.

CANDY: "Us?"

ZIGGIE: His home folks. They named the track after him so he come home t'give us a thrill.

CANDY: *(Bored)* Well, I must be missin' somethin'.

P.A.: *(Off)* An' Billy Harland is a qualifier. *(Lethargically)* Atta boy, Billy.

ZIGGIE: Always was a class guy. When my daddy got killed...he kinda took me under his wing. Like a big brother. We'd go huntin'. Fishin'. Once I hooked me this big ole channel cat. Thought it was a whale... pulled me right in. *(Laughs)* Couldn't swim a lick. He just laughed. He watched me thrash around until I was about t'go under. Then he scooped me up by the seat a'my jeans. I don't remember if I was more hurt than pissed. But, I know one thing. Next week I hitched t'the county "Y"... an' I started t'learn how t'swim. *(Beat)* I grew older, he taught me cars. Taught me all I know. *(He reflects.)*

CANDY: Ricky Roo says he's spooked.

ZIGGIE: Huh?

CANDY: Ricky says Speed is chickenshit, now.

ZIGGIE: HE WHAT???

CANDY: *(Retreating)* I'm merely conveyin'...repeatin'.

*(*SLIME *re-enters cautiously, with a bottle of cheap wine.)*

SLIME: What'd I miss?

CANDY: *(Happy to change the subject)* Guy just qualified.

SLIME: No shit!

CANDY: Billy somebody.

SLIME: No shit!

ZIGGIE: Where'd you hear Ricky Roo talk that kinda talk?

CANDY: You weren't there.

ZIGGIE: *(Impatiently)* Naturally. If I was there, I wouldn't hafta ask.

CANDY: We were up at Provosnik's Paradise on 379 droppin' reds an' drinkin' "Rocks" when we started talkin' about Speed an' how he's the only one ever made it big outta here. *(Starting to savor the event)* An' I says, "How 'bout Marsha Enright on *Return To The Edge of The Storm*? An' bigmouth Bo says, "She usta wear the biggest braces in town." An' I says, "Looked like the grill of a Cadillac." Oh, everybody laughed at that one. An Bigmouth says, "Underneath that make-up, she got more craters than "The Man In The Moon'." Nobody laughed. But they perked up when I says, "Marsha's a dyke. Everybody knows that." They all agreed. Then Bo—

ZIGGIE: *(Angry exasperation)* Fuck Marsha Enright!!!

CANDY: Not likely, Zig. She's a dy—

ZIGGIE: TELL ME ABOUT RICKY!!!!!!!

SLIME: *(Nervously)* Here's your wine, Zig. I forgot t'pee. *(He starts to hustle off.)*

ZIGGIE: GET BACK HERE!

(SLIME returns reluctantly and sits on the front row. He rivets on the track. ZIGGIE stares at CANDY.)

CANDY: Well, ya gotta realize Ricky was flyin' high an' he just come out an' said ... You tell 'im, Slimebucket.

SLIME: I dunno nothin'.

CANDY: *That* we know. But you *can* hear.

ZIGGIE: Look, if one or the other of you turkeys—

CANDY: O.K., O.K. .... Well, Rick said Speed's been spooked since the accident. No heart no more.

SLIME: No balls.

ZIGGIE: Ricky said that about *Speed*?

SLIME: *(To CANDY, half-amused)* 'Member he said his differential's fallin' apart?

ZIGGIE: What's 'at supposed t'mean?

SLIME: *(Sobers)* Ah dunno. But it sounded like a gooder at the time.

CANDY: Said Speed'll be doin' hot rods, soon. Said he's playin' minor leagues now, headin' for the sandbox.

SLIME: *(Correcting her)* Sandlots ... sandlots ...

ZIGGIE: Was Glenna there?

CANDY: Sorta. She was sleepin' one off on the shuffleboard.

P.A.: *(Off)* O.K., folks, let's hear it for L.A. Carpenter from Huntsville, Alabama drivin' his Leopard 27X.

(SLIME has opened the bottle of wine and is about to swig. ZIGGIE intercepts. The car zooms away from the starting line.)

ZIGGIE: Hey, I told you before, you drink last from a bottle. That's all!

CANDY: You're unhygenic, Slime.

(ZIGGIE swigs and passes it on to CANDY, who swigs reluctantly, then grimaces.)

SLIME: *(Watching the track)* Boy's doin' purty good.

ZIGGIE: That "boy's" old enough t'be your father. An' he's nothin' more than a meatball drivin' a bucket a'grease.

CANDY: Then Speed oughtta whip him, huh?

ZIGGIE: Hmph! *(To SLIME)* 'Member when we was just peanuts an' we'd climb over that fence *(Thumbing over his shoulder)* t'watch Speed when he was just startin' out?

CANDY: I guess I can't get it up for racin' cause I wasn't raised up here.

ZIGGIE: The loss is yours, Candy. Speed had a special feelin' for his piece. Like him an' his machine were welded together.

SLIME: Like they was true lovers, almost.

CANDY: "Feelin' his piece" ... "Welded together" ... "True lovers". I know you guys are a little kinky but don't lay that rap on Speed.

P.A.: *(Off)* Sorry, L.A., yer off by a whisker.

SLIME: *(Shouts)* SORRY, L.A. *(Beat; afterthought)* SORRY LARD ASS! *(Laughs)*

CANDY: Stop talkin' t'yerself.

(Four others have entered from the upstage area. They have a couple more bottles with them. The women are attractive, although GLENNA RAE is a bit disheveled. BO PEEP carries a guitar. RICKY RUANE wears a lightweight sleeveless jacket. On the back is a map of Vietnam and the inscription, "When I die I'll go to Heaven cause I spent my time in Hell." Below that reads, "Vietnam". Finally, SLICK is one of those guys who's convinced that stoicism plus thumbs in beltloops plus a tooth-

pick plus sunglasses equals machismo. All wear clothing and hair that the townsfolk are convinced would be more appropriate elsewhere. They are undetected until GLENNA RAE *screams into* CANDY'S *ear . . .)*

GLENNA RAE: Eeeeeee!

*(*CANDY *leaps in terror to* ZIGGIE, *as does* SLIME. ZIGGIE *is unruffled. He stares at happy-go-lucky* RICKY. *The other newcomers are equally "loose" (except for* SLIME, *who rarely registers anything).* CANDY *recovers and heads for* GLENNA RAE, *who slips away, laughing.)*

CANDY: BITCH!

(Suddenly, GLENNA RAE *wheels and stops as if to meet* CANDY'S *challenge.* CANDY *halts and* SLIME *intervenes by holding* CANDY. *She shakes him off in no uncertain terms.)*

CANDY: Don't you touch me again! *(To* GLENNA RAE*)* You coulda made me deaf.

GLENNA RAE: I'd've done you a favor. You'd never hafta hear yourself again.

SLIME: Damn, Glenna Rae. You scared the shit outta me.

GLENNA RAE: If that was true, we'd be buried up to our necks.

BO PEEP: Governor'd declare a state of emergency. Record shitstorm!

SLIME: How you doin', boy?

SLICK: Ahm doin' O.K. How you doin?

SLIME: Ahm O.K.

ZIGGIE: Where you guys been? *(To* GLENNA RAE*)* You! Years since you seen Speed an' you come late an' drunked up t'boot.

GLENNA RAE: Maybe I don't care about him anymore.

ZIGGIE: Maybe you're scared how much you do! Who's got my stuff?

*(*RICKY *confidently produces a pouch.)*

GLENNA RAE: Maybe I don't need an old lover when I can have a couple of young ones.

(She looks in the direction of SLICK *and* RICKY.*)*

CANDY: Is that separately or together?

GLENNA: Two's better than none at all. You'll find that out when Ziggie cuts you loo—

ZIGGIE: YOU TWO SHUT UP! Drownin' out the damn cars.

P.A.: *(Off)* An' now, an ole favorite from Walla Walla, Washington, drivin' his Coyote Timberwolf Q 22, Mackie Morris.

(SLIME is the only one paying undivided attention. The others will smoke ... drink ... gab ...)

SLIME: Hey, ole Mackie Morris, Zig. An' his Coyote Timberwolf.

(SLIME delivers his Coyote Timberwolf "hoot". ZIGGIE gestures to RICKY for the pouch. RICKY winds up and feigns a throw. ZIGGIE starts towards him. RICKY tosses the pouch with a smile. ZIGGIE catches and opens it.)

ZIGGIE: Who's been inta this stash?

GLENNA RAE: Bo Peep, whata you know about this travesty of justice?

BO PEEP: I'm innocent as a virgin.

(Hoots from all but ZIGGIE.)

BO PEEP: Only a figure a'speech.

(The car takes off and soon roars past. All but ZIGGIE turn to watch but with no great enthusiasm. After a moment ...)

BO PEEP: How 'bout you, Slick?

(SLICK just spits to his left.)

BO PEEP: Hey Glenna, is a spray t'his left a "yes" or "no"?

GLENNA: It means, "I know who did it but I ain't talkin'."

RICKY: I cannot tell a lie, Zig. I dunnit. We're pals, huh? Share alike?

(He takes a swig. ZIGGIE grabs it and the contents dribble down his chin.)

ZIGGIE: Right, pal.

(He methodically wipes the rim clean and takes a swallow.)

RICKY: I been meanin' t'ask why you're the custodian, since we all threw in equal.

(ZIGGIE wipes the nearly empty bottle under his armpit and returns it to RICKY. RICKY hands it to SLIME. He wipes it clean and swigs.)

ZIGGIE: You suggestin' I'm rippin' off?

RICKY: I didn't say—

(ZIGGIE feigns attack. The others scramble away. They're engaged in horseplay that could get ugly.)

ZIGGIE: Anybody suggestin' I'm rippin' off?

GLENNA RAE: Slime did.

SLIME: *(Panicky)* No I didn't, Zig. She's a lyin' bitch.

(Laughter from all but ZIGGIE.)

ZIGGIE: Y'all don't seem t'appreciate the trouble I go to. I prō-cure the best stuff in these parts for you.

BO PEEP: *(Tongue-in-cheek)* 'Preciated, Zig.

ZIGGIE: 'Member our little agreement? I take the risks, I hold the goods. If I get busted, I take the rap. Right?

P.A.: *(Off)* Nice ride, Mackie. Ya got room t'spare.

SLIME: 'Nother qualifier.

GLENNA RAE: You're a qualifier for the pig farm.

(The women snort and "oink" at him.)

RICKY: Why're you so good t'us, Zig?

ZIGGIE: Cause you're like little kids. You need someone t'wipe yer noses.

(GLENNA RAE and BO PEEP go through a little ritual of wiping each other's nose. ZIGGIE is beyond paying attention to them.)

SLIME: We ain't kids no more, Zig.

ZIGGIE: *(To RICKY)* I'm in charge. That's the order of things. *(To SLICK)* Hey Slick, wake up, boy! How was that stuff Ricky Roo picked up a coupla months ago?

SLICK: Like somethin' between Slime's toes.

(Laughter. SLICK likes what he hears.)

ZIGGIE: *(Relaxing)* Now, I suggest we all sit back an' relax an' take in the action.

(They will all settle down, drink and smoke. In general, they watch the track indifferently. They are getting high as well as bored.)

SLIME: Hey Slick, gimmee a toothpick.

RICKY: Give us all a toothpick.

(SLICK dutifully distributes toothpicks wrapped in tissue to the males only. ZIGGIE tosses his away. SLICK looks at him as though he's a bit cracked. He retrieves it. BO PEEP gestures for it but she's ignored.)

SLIME: They're not ladylike.

(SLICK, RICKY, and SLIME go through a ritual of tearing off the tissue, inserting the toothpick and savoring the flavor. It should not be in unison but it should be done fairly simultaneously. The women watch in bemusement.)

SLIME: Ummm! Mint!

BO PEEP: Whatta you guys need toothpicks for? You ain't just eaten.

SLIME: So what, we ain't just eaten?

BO PEEP: Ain't that what they're for? Diggin' food outta your choppers?

SLIME: *(Nodding emphatically)* NAW!

BO PEEP: Then what're they for?

SLIME: Nothin' you'd unnerstand. *(Beat)* Hey, Zig, I ain't a kid. I'm a man.

BO PEEP: A kid's a baby billygoat. That's you, rootin' through the garbage.

SLIME: *(To BO PEEP)* I'm just lookin' for my silver. *(He produces the ball of tin foil.)* I don't eat the junk like a billy does.

BO PEEP: What're you gonna do with alla that silver? Open up a jewelry store?

SLIME: Silver *foil.* *(Beat)* My daddy tole me that in the last war, people got paid for turnin' this in.

BO PEEP: What? I don't remember that. Hell, I'd a been out at the town dump every day if I thought I'd be gettin' paid.

SLIME: Natcherly, you don't remember. You weren't even alive in World War II.

GLENNA: That was *hardly* the last war.

SLIME: The last *real* war.

RICKY: *(Irritably)* You tell my dead buddies they weren't fightin' a real war. Tell 'em they got hit with buckshot.

SLIME: Well, I'm savin' this silver for the next war.

GLENNA RAY: Silver won't help.

BO PEEP: Nothin' will.

(There is a lull. Clearly they are becoming restless.)

CANDY: This is the life.

GLENNA RAE: Sittin' here in the ole ...

RICKY: Oval.

GLENNA RAE: Yeah, oval. *(Beat)* Why d'they call it an oval, Rick?

RICKY: Cause it's shaped round, I guess.

GLENNA RAE: Why don't they call it a zero, then?

CANDY: That'd sum up this whole damn sport.

GLENNA RAE: Or a doughnut?

BO PEEP: Here comes "Speed" Constant once around the ole doughnut.

GLENNA RAE: Hey Zig, when's Speed's time trial comin' up?

ZIGGIE: Awhile.

GLENNA RAE: That's what I like about you. You're so specific.

SLIME: They's savin' the best for last.

RICKY: *(To* ZIGGIE*)* So how come you were worried about us not showin' up at the crack a'dawn?

BO PEEP: He wasn't worried about us. He was frettin' over what was missin'.

CANDY: God, I gotta stay straight this weekend.

BO PEEP: You?

GLENNA RAE: How?

CANDY: I didn't show up again, last Monday. Ole Miz Wilcox gave me hell. You know what a sarcastic bitch she can be, Glenna.

GLENNA RAE: Believe me, honey, I know. I was in an' outta that job faster than a preacher in a cathouse.

CANDY: Tuesday mornin' she greets me with *(Parodies with bucked teeth and crossed eyes)* "Well, if it isn't Miss Terrell, Queen of the Quarry."

P.A.: *(Off)* From Bem...Bemid...*(Evidently consulting a partner)* How you say that? *(Beat)* Bem-id-jee? That's a new one on me. *(Back to his microphone demeanor)* From Bemidji, Minnesota, drivin' a Super Mongoose Special, Freddy D. Handy.

BO PEEP: *(Totally unimpressed)* Wow! A Super Mongoose Special.

GLENNA RAE: So far we've seen a mongoose, a coyote timberwolf, a... what else?

CANDY: A panther...a leopard.

BO PEEP: This is better than Wild Kingdom.

SLIME: Ole Freddie D. Handy. Saw him crash, once.

RICKY: Maybe it'll happen again.

BO PEEP: That what you're wishin' for, Ricky Roo? Quench your appetite for violence?

RICKY: I could always punch the teeth outta that big hole in your face, Bo.

ZIGGIE: It's always a possibility. Ain't that what you're sayin', Rick?

RICKY: *(Coolly)* More or less, Zig. More or less.

(The car starts and all watch until it passes and the sound fades.)

CANDY: Hey, don't anybody wanna hear about me an' ole Wilcox?

BO PEEP: Yeah, Candy, we're hangin' on your every word.

CANDY: Where was I?

RICKY: "Queen of The Quarry"

CANDY: So she says, "I know it would be a staggerin' blow t'J. C. Penney—" *(Aside)* Who's dead anyway, that's how much she knows— "But I think the firm might survive if you'd like t'retire to your retreat on the outskirts of town with your sophisticated friends."

SLIME: We ain't so sophisticated.

BO PEEP: She wasn't includin' you.

CANDY: So, y'know what I says t'her?

RICKY: *(Referring to the track)* Think he made it, Zig?

ZIGGIE: Dunno, it's pretty damn close. Didn't nobody bring a stopwatch?

SLICK: Ah got one.

(He removes a stopwatch from his pocket.)

ZIGGIE: *(Irritably)* Well, speak up, ya damn dummy. We wouldn't hafta wait for ole Casey's announcement. Goddam wino's probably wrong half the time, anyway. *(Grabs the watch)* Gimmee.

CANDY: *(Irritably)* So y'know what I said t'her?

BO PEEP: Didn't nobody bring no music? Jeez, what a pack a'limp-dick deadbeats. We could be listenin' t'some good music all this time we been waitin'.

SLIME: There's music in them motors, Bo, songs in them screechin' tires.

BO PEEP: *(After a stare)* You believe why you just said?

SLIME: *(Shrugs)* Not exactly. But it sounds pretty good.

P.A.: *(Off)* And Freddy D. Handy makes it just under the wire.

ZIGGIE: He ain't gonna be no problem.

(There is a lull. CANDY *surveys the situation and grabs the moment.)*

CANDY: So I says, "Miz Wilcox, you oughtta truck your own boney ass out t'the quarry, sometime. You might enjoy it more'n your Bible classes on Sunday mornin'. You can get yourself stoned, do a little skinny-dippin', screw a few guys. Then you know what I told 'er?

(No response because there's no interest.)

CANDY: YOU BASTARDS KNOW WHAT I TOLD 'ER?

(The others pop to life.)

GLENNA RAE: Sure, Candy, ya told her t'fuck off.

*(*CANDY *thinks a moment, then decides that she'll buy that.)*

CANDY: Why, Glenna, you must be psychic. That's exactly what I said.

The very same thing you said t'her ratty face a while back. I said it loud and clear then turned on my heel and walked down the aisle an' went behind my counter an put on my little pink apron an' started shuckin' jelly beans inta the bags in anticipation of my customers.

GLENNA RAE: Now, Candy, you know you're just tellin' a bold-faced lie. Else you wouldn't have t'worry about goin' t'work on Monday.

CANDY: Truth. God's honest.

GLENNA RAE: Swear it on your momma. C'mon, get yer hand up.

CANDY: *(Reluctantly)* I don't . . . I don't do such a thing.

GLENNA RAE: You don't swear?

CANDY: Not on my momma. Only dirty.

GLENNA RAE: Your momma ain't dirty?

(CANDY is hurt. RICKY rises.)

RICKY: Whoo-ee! I'm gettin' high . . . gettin' high . . . gettin' high . . .

SLIME: That's cause you didn't sleep last night, Rick.

RICKY: If I did you'd've tried t'get inta Bo Peep's drawers.

BO PEEP: He'd'a wound up with a massive rupture.

SLIME: Bull t'both a'those notions.

RICKY: I gotta take me a leak.

ZIGGIE: You sure you're arright, Rick?

RICKY: Long way t'go.

(He starts off.)

GLENNA RAE: All downhill for you.

RICKY: You'll be there when I hit rock bottom. *(Exits)*

ZIGGIE: Yeah, I gotta go myself.

(As ZIGGIE exits, he hands the binoculars to CANDY, kisses her, and heads off. She is elated and watches him leave through the glasses.)

P.A.: *(Off)* From Dearborn, Michigan, drivin' a Prairie Dog V–50, Junior McCandless.

SLIME: Here he is, Slick.

SLICK: *(Spitting with profound disgust)* Sheeee-it! (BO PEEP *grabs the binoculars from* CANDY, *peers, then laughs.)*

BO PEEP: I'll be damned.

CANDY: What's up, Bo?

(BO PEEP hands the glasses to GLENNA RAE. She peers.)

GLENNA RAE: *(Giggles)* Damn! Wonder if Speed knows this guy.

SLIME: Can I see?

(GLENNA RAE *weighs giving the glasses to* SLIME *or* CANDY. *Finally she hands them to* SLIME. CANDY *scrambles to him so she can share.*)

SLIME: Almost looks like the others with that face mask.

(SLICK *comes alive for the first time. He leaps to* SLIME *and takes the glasses.*)

SLICK: Well he ain't like the others. *(Adjusting the focus)* What's wrong with these damn—

SLIME: Focus off, maybe.

BO PEEP: Your focus is way off, Slick. You been viewin' the world with blurred vision since you were a little stubby.

CANDY: What's Slick so cankered about? They're inta every other sport.

SLICK: Car racin's ours.

GLENNA RAE: I always thought they were too smart for this.

(SLICK *sneers at her.* MCCANDLESS *is off and for the first time there is interest by all.*)

SLIME: *(Referring to the stopwatch)* He's doin pretty good.

SLICK: That's cause he's out there by himself. No competition.

SLIME: Still, he gotta beat the clock.

CANDY: Yeah, he gotta zip round t'the nut wavin' the tablecloth.

SLICK: They got reflexes. I'll give 'em that.

GLENNA RAE: Everybody's got reflexes. He's only human.

SLICK: Not everybody's got guts, though. And brains, too. Don't forget that little ingredient.

BO PEEP: You got 'em, Slick . . . that *little* ingredient.

SLICK: *(Ignoring her)* Some of 'em got guts. A few got brains. But none that I ever come across had both.

GLENNA RAE: Yeah, me'n Speed had some real intellectually stimulatin' conversations.

BO PEEP: *(Good naturedly)* Like who does what t'who, an' how.

SLICK: *(Smile)* Maybe he oughtta be drivin' a Cadillac that's three months behind in payments. *(Laughs aloud)* First prize would be a truck-load a'watermelons. *(Laughs again)*

(ZIGGIE *enters, sees them all focused on the track, and rushes to the front of the bleachers.*)

ZIGGIE: Speed???

SLIME: Naw, it's McCandless.

ZIGGIE: *(Shrugs)* 'Zat all?

SLICK: 'Zat all? You know what this means?

ZIGGIE: I dunno that it *means* anythin'.

SLICK: This guy's Jackie Robinson.

SLIME: McCandless . . . McCandless, Slick!

(SLICK kicks at SLIME, who barely scampers out of the way, at a loss to explain what provoked the action.)

SLICK: Now they'll all be comin' in.

GLENNA RAE: They'll break alla racin' records, too.

BO PEEP: Every dark cloud has a silver linin'.

SLIME: *(Giggling)* Hey, that's pretty good, Bo. That tickles me.

P.A.: *(Off) (Lethargically)* McCandless qualifies.

(The women cheer, but SLICK dismisses them. SLIME refers to the watch.)

SLIME: Qualifies? Hell, he got the best time so far. ATTA BOY, JUNIOR!
(He claps, whistles and turns to face SLICK's wrath. He subsides.)

BO PEEP: You might say he's a *threat!*

SLICK: *(To BO PEEP)* You favor them, dontcha?

BO PEEP: No more'n I favor you.

GLENNA RAE: I swear, Slick, you're the youngest man I know still feels that way.

SLICK: *(Nods)* It gets lonely, sometimes. *(Beat)* Zig, don'tcha get burned by this?

ZIGGIE: *(Wearily)* What good's it do? Who're we? You think I like it when they drive up t'the station in a big car an' says, "Fill 'er up, *boy*. An' check out the water an' oil an' tires an' windshield." An' once in a while they'll tip ya a buck. An I sez . . . I sez . . . *(With difficulty)* "Thank ya', sir." An' I pocket the bill. *(Beat)* People like us . . . the world's got our balls in its pocket.

SLIME: Not me. I'm gonna get outta here. An' I'm gonna get rich.

ZIGGIE: Thass why we gotta look up t'Speed. He saw the light an' he made his move an' he made it through.

SLIME: He reached for the gold ring, an' he got it. *(Explaining himself, as if anyone cared.)* Y'know like on the carōūsel out at Hunt's Park?

GLENNA RAE: At Hunt's Park, it's a brass ring . . . an' it's a merry-go-round.

(RICKY staggers onstage, his lip bloodied and holding his sides. All, save ZIGGIE, rush to him.)

GLENNA RAE: Ricky!

SLIME: Jeez!

CANDY: What the hell happened t'you?

GLENNA RAE: *(To ZIGGIE)* What d'you know about this?

ZIGGIE: I don't tend t'Ricky Roo. Anythin' could've happened in his condition. Coulda fell. Coulda pissed on some guys shoes inna can. Guy could've clocked 'im.

(CANDY looks to ZIGGIE's shoes.)

GLENNA RAE: You did a number on him.

ZIGGIE: I don't do numbers on punks. I let guys like Ricky do 'em for me. I didn't touch 'im. Rick, tell Glenna Rae right straight out—

RICKY: *(Staring directly at ZIGGIE)* Stoned . . . should'na drank so fast.

(The P.A. ("CASEY") seems to be getting drunk.)

P.A.: *(Off)* This here's Duane Fields from Chuly Vista, California . . . drivin' a . . . le's see here . . . drivin' a Killershark Unlimited. Sure, what the hell else would he be drivin'?

ZIGGIE: *(To GLENNA RAE, indicating RICKY)* See, what'd I tell ya?

CANDY: C'mon girls, le's get 'im down t'the infirmary. *(BO PEEP helps out. SLICK and SLIME remain behind.)*

GLENNA RAE: Y'mind if I stay, girls? In case Speed—

CANDY: It's O.K., honey. *(Lugging RICKY)* He's a heavy sonofabitch.

BO PEEP: He don't feel this heavy when he's on top of ya.

ZIGGIE: *(To SLICK and SLIME)* Hey, what's ailin' you two? Get your asses up and give a hand. Where's your compassion for yer fellow man?

SLIME: Ain't got none.

ZIGGIE: Well, you better get some. You give us gentlemen a bad name.

(They cross to help, reluctantly.)

CANDY: Don't hurt him.

SLIME: He's arready hurt.

(The four exit with RICKY.)

GLENNA RAE: You didn't hafta do that.

ZIGGIE: Those boys're takin' you women for granted. They shoulda helped Rick down—

GLENNA RAE: Cut it, Zig. You're not talkin' t'Candy.

ZIGGIE: Now, I tole ya, Ricky, tole ya—

GLENNA RAE: Just cause he ripped off a little bit?

ZIGGIE: Rick's gettin' a little too big for his britches. I'm not surprised he got tapped.

GLENNA RAE: You better not sell Ricky short, Zig. He's not gonna take that shit in four months when his probation expires.

ZIGGIE: I'm ready. *(Beat)* Hey, how come you're so concerned about Rick? Maybe you're fallin' for him.

GLENNA RAE: Ricky's just *there* ... like Slick.

ZIGGIE: Y'know, he was sayin' that Speed's spooked causa' the accident.

GLENNA RAE: I *know* he's scared.

ZIGGIE: What???

GLENNA RAE: His brother tole me the same thing. Handwritin's on the wall. His times're fallin' off. Hell, he's 36 ... 37, now. Nothin t'be ashamed of. Damn near got himself killed two years ago.

ZIGGIE: Then why's he riskin' his neck on a dinky-ass track like this? I mean, he was at Indianapolis back in May.

GLENNA RAE: Yeah ... didn't finish.

ZIGGIE: Engine broke down.

GLENNA RAE: Bullhocky, Zig! Fatigue. Nervous exhaustion. Randall says he wants t'throw it in. He's only here t'win big so the Jackrabbit Motor Company'll set him up with a local franchise. He won't really run it. They wanna call it, "Constant Brothers Jackrabbit Sales" so Randall can manage and Speed can shake hands. Once in awhile, they'll fly 'im out t'Michigan t'test a new car.

ZIGGIE: Speed wants t'come back here? After all he's done? After all he's seen?

GLENNA RAE: Hey, he'll be a big turd in a small cesspool. Anyway, he's broke. That ole mansion he was buildin' for his daddy is still standin' half-finished.

ZIGGIE: Damn! We're fightin' t'get out an' he wants back in.

GLENNA RAE: We really fightin' t'get out? *(Pause)* So, I'm playin' a long-shot. If I get t'see him ... see how he feels about me after ten years ... well, I'm told he wants t'settle down ... find a good woman ...

ZIGGIE: *(Snickers) Good* woman.

GLENNA RAE: Shut up, you ... I'd like that ... have kids ... raise a family.

I'd make a good mother. Hell, the only thing I got t'look forward to around here is my Golden Age Discount Card.

ZIGGIE: *(Sincerely)* Glenna, you think he's even gonna remember you? *(Sarcastically)* What were you, about eight years old?

GLENNA RAE: *(Punches him lightly)* He'll remember. He still asks how I am.

ZIGGIE: Why doesn't he ask *you* about how you are?

GLENNA RAE: First night was my fifteenth birthday. He was a sorta present from my big brother. When L. Henry told me that the *the* Speed Constant was in the hayloft...waitin' just for me...I trembled an' shook all over. Hit the sky with my very first lover. Ain't been there again since the day he rode outta town.

ZIGGIE: Ain't because you ain't been tryin'.

GLENNA RAE: Well, if I can't make it with the one that I loved, then I wanna be at the quarry with a few that I like.

P.A.: *(Off)* From Flagstaff, Arizona drivin' that flashy Chickenhawk V—

VOICE: *(Off)* Five. Chickenhawk Five.

P.A.: *(Off)* Well, why don't they write five instead of "V"?

ZIGGIE: Never could figure you out. You're a smart, good-lookin' chick. You wanna sling hash in the Camelot Diner alla your life? *(Half-seriously)* Maybe you should go t'some big city an' sell what you been givin' away.

(At first she looks at him critically, then decides to play along with his little game)

GLENNA RAE: That'd take alla fun out of it.

ZIGGIE: High-class call girl makes a pile a'scratch. Don't hafta work too hard. Get them teeth fixed that're goin' bad.

GLENNA RAE: *(Concerned)* It shows.

ZIGGIE: *(Shakes his head)* Ya told me.

(The car takes off. They pause to watch. When the brief noise subsides...)

GLENNA RAE: *(Continuing what may be his little game.)* Welllll, no dice. I'd need a man t'protect me.

ZIGGIE: *(Smiles)* That'd be a piece a'cake for me.

(They are shoulder to shoulder as they discuss their scenario, which is starting to seem within the realm of possibilities, if circumstances were right.)

ZIGGIE: So, if things don't work out for you with Speed...

GLENNA RAE: I'll be sure t'give it some thought, Zig.

ZIGGIE: Yeah, me too. But I gotta lotta things t'consider.

GLENNA RAE: What's t'consider? 'Fraid you might get bored after this place?

(ZIGGIE *shrugs ... shakes his head.*)

GLENNA RAE: *(Coyly)* Maybe ole Zig's fallen in love with Candy.

(ZIGGIE *just smirks and shakes his head again.*)

GLENNA RAE: Maybe it's your super job as manager of the Econodrive gas station. You even pick up a little extra riflin' the cigarette machine.

ZIGGIE: I ain't talkin' about money, necessarily. I mean ... who'd know me in a strange city?

GLENNA RAE: In a *strange* city, you'd be right at home. Run for mayor. Win hands down.

ZIGGIE: It's tough breakin' into a new town.

GLENNA RAE: Yeah, everybody knows you here but for all the wrong reasons. Anyway, how d'you know how tough it is? You never tried. 'Member the day you got your first car? You said, "Farewell, folks, I'm up an' outta here." You an' that ole heap were back by sundown.

ZIGGIE: *(Evasively)* Wasn't a heap when I got through with 'er.

GLENNA RAE: *(Reminiscing)* Lord, remember we'd pile in that thing on a Friday night an' drive a coupla hundred miles. Only we traveled all that distance in a thirty mile radius. Cruisin' around all night ... all day ... back 'n' forth ... east 'n' west ... north 'n' south, like rats caught in a maze.

(ZIGGIE *looks at her with disdain.*)

GLENNA RAE: Nothin' personal. Figure of speech. *(Beat)* Lu Jean is goin' through that phase right now. Drivin' Momma crazy all over again. She's gone from Friday night till Monday mornin' when she stops in for her schoolbooks. I stopped by the house the other night an' she says t'me, "We eat, sleep, screw, an' go t'the movies in the car. We only get out t'go t'the can. What kinda crummy existence is that?" So I said, "Don't cry on my shoulder, honey. I been there ... an' I made it through."

(*They're pretty much nuzzling each other by now. He turns his head to her.*)

ZIGGIE: You made it through?

(*She turns her head to him, as* CANDY *re-enters.*)

CANDY: Well, well, lookee here! Hope I ain't bustin' up anythin' by my intrudin'.

GLENNA RAE: Nothin' that can't be re-established when your back is turned.

CANDY: 'Zat right? Well, lemmee turn my back around so you can go 'bout your business. *(She turns around.)*

ZIGGIE: Cut it out, Candy. Me an' Glenna gonna mess around, we can do it in private.

CANDY: Not necessarily. Glenna Rae's been known t'do it in fronta appreciative audiences.

GLENNA RAE: You've been known t'do it *with* appreciative audiences.

(CANDY feigns a move at GLENNA RAE but ZIGGIE intervenes.)

ZIGGIE: How's Ricky comin' along?

CANDY: Nurse is takin' care of him, as if you cared.

ZIGGIE: Rick's my main man.

CANDY: Humpfh! *(Beat)* Hey, you two ain't gonna guess inna hundred years who I seen on my way back here.

GLENNA RAE: Speed? Y'seen Speed?

CANDY: Speed? I dunno. What's he look like?

GLENNA RAE: The Pope? Y'seen The Pope under the grandstand drinkin' "Yoo Hoo" an' eatin' "Funny Bones."

CANDY: C'mon!

GLENNA RAE: I give up.

CANDY: You give up, Zig?

ZIGGIE: *(Wearily)* Lord yes, I give up.

CANDY: I don't wantcha t'give up. I wantcha t'keep guessin'.

ZIGGIE: I know. That's why I give up.

CANDY: O.K., I seen...I seen...I seen...

GLENNA RAE: WHO THE HELL DID YOU SEE?

CANDY: CHARLENE DRAKE!

(Dead pause. ZIGGIE and GLENNA RAE look to one another, then to CANDY.)

GLENNA RAE: You're kiddin'. *(Beat)* Nah, probably not. You don't have that much imagination.

ZIGGIE: I thought we seen the last of her.

CANDY: No such luck. *(Pointedly, to ZIGGIE)* She's back...*an' with a husband*. An' guess what about him?

GLENNA RAE: Give up.

ZIGGIE: Ditto.

CANDY: Wow! This is my day for stumpin'. Well, ole Charlene got herself hitched to an Englishman. An' he sure doesn't talk like us.

GLENNA RAE: That's cause he's English.

CANDY: I know, dummy! That's what I just got through sayin'.

P.A.: *(Off)* And Davey Lane of Flagstaff, Arizona is our latest qualifier. *(Beat)* Long! That's Davey *Long*, folks. Shorry about that, Davey.

ZIGGIE: Well, that figures. Charlene always thought she was too good for anyone in town.

GLENNA RAE: Anybody in the whole country, I guess.

CANDY: She chased after you like a bitch in heat, Zig.

GLENNA RAE: Yeah, all her highfallutin' ways went down the drain after a night with you.

CANDY: Her an' her fat ole daddy's money.

GLENNA RAE: Her little red sports car.

CANDY: Summers in Europe.

GLENNA RAE: Snooty New England college.

CANDY: Hey, Glenna, you were twice as smart as her at Robert E. Hell, even Bo was smarter. An' le's not forget about my scholarship t'State.

GLENNA RAE: *(Throwaway)* Cheerleadin'.

CANDY: I'da gone but they didn't have my subject of interest.

GLENNA RAE: Cosmetology.

CANDY: Her daddy woulda shot you 'cept he knew Charlene mighta shot him.

ZIGGIE: She changed any?

CANDY: Nah, I ast 'er ... I said, "What brings the likes a'you back here, Charlene?" An' she says—y'know, real snotty-like— *(Fingers pinching her nose)* "Why, I thought I'd show Rudolph a little of the local color." So, I says, "Why don'tcha go t'Coontown?" An' she turns t'Rudolph an' says, "See what I mean, dear?"

ZIGGIE: Rudolph. *(Grins)* Only Rudolph I ever heard of was a reindeer.

CANDY: There was Rudolph Valentino.

GLENNA RAE: Rudolph Nuryev.

CANDY: *(Blankly)* Right, Now, ya wanna hear about Charlene?

GLENNA RAE: Do we have a choice?

CANDY: I can hold my peace. I ain't obsessed with gossip. *(Pause, then energetically)* However, this is fact, not gossip. And since Ziggie's curious about his ole flame—

ZIGGIE: Whoa, baby! Cut the "ole flame," business. We had a...mutual relationship. We were both "off limits" t'one another. That's what appealed t'me. Draggin' 'er down an' her lovin' it. Most folks never saw that side of 'er. Worked out terrific. I think we detested each other, personally. That way, we knew nothin' would ever come of it 'cept the animal stuff. That's a good way t'have it.

CANDY: *(Quietly)* You feel that way about me, Zig?

(He embraces her casually.)

ZIGGIE: Naw...naw, Candy. Nothin' about you that's outta reach. I feel different about you.

GLENNA RAE: Ain't you two cute.

CANDY: *(To GLENNA RAE)* You'd like t'be in my shoes right now. *(To ZIGGIE)* What you just said is very nice, Zig. I think. Incidentally, I told Charlene you were up here, but she declined a social call.

GLENNA RAE: *(To ZIGGIE)* You'n her ole man could compare notes.

CANDY: *(Enthusiastically)* An' me'n Charlene could compare notes.

GLENNA RAE: *(To ZIGGIE)* That limey's profitin' from your perverse imagination.

(The others start to file back in from the infirmary. SLICK pulls SLIME by the end piece of gauze that completely covers his face, and provides for a makeshift sling. Everyone laughs at this. When SLIME unwraps himself, he will enlighten everyone with a simple...

SLIME: It's me!

(BO PEEP and RICKY follow. RICKY's lip is repaired. He has a six-pack.)

SLIME: We miss anythin'?

GLENNA RAE: Nope. And we didn't miss you, neither.

CANDY: *(To SLIME)* Ya missed...ya gotta guess who ya missed.

ZIGGIE: *(Unemotionally)* Charlene Drake.

BO PEEP: Charlene!

CANDY: Aw damn, Zig! Ya hadda go an' ruin things.

ZIGGIE: *(Ignoring her)* She's married to a British guy named Rudolph.

P.A.: *(Off)* Innerducin' Gunther Sherman of Chambersburg, P-A, drivin' a PL8 Lightnin' Bug.

GLENNA RAE: *(Indicating CANDY)* You sabotaged her conversation for a month, Zig.

BO PEEP: Charlene? That bitch!

CANDY: Yeah, she's still doin' the "hurt dance."

ZIGGIE: *(To* RICKY*)* How you doin', boy?

RICKY: Gimmee a drink.

ZIGGIE: Just answered my question.

(We hear a car take off. RICKY *grabs the bottle* ZIGGIE *offers.)*

SLIME: Hell, this place ain't fillin' up so good for Speed.

GLENNA RAE: It's only the trials. Wait'll tomorra for the real thing.

(Suddenly we hear the screech of a skidding car. The group absolutely bolts alive. They all freeze except for their heads, which follow the car as it skids past and stops beyond them. ZIGGIE *has had the glasses on the driver. They subside.)*

SLIME: Whoo-ee! Nearly had one that time.

P.A.: *(Off)* Shteady there, boy. Just a little tailshpin, folks.

ZIGGIE: Who wuzzat?

BO PEEP: Some guy from Pennsylvania, someplace.

SLIME: Sixty-eight.

*(*ZIGGIE *looks at* SLIME *in customary disbelief.)*

BO PEEP: Long ways t'come t'get knocked out inna time trial.

SLIME: He don't come alla way from P.A. He travels the circuit just like these otha mothas.

BO PEEP: Well, he musta come from somewheres, originally.

SLIME: Maybe originally. Not lately.

BO PEEP: Wish I could go t'Pennsylvania. They must have record companies in Pittsburgh ... Philly ...

GLENNA RAE: Got nobody t'take care of Peggy Sue.

CANDY: I would, Bo.

BO PEEP: You'd be feedin' her a diet of licorice and soda pop.

CANDY: Never hurt me none. *(Thrusting)* Developed my body.

GLENNA RAE: Corroded your brain.

BO PEEP: Wish my momma'd care for her till I got on my feet.

GLENNA RAE: You'd be a top composer in a music town, Bo.

CANDY: Folks'd forget about Marsha Enright.

BO PEEP: *(Imitating)* "The day you brung that lil' bit home was the day you bound your ties t'her. You disgrace me then you expect me t'care for that poor creature."

CANDY: Well, she coulda kicked you out.

BO PEEP: Then who'd tend t' the sheep?

GLENNA RAE: Havin' an illegitimate child around here's no disgrace. It's a diversion.

BO PEEP: Hey Slick, wake up, boy.

P.A.: *(Off)* Let's have a hand for the veteran from Mercury, South Dakota drivin' an Ocelot, Shuper Midget, Murray Hammond...Kick ass, Murray.

BO PEEP: When you were in New York did you meet any music people?

SLICK: Yeah, me'n Frank Sinatra are good ole buddies. Elvis invited me t'his concert at The Madison Square Garden.

(Everyone gets a kick out of this.)

SLICK: That was a big surprise t'me.

RICKY: Elvis's concert?

SLICK: *(Somberly shakes his head)* The Madison Square Garden. *(Beat)* It's round.

(Various reactions.)

RICKY: Closest you ever got t'Elvis was the juke box at The Shangri-la.

(The car roars away.)

CANDY: Did ya get t'any rock 'n roll concerts?

SLICK: *(Shakes his head)* They got people play the streets for free.

SLIME: For free?

SLICK: Well, they pass the hat.

SLIME: You give 'em anything?

SLICK: *(Shakes his head)* They wasn't *that* good. Anyway, who ast them?

ZIGGIE: What the hell did you do up there except spit through your teeth and comb your greasy hair?

SLICK: Rode the subway a lot. All around town an' back t'Queens. That's where my brother kept his trailer and his wife. Then rode back downtown the next day. Times Square, maybe.

BO PEEP: *(Smartly)* Is Times Square round?

SLICK: No, it's flat, like your chest! *(Beat)* Played a lotta pinballs. Seen a lotta movies. Hundred different movies runnin' all night long. Seen Coney Island. Rode the rolley coaster. Stood up all the way. Held on, of course...but I stood up. Seen Greenwich Village. They's all faggots, there. Got my ass outta there inna hurry.

GLENNA RAE: How 'bout The United Nations?

SLICK: Naw, we seen it inna movie in Civics class. 'Member, Bo? Miss Graham made us watch it.

(SLIME—who has been playing with the gauze he stole—improvises a noose when he hears "Miss Graham". ZIGGIE kicks him in the rear.)

ZIGGIE: *(Angrily)* Hey, that's gross a'you, boy.

GLENNA RAE: It's teachin' the likes of you that made 'er do it.

SLIME: *(Half-heartedly)* Sorry.

BO PEEP: *(Back to SLICK)* How 'bout The Statue of Liberty?

SLICK: *(Nods)* From a distance.

BO PEEP: Any plays?

(SLICK shakes his head.)

GLENNA RAE: Museums?

SLICK: *(Reflects)* Saw what you might call a museum. The Bronx Zoo. I ambled past this modern art museum one day an' looked in the window. Just outta curiosity, I went in an' asked how much was admission. An' this lil' girl says, "Pay what you wish today." An' I says, "Honey, I don't care t' pay nothin' which is about what one a' them paintin's are worth."

GLENNA RAE: A real cultural butterfly, Slick.

SLICK: Seen some dirty bookstores, huh, Slick? He brung me back a dirty book.

GLENNA RAE: You guys have real style . . . real class . . .

SLIME: Showed it t'Zig . . . huh, Zig.

ZIGGIE: You showed me the few parts you hadn't soiled.

BO PEEP: That's disgustin', Slime.

GLENNA RAE: Slime wouldn't dig it if it wasn't disgustin'.

(It's time for them to taunt SLIME, the natural scapegoat. It's a periodic ritual and he's come to the point over the years whereby he accepts his role as inevitable, and almost with a sort of goofy pride. The jibes come fast and furious.)

RICKY: Hey Slime, when're you goin t'the big city?

GLENNA RAE: Make the big name for yourself?

BO PEEP: Spin our minds with your plans.

GLENNA RAE: How're you gonna leave, inna Rolls Royce?

CANDY: In the back of a white van in a straight jacket.

ZIGGIE: Where're you gonna live when you're on top?

SLIME: *(Abruptly)* Sweden!

BO PEEP: Right. Sweden.

SLIME: My cousin Delmer tole me—

GLENNA RAE: Your cousin who?

SLIME: Delmer!

BO PEEP: Who?

SLIME: Delmer!!

CANDY: Who?

SLIME: DELMER!!! *(Beat)* Why're you nitwit broads always pullin' this crap?

GLENNA RAE: 'Cause we love you, Slime.

BO PEEP: Infatuated by you, Slime.

(He smiles, coyly.)

CANDY: And we'd like t'meet your cousin Delmer.

GLENNA RAE: 'Cause we don't know this mysterious cousin Delmer. Do we, Bo?

SLIME: Sure y'do. He lives over on Jefferson up from the slaughterhouse.

RICKY: *(Mock surprise)* You mean, "TOAD"???

P.A.: *(Off) (Faintly, as the characters speak over him)* From Strasburg, Virginia, drivin' an XDA Screamin' Vulture, Buddy Freeman.

SLIME: Yeah...Toad.

BO PEEP: He shed that handle like a snake sheddin its skin.

CANDY: That's appropriate. We shoulda called 'im "Snake."

RICKY: 'Member years ago, we took you two down t'the river and re-baptized you?

GLENNA RAE: You came t'the surface as "Slime".

BO PEEP: He came t'the surface as "Toad".

SLIME: Our family never accepted—

ZIGGIE: *(Still peering trackward)* We're your *real* family, Slime.

(SLIME pauses in frustration. He reflects on the designation and, since it came from ZIGGIE, he accepts.)

SLIME: Yeah...of sorts.

CANDY: Good boy, Slime. Now tell us about Sweden.

SLIME: Yeah, Delmer says—

ALL THREE WOMEN: WHO???

SLIME: *(Quietly)* Toad. He tole me about them Swedish broads. From bein' in the Navy. All you gotta do is stand onna sidewalk, like this.

(In a pathetic rendition of his cousin's technique (which was probably fairly pathetic when TOAD rendered it) he loops his thumbs in his belt and the remaining eight fingers point in the direction of the crotch. Everybody—save ZIGGIE—takes up the modus operandi.)

SLIME: Then when you see the one you want you mosey over an' give a nod, like so.

(SLIME jerks his head. He's incapable of anything as subtle as a nod. The others take it up. They wander to one another following SLIME's cue, and "nod". At one point, ZIGGIE turns and sees his six spastic companions strutting and nodding. He separates from them, sits and buries his head in his hands in embarrassment.)

P.A.: *(Off)* Atta boy, Freeman. You're in t'spare.

RICKY: *(Still strutting)* What happens now?

SLIME: She whips you right t'bed.

GLENNA: How long did it take Toad t'score?

BO PEEP: He didn't. He got a wrenched neck an' fallen arches. *(Laughter all around.)*

CANDY: Hey, Bo Peep, how 'bout the song.

SLIME: *(Whining)* Aw c'mon, you're mockin' me with that song.

CANDY: You mock *youself*, Slime. The song is a tribute. A genuine artist went an' composed a song for you an' you wanna press the reject button.

BO PEEP: I'm hurt, Slimey.

(The others—ZIGGIE excepted—start to bang out the country-rock rhythms of SLIME's SONG. One of them pulls out a harmonica. Another bangs two beer cans together, perhaps. Another could tap a bottle with a penknife. Another may simply stomp feet. Everyone with free hands will clap. When they are all into the beat, Bo Peep will begin singing as a makeshift circle forms around SLIME. SLIME reacts paradoxically as he is treated like some moronic deity. He gives the impression, initially, that he resents the ritual, yet he savors the recognition. He slowly gives into the rhythm of the number.)

(ZIGGIE is the only nonparticipant. He remains furthest downstage while the others cavort. When he spots SPEED, he stands on the bleachers. Only then will the song fade as the others start to rivet on the track.)

SLIME's SONG: *(BO PEEP accompanies herself on the guitar. The others sing the chorus.)*

If you ever take a wrong turn and stop in on my home town,
Take a minute to discover, you don't wanna hang around.
The people who talk friendly are just rotten through and through,
But there's a guy you hafta meet cause he's too weird t'be true.

CHORUS

Slime, Slime, remember his name,
Cause this ole boy is headed for the loser's hall of fame.
Slime, Slime, he's really outta sight.
His body's thin and dirty and his face is just a fright.

Well, my home folks are self-righteous as they talk their platitudes,
And when you come right down to it, they're narrow-minded prudes.
They'll gossip, curse and cheat you 'bout each an' every time,
But the worst of them is twice as good as disgustin' Mr. Slime.

CHORUS REPEATED

So when you think you've seen enough and your headin' on your way,
Don't forget t'count your blessin's that you didn't hafta stay.
Cause a Godforsaken place like this you may live to see once more.
But Slime's a thing you'll never see till you're at ole Satan's door.

CHORUS REPEATED

(Almost immediately into the final chorus, RICKY notices ZIGGIE and breaks from the crowd. He reaches for the binoculars but ZIGGIE brushes him off. BO PEEP abandons the song as do the others, midway into the second line of the chorus. We hear cheering. Only SLIME doesn't react. He has been ecstatically skipping in circles, his eyes closed, his jaw agog. He is truly betranced until he pops awake a few lines into the announcement and rejoins the others.)

P.A.: *(Off)* And here he is, folks ... the guy we've all been waitin' for ... the international native son an' namesake of this very same track, Mr. Speed Constant ...

(While CASEY describes the car, SLICK, RICKY and (belatedly) SLIME are enthralled with the details. CANDY and BO PEEP satirize their enthusiasm, CANDY to the point of faking orgasm. ZIGGIE and GLENNA RAE stand next to one another and focus on the track. ZIGGIE remains cool after the completion of the somewhat slurred announcement while all the others go nuts.)

P.A.: *(Off)* ... drivin' his Super Special TP–78 Golden Tiger Cat, with the dynamometer fantail outlet as well as the turbo-charged 8.1 litre mid-engine feature triple X19 cam shafts with free-flow exhaust manifolds, silver-studded radial traction grip masters and including a high dead back axle ration with three crown wheel and pinions, a lightened flywheel, piston-patterned shock absorbers, an extra-long steel drop-arm, rack-and-pattern steering, front struts, zodiac running gear, Apollo linkage, vertical dampers, coil springs, tandem brake master cylinders and a Sears and Roebuck tape deck.

RICKY: Looka that damn car!

BO PEEP: Only midgets could make love in that thing.

CANDY: It is pretty. I wonder who chose the colors.

P.A.: *(Off)* And now our ole hometown buddy-boy Shpeed has consented t'take one lap around the track before his run so's t'acknowledge his old pals. Then he'sh gonna line up for hish time trial and show ush what the world hash been witnesshin'. So, give 'im a hand and a wave when he passhesh ya.

(They follow his approach from their left. They whistle, cheer, stomp—anything to get his attention. We hear scattered cheering in the background. ZIGGIE—using the glasses—glows at SPEED's approach. But his smile fades drastically when SPEED is dead in front of them, and he lowers the binoculars in a semi-horrified state. GLENNA picks up on this and she snatches the glasses. Before ZIGGIE can recover his composure—and his binoculars from GLENNA RAE—she too has seen. He snatches them back as much to keep them from the others as anything. But GLENNA knows and they engage in a verbal debate that is drowned out by the engine and the cheering. All we can tell is that GLENNA shakes her head in vehement negation. Eventually, the heart for argument goes out of ZIGGIE and he sits tiredly and morosely. The cheering fades and the others settle down to wait for the run.)

RICKY: *(Excitedly)* Damn! Gimmee a beer.

(Some go for a beer—but not ZIGGIE.)

BO PEEP: *(To the intense GLENNA RAE)* It's only a man, honey.

(She hands GLENNA RAE a beer.)

SLIME: How's he look, Zig?

ZIGGIE: *(Gloomily)* Good. Same as always.

SLIME: *(Shaking his head)* Same? After alla these years? Tarnation!

BO PEEP: Did he see us when he passed by, honey?

GLENNA RAE: He saw us. Didn't he Zig?

SLIME: I thought I saw 'im wave. Right, Zig?

ZIGGIE: Y'might say that.

RICKY: Hey Bo, you think Speed could inspire a song in you?

BO PEEP: Happens I'm workin' one up. *(Sarcastically)* Speed's a real muse.

SLIME: *(Excitedly)* What'd you call him???

BO PEEP: A muse. A muse is an artist's inspiration, you dumb turd.

SLIME: Like "dope" or somethin'?

CANDY: Dope is you. All you'd inspire is nausea.

SLIME: *(Ignoring her)* Then "Speed" 's a good name for Speed. He's like speed t'us.

RICKY: Shut your holes down. He's gettin' ready t'lay rubber.

(ZIGGIE peers as we hear the motor in the distance.)

GLENNA RAE: Ziggie, I wonder if I—

ZIGGIE: Sorry, Glenna, shoulda brung your own.

P.A.: *(Off)* Here we go, folksh! Billy Ray Jenks is gettin' ready t'drop the checkered flag.

SLIME: Boy, I'm nervous. You nervous, Slick?

(SLICK just spits. SLIME follows the flight, then looks at SLICK.)

SLIME: Wisht I could be that cool. You cool as a bitch, Slick.

BO PEEP: Fire'n'ice, those two.

P.A.: *(Off)* AND HE'S OFF!!!

(They all observe. GLENNA is quiet but intense. ZIGGIE watches through the binoculars. SLIME is the only one overly excited but all eyes are on the car. The noise from the car becomes unbearable as it passes. SLIME's shouts of encouragement are drowned out. After the noise diminishes the others urge him on. By now, RICKY is using the stopwatch.)

SLIME: *(From AND HE'S OFF!!!)* Ow, c'mon boy...c'mon, ole Speed Constant...do it for us...do it for your fans...Burn the guts outta that machine...do it for all of us...for Ziggie and Glenna Rae and Candy and Ricky Roo Roo and Bo Peep and Slick and FOR ME! FOR ME! FOR ME!

GLENNA RAE: *(After the noise relents)* How's he doin', Rick?

RICKY: Zero t'sixty in six.

CANDY: Zat good?

SLIME: *(Almost panicky and watching)* Certainly, it's good, y'dumb bitch.

CANDY: *(Watching)* Don't you call me names, super-shit.

SLIME: *(Watching)* Half-dollar whore.

CANDY: *(Watching)* Bug fucker.

SLIME: *(Watching)* Horse humper.

(The insults are almost an afterthought, as all are riveted.)

GLENNA RAE: How's he doin', Rick?

RICKY: He's gonna make it!

BO PEEP: Zat all?

RICKY: No, that's not all. He's gonna break the all-time track record. BREAK IT IN A TOUSAND PIECES!!!

(They start to chant. All but ZIGGIE, who has been silent throughout, pick up the rhythm. They quickly build to a frenzy ("Speed, Speed, Speed, SPEED, SPEED, SPEED, etc.) until RICKY celebrates the new record joyously. They leap up, embrace, celebrate and, for the most part, take their attention from the track. Again, ZIGGIE's

been above the crowd. Suddenly we hear a terrific CRASH! All leap to the downstage wall, save GLENNA RAE *and* ZIGGIE, *who remain in the grandstand (thus elevated). Some straddle the wall, some lean over. Only* GLENNA RAE *and* ZIGGIE *are not shocked. As a flame effect catches the frozen caged faces, an ambulance siren starts up in the distance.)*

P.A.: *(Off)* Great God Almighty!

Fadeout

Act Two

(The act opens to rural night sounds. Periodically, we will hear a dog bark. The stage is dimly lit, save the illumination from two flashlights manipulated by Slime *and* Candy.*)*

(We are in an automobile graveyard. The flashlight beams play from face to face to Speed's *car—or the auto collage that serves as a representation of the car. Strewn about are left-over or discarded parts of other cars. If played on a proscenium or thrust stage, perhaps the backdrop can suggest the automobile graveyard motif. If possible, it could be a hugh, blown-up photo of a "yard" at night.)*

Candy: Poor sonofabitch never had a chance.

Slime: Yeah, soon's I seen it happen, I had a powerful hunch he was a goner.

Candy: Shrewd! Man bashes into a concrete wall at 120 MPH, flips over eleven times, blows up, and you had a "hunch" he mighta cashed it in.

Slime: I said a *powerful* hunch.

Candy: When were you sure he was worm bait? When the county coroner sent you a telegram?

Slime: He don't even know me.

Candy: He oughtta know ya since you're brain dead. *(Surveying the scene)* God, this place gimmee the creeperoos.

Slime: How come?

Candy: How come? I'm out here with Speed dead an' you alive. If that ain't enough t'spook the shit outta you . . .

Slime: *(Sincerely)* You know I wouldn't hurt you.

Candy: *(Beam offstage)* Where's Zig?

Slime: Zig'll come back. Zig always comes back.

Candy: *(Beam off in another direction)* Hey Slime, who belonged t'that ole T-Bird?

Slime: Oh, "Red Rocket"?

Candy: Who's "Red Rocket"?

Slime: The car was "Red Rocket". The owner was A.O. Purdy.

Candy: Who's A.O. Purdy?

Slime: He was before your time around here. He was a heller.

Candy: Am I to assume that A.O. is in the happy huntin' ground, or did he set out for greener pastures?

Slime: You think he survived that? Got it on 265 one night. Lotsa folks were glad. Not me, though.

CANDY: Whyzat?

SLIME: He stripped that motha clean, souped it back up, dropped the mufflers, then he'd barrel through town 'bout 3 A.M. wakin' alla babies. That's why they called him "Nightmare". A.O. "Nightmare" Purdy.

CANDY: Sonofabitch!

SLIME: Naw! Just a good ole boy.

CANDY: Ain't that Lettie Grissom's Chevy over there?

SLIME: What's left of 'er. Member the night she stumbled outta Provosnik's "Paradise" and smacked inta those folks?

CANDY: She didn't smack inta those folks. Her car did.

SLIME: *(Adamantly)* You gonna tell me that one about "Lefty's Fill'er Up" and the cigarettes?

(By now each has his/her beam in the other one's face.)

CANDY: God's honest truth.

SLIME: If it was true, she'd be in jail.

(During this, SLIME will nod tiredly and mouth "Yeah, yeah, yeah"—as though he's heard it all before.)

CANDY: Lettie stopped at Lefty's for some butts and she was so drunk she forgot to pull the emergency on an' her car rolled back onna road right at the ridge an' killed those folks drivin' cross country like their ass was on fire. *(Dramatically clapping)* WHAM! BAM! That's all she wrote!

SLIME: You believe every half-ass rumor you hear?

CANDY: Weren't no rumor. I did some personal investigation on my own.

SLIME: *(Excitedly)* Then how come Lefty tole everybody that he seen it an he helped Lettie outta her car an' it was a miracle she was only shook up some. That's what he tole Merle Hooper on The Sentinal an' thass what he tole the court!

(They are heating up.)

CANDY: Everybody knows that Lettie paid Lefty five hundred dollars t'tell that tall tale!

SLIME: BULL! Lefty's a church deacon!

CANDY: So was Lamar Wylie before he blinded his mother with lye!!!

SLIME: If Lamar hadn'ta done it, somebody else woulda. OLE LADY WYLIE DESERVED IT!!!

(Things subside as CANDY reminds herself who she's up against.)

CANDY: I swear you're the only one believes that stuff an' nonsense t'this day.

SLIME: What about the jury, Miss Smartypants?

CANDY: They felt sorry for Lettie. Her car was totaled. An' she was drunk. It wasn't a purposeful act. An' the folks were outsiders. If they were local, with kin an' all . . .

SLIME: (Nods) Different story.

(CANDY nods.)

SLIME: Least it got Lettie t'stop drivin'.

CANDY: Didn't get her t'stop drinkin'.

SLIME: Way she drove, she'll live longer doin' a quart a day.

(We hear a car approach.)

CANDY: Hey, somebody's comin'.

SLIME: Ricky Roo.

CANDY: How can ya tell?

SLIME: Hell, girl, who else around here rolls with double camshaft an' twin glass packs?

CANDY: I don't pay no mind t'such truck.

(RICKY pulls in with a roar. Offstage lights illuminate the area and we become aware of some dismantling paraphernalia (toolbox, crowbar, wrench, blowtorch). We hear four doors slam offstage as the headlights go out and the stage goes dim. SLIME and CANDY have their beams pointed offstage. They, in turn, are illuminated by the beams of the newcomers. This sort of manually manipulated light show will continue well into the act when finally the stage will be lit by RICKY's headlights.)

SLIME: (Enthusiastically) Hey Rick, how ya doin'?

BO PEEP: (Entering with tape deck) Since you last seen 'im, he came down a corony, a nervous breakdown, and herpes.

SLICK: (Handing SLIME a beer cooler) How ya doin', boy?

SLIME: Ah'm O.K., How you doin'?

SLICK: (Nonchalantly) Ah'm O.K.

RICKY: (Enters) Where's Zig?

BO PEEP: He left the quarry before us.

CANDY: (Surprised) The quarry? What'd he go back there for? When he dropped (Indicating SLIME) us off here he said he was goin t'town for booze, bennies, an' butts. (Strutting in imitation) "Booze, bennies an' butts."

(Silence. Each newcomer looks to each other.)

BO PEEP: He musta made a wrong turn.

CANDY: He knows this county like the back of—

RICKY: *(Specifically interrupting)* Whoooeee, looka what we got here.

(He drops his own toolbox and leaps upon the wreck, or rocks it with one foot.)

GLENNA RAE: *(Drunkenly)* I wish you could have a little more respect for the recently deceased, Ricky.

RICKY: Like me an' my buddies usta say, "What's dead is dead."

GLENNA: I am a woman in mournin'.

RICKY: *(Crossing away from the wreck)* Bull-shit!

GLENNA RAE: Damn, what a mess!

SLIME: That wasn't no haystack he hit out there today.

BO PEEP: You just ooze with compassion.

CANDY: And sweat.

BO PEEP: *(To* GLENNA RAE*)* Let it out, honey. Have youself a cry.

SLICK: Least he didn't suffer none.

GLENNA RAE: Thank God. *(Skyward, with a vengeance)* Thanks, God! I wish you would let us know what is in your scheme of things. You have one humdinger sense of humor.

RICKY: Easy, Glenna. Speed was a racin' man. He wouldna felt bitter about today.

GLENNA RAE: Then he'd be a damn fool. He got cheated outta half a lifetime. He's cheated in death. We're cheated in life.

BO PEEP: Hey Glenna, only a handful lived a fuller life an', like you said, he did it in half the time

GLENNA RAE: That's not what I said.

BO PEEP: He's a hero. Lived fast, died young. That's what it takes.

RICKY: *(Reacting to the pall)* Hey, hey, hey, Speed wouldn't want us mopin' around like this. Hey Bo, how's that song you been workin' up for Speed?

BO PEEP: Real good. Pretty much the same little ditty I was workin' on before the accident. I just changed the tense from alive t'dead.

SLIME: That's 'propriate.

RICKY: *(Flourish)* O.K. now, our own artist of the first water, Miss Bo Peep Braxton is ready with a song.

BO PEEP: *(Picking up her guitar)* Well, thank you Mr. Ruane for that warm introduction. Now, unnerstand kids, this thing ain't polished yet. I just banged it out as I was—

RICKY: It's the feelin' that counts, Bo.

BO PEEP: It ain't easy composin' like this, y'know ... on the spur a'the mo—

RICKY: *(Impatient smile)* Play away, Bo.

BO PEEP: Usually, I gotta wait for some inspiration before—

RICKY: You need some inspiration??? PLAY THE FUCKIN SONG! *(Beat)* There. There's your inspiration.

(Bo sings Speed's Lament)

BO PEEP: Speed Constant came from my home town, I'm awful proud t'say.
He was the fastest drivin' man in the whole USA.
No other man would take such risks and wake up the next day.
But Speed was pure and he had God to guide him on his way.

(The others mutter lines of approbation ("Lovely", "Touching").)

One hot ole day not long ago, Speed drove back into town.
The local folks were mighty pleased he hadn't let them down.
For Speed had seen the world y'see, he'd surely been around.
But a humbler man you've never seen, even though he wore the
    crown.

(SLIME utters "What crown?". The others SSSSHHHH him.)

The stage was set for Speed's big race, his was the favored car.
Our home town boy would win the day folks said from near an' far.
But God had other plans for Speed an' despite a valiant try,
Our hero's layin' rubber at that speedway in the sky.

(CANDY whimpers.)

BO PEEP: Now, here comes the chorus.

(After a "Sing it, girl!" and a "Truly a masterpiece!" she rips into a raucous rhythm that is an exact duplicate of "Slime's Song" in Act One. The others turn and stare in disbelief as the rhythm becomes recognizable.)

BO PEEP: Speed, Speed, remember his name
Cause this ole boy is headin' for the winner's Hall of Fame.
Speed, Speed was really outta sight.
His car was super special and his heart was fulla fight.

Speed, Speed, remember his name
Cause this ole boy is headin' for the winners' Hall of Fame
Speed, Speed—

SLIME: *(Interrupting excitedly)* Hey, Hey, Bo! That's *my* chorus!

GLENNA RAE: Whataya call that?

BO PEEP: Well, "Speed's Lament". Y'know, workin' title.

RICKY: Well, if you work on anythin', work on the chorus.

BO PEEP: You don't like the chorus?

SLIME: Not in no way, form, or shape!

BO PEEP: Thought I could sneak it past ya.

RICKY: That's like tryna sneak a freight train past us.

BO PEEP: I have trouble with choruses.

RICKY: The rest of the piece ain't solid gold, either.

GLENNA RAE: Pay no mind, Bo. It was real nice. If Speed heard it, he woulda been thankful.

CANDY: *(Innocently)* If Speed coulda heard it, Bo wouldna hadda sing it.

(At the end of her rope, GLENNA RAE lunges at CANDY.)

GLENNA RAE: Candy, I swear t'God—

(She's restrained by RICKY as CANDY flees.)

RICKY: Hey, what're we out here for? T'cry in our beer an' go t'war with each other?

SLIME: Naw, we came out for relics. *(RICKY gives him an odd stare.)*

CANDY: *(Returning)* To take relics from the car . . . that's what Zig said.

RICKY: Well, I came out t'party. We're gonna cut loose tonight.

BO PEEP: Yessiree, here we are in The Grand Ballroom of Caesars Palace on the beautiful Las Vegas strip. *(To CANDY and SLIME)* You guys left the quarry too early.

SLIME: Too damn crowded.

CANDY: I was enjoyin' myself.

RICKY: But Ziggie wanted t'leave so you two follow behind, waggin' your tales.

(SLIME and CANDY shrug. By now, all are sprawled around, passing a joint. SLIME can't participate until it's nearly exhausted. Then it's his to the end. There seems to be a certain sense of exhilaration that doesn't evidence itself when Ziggie's around.)

BO PEEP: Sure see a lotta old faces on race weekend.

CANDY: Mostly ugly ones by my accountin'.

RICKY: Alla them bastards tryna relive old times at the quarry. Come Sunday, they truck their asses back t'their families . . . their brats.

CANDY: Some go back t'their farms. Don't see 'em for a whole year.

SLICK: 'Cept for Sundays on their way t'First Baptist.

SLIME: That don't count.

CANDY: Some go back t'their stinkin' cities an' their itty-bitty apartments.

SLICK: After they tell ya how good they're doin'.

RICKY: Not that anybody ast 'em. They go away, they should stay away. The quarry's ours, now.

BO PEEP: Seen Baby Jean Fletcher out there.

GLENNA RAE: Baby Jean. A walkin' douche bag.

RICKY: Sonny Boy Brockett

(RICKY and SLIME simulate a football pass with a beer can.)

SLIME: Sonny Boy. Figured he'd play out his option with The St. Paul Savages so's he could sign with The Montgomery Mongols. Broke his leg the last game...*(Laughs)* last two minutes. *(Laughs loudly)* Now, nobody wants him. *(Shakes his head.)* What a loser.

BO PEEP: Charlene put 'er foot in 'er mouth out there, tonight.

GLENNA RAE: 'Mong other things by now, I betcha.

CANDY: *(Surprised)* Charlene??? Was Charlene out there?

BO PEEP: *(Defensively)* Well...uh...yeah, she stopped by.

CANDY: Did Ziggy...

BO PEEP: She came over and tried t'make a pass.

GLENNA RAE: He looked right past 'er.

CANDY: *(Brightening)* Heyyyyy...that ain't easy, considerin' alla room she takes up.

(They all laugh, more or less supportively.)

BO PEEP: Matter of fact, he said, "Fuck off, Fatso!"

CANDY: *(Elated)* He did? He said that? *(Imitating)* "Fuck off, Fatso!" That's real nice. *(Beat)* Did that bitch bring Rudy along?

GLENNA RAE: Nah, she said he was home in bed.

CANDY: Yeah, I guess a go-round with "Charlene The Machine" leaves that little raggedy-ass bastard in a state of terminal collapse. *(Slight pause)* Hey Bo, what was it you said Charlene took up at college? Big long word.

BO PEEP: Anthrypology.

CANDY: Yeah, that's diggin' up bones, Glenna?

GLENNA RAE: Well, on one level, yeah.

CANDY: This mornin' I said, "Where'd ya find Rudy, on a bone diggin' expedition?" Oh, was she pissed. She always was jealous of me since I was second runner-up in the state beauty pageant. She stills calls it a "contest", tryna get my goat. What would she know of "pageantry"?

BO PEEP: You woulda won honey, if you'd let me teach you guitar.

CANDY: *(Shrugs)* I figured my looks were enough. 'Side, I mighta lost beauty points if I hadda cut my nails.

RICKY: You were doin' O.K. on "Pop Goes The Weasel" till you dropped the spoons.

(All laugh, including CANDY, at what may or may not have been true.)

GLENNA RAE: Hey Slick, tell Candy how ya greeted Charlene.

SLIME: C'mon Slick, let's hear it.

SLICK: You can't hear it. You don't conjure one up at the drop of a hat. She said, "Hey Slick, You still go all day with nothin' more'n a fart outta you?"

BO PEEP: So he says—

SLICK: *(Exploding)* I'M TELLIN' IT!

(Everyone reacts. He continues.)

SLICK: So, I says, "Yeah, an' I saved today's especially for you." Then I about faced an' let 'er fly.

(The others absolutely love it. Fingers to noses, waving to clear the air, imitative sounds and above all, laughter. Things settle.)

SLICK: Then she called me a "marginal dummy". I said I ain't a dummy. I can talk. I just don't care t' talk t'you. That makes me a smarty."

(All laugh mildly but SLIME, who's obviously affected. GLENNA RAE catches on, then Bo. Finally, an uneasy silence.)

SLIME: She's not a "dummy." She's a cata-tonic.

SLICK: Hey Buddy, I shouldn'a said that. I wasn't—

SLIME: *(Without self-pity)* A dummy is born mute. She just stopped talkin'. But she talks t'me through her eyes. Every night when I take 'er dinner up to 'er, she turns from the TV an' I tell 'er my day. An she answers me with looks an' blinks an' stares an such. Told her about Speed tonight an' she let me know she heard. Said she was prayin' for his soul an' his family. That's *all* that's wrong with her. When ya remember she had eleven kids an' we live on a poor, dirt farm, can't hardly feed us ... well, she coulda done somethin' worse than just clam up. Lots worse. Lots have.

(Silence all around. Finally...)

BO PEEP: Charlene was askin' for you, Slime.

SLIME: G'wan, for me? Charlene?

BO PEEP: Figures you was long gone by now what with all your "movin' on" talk.

SLIME: *(Matter-of-factly)* Got my bags packed, waitin' onna chance.

BO PEEP: She says, "Travel's broadenin'," an' then—

RICKY: Glenna says, "From the looks a'your ass, you been around the world."

(Laughter)

BO PEEP: Maybe you shouldna said that. I mean, she consoled you on accounta Speed's misfortune.

GLENNA: If it takes death t'make her act decent, she can piss up a rope.

RICKY: I won't forget that crack she scored on me.

BO PEEP: It wasn't like you were a real criminal. You were just afflicted with a severe case of joyridin'.

RICKY: Her daddy steals poor people blind. Didn't figure he'd miss that ole Lincoln. He had three other cars.

CANDY: You shouldna blowed alla that dough at one time.

BO PEEP: Rick, when you spend $1200 in one weekend at The Paradise, the accusin' finger pokes you every which way.

SLICK: How was you t'know you were dancin' with the state police?

RICKY: They got broads doin' everythin', now. Hey Slime, how many a'them shrimp cocktails did you eat?

SLIME: Twenty-four.

GLENNA RAE: Then you barfed 'em all over the parkin' lot. Acquired a taste for them and lost it, all in one night.

RICKY: Member Billye threw the pool cue through the juke box?

SLICK: Provosnik nearly croaked when Ricky hands him two C-notes an' says, "Get some new records while you're at it."

GLENNA RAE: Poor Billye.

SLIME: Billye was the best swimmer the quarry's ever seen.

BO PEEP: Who woulda thought she'd've died one night at The Miami Beach Ramada Inn.

SLIME: Who woulda thought the pool had been drained? *(He mimes her fatal dive with his fingers.)* Splat!

CANDY: I been meanin' t'get down there an' do some personal investigation on my own. She was too pretty t'just have an accident.

BO PEEP: Samson Steele's still conceited as ever.

GLENNA RAE: He is a powerful hunk a'young manhood, though, with all them muscles.

SLIME: He wasn't so powerful the night Ziggie cold-cocked him with one punch. He sure looked funny sippin' Ripple through a straw.

CANDY: *(Sneering)* Charlene always pushed Ziggie t'fight for her honor.

GLENNA RAE: A fight for her honor is a no-win proposition.

BO PEEP: Like Slime fightin' for The Heavyweight Championship.

SLIME: *(Seriously)* I am a lover, not a fighter.

CANDY: Ziggie!

RICKY: I don't hear nothin'.

BO PEEP: Wait, I think I hear somethin!

(We hear a car in the distance.)

CANDY: Ziggie for sure. I can hear his car ten miles off.

(The men grab their gear and start to work on the car. RICKY is clearly disgruntled. ZIGGIE's car pulls in offstage with a tremendous screech. For a moment, the stage is illuminated from his headlights. Then it goes dim again.)

RICKY: *(Calling)* Hey Zig, your lights'd help considerable.

(ZIGGIE enters with a bottle. He is clearly stoned.)

SLIME: OOOOOOOEEEEE, Zig, are you smashed?

(ZIGGIE reacts violently, grabbing the terror-stricken, SLIME.)

ZIGGIE: *(Indicating the car)* Given the circumstances, that's not very 'propriate.

SLIME: *(Squirming)* Yer right, Zig. I shouldna said no such—

(ZIGGIE laughs heartily and cuffs SLIME like a puppy. He hands SLIME what little is left of the bottle.)

SLIME: Thanks, Zig. I think I'll partake seen's you just shook me up some.

(After he swigs, SLIME offers the bottle back to ZIGGIE. ZIGGIE eyes the slovenly twerp, then the bottle, then SLIME again. He thinks better of reaccepiance.)

ZIGGIE: Thass O.K., it's a present.

(SLIME is elated, more over the gesture than the liquor.)

RICKY: Zig?

ZIGGIE: *(Ignoring him)* How's the work comin' along?

(Sensing something potentially explosive, the flashlight beams will play off the two antagonists, as each one speaks.)

RICKY: Zig?

ZIGGIE: Not makin' much progress.

RICKY: Hey, Zig!

ZIGGIE: Yoo?

RICKY: Lights. *(Pointing off to ZIGGIE's car)*

ZIGGIE: Can't!

RICKY: Why?

ZIGGIE: I beat you.

RICKY: What?

ZIGGIE: Up here.

RICKY: You left.

ZIGGIE: I came back.

RICKY: You forfeited.

ZIGGIE: I don't forfeit.

RICKY: What's this shit?

ZIGGIE: Your lights, Rick!

RICKY: *(Shaking his head)* What the—

ZIGGIE: High beams!

RICKY: Low beams.

ZIGGIE: I'll give us your high beams.

(He starts off. RICKY steps in front of him. Pause.)

RICKY: No livin' man touches my car.

(RICKY slowly exits. Momentarily, his lights come on.)

SLIME: Shrewd thinkin', Zig.

ZIGGIE: Shaddap!

CANDY: He musta won that Purple Heart in a card game.

ZIGGIE: Killin' gooks ain't like fightin' friends.

(RICKY re-enters. ZIGGIE is a changed man.)

ZIGGIE: Now, that wasn't so hard, was it, ole Buddy? *(Gesturing to the wreck)* You're the body and fender man of record, here. How 'bout an expert's eye-view?

RICKY: *(Grumpily)* We charge for estimates.

ZIGGIE: *(Smiles, shakes his head.)* "We charge for estimates." That almighty dollar comes between friends, again. Whatcha workin' on?

RICKY: Gettin' me a door, here.

ZIGGIE: Atta boy, think big. *(Turns)* Slime?

SLIME: I been workin' on this door handle ever since we arrived.

(The others snicker.)

ZIGGIE: Since you arrived, huh? Maybe you're doin' somethin' wrong.

SLIME: Gonna put it on my own buggy.

CANDY: What an obscenity. *(Beat)* My Uncle Luscious had a car two days an' the handle came off in his hand.

(Absolutely no reaction to her mini-tale. She shrugs, sips a beer.)

ZIGGIE: *(To SLIME)* See, this car's custom. Speed supervised its creation. Read about it in *Auto Freak News.* His boys had pride. A vanishin' breed. Those 'sembly line guys . . . they don't give a damn. *(Beat)* Slick?

(SLICK points to a fender and murmurs something that sounds like . . .)

SLICK: Fnrr.

ZIGGIE: "Fnrr," huh? You oughtta talk more, boy. You're losin' your ability to communicate.

BO PEEP: Naw, Zig. Slick's traveled a lot, seen a heap. He only knows highfalutin' words.

SLICK: *(Threateningly, with a screwdriver)* Keep it up.

BO PEEP: Whooooaaa! "Keep it up?" That's wishful thinkin' on your part after last night, Slick.

(The others deride SLICK.)

SLICK: Take more'n a bimbo like you t'wear me down, Bo.

SLIME: Atta boy, buddy boy!

BO PEEP: You shut up, pigshit. One of my sheep . . . name's Daisy . . . I believe you know her. She says you *are* a lover, at that.

(The others turn on SLIME, who feels compelled to shake his head vehemently and in all seriousness. ZIGGIE's had enough of this frivolity.)

ZIGGIE: Hey, hey, show some respect for the deceased.

CANDY: Just tryna pass the time, Zig.

ZIGGIE: Passin' time is your only activity.

CANDY: *(Coyly)* You know that ain't true.

ZIGGIE: Biggest event of your day is that hour in fronta the mirror every mornin'.

CANDY: I'm prouda my looks.

ZIGGIE: Well, I'm ashamed a'your brain. One cancels out the other.

CANDY: Girls don't need brains if they have other...*(Shaking her rear)* ass-ets.

BO PEEP: You are the livin' embodiment of that, honey.

CANDY: *(Brightly)* Thank you, Bo.

ZIGGIE: An' aside from Speed, you could show concern for sister Glenna there...drownin' in 'er sorras.

GLENNA RAE: Don't be so melodramatic. I'm drinkin' cause I like it.

ZIGGIE: *(To GLENNA)* You gotta funny way a'sufferin'. *(To the others)* Let's get back t'work.

RICKY: *(With a beam on the motor area)* What about this engine, Zig? Smashed beyond repair. Even got bits an' pieces of his flesh hangin' off.

(The women react with revulsion and retreat. The men rally around RICKY and peer into the area in focus.)

BO PEEP: Damn!

ZIGGIE: A frightinin' sight, Rick. *(Turning)* Hey Glenna, come see what I'm so "meladramatic" about. *(Beat)* They say that ole movie star got killed—James Dean—they say when they dug him outta his Porsche the speedometer was buried in his belly. When they pried 'er loose, she read one-thirty.

CANDY: Maybe it was the clock. Maybe he got killed at one-thirty.

(All look to her as if they can't believe her idiocy. She retreats.)

RICKY: Slime, move over an' make room in the idiot box for Candy.

SLIME: *(Disregarding)* I seen pitchers of that Porsche somewheres. *(Beat)* Auto Freak News.

(The dog barks offstage. ZIGGIE takes some ribs from the cooler and starts off with the crow bar in his other hand.)

GLENNA RAE: *(In pursuit)* Ziggie! Don't! He's only barkin'. Dogs bark!

ZIGGIE: It's only the junkman's half-dead, pit bull. He's barkin' from pain. This'll be an act of mercy.

(He exits. GLENNA RAE returns frustrated, anguished, pained. Her fists and teeth are clenched. BO PEEP starts to cross.)

BO PEEP: Don't let it get t'you, Gl—

GLENNA RAE: GET AWAY FROM ME! ALLA YOU!

(She crosses angrily, grabs her bottle, and swigs.)

RICKY: You should care for yourself like you care for that dog.

SLICK: *(Pulling* SLIME's *leg)* Wasn't *Auto Freak News.*

SLIME: Wasn't?

*(*RICKY *and* SLICK *shake their heads.)*

SLIME: *Gearbox Monthly?*

(The other two shake their heads again. SLIME *is in a quandary.)*

SLIME: *Racin' Review?*

RICKY: You seen it in *The Checkered Flag.*

SLIME: *(Puzzled) The Checkered Flag?* I dunno that one.

SLICK: You're not lookin' hard enough.

RICKY: Lotta valuable information.

SLICK: You're shortchangin' yourself.

RICKY: Missin' the boat.

SLICK: Droppin' the ball.

RICKY: Start gettin' *The Checkered Flag.*

SLIME: *(Befuddled; he nods.)* Thank ya, boys. *(Beat, he revives)* Hey, I seena old movie with that James Dean fella a coupla years back at The ElDorādo Drive-In. He was this new kid in town an everybody's out t'get 'im cause he mumbles a lot an' he balls the prettiest girls in town an' he got hisself a souped up ole Hudson.

CANDY: What's a Hudson?

BO PEEP: Nobody balled inna movies back then.

SLIME: They was soul kissin'. That's how the audience knew on the Q.T. they was ballin'. It was a...What wuzzat word we learned in English class back at Robert E.?...Same as a musical instrument?

*(*SLIME *mimes a cymbal effect.)*

BO PEEP: Accordian?

GLENNA RAE: *(Knowingly)* Cymbal.

SLIME: Yeah, thassit. *(Beat)* Where was I?

CANDY: Soul kissin' Natalie Wood.

(An offstage "Yelp" is heard, then another. then a sort of whimper, then nothing. Everyone shudders a bit. GLENNA *distanced from the others—seems to wrap herself in a ball of pain and shakes a bit.* CANDY—*in one of her few moments of enlightenment—decides it's best to continue.)*

CANDY: *(Slight pause)* First time...First time I got soul kissed, I ran home an' washed my mouth out with a whole bottle a' Listerine.

CANDY AND BO PEEP: *(Simultaneously)* "Family size."

CANDY: *(Troubled, looking off in the direction of the incident)* Now, I do it . . . alla time. *(Painfully)* Sometimes . . . I wonder . . . why.

(All—save GLENNA RAE—are focused on her. This time BO PEEP breaks the ice.)

BO PEEP: My momma musta had the hots for James Dean. She'd talk a streak about him when I was growin' up. So when they had that James Dean Festival at The ElDorādo, I went. I saw that *East of The Garden of Eden*. Didn't show *me* much. I said "Shit!" That was my only comment.

SLIME: Shit?

BO PEEP: Right! "Shit!" Hell, when Buddy Holley an' Richie Vallens an' The Big Bopper went down in that plane, all three at once . . . now that was a true tragedy. Mr. Shakespeare couldna dreamed up a sadder one than that. Truly a loss t'music.

(ZIGGIE enters, stands. All eyes are on him. After a long moment, the dog barks. ZIGGIE "Yelps," just as we heard him do offstage a few moments ago. Everyone is relieved, smiling. SLIME gives a bad imitation of the yelp. GLENNA RAE bounds toward ZIGGIE.)

GLENNA RAE: *(Half-laughing)* You son of a bitch, Zig. You sure had us—

ZIGGIE: *(Directly to her, and in no uncertain terms)* You take me for a neanderthal, don't ya? How come you never thought t'feed 'im?

GLENNA RAE: *(Thrown by this)* No, Zig, I knew you wouldn't do—

ZIGGIE: You ever ask yourself why you wound up hangin' around with us? I mean, nobody expected too much from us. But you . . . your brains . . . your promise . . . your values . . . You're the real wash-out, Glenna.

(He heads back to the car. She stands with bottle in hand but without indicating it any more than BO would indicate her guitar—i.e., it's a given. He's crossed, so she talks in a vacuum.)

GLENNA RAE: My mind and my ambition were at opposite ends. *(But, after a pause she characteristically rebounds.)* I knew you wouldn't hurt a pit bull. You're two of a kind.

ZIGGIE: *(Turns, smiles)* I'll take that as a compliment.

GLENNA RAE: That's how it was intended. *(Smiles)*

(RICKY gestures to ZIGGIE, who steps forward and knocks the car door loose with the crowbar. ZIGGIE nearly stumbles drunkenly as he lifts the door above his head.)

RICKY: Take 'er easy, Zig.

ZIGGIE: Hang this right over the door of the station.

BO PEEP: If Pete'll let you hang it there.

ZIGGIE: Pete'll let me hang it there. *(Indicating his toolbox)* Ricky, hand me that greasy ole box over there.

RICKY: *(Broad smile, indicating both* GLENNA RAE *and* BO PEEP*)* Which one?

GLENNA RAE: *(Outraged)* C'mon, let's get outta here, girls.

RICKY: Sit down an' shut up.

GLENNA RAE: Fuck you, Roo Roo.

CANDY: You made a poem, Glenna.

GLENNA RAE: *(To* RICKY*)* You're not talkin' t'your mother, now.

("Owwwww's," "Uh-ooooo's" all around.)

RICKY: You keep my momma outta this.

BO PEEP: Like she been kept outta every barroom in the county?

*(*SLICK *and* SLIME *are amused.* RICKY *spots them.)*

RICKY: You two're supposed t'be on my side.

SLIME: Not if you're gettin' whupped.

CANDY: None a'the three of you got the brains t'keel over if you was struck dead.

RICKY: *(to* BO PEEP*)* You keep kin outta this. If your kid grows up and has a child legit, she'll be breakin' family tradition.

(She swings at him and misses.)

RICKY: *(Dancing away)* No chance a'that, though. Peggy Sue'll soon start peddlin' out t'the quarry on her tricycle lookin' for a little—

*(*BO PEEP *throws a can at him.* RICKY *grabs the crowbar and starts off after her as she scampers away. Everyone knows he'd never use it (or really hurt her in any way, for that matter) and they hoot with pleasure. All do so except the grim-visaged* ZIGGIE, *who intercepts* RICKY *by stepping into his path. Everyone tenses.* ZIGGIE *pushes* RICKY *once, twice, three times.* RICKY *raises the crowbar.* ZIGGIE *doesn't resist . . . doesn't even defend. He lowers his head.)*

ZIGGIE: Go on . . . go on, Ricky. *(He isn't taunting, now—he's asking.)* You have the guts t'do it, Ricky Roo Roo?

*(*RICKY *and the others give him an odd stare. Suddenly* RICKY *"does it" amid screams. However, he purposely misses his adversary and slams the crowbar onto the car. He leaves it behind and walks away.* ZIGGIE *picks it up and follows. The others are dumbstruck.)*

GLENNA RAE: *(Fearfully)* Careful, Zig.

*(*RICKY *turns.* ZIGGIE *is directly in front of him with the crowbar.)*

RICKY: You gonna stick that t'me?

ZIGGIE: *(Offering the crowbar)* I wanna give it t'you.

(RICKY takes it but doesn't threaten.)

RICKY: Zig, I know you're flyin' high right now but I think somethin' happened t'you out there today. Somethin' you're not likely t'get over. *(Beat)* You're just lucky you're facin' a man right now. Not some punk like Samson Steele. He'd scramble your brains like Speed did that car.

(He drops the crowbar, walks away again. ZIGGIE looks around at the observers. Then, after a deep breath...)

ZIGGIE: I think it's prayer time. Let's all gather round this here machine...what's left a'her. I'd like t'express myself in a tribute...a kind of a...

BO PEEP: Eulogy?

(Only SLIME and CANDY partake thoroughly. ZIGGIE will stammer with the words a bit but he will invest the speech with a passion that is uncharacteristic and fascinates, disturbs even, the four on the perimeter.)

ZIGGIE: Thank you, Bo...a eulogy...We place our hands on this once-proud machine, in tribute to its once-proud driver, the late, great, and lamented Hollis "Speed" Constant, idol and inspiration to us all. He was a man who summoned up the old virtues of bravery and financial pursuit and faith in The Lord to become one of the world's genuine heroes. His flame flickered briefly on this earth but it blazed like the devil's own inferno.

(GLENNA RAE, RICKY, SLICK, and BO PEEP look quizzically to one another.)

Unlike other recent and so-called martyrs in this great land of ours, Speed was no self-seeking merchant of special interests and propaganda. No siree, he never forgot that he was a common man, even after tasting caviar and champagne and movie stars.

(This breaks BO up, although she manages to suppress her laughter.)

Yes he made the the small feel tall...

(RICKY points to SLIME, who's in a state of euphoria.)

...the country folk feel city. But most of all, Speed Constant did what nobody else does anymore in this great land of ours...

SLIME: Whassat, Zig?

ZIGGIE: He kept our dreams alive.

(SLIME can't quite comprehend this. He scratches his head, looks bewildered.)

CANDY: Amen, Zig. You said a mouthful.

BO BEEP: *(Half-giggling)* Reverend Selby Baxter couldna said it no better.

GLENNA RAE: Bull shit!

ZIGGIE: You slut. He shoulda meant somethin' t'you.

GLENNA RAE: He did. Somethin' long dead.

SLIME: *(Approaching diplomatically)* Zig, she's just upset. She din't mean no harm.

(ZIGGIE kicks at him and he skips away in retreat.)

GLENNA RAE: Ziggie, *we* know the story out there, today.

ZIGGIE: What "story"?

GLENNA RAE: I hafta tell ya?

ZIGGIE: Hey, the resta you ... take five.

(All head off slowly in the direction of ZIGGIE's car.)

ZIGGIE: Naw ... naw, not that way. Other way.

(All head off in the opposite direction except for RICKY, who continues off.)

ZIGGIE: Hey Bo, play your music. Play t'your heart's content.

BO PEEP: *(Sarcastically, as she hits the button.)* Thanks, Zig.

(We hear country and western. When BO PEEP, CANDY, SLIME, and SLICK have exited, and the music has grown faint...)

ZIGGIE: Now, whatchoo babblin' about?

GLENNA RAE: You saw. You had the glasses. You saw how he stared at us.

ZIGGIE: He reckanized us.

GLENNA RAE: He had that look on his face said, "Death time, folks ..."

ZIGGIE: *(At a loss for a moment, THEN:)* Bullshit! He was happy. Rarin' t'go.

GLENNA RAE: Kept shakin' his head real slow.

ZIGGIE: He always shook his head when he laughed.

GLENNA RAE: *(One thumb down)* Then he gave us the "thumbs down" sign.

ZIGGIE: *(One thumb up)* The high sign ... the high sign ...

GLENNA RAE: Then he came 'round that startin' line, opened up that beautiful Golden Tiger Cat, went once around and broke the all-time record. But he just kept foot t'floor and hit that concrete wall head-on.

ZIGGIE: Naw, naw, you're sufferin' from a fantasy causa what he meant t'ya. *(Shouting)* BO! TURN THAT THING UP!

BO PEEP: *(Off)* Why Zig, I didn't know you were a music lover.

ZIGGIE: He crashed cause the steerin' column locked. Was onna news ...was inna Sentinal.

GLENNA RAE: How d'you check that out in a mess like this? *(Beat)* Aw, Zig, it was no shameful thing. He was a man comin' apart...a man that lost the handle...

ZIGGIE: *(Disconcerted)* He was a champion. Our champion! Champions don't go out like that.

GLENNA RAE: Whata we know about champions?

ZIGGIE: *(Desperately)* HEY, BO. TURN THAT RACKET OFF AN' GET IN HERE!

BO PEEP: *(After she's turned the music off and begun to re-enter.)* Your brain is baked tonight, Zig.

(The other three enter behind her. RICKY slouches in from the opposite side with a big grin.)

ZIGGIE: Seems there's a misunderstandin' about events, today. We all seen true an' clear, 'cept for Glenna. I think her point of view is influenced by her...previous relationship with Speed.

RICKY: What's that point of view, Zig?

ZIGGIE: Well, Glenna thinks the accident was no accident. Thinks Speed was "death wishin' " it out there.

SLIME: *(Awed)* Soo-icide?

ZIGGIE: *(Nods)* How d'you feel about that?

SLIME: Well...I dunno...I, uh—

ZIGGIE: Whose side're you gonna take?

SLIME: Well, uh...Hell, I gotta go with you, Zig. Glenna's thinkin' don't carry no more weight than a cup fulla cotton.

ZIGGIE: Candy?

CANDY: You decide for me, Zig. Y'know I don't like decisions.

ZIGGIE: Looks like twelve peepers seen what your two seen. An' ours all viewed a mechanical failure.

(BO PEEP is irritated; RICKY is amused.)

SLICK: I think I'd like t'say—

ZIGGIE: *(Purposely ignoring him)* Well, sun's gonna be comin' up soon. Then we sashay out t'the track.

GLENNA RAE: *(Excitedly)* We goin' out there again, today?

ZIGGIE: Today's race day. Gotta go.

GLENNA RAE: *(Angrily)* Gotta go? Who gotta go? I don't gotta go. Maybe you gotta go. I don't gotta go!

SLIME: *(After a dead-eyed pause)* You don't wanna go?

ZIGGIE: Two reasons why we gotta go. *(Index finger raised)* When a tragedy occurs, you jump right back in. Gotta overcome the fear or you'll never return. Right, Rick?

RICKY: S'been my experience.

GLENNA RAE: If everybody stayed away, then Speed would be alive today.

ZIGGIE: That ain't human nature. *(Raises a second finger)* 'Sides, Speed would want us out there today. It's the duty of a fan.

(In disgust, GLENNA goes for her bottle.)

ZIGGIE: How 'bout the resta you? Slime?

SLIME: I'm with you, Zig. Like always.

ZIGGIE: Atta boy. Candy?

CANDY: *(A certain self-knowledge)* I react t'the snap of your fingers.

ZIGGIE: Right. We've been waitin' 364 days for today and there's no—

SLIME: 3–6–5. This here's leap year.

(Smiles, amusement all around (GLENNA excepted).)

ZIGGIE: You get smarter every day. Now, let's have a beer an' get back t'work.

(CANDY dutifully distributes beer. She tosses SLIME's at him and it foams when he opens it.)

SLICK: Hey, Zig, I'd like a say.

ZIGGIE: Well, as I live and breathe. Have yourself a say, Slick.

(Long pause, as though he's about to say something profound. Then—)

SLICK: I'm in.

ZIGGIE: Good boy, Slick.

(ZIGGIE's car horn sounds. All but ZIGGIE and RICKY are surprised. RICKY—having just been in the vicinity—wears a wide grin.)

RICKY: I think you're bein' paged, Zig.

GLENNA RAE: *(Drunkenly)* She been out there all this time?

BO PEEP: Dirty trick, Ziggie.

CANDY: BLOW IT OUT YOUR ASS!!! All that education an' she's still a shitkicker. ZIGGIE'S PAYIN' HOMAGE T'SPEED! WHY DON'TCHA

HAUL ASS? YOU DON'T BELONG! *(As she starts to weep quietly)* Bitch ain't got an ounce of pride. Think somebody like her who's been everywhere, done everythin', would hate t'come back t'this one-horse armpit of a town. *(To* ZIGGIE*)* When she leaves here with that fruitcake she's married to, she's gonna look down her nose at people like you . . . like me . . . like alla us, just like always. She's gonna sneer at us at gas pumps and luncheonettes. We're gonna tend t'her garden . . . collect her trash . . . don't matter it's England. But when she starts bitchin' about the service, I just hope she remembers she flew thousands of miles t'*beg* for service from the likes of one of us.

ZIGGIE: She'll remember! An' you make your point known, Candy. Eloquently. *(He crosses and holds her affectionately.)* An' you just hit on why I do it *to* her, never *for* her. *(Beat)* So, I gotta retreat briefly for a bit of a sojurn.

CANDY: *(Clinging, as she calls off)* ZIGGIE'S SPOKEN FOR! ZIGGIE'S SPOK—

(He wheels and slaps her hard enough that she goes down.)

SLIME: *(Rushing across)* Zig, Candy's one a'us—

(ZIGGIE punches SLIME in the belly. He doubles up. RICKY chops him. SLIME goes down. SLICK approaches. Both back away. SLICK looks down at SLIME. He looks up at the pair. They do nothing.)

RICKY: *(Hysterically)* I dunno why we have him hangin' on us like a ball 'n' chain. We've been chained from the beginnin'. I'm sick of that kinda life.

ZIGGIE: *(Looking at* SLIME*)* He's got his good points.

(The car horn sounds again.)

ZIGGIE: I COME WHEN I'M READY!!!

CANDY: *(Whimpering)* Can say that, again.

(CANDY is recovering, SLIME is starting to come around. In short, there was no attempt to "injure" or maim either. One gets the impression it's happened before . . . and will happen again.)

RICKY: Hey Zig, we're comin, too.

ZIGGIE: *(Pause, reflects)* Why, y'all come, Rick. This here's America . . . a free country.

(RICKY has stayed sober and ZIGGIE certainly has not. And, since RICKY expected another response from ZIGGIE, he slugs one, two, three times to ZIGGIE's arm with the same kind of dangerous horseplay displayed earlier in the play. A fourth punch to ZIGGIE's upper arm means business. ZIGGIE just stares, and turns to exit, leaving RICKY frustrated with a pyrrhic victory.)

RICKY: *(Assuming command)* C'mon, alla ya. We're headin' for the quarry. Grab the gear. Hey, Zig!

(ZIGGIE turns at the edge of the stage. RICKY points to the car door. ZIGGIE gives a look to the door, then a look to the wreck.)

ZIGGIE: Fuck it!

(ZIGGIE turns at the edge of the stage. RICKY points to the car door. ZIGGIE gives a look to the door, then a look to the wreck.)

ZIGGIE: Fuck it!

(RICKY laughs crazily, uproariously, triumphantly. All the others look at him. His laugh diminishes. He collects himself and picks up the door.)

RICKY: This here's gonna look real good over the door of the body shop. *(He heads off.)*

GLENNA RAE: *(Drunkenly, to CANDY)* You O.K., honey?

CANDY: I'm in better shape than you. Not that you give a damn.

BO PEEP: We give a damn. We just got no say. *(Heads off)*

CANDY: *(To BO PEEP)* Than why're you leavin' with 'em?

BO PEEP: *(Turns)* They're the only game in town. *(Turns, exits)*

CHARLENE: *(Off, shouts)* Don't worry, Candy, you're still the prettiest girl hereabouts.

CANDY: *(Shouting off)* Don't count for much when your competition's the biggest slut hereabouts.

CHARLENE: *(Off, shouts)* YOU CHEAP LITTLE—

ZIGGIE: *(Off, to CHARLENE)* SHUT UP! SHE JUST HIT THE NAIL ON THE HEAD, CHARLENE!

(GLENNA—who is sitting in or laying on the wreck—laughs. CANDY—who is still on the ground—smiles through her tears.)

CANDY: *(To herself)* Atta boy, Zig.

BO PEEP: *(Off)* Hey Zig, open the door.

ZIGGIE: *(Off)* Ride with Ricky. See you half-wits later.

(ZIGGIE howls the last laugh. There's a tremendous screech as he pulls away. Because it's nearly sunup, the stage lights diminish only slightly when RICKY turns his car lights off. SLICK—who has been collecting equipment and the cooler—goes to SLIME who is still prone, but recovering. He extracts a beer and lays it next to SLIME's head. Then, as he rubs his pal's hair, SLIME touches his hand, in a fleeting gesture of friendship.)

SLICK: See ya, boy.

(He heads off. As he's nearing the exit:)

RICKY: *(Off)* That a beer of mine you gave 'im, Slick?

SLICK: Yeah. You hurt 'im. You pay. *(Exits)*

(We hear the weak groan of RICKY'S *battery.* CANDY *smiles.)*

RICKY: *(Off)* That sonofabitch! I shoulda put him t'sleep early on tonight. C'mon, let's walk it.

CANDY: You may be a body an' fender man but ya sure don't know batteries.

(An empty beer can comes flying onstage. She scrambles comically, then goes to SLIME.*)*

CANDY: How you doin', boy?

SLIME: Oh, I'm O.K. How're you doin'?

CANDY: I'm O.K.

SLIME: Betcha I piss blood.

CANDY: That's the wound you got for comin' t'my defense.

SLIME: Wisht they hit my face so you'd be reminded.

CANDY: I don't need remindin'.

SLIME: Wisht I had a scar even, maybe. Now I just gotta piss my wound away.

(She smiles and helps him up. They are as oblivious to passed out GLENNA RAE *as she is to them.)*

CANDY: Well, no point stayin' here.

SLIME: Naw. Hey, Candy, if you went with them you'd just do booze an' dope all day an' catch it from ole Wilcox tomorra.

CANDY: Is that the silver linin' I'm supposed t'look for? Well, maybe I quit J. C. Penney's. Maybe I quit this town. Right now!

SLIME: Well, Ziggie's hard on you but I betcha he's worse on her.

CANDY: But she likes that. I don't!

SLIME: He'll be on the phone callin' you tomorra.

CANDY: Should that make me wanna stay here?

SLIME: How would you get out? Can't take your daddy's car. No Sunday bus.

(She strikes a hitchhiking pose, her rear cutely angled. He mimes a driver screeching to a halt.)

SLIME: My chariot is your chariot, my lovely princess.

CANDY: Well, thank you, my handsome Prince of The Turnpike.

(They giggle like two kids.)

CANDY: I could make it t'some big city. Get a job dancin' . . . show business, modelin'...somethin' like that. Then I'll come back in a coupla years loaded down with furs an' finery. Stuff *earned*, not *given* by my daddy.

SLIME: *(Grins)* Not even your sugar daddy.

CANDY: *(Smiles, shrugs)* Maybe a bauble or two. I won't go chasin' after Zig, though, when I come back. I'll 'knowledge him. I'll 'knowledge alla you. But we won't have much in common cause you'll still be doin' the same damn things. I mean you...you talk about Switzerland and gettin' out an—

SLIME: Sweden!

CANDY: What'sa difference?

SLIME: Sweden's north a' Switzerland. I looked it up onna map. *(Beat)* It's easy for you t'leave. You make friends real easy. But, me...these're the only pals I ever had.

(CANDY shakes her head.)

What they just done t'me...it was the teachin' of a lesson.

CANDY: So, you wouldn't defend me again?

SLIME: I would. Like always, I have trouble rememberin' some lessons. Anyway, defendin' you...it's instink.

CANDY: *(Smiles, shakes her head)* Well, I'm splittin'. You wouldn't have a mirror?

SLIME: Don't use one.

(She gives a little wave, turns and heads off.)

SLIME: Hey, you're goin' the wrong way. 265 is North.

CANDY: You dumb, peckerwood bastard. You think I'm leavin' with the clothes on my back?

(He approaches, reaches into his pocket, and extracts his "silver ball" and holds it out to her in the palm of his hand.)

CANDY: You tryna be funny? Get away from me with that Slimeball.

(She whacks it out of his hand. He watches until it comes to rest. Then, like an obedient pup, he scampers after it, "fetches," and returns to retreating CANDY.)

SLIME: It's all I have for your goin' away.

CANDY: *(Stops. Realizes. Turns.)* Well, what about...I thought you were savin' for the war.

SLIME: *(Shrugs shyly)* I'd rather give it to someone beautiful...than save it for somethin' terrible.

CANDY: *(Genuinely)* You're a real romantic guy, Slime.

SLIME: *(Brightly)* Yeah? *(Stammers)* I ... I ... alw— ... always ... I always ...

CANDY: I know. *(Touching him gently)* I've always known.

SLIME: You did? Then why are you always so mean t'me?

CANDY: *(Apologetically, nervously)* I dunno. I never meant t'be. I just ... I just didn't want wanna encourage you.

SLIME: *(Nods, thinks a moment)* Yeah ... I wouldna encouraged *me*.

(She kisses him gently on the lips. They separate.)

SLIME: Well ... see ya, Florinda.

CANDY: *(Momentarily irritated)* You know how much I hate that name ... *(Smiles)* Carlton.

(Both smile as she turns and exits. We are vaguely aware of early morning sounds. He watches her for awhile then turns, jams his hands in his pockets, kicks a beer can, and looks to the wreck.)

SLIME: I didn't know you was still here, Glenna. You gonna be arright? Need some help home?

(No response, of course. GLENNA has still got her bottle in tow.)

SLIME: Glenna always makes it home.

(He heads for the exit opposite CANDY's, stops, remembers something, returns to the wreck, and picks up the door handle. He shines it on his shirt, huffs on it, buffs it on his shirt again and, satisfied, stuffs it in his pocket. He looks skyward.)

SLIME: *(To himself)* Gonna be hot as a bitch t'day.

(He skips off in the direction of the "walkers." The lights stay up on GLENNA RAE for a long moment, then ...)

FADEOUT

Miguel Piñero

Short Eyes

MIGUEL PIÑERO, former burglar, mugger, shoplifter, and drug addict, began writing when he was in Sing Sing, serving a five-year sentence for armed robbery. He was discovered and encouraged by Marvin Felix Camillo, who conducted a drama workshop at the prison. Camillo's workshop grew into an acting company of ex-convicts called "The Family," members of which made up most of the cast in Joseph Papp's production of *Short Eyes* at Lincoln Center. Mr. Piñero recently performed on television's *Miami Vice*.

For information regarding stock and amateur production rights, contact: Samuel French, Inc., 25 West 45th Street, New York, NY 10019. For all other rights, contact: Cohn, Glickstein, Lurie, Ostrin & Lubell, Esqs., 1370 Avenue of the Americas, New York, NY 10019.

Original Production Notes

Cast
(in alphabetical order)

Mr. Brown	Hollis Barnes
Sergeant Morrison	Chuck Bergansky
Juan Otero	Bimbo
Charlie "Longshoe" Murphy	Joseph Carberry
Clark Davis	William Carden
Julio "Cupcakes" Mercado	Tito Goya
John "Ice" Wicker	Ben Jefferson
William "El Raheem" Johnson	J. J. Johnson
Blanca	Chu Chu Malave
Mr. Frederick Nett	Robert Maroff
Gypsy	Rick Reid
Omar Blinker	Kenny Steward
Paco Pasqual	Felipe Torres
Captain Allard	H. Richard Young

The play was directed by Marvin Felix Camillo, with sets designed by David Mitchell, costumes designed by Paul Martino and supervised by David Mitchell, and lighting by Spencer Mosse. Producer, Joseph Papp; Associate Producer, Bernard Gersten.

Short Eyes was first produced by the Theatre of the Riverside Church on January 1, 1974, for 22 performances. There it was seen by Joseph Papp, who took it to his Anspacher Theater and then, after a two-week run at the Zellerbach Theater in Pennsylvania, for a total of 54 performances. Papp then took it to the Vivian Beaumont Theater at Lincoln Center, where it opened as part of the New York Shakespeare Festival on May 9, 1974, with the above cast. It closed there on August 4, 1974, after 86 performances and 16 previews.

The People

JUAN   *A Puerto Rican in his early thirties*
CUPCAKES   *A Puerto Rican pretty boy of twenty-one who looks younger*
PACO   *A Puerto Rican in his early thirties with the look of a dope fiend*
ICE   *A black man in his late twenties who looks older*
OMAR   *A black amateur boxer in his mid-twenties, virile*
EL RAHEEM   *A black man in his mid-twenties with regal look and militant bearing*
LONGSHOE   *A hip, tough Irishman in his mid-twenties*
CLARK DAVIS   *A handsome, frightened white man in his early twenties*
MR. NETT   *An old-line white prison guard in his late forties*
CAPTAIN ALLARD   *Officer in House of Detention. Straight and gung-ho*
MR. BROWN   *An officer in the House of Detention*
SERGEANT MORRISON   *Another officer*
BLANCA AND GYPSY   *Walk-on, nonspeaking parts*

(The entire play takes place in the dayroom on one of the floors in the House of Detention.)

Act One: Early morning, lock-in after breakfast
Act Two: Same day at 3:00 p.m.
Epilogue: Same evening

Act One

(Dayroom in the House of Detention. Upstage right is entrance gate. Upstage left is gate leading to shower room and slop sink. Upstage center is a toilet and drinking fountain. Above is a catwalk. Stage left is a table and chairs. Downstage right is a garbage can. Upstage right is a TV set on a stand. Early-morning lock-in after the morning meal.)

(Early-morning light.)

(Inmates' voices can be heard: various ad-libs, calling out to each other, asking questions, exchanging prison gossip, etc.)

MORRISON: All right, listen up ... I said listen up. *(Whistle)* When I call your names, give me your cell location. *(Catcalls)* Off the fucking noise. Now if I have to call out your name more than once, pray—cause your soul may belong to God, but your ass is mine. *(More catcalls. House lights go out.)* Williams, D.

VOICE RESPONSE: Upper D 14.

MORRISON: Homer, J.

VOICE RESPONSE: Lower D 7.

MORRISON: Stone, F.

VOICE RESPONSE: Lower D 5.

MORRISON: Miller, G.

VOICE RESPONSE: Upper D 3.

MORRISON: Lockout for criminal court ... *(Whistle)* "A" side dayroom. All right, already! ... knock it off. Supreme Court. *(Whistle)* Johnson.

INMATE VOICE: Who?

MORRISON: Johnson.

TWO INMATE VOICES: Who?

MORRISON: Johnson.

A LOT OF VOICES: Who? ... who? ... who? ... who? ...

MORRISON: Aw, come on, fellas, give me a break.

INMATE VOICE: Your brains may belong to the state, but your sanity belongs to me.

INMATE VOICE: Aw, come on, fellas, give the fella a break.

INMATE VOICE: Break ... *(Bronx cheer)*

MORRISON: Johnson.

INMATE VOICE: Upper D 15.

MORRISON: *Corree*-a.

INMATE VOICE: *Can't you say my name right? (Giving proper pronunciation.)* Correa ... Correa ... Correa.

MORRISON: You guys go to the "C" side dayroom *(Whistle)* Sing Sing reception center. Gomez, A.

VOICE RESPONSE: Lower D 9.

MORRISON: Shit-can-do. *(Catcalls)*

VOICE RESPONSE: Scicando ... Lower D 11.

MORRISON: Bring all your personal belongings and go to the "B" side dayroom. *(Catcalls)* All right, you guys want to play games, you guys don't let up that noise, you guys ain't locking out this morning.

INMATE VOICE: You got it.

(Ad-libs continue until OMAR speaks.)

ICE: Fuck you, sucker.

(Silence. Sound of prison gate opening is heard.)

MORRISON: *(Whistle—dayroom lights come on)* All right, on the lockout.

(Enter OMAR, LONGSHOE, EL RAHEEM, PACO, and ICE. Each runs toward his respective position. Ad-libs.)

(Then JUAN walks slowly toward his position.)

(CUPCAKES is the last to come in. The MEN accompany him with simple scat singing to the tune of "The Stripper." Ad-libs.)

JUAN: Why don't you cut that loose? Man, don't you think that kid get tired of hearing that every morning?

PACO: Oh, man, we just jiving.

ICE: Hey, Cupcake, you ain't got no plexes behind that, do you?

CUPCAKES: I mean ... like no ... but ...

PACO: You see, Juan, Cupcake don't mind.

CUPCAKES: No, really, Juan. Like I don't mind ... But that doesn't mean that I like to listen to it. I mean ... like ... hey ... I call you guys by your name. Why don't you call me by mine? My name ain't Cupcakes, it's Julio.

EL RAHEEM: If you would acknowledge that you are God, your name wouldn't be Cupcake or Julio or anything else. You would be Dahoo.

LONGSHOE: Already! Can't you spare us that shit early in the a.m.?

EL RAHEEM: No...one...is...talking...to...you...Yacoub.

LONGSHOE: The name is Longshoe Charlie Murphy... *Mister* Murphy to you.

EL RAHEEM: Yacoub...maker and creator of the devil...swine merchant. Your time is near at hand. Fuck around and your time will be now. Soon all devils' heads will roll and now rivers shall flow through the city—created by the blood of Whitey...Devil...beast.

OMAR: Salaam Alaikum.

PACO: Salami with bacons.

ICE: Power to the people.

LONGSHOE: Free the Watergate 500.

JUAN: Pa'lante.

CUPCAKES: Tippecanoe and Tyler too.

PACO: *(On table, overly feminine.)* A la lucha...a la lucha...que somo mucha...

OMAR: Hey! Hey...you know the Panthers say "Power to the people."

MR. NETT: On the gate.

OMAR: *(Strong voice)* Power to the people. And gay liberators say... *(High voice, limp wrist in fist.)* Power to the people.

(Enter NETT.)

MR. NETT: How about police power?

JUAN: How about it? Oink, oink.

MR. NETT: Wise guy. Paco, you got a counsel visit.

PACO: Vaya.

OMAR: Mr. Nett?

MR. NETT: Yeah, what is it?

OMAR: Mr. Nett, you know like I've been here over ten months—and I'd like to know why I can't get on the help. Like I've asked a dozen times ...and guys that just come in are shot over me...and I get shot down ...Like why? Have I done something to you? Is there something about me that you don't like?

MR. NETT: Why, no. I don't have anything against you. But since you ask me I'll tell you. One is that when you first came in here you had the clap.

OMAR: But I don't have it any more. That was ten months ago.

MR. NETT: How many fights have you had since the first day you came on the floor?

OMAR: But I haven't had a fight in a long time.

MR. NETT: How many?

OMAR: Seven.

MR. NETT: Seven? Close to ten would be my estimation. No, if I put you on the help, there would be trouble in no time. Now if you give me your word that you won't fight and stay cool, I'll give it some deep consideration.

OMAR: I can't give you my word on something like that. You know I don't stand for no lame coming out the side of his neck with me. Not my word...My word is bond.

EL RAHEEM: Bond is life.

OMAR: That's why I can't give you my word. My word is my bond. Man in prison ain't got nothing but his word, and he's got to be careful who and how and for what he give it for. But I'll tell you this, I'll try to be cool.

MR. NETT: Well, you're honest about it anyway. I'll think it over.

(PACO and MR. NETT exit.)

EL RAHEEM: Try is a failure.

OMAR: Fuck you.

EL RAHEEM: Try is a failure. Do.

OMAR: Fuck you.

EL RAHEEM: Fuck yourself, it's cheaper.

CUPCAKES: Hey, Mr. Nett—put on the power.

MR. NETT: *(From outside the gate)* The power is on.

CUPCAKES: The box ain't on.

MR. NETT: Might be broken. I'll call the repairman.

JUAN: Might as well listen to the radio.

ICE: The radio ain't workin' either, Juan. I tried to get BLS a little while ago and got nothin' but static, Jack.

CUPCAKES: Anyone wants to play Dirty Hearts? I ain't got no money, but I'll have cigarettes later on this week.

OMAR: Money on the wood makes bettin' good.

ICE: Right on.

(LONGSHOE gives CUPCAKES cigarettes.)

JUAN: Hey, Julio.

(Throws CUPCAKES cigarettes.)

(BROWN *appears outside entrance gate.*)

BROWN: On the gate.

(*Gate opens and* PACO *enters. Gate closes and* BROWN *exits.*)

CUPCAKES: Shit. That was a real fast visit.

PACO: Not fast enough.

LONGSHOE: What the man say about your case?

PACO: The bitch wants me to cop out to a D—she must think my dick is made of sponge rubber. I told her to tell the D.A. to rub the offer on his chest. Not to come to court on my behalf—shit, the bitch must have made a deal with the D.A. on one of her paying customers. Man, if I wait I could get a misdemeanor by my motherfucking self. What the fuck I need with a Legal Aid? Guess who's on the bench?

ICE: Who they got out there?

PACO: Cop-out Levine.

ICE: Wow! He give me a pound for a frown.

PACO: First they give me a student, and now a double-crossin' bitch.

LONGSHOE: We all got to make a living.

PACO: On my expense? No fucking good.

EL RAHEEM: You still expect the white man to give you a fair trial in his court? Don't you know what justice really means? Justice... "just us"... white folks.

PACO: Look here, man. I don't expect nothing from nobody—especially the Yankees. Man, this ain't my first time before them people behind these walls, cause I ain't got the money for bail. And you can bet that it won't be my last time—not as long as I'm poor and Puerto Rican.

CUPCAKES: Come on, let's play... for push-ups.

JUAN: How many?

CUPCAKES: Ten if you got just one book, fifteen if you got two.

PACO: I ain't playing for no goddamn push-ups.

ICE: Hey—come on, don't be like that.

PACO: Said ain't playing for no push-ups. Tell you what, let's play for coochie-coochies.

ICE: What the hell is coochie-coochies?

JUAN: It's a game they play in Puerto Rico. You ever see a flick about Hawaii? Them girls with the grass skirts moving their butts dancing? That's coochie-coochies.

ICE: I thought that was the hula-jack.

PACO: Put your shirt on your hips like this and move your ass. Coochie-coochie-coochie . . .

CUPCAKES: That's out.

PACO: You got a plexes?

CUPCAKES: Told you before that I don't have no complexes.

JUAN: You got no plexes at all?

CUPCAKES: No.

JUAN: Then why not let me fuck you?

CUPCAKES: That's definitely out.

JUAN: People without complexes might as well turn stuff.

OMAR: Thinking of joining the ranks? Cruising the tearooms?

EL RAHEEM: What kind of black original man talk is that? Cupcakes puts the wisdom before the knowledge because that's his nature. He can't help that. But you are deliberately acting and thinking out of your nature . . . thinking like the white devil, Yacoub. Your presence infects the minds of my people like a fever. You, Yacoub, are the bearer of three thousand nine hundred and ninety-nine diseases . . . corrupt . . . evil . . . pork-chop-eating brain . . .

LONGSHOE: Look.

EL RAHEEM: Where?

LONGSHOE: I'm sick and . . .

EL RAHEEM: See, brothers, he admits he is sick with corruption.

LONGSHOE: Who?

EL RAHEEM: You're not only the devil, you're also an owl?

LONGSHOE: Why?

EL RAHEEM: "Y"—why? Why is "Y" the twenty-fifth letter of the alphabet?

LONGSHOE: You . . . son of . . .

EL RAHEEM: You . . . me . . . they . . . them. This . . . those . . . that . . . "U" for the unknown.

LONGSHOE: I . . . I . . .

EL RAHEEM: Eye . . . I . . . Aye . . . Aye . . . Aiii . . . hi . . .

LONGSHOE: Games, huh?

EL RAHEEM: The way of life is no game. Lame.

LONGSHOE: G...O...D ...D...O...G...God spelled backward is dog
...dog spelled backward is God...If Allah is God, Allah is a dog.

EL RAHEEM: Allah Akbar. *(Screams, jumps on him.)* Allah Akbar.

(MR. NETT and BROWN appear outside entrance gate.)

MR. NETT: On the gate.

(BROWN opens gate. MR. NETT and BROWN enter. MR. NETT breaks them apart.)

MR. NETT: What the hell is going on here?

OMAR: Mr. Nett, let these two git it off, else we's gonna have mucho
static around here.

ICE: Yeah...Mr. Nett...they got a personality thing going on for weeks.

MR. NETT: Fair fight, Murphy?

LONGSHOE: That's what I want.

MR. NETT: Johnson?

EL RAHEEM: El Raheem. Johnson is a slave name.

(Nods)

May your Christian God have mercy on your soul, Yacoub.

*(BROWN closes gate. EL RAHEEM and LONGSHOE square off and begin to fight...
boxing...some wrestling. LONGSHOE is knocked clean across the room.)*

LONGSHOE: Guess you say that left hook is Whitey trickology?

EL RAHEEM: No, honky, you knocked me down. My sister hits harder
than that. She's only eight.

(They wrestle until EL RAHEEM is on top. Then NETT breaks them apart.)

OMAR: Why didn't you break it up while Whitey was on top?

MR. NETT: Listen, why don't you two guys call it quits—ain't none of
you really gonna end up the winner...Give it up...be friends...shake
hands...Come, break it up, you both got your shit off...break it up.
Go out and clean yourselves up. Make this the last time I see either of
you fighting. On the gate. Next time I turn on the water.

(BROWN and NETT exit, gate closes.)

(The RICANS go to their table and begin to play on the table as if it were bongos.)

ICE: You two got it together.

EL RAHEEM: I am God...master and ruler of my universe...I am always
together.

OMAR: Let me ask you one question, God.

EL RAHEEM: You have permission to ask two.

OMAR: Thank you...If you're God, why are you in jail? God can do anything, right? Melt these walls down, then create a stairway of light to the streets below . . . God. If you're God, then you can do these things. If you can't, tell me why God can't do a simple thing like that.

EL RAHEEM: I am God . . . I am a poor righteous teacher of almighty Allah and by his will I am here to awaken the original lost in these prisons . . . Black original man is asleep . . . This is your school of self-awareness. Wake up, black man, melt these walls? You ask me, a tangible god, to do an intangible feat? Mysterious intangible gods do mysterious intangible deeds. There is nothing mysterious about me. Tangible gods do tangible deeds.

(PUERTO RICAN GROUP goes back to playing. "Toca, si, va, tocar.")

CUPCAKES: *(On table, M.C.-style)* That's right, ladies and gentlemen . . . damas y caballeros . . . every night is Latin night at the House of Detention. Tonight for the first time . . . direct from his record-breaking counsel visit . . . on congas is Paco Pasqual . . . yeaaaaaa. With a all-star band . . . for your listening enjoyment . . . Juan Bobo Otero on timbales . . . On mouth organ Charles Murphy . . . To show you the latest dancing are Iceman, John Wicker . . . and his equally talented partner, Omar Blinker . . . yeaaaaaa. While tapping his toes for you all . . . moving his head to the rhythm of the band is the mighty El Raheem, yeaaaaaaa. Boooooooo. Yes, brothers and sisters, especially you sisters, don't miss this musical extravaganza. I'll be there too . . . to say hello to all my friends . . . So be there . . . Don't be the one to say "Gee, I missed it" . . . This is your cha-cha jockey, Julio . . .

ALL: Cupcakes . . .

CUPCAKES: Mercado . . . Be sure to be there . . . Catch this act . . . this show of shows before they leave on a long extended touring engagement with state . . .

(PACO pinches CUPCAKES's ass.)

Keep your hands off my ass, man.

(CUPCAKES moves stage left, sits pouting. Ad-libs.)

PACO: Hey, kid, do one of those prison toasts . . .

(They urge him on with various ad-libs.)

CUPCAKES: All right, dig . . . You guys gotta give me background . . . Clap your hands and say . . . Mambo tu le pop . . . It was the night before Christmas . . . and all through the pad . . . cocaine and heroin was all the cats had. One cat in the corner . . . copping a nod . . . Another scratching thought he was God . . . I jumps on the phone . . . and dial with care . . . hoping my reefer . . . would soon be there . . . After a while . . . crowding my style . . . I ran to the door . . . see what's the matter . . . And to my

surprise ... I saw five police badges ... staring ... glaring in my eyes ...
A couple of studs ... starts to get tough, so I ran to the bathroom ... get
rid of the stuff ... narc bang ... bang ... but they banged in vain ... cause
you see ... what didn't go in my veins went down the drain ... Broke
down the door ... knock me to the floor ... and took me away, that's the
way I spent my last Christmas Day ... like a dirty dog ... in a dark and
dingy cell ... But I didn't care cause I was high as hell ... But I was cool
... I was cool ... I was cool ... You people are the fools ... cream of the
top ... cause I got you to say something as stupid as Mambo tu le pop.

(GROUP *chases* CUPCAKES *around stage.* BROWN *and* CLARK DAVIS *appear outside entrance gate.*)

BROWN: On the gate.

(*Gate opens and* CLARK DAVIS *enters, goes to stage center.* BROWN *closes gate and exits.*)

CUPCAKES: Hey Longshoe ... one of your kin ... look-a-like sin just
walked in ...

EL RAHEEM: Another devil.

LONGSHOE: Hey ... hey, whatdayasay ... My name's Longshoe Charlie
Murphy. Call me Longshoe. What's your name?

CLARK: Davis ... Clark ... Ah ... Clark Davis ... Clark is my first name.

PACO: Clark Kent.

CUPCAKES: Mild-mannered, too.

OMAR: No, no, Superman.

(*Other ad-libs: "Faster than a speeding bullet," etc.*)

PACO: Oye ... Shoe ... Está bueno ... Pa' rajalo ...

LONGSHOE: Back ... back ... boy ... no está bueno ... anyway, no mucho
... como Cupcake.

PACO: Vaya.

LONGSHOE: Pay them no mind ... crazy spics ... where you locking?

CLARK: Upper D 15.

LONGSHOE: Siberia, huh? ... Tough.

CLARK: First time in the joint.

LONGSHOE: Yeah? Well, I better hip you to what's happening fast.

ICE: Look out for your homey, Shoe.

OMAR: Second.

LONGSHOE: Look here, this is our section ... white ... dig? That's the

Rican table, you can sit there if they give you permission ... Same goes
with the black section.

ICE: Say it loud.

OMAR: I'm black and proud.

ICE: Vaya!

LONGSHOE: Most of the fellas are in court. I'm the Don Gee here. You
know what that mean, right? Good ... Niggers and the spics don't give
us honkies much trouble. We're cool half ass. This is a good floor. Dynamite hack on all shifts. Stay away from the black gods ...

(NETT *appears outside gate.*)

NETT: On the gate.

LONGSHOE: You know them when you see them.

(NETT *opens gate and enters*)

NETT: On the chow.

ICE: What we got, Mr. Nett?

NETT: Baloney à la carte.

ICE: Shit, welfare steaks again.

(*All exit except* CLARK *and* LONGSHOE. *Gate stays open. The men reenter with
sandwiches and return to their respective places.* NETT *closes gate and exits.*)

LONGSHOE: Black go on the front of the line, we stay in the back ... It's
okay to rap with the blacks, but don't get too close with any of them.
Ricans too. We're the minority here, so be cool. If you hate yams, keep
it to yourself. Don't show it. But also don't let them run over you. Ricans
are funny people. Took me a long time to figure them out, and you know
something, I found out that I still have a lot to learn about them. I rap
spic talk. They get a big-brother attitude about the whites in jail. But
they also back the niggers to the T.

ICE: *(Throws* LONGSHOE *a sandwich.)* Hey, Shoe.

LONGSHOE: If a spic pulls a razor blade on you and you don't have a
mop wringer in your hands ... run ... If you have static with a nigger
and they ain't no white people around ... get a spic to watch your back,
you may have a chance ... That ain't no guarantee ... If you have static
with a spic, don't get no nigger to watch your back cause you ain't gonna
have none.

OMAR: You can say that again.

ICE: Two times.

LONGSHOE: You're a good-looking kid ... You ain't stuff and you don't

want to be stuff. Stay away from the bandidos. Paco is one of them . . .
Take no gifts from no one.

(NETT *appears outside entrance gate.*)

NETT: Clark Davis . . . Davis.

CLARK: Yes, that's me.

NETT: On the gate. (NETT *opens gate, enters with* CLARK's *belongings,
leaves gate open.*) Come here . . . come here . . . white trash . . . filth . . . Let
me tell you something and you better listen good cause I'm only going
to say it one time . . . and one time only. This is a nice floor . . . a quiet floor
. . . There has never been too much trouble on this floor . . . With you, I
smell trouble . . . I don't question the warden's or the captain's motive
for putting you on this floor . . . But for once I'm gonna ask why they put
a sick fucking degenerate like you on my floor . . . If you just talk out the
side of your mouth one time . . . if you look at me sideways one time . . . if
you mispronounce my name once, if you pick up more food than you can
eat . . . if you call me for something I think is unnecessary . . . if you over-
sleep, undersleep . . . if . . . if . . . if . . . you give me just one little reason . . . I'm
gonna break your face up so bad your own mother won't know you . . .

LONGSHOE: Mr. Nett is being kinda hard . . .

NETT: Shut up . . . I got a eight-year-old daughter who was molested by
one of those bastards . . . stinking sons of bitches and I just as well pretend that he was you, Davis, do you understand that . . .

PACO: Short eyes.

LONGSHOE: Short eyes? Short eyes . . . Clark, are you one of those short-
eyes freaks . . . are you a short-eyes freak?

NETT: Sit down, Murphy . . . I'm talking to this . . . this scumbag . . . yeah,
he's a child rapist . . . a baby rapist, how old was she? How old? . . . Eight
. . . seven . . . Disgusting bastard . . . Stay out of my sight . . . cause if you
get in my face just one time . . . don't forget what I told you . . . I'll take
a night stick and ram it clean up your asshole . . . I hope to God that
they take you off this floor, or send you to Sing Sing . . . The men up there
know what to do with degenerates like you.

CLARK: I . . . I . . .

NETT: All right, let's go . . . Lock in . . . lock in . . . for the count . . . Clark,
the captain outside on the bridge wants to see you. I hope he takes you
off this floor . . .

LONGSHOE: Hey, Davis . . .

(*Walks up to him and spits in his face. Men exit.*)

NETT: Juan, stay out and clean the dayroom. Omar, take the tier.

(CAPTAIN ALLARD appears on the catwalk above. CLARK joins ALLARD and they carry on inaudible conversation. Crossing from stage right to stage left on the catwalk are CUPCAKES, ICE, and LONGSHOE, followed by MR. BROWN. As LONGSHOE passes, he bumps CLARK.)

(MR. BROWN stops beside CLARK, and CAPTAIN ALLARD chases after LONGSHOE to catwalk above left.)

ALLARD: Hey, just a minute, you. That's just the kind of stuff that's going to cease.

(BROWN and CLARK exit catwalk above right and appear at entrance gate stage right.)

BROWN: On the gate.

(BROWN opens gate, CLARK enters dayroom, BROWN closes gate. CLARK says something inaudible to BROWN.)

BROWN: You're lucky if you get a call before Christmas.

(BROWN exits. CLARK leans on gate.)

LONGSHOE: Get off that fuckin' gate.

(While the above was going on, JUAN has taken his cleaning equipment from the shower upstage left and placed can of Ajax and rag on the toilet area upstage center, and broom, mop, bucket, dustpan, dust broom, dust box in downstage left corner. JUAN sits at table, CLARK at window. JUAN pours coffee, offers CLARK a sandwich. CLARK crosses to table and sits.)

JUAN: Hey, man, did you really do it?

(OMAR starts chant offstage.)

CLARK: I don't know.

JUAN: What do you mean, you don't know? What you think I am, a fool, or something out of a comic book.

CLARK: No...I don't mean to sound like that, I...I...

JUAN: Look, man, either you did it or you didn't. *(He stands.)* That all there is to it...

CLARK: I don't know if I did it or not.

JUAN: You better break that down to me *(Sits)* cause you lost me.

CLARK: What I mean is that I may have done it or I may not have...I just don't remember...I remember seeing that little girl that morning ...I sat in Bellevue thirty-three days and I don't remember doing anything like that to that little girl.

JUAN: You done something like that before, haven't you?

CLARK: I...ye...yes...I have...How did you know?

JUAN: Your guilt flies off your tongue, man. *(Stands)* Sound like one of those guys in an encounter session *(Starts to sweep.)* looking to dump their shit off on someone...You need help...The bad part about it is that you know it...

CLARK: Help? I need help? Yes...yes, I do need help...But I'm afraid to find it...Why?...Fear...just fear...Perhaps fear of knowing that I may be put away forever...I have a wife and kid I love very much... and I want to be with them. I don't ever want to be away from them ...ever. But now this thing has happened...I don't know what to do ...I don't know...If I fight it in court, they'll end up getting hurt...If I don't it'll be the same thing...Jesus help me...God forgive me.

JUAN: Cause man won't. *(JUAN at downstage left corner, sweeping up dust.)*

CLARK: No, man won't...Society will never forgive me...or accept me back once this is openly known.

(JUAN begins to stack chairs stage right. CLARK hands JUAN a chair.)

CLARK: I think about it sometimes and...funny, I don't really feel disgusted...just ashamed...You wanna...

JUAN: Listen to you? It's up to you...You got a half hour before the floor locks out unless you wanna go public like A.A. *(He picks up stool.)*

CLARK: No...no...no...I can't...I didn't even talk with the psychiatrist in the bughouse.

JUAN: Run it...*(He puts down stool.)*

CLARK: You know, somehow it seems like there's no beginning. Seems like I've always been in there all my life. I have like little picture incidents running across my mind...I remember being...fifteen or sixteen years old...

(JUAN crosses upstage center to clean toilet.)

CLARK: ...or something around that age, waking up to the sound of voices coming from the living room...cartoons on the TV...They were watching cartoons on the TV, two little girls. One was my sister, and her friend...And you know how it is when you get up in the morning, the inevitable hard-on is getting up with you. I draped the sheet around my shoulders...Everyone else was sleeping...The girl watching TV with my sister...yes...Hispanic...pale-looking skin...She was eight ...nine...ten...what the difference, she was a child...She was very pretty—high cheekbones, flashing black eyes...She was wearing blue short pants...tight-fitting...a white blouse, or shirt...My sister...she left to do number two...

(JUAN *returns to stage right.*)

CLARK: She told her friend wait for me, I'm going to do number two, and they laughed about it. I sneaked in standing a little behind her... She felt me standing there and turned to me... She smiled such a pretty little smile... I told her I was a vampire and she laughed... I spread the sheets apart and she suddenly stopped laughing... She just stood there staring at me... Shocked? surprised? intrigued? Don't know... don't know... She just stood and stared...

(JUAN *crosses to downstage left.*)

CLARK: I came closer like a vampire... She started backing away... ran toward the door... stopped, looked at me again. Never at my face... my body... I couldn't really tell whether or not the look on her face was one of fear... but I'll never forget that look.

(BROWN *crosses on catwalk from left to right with a banana. Stands at right.*)

CLARK: I was really scared that she'd tell her parents. Weeks passed without confrontation... and I was feeling less and less afraid... But that's not my thing, showing myself naked to little girls in schoolyards.

(JUAN *crosses to downstage right corner and begins to mop from downstage right to downstage left.*)

CLARK: One time... no, it was the first time... the very first time. I was alone watching TV... Was I in school or out... And there was this little Puerto Rican girl from next door... Her father was the new janitor... I had seen her before... many times... sliding down the banister... Always her panties looked dirty... She was... oh, why do I always try to make their age higher than it really was... even to myself. She was young, much too young... Why did she come there? For who? Hundred questions. Not one small answer... not even a lie flickers across my brain.

OFFSTAGE VOICE: All right, listen up. The following inmates report for sanitation duty: Smalls, Gary; Medena, James; Pfeifer, Willis; Martinez, Raul. Report to C.O. grounds for sanitation duty.

CLARK: How did I get to the bathroom with her? Don't know. I was standing there with her, I was combing her hair. I was combing her hair. Her curly reddish hair...

(JUAN *crosses upstage right, starts to mop upstage right to upstage left.*)

CLARK: I was naked... naked... except for these flower-printed cotton underwears... No slippers, barefooted... Suddenly I get this feeling over me... like a flash fever... and I'm hard... I placed my hands on her small shoulders... and pressed her hand and placed it on my penis... Did she know what to do? Or did I coerce her? I pulled down my drawers

...But then I felt too naked, so I put them back on...My eyes were closed...but I felt as if there was this giant eye off in space staring at me...

(JUAN *stops upstage left and listens to* CLARK, *who is unaware* JUAN *is in back of him.*)

CLARK: I opened them and saw her staring at me in the cabinet mirror. I pulled her back away from the view of the mirror...My hands up her dress, feeling her undeveloped body...I...I...I began pulling her underwear down on the bowl...She resisted...slightly, just a moment... I sat on the bowl...She turned and threw her arms around my neck and kissed me on the lips...She gave a small nervous giggle...I couldn't look at her...I closed my eyes...turned her body...to face away from me...I lubricated myself...and...I hear a scream, my own ...there was a spot of blood on my drawers...I took them off right then and there...ripped them up and flushed them down the toilet...She had dressed herself up and asked me if we could do it again tomorrow... and was I her boyfriend now...I said yes, yes...

(JUAN *goes to center stage, starts mopping center stage right to stage left.* BROWN *exits from catwalk above right.*)

CLARK: I couldn't sit still that whole morning. I just couldn't relax. I dressed and took a walk...Next thing I know I was running—out of breath...I had run over twenty blocks...twenty blocks blind...without knowing...I was running...Juan, was it my conscious or subconscious that my rest stop was a children's playground...Coincidence perhaps...But why did I run in that direction, no, better still, why did I start walking in that direction...Coincidence? Why didn't my breath give out elsewhere...Coincidence?

(JUAN *moves to downstage left,* CLARK *moves to upstage center and sits on window ledge.*)

CLARK: I sat on the park bench and watched the little girls swing... slide...run...jump rope...Fat...skinny...black...white...Chinese ...I sat there until the next morning...The next day I went home and met the little Puerto Rican girl again...Almost three times a week... The rest of the time I would be in the playground or in the children's section of the movies...But you know something? Er, er...

(*He moves toward* JUAN, *who is in downstage left corner.*)

JUAN: Juan.

CLARK: Yes, Juan...Juan the listener...the compassionate...you know something, Juan...I soon became...became...what? A pro? A professional degenerate?

(The sound of garbage cans banging together is heard offstage.)

CLARK: I don't know if you can call it a second insight on children. But
... I would go to the park ... and sit there for hours and talk with a little
girl and know if I would do it or not with her ... Just a few words was
all needed ... Talk stupid things they consider grownup talk ... Soon my
hand would hold hers, then I would caress her face ... Next her thighs
... under their dress ... I never took any of them home or drove away
with them in my car ... I always told them to meet me in the very same
building they lived in ...

OFFSTAGE VOICE: On the sanitation gate. *(Sound of gate opening.)*

CLARK: On the roof or their basements under the stairs ... Sometimes
in their own home if the parents were out ... The easiest ones were the
Puerto Ricans and the black girls ... Little white ones would masturbate
you right there in the park for a dollar or a quarter ... depending on
how much emphasis their parents put in their heads on making money
... I felt ashamed at first ... But then I would rehearse at nights what
to do the next time ... planning ... I ...

(JUAN starts moving slowly from downstage left to upstage left.)

CLARK: ... couldn't help myself ... I couldn't help myself ... Something
drove me to it ... I thought of killing myself ... but I just couldn't go
through with it ... I don't really wanna die ... I wanted to stop, really I
did ... I just didn't know how. I thought maybe I was crazy ... but I read
all types of psychology books ... I heard or read somewhere that crazy
people can't distinguish right from wrong ... Yet I can ... I know what's
right and I know what I'm doing is wrong, yet I can't stop myself ...

JUAN: Why didn't you go to the police or a psychiatrist?

(He crosses to shower room upstage left.)

CLARK: I wanted to many a time ... But I know that the police would
find some pretext to kill me ... And a psychiatrist ... well, if he thought
he couldn't help me he'd turn me over to them or commit me to some
nut ward ... Juan, try to understand me.

(JUAN comes out of shower room and starts putting away his cleaning equipment.)

JUAN: Motherfucker, try to understand you ... if I wasn't trying to, I
would have killed you ... stone dead, punk ... *(At downstage left corner,
picks up broom and bucket.)* The minute you said that thing about the
Rican girls ... If I was you I'd ask transfer to protection ... cause *(Returns
to shower room.)* if you remain on this floor you're asking to die ... You'll
be committing involuntary suicide ... *(He again crosses to downstage left
corner, picks up remaining equipment, crosses to toilet, picks up Ajax and*

rag, and crosses to shower room.) Shit, why the fuck did you have to tell me all of it ... You don't know me from Adam ... *(He comes out of shower room and crosses to* CLARK, *stage center.)* Why the hell did you have to make me your father confessor? Why? Why didn't you stop, why?

CLARK: Cause you asked. Cause you ... What I told you I didn't even tell the doctors at the observation ward ... Everything is coming down on me so fast ... I needed to tell it all ... to someone ... Juan, you were willing to listen.

(Whistle blows.)

MR. NETT: *(Offstage)* All right, on the lockout ... *(Whistle)*

OTHER VOICES: On the lockout.

*(*BROWN *appears outside the gate).*

BROWN: On the gate.

(Enter EL RAHEEM, PACO, OMAR, ICE, CUPCAKES, *and* LONGSHOE. BROWN *closes gate and exits.* ICE *and* OMAR *get one chair and cross to table.* OMAR *starts playing cards.* LONGSHOE *gets his stool and crosses to behind table.* CUPCAKES *does push-ups on chair stage right.)*

ICE: You're gonna be on the help for good, Omar.

OMAR: No, the man said just for today ... But he put me on top of the list.

ICE: You gonna look out for me, heavy homeeeeey?

OMAR: Since when did we become homeeeeeys? Shit, man—you're way out there in Coney Island somewhere ... and I'm way in Bed-Stuy.

ICE: How you gonna show, brother man? It's the same borough, ain't it?

OMAR: It's the same borough, Iceman ... but it's a different world.

ICE: Ain't this a bitch? I comes on this here floor with this man ... There was nothing but Whiteys on the floor. It was me and him against the world ... I come out every night and stand by his side, ready to die ... to die ...

PACO: Yeah, cause you no wanna die alone.

ICE: That has nothing to do with nothing.

OMAR: It has everything to do with everything.

ICE: How you going to show? How you do this to me, Omar, homey.

OMAR: Being how you mentioned it, perhaps it's not a bad idea. Save me some money when you go to the store.

ICE: I ain't gonna argue that ... cause this is me, the Iceman, talking—

my hand don't call for this type of talking, man. Your main mellow-man, this is too strong...Contracts...

OMAR: Who said anything about contract? I didn't say anything about contract...Anybody here said anything about a contract?...

CUPCAKES: I didn't hear anybody say anything...I didn't say it.

PACO: Me neither...

LONGSHOE: Who could say anything with a swollen lip.

JUAN: I mind my own business.

OMAR: See, you must be hearing things.

ICE: You didn't say it...but you implied it...You was leading right up to it.

OMAR: Well, now that you mentioned it...perhaps it's not a bad idea...

ICE: How you gonna do this to me? Omarrrrr...homeeey...

OMAR: Did it to yourself...You knew I'd always look out...but now you put these ideas into my head...and it sounds kinda...

ICE: Omar...my pretty nigger...even if you get no bigger, you'll always be my main nigger...And if you get any bigger, you'll just be my bigger nigger...

OMAR: Better run that shit on the judge...You know what you can do for me...give me a softshoe.

ICE: Yes sir, boss, captain, your honor, mister, sir. *(Fast softshoe)*

OMAR: Hey, freak. *(To* CLARK*)* You're sittin' on my Chinese handball court...

(CLARK moves to upstage right.)

ICE: That there is where I hangs my wet clean clothes...and I don't wanna have them sprayed. Move...creep.

(CLARK moves to stage center.)

EL RAHEEM: You're in God's walking space.

(CLARK moves to lower stage right.)

PACO: That's Paco's walking space.

CUPCAKES: Hey, Clark...that spot's not taken...Right over there... Yeah, that's right...The whole toilet bowl and you go well together.

CLARK: I'm not going to stand for this treatment.

PACO: Did you say something out of your mouth, creep...

OMAR: You talking to everyone, or to someone in particular?

LONGSHOE: I know you ain't talking to me.

ICE: You got something you wanna say to someone in this room, faggot?

CLARK: I was talking to myself.

EL RAHEEM: Well, don't talk to yourself too loud.

CUPCAKES: Talk to the shitbowl...You'll find you got a lot in common with each other...

JUAN: Drop it...Cut it loose...

PACO: ¿Donde está La Mancha?...or did Sancho go to another floor?

JUAN: Paco...one of these days you gonna get me very very angry.

PACO: I'm trembling, man...whooo, I'm scared...Can't you smell it, I'm shitting bricks...

ICE: Juan...be cool...don't know why you wanna put front for that freak...But, man...if you don't wanna vamp...don't go against your own people...You be wrong, man...

JUAN: Ain't going against my own brother man...But if the dude is a sicky...cut him loose...All that ain't necessary...Ice.

ICE: It ain't your place, Juan, and you know it...You're out of time...

PACO: I think he has a special interest.

ICE: Don't come out of your face wrong, Paco.

PACO: Ice.

ICE: You're interrupting me, Paco...Me and you both know where you're coming from...Don't make me put your shit in the streets... And, Juan, you know you're out of order. This ain't your turn, man...

CUPCAKES: Let's go do up them clothes, Juan.

JUAN: Yeah. O.K., kid...go get the buckets...I'll be down the tier.

(BROWN appears outside gate.)

CUPCAKES: On the gate.

BROWN: On the gate. (He opens gate and CUPCAKES and JUAN exit. He closes gate and exits.)

PACO: Man thinks he El grande Pingú...

ICE: Squash it...

LONGSHOE: (Goes over to toilet, where CLARK is.) Hey, man...don't leave. I want you to hold it for me...while I pee.

CLARK: What...wha...

LONGSHOE: I want you to hold my motherfucking dick while I pee, sucker, so I don't get my hands wet . . . *(Laughter)* Well?

CLARK: No . . . no . . . I can't do that . . .

LONGSHOE: Oh. You can't do that . . . but you can rape seven-year-old girls.

CLARK: I didn't rape anybody. I didn't do anything.

LONGSHOE: Shut up, punk. *(Pushes CLARK's chest.)* What's this—smokes.

CLARK: They're all I have . . . but you're welcome to some.

LONGSHOE: Some? I'm welcome to all of them, creep.

CLARK: What about me?

LONGSHOE: What about you?

CLARK: They're all I have.

LONGSHOE: Kick.

CLARK: But . . .

ICE: Kick, motherfucker, kick.

LONGSHOE: Kick . . . hey, let me see that chain . . . gold . . .

CLARK: Yes.

LONGSHOE: How many carats?

CLARK: Fourteen.

ICE: Damn, Shoe . . . if you gonna take the chain, take the chain.

LONGSHOE: I . . . me . . . take . . . Who said anything about taking anything. That would be stealing and that's dishonest, ain't it, Clarky baby . . . You wanna give that chain, don't you . . . After all, we're both white and we got to look out for one another. Ain't that true, Clarky baby . . . You gonna be real white about the whole thing, aren't you, Clarky baby.

CLARK: It's a gift from my mother.

ALL: Ohhh.

LONGSHOE: I didn't know you had a mother . . . I didn't think human beings gave birth to dogs, too.

OMAR: Looks like the freak ain't upping the chain, Shoe.

LONGSHOE: Oh man, Clarky baby, how you gonna show in front of these people? You want them to think we're that untogether? What are you trying to say, man? You mean to stand there in your nice cheap summer suit looking very white and deny my whiteness by refusing to share a gift with me? That totally uncool . . . You're insulting me, man.

OMAR: Man's trying to say that you're not white enough.

LONGSHOE: You're trying to put a wire out on me, creep?

OMAR: Man saying you're a nigger-lover.

LONGSHOE: You saying that I'm a quadroon?

EL RAHEEM: What? Freak, did you say that devil has some royal Congo blood in his veins?

ICE: I ain't got nothin' to do with it, Shoe, but I swore I heard the freak say that you were passing, Shoe.

CLARK: I didn't say that . . . I didn't say anything.

ICE: You calling me a liar.

CLARK: No, no . . . no.

LONGSHOE: Then you did say it?

(They all push CLARK around.)

CLARK: Please, please, here take this chain, leave me alone.

ICE: *(Yanks chain from around neck.)* Pick the motherfucking chain up, freak.

EL RAHEEM: That's right . . . You tell that man he ain't good enough to talk to.

LONGSHOE: First I'm a nigger-lover . . . then a quadroon . . . Now I'm not even good enough to talk to.

EL RAHEEM: Boy, I told you about being in God's walking space, didn't I?

ICE: You better answer God when he speaks, boy.

LONGSHOE: Don't you turn your back on me, motherfucker.

(Strikes CLARK. He falls against EL RAHEEM, who hits him too.)

(OMAR begins kicking him.)

(MR. NETT appears outside gate.)

MR. NETT: On the gate. *(He opens gate, enters.)*

OMAR: Mr. Nett.

EL RAHEEM: Mr. Nett, Mr. Nett, the man started a fight with Omar and we just broke it up.

ICE: That's right, Mr. Nett.

MR. NETT: You guys shouldn't whip his face. Omar, you are on the help permanently. The Torres brothers beat their case this morning.

OMAR: Right on . . . Bet them two are high as all hell by now.

MR. NET: Yeah, and they'll be back, mark my words . . . Listen, get this man off the floor . . . You guys know the rules . . . No sleeping on the floor. *(He closes gate and exits.)*

ICE: You guys oughta learn how to touch up a dude.

OMAR: I'll get a bucket of water.

LONGSHOE: Fuck the bucket of water, Omar. Put the sucker's head in the toilet bowl. There's water there.

EL RAHEEM: He's still a devil...I won't do that to no man.

LONGSHOE: We could get it on again.

EL RAHEEM: That don't present me no problems...

ICE: Squash it, man...both of you...

LONGSHOE: Come on, Omar, grab his other side...

OMAR: Hey, there's still piss in there.

LONGSHOE: Put his head in and I'll flush it.

EL RAHEEM: Omar...let me put his head in there and you flush it.

LONGSHOE: Makes me no difference...flush the motherfucker, Omar.

(OMAR, LONGSHOE, PACO *pick up* CLARK *to put his head in toilet bowl. They use him as a ramrod, making three runs at the toilet,* CLARK *screaming. On third ram, toilet is flushed, and lights fade.)*

Act Two

(Same scene. Half an hour later. JUAN is playing chess with ICE. PACO is seated at table, watching ICE and JUAN play chess. OMAR and CUPCAKES are doing exercises. EL RAHEEM is writing, talking to himself. LONGSHOE is reading.)

ICE: You know, it's kinda like a shame what these dudes did to that poor ugly misbegotten son of a bitch. I feel almost sorry for the slob. They do that to me or even think of doing it . . . it's war . . . to the bitter end.

JUAN: Spare me . . . Where they take him?

ICE: Don't know . . . don't care . . . and don't give a fuck . . .

OMAR: They took him down for P.I. . . .

CUPCAKES: Pi?

OMAR: Positive Identification . . . stupid.

CUPCAKES: Your mama.

OMAR: My mama don't play that shit . . . and neither do I . . .

EL RAHEEM: I hope they don't bring him back on the floor . . .

JUAN: Who, Short Eyes?

EL RAHEEM: Yeah . . . I got the feeling . . . and the knowledge working full and I feel it . . .

ICE: Feel what, man?

JUAN: You know as well as I do what . . . Go on, it's your play . . .

ICE: Looks like you made the wrong move there, governor . . . it seems that I am going to have to prove to you young whippersnapper that you can't fool around with an old man . . .

JUAN: You sure talk a lotta shit, Ice.

ICE: You're in check, my good fellow—chip, chip, cheerios and all that shit . . . Ten months, and finally I beat that motherfucker.

LONGSHOE: I hear you talking, Ice . . . git em . . .

ICE: Excuse me, my good man, while I answers nature's call . . . I shall return shortly . . . Motherfucker, you better not cheat . . . Let me cop that heist when you're through . . . Shoe.

LONGSHOE: You're on it second . . . Cupcakes cracked already.

EL RAHEEM: I don't understand you niggers, sometimes . . . Here you got an opportunity to learn about yourselves . . . about the greatness of the black man. And what you do? . . . Spend your time reading filthy books . . . talking negative shit . . . beating your meat at night . . . Nothing that'll benefit you in the future world of the black man...The time for the devil is almost up...He was meant to rule for a certain time and his time is near, almost too near.

LONGSHOE: El, let me tell you something. I'm a hope-to-die dope fiend ...not cause I'm black...or cause I have some personality disorder, but because I like being a dope fiend. I like being a dope fiend. And nothing is gonna change that in me...If Allah comes down from wherever he is...and he ain't doing good dope...I ain't gonna cop from him...And I'll put out a wire that his thing is cut with rat poison...Why don't you go back into your lessons and git off my motherfucking back...Cause I do as I please when the day comes that I wanna become a black god, a Panther or a Muslim, then I will become one...Right now all this shit you keep running about us being niggers—stupid and ignorance ain't gonna get you nothing, but a good kick in the ass...

ICE: *(Continuing)* Let me cop that heist, Cupcake—

CUPCAKES: When you gonna learn that I'm número uno.

OMAR: Come on, número uno...do me número ten push-ups—

PACO: Uno, do, tre, quatro...

OMAR: Hey, will you look at this. What kinda push-ups are those suppose to be—his ass all up in the air.

PACO: El culito está cojiendo ire.

CUPCAKES: I hope Geraldo Rivera gives you the shock of your life.

OMAR: Weak—weak.

LONGSHOE: Better get some friends to burn some candles for you.

PACO: Corny little guy, ain't he?

CUPCAKES: It's better than saying I hope he gets electrocuted, isn't it?

LONGSHOE: Go back to clown's college.

ICE: I told you dudes about letting him see too much TV. The boob-tube gives cancer of the eyeball—but in your case—

OMAR: Weak—weak boo-boo.

(All join in booing ICE.)

CUPCAKES: Holy dingleberries, Batman—your shit stinks too.

JUAN: O.K., everybody, let give them something for effort—two ha-ha's for Ice and one tee-hee for Cakes...Ready...tee-hee, ha-ha.

(NETT appears outside gate.)

NETT: On the gate. *(He enters.)*

JUAN: ...And one boo for Mr. Nett.

ALL: Boo...

CUPCAKES: Fuck this, I'm going to take a shower.

(He goes into shower.)

MR. NETT: *(To* JUAN*)* Poet, you've got a visit.

JUAN: 'Bout time—I know Mamy ain't gonna let me swim this ocean by my lonesome—

MR. NETT: You too, Murphy—

JUAN: Come on, let's not keep the people waiting.

LONGSHOE: I refuse my visit, Mr. Nett.

MR. NETT: That's up to you.

JUAN: You what? Man, what kinda talk is that about—your people hustled out here from the Island and you refuse? You gonna show like Cagney?

LONGSHOE: Juan, I like you, but don't go in my kitchen without my permission.

JUAN: Solid on that...later...

(Enter BROWN.*)*

BROWN: All right, listen up. Anyone for religious services?

EL RAHEEM: Yeah, I'm going, Mr. Brown.

(Various ad-libs)

OMAR: How about some pussy?

BROWN: You better watch your mouth, punk, or I'll put my foot up your ass.

(Exit BROWN *and* EL RAHEEM.*)*

LONGSHOE: Juan—wait...it's cool, man...

JUAN: Sure—sure, man—it's cool. Me and you's all right...

LONGSHOE: Juan—wait, don't make your visit—don't go, man...

JUAN: What? Not to make my visit...You must be out of your mind, Shoes...

LONGSHOE: Don't, man...The freak...He's gonna...man, like I feel it ...You gonna seem out of place when you show back—it's gonna be like when you step out of the joint...The impact...Everything's coming down...and bang, knocks you dead on your ass...And you fight to get up...And all you can do is throw a brick...cause that's the only thing that carries any weight...Dig where that's at, Juan...You in the life ...you know.

JUAN: Only thing I know is that you been fucking with them A trains, again.

OMAR: Yeah, and that goddamn homemade wine.

LONGSHOE: That's right ... But you know like everyone else knows that I know what I'm saying even if I don't say it out loud ...

MR. NETT: Murphy, you're lucky I don't lock you up for being stoned.

LONGSHOE: You wouldn't do that, Mr. Nett. Mr. Nett ... you wouldn't do that, Mr. Nett ... What would happen to your bread on the white side of the road.

PACO: Hey man, be cool, Shoe.

LONGSHOE: I said white side, Paco, not Puerto Rican ...

MR. NETT: Murphy ...

LONGSHOE: I should have you call me *Mister* Murphy ... *Mister* Nett ...

MR. NETT: Don't push it, Murphy.

PACO: If I blow ... you gonna answer.

MR. NETT: Listen, Murphy, if you don't want your visit, that all right with me ... I give less than a fuck ... That's your right ... Coming, Juan?

LONGSHOE: No.

JUAN: Don't do that ... Don't ever do that again ... Don't ever attempt to think for me. I don't know where your head's at ... But I can't see what the freak has to do with ...

NETT: *(Crossing to shower.)* Mercado.

LONGSHOE: Man, he has everything to do with it ... Don't you see he has the mark on ... Like I said before, it's the same thing as coming out of the joint ... You're branded ... A week ... a month ... sooner or later they're gonna take you off the count ... You know that ... What makes you think his place is any different ... It's all the same thing ...

JUAN: You lost me, but keep me lost ... cause I gotta feeling I ain't gonna like it if you find me ...

LONGSHOE: Go on, get your part of it ... But don't bring it back on the floor cause if you do you better walk pretty hard, Juan ...

JUAN: No, Shoes ... I walk soft but I hits hard ... Dig this ... visits and mail ... that's my ounce of freedom and I ain't gonna give it up for nobody.

(NETT and JUAN exit, gate closes. LONGSHOE gets sick and vomits into toilet, upstage center. ICE and OMAR cross upstage to Longshoe.)

ICE: You better get Mr. Nett.

OMAR: Hey, Mr. Nett. You better come in here, Shoe is sick.

(NETT *appears outside gate.*)

NETT: On the gate *(Gate opens, he enters.)*

(OMAR, ICE, *and* NETT *help* LONGSHOE *to gate, exit. Gate closes.*)

(PACO *alone in room, with* CUPCAKES *in shower.* PACO *flushes toilet and waits until men have crossed catwalk above. He enters shower and joins* CUPCAKES *singing.* PACO *sneaks up on* CUPCAKES *and embraces and kisses him on the neck.*)

CUPCAKES: What the fuck ... Hey, git the fuck off me, motherfucker ... Paco ... man, what's the matter with you ...

PACO: Matter? What's the matter with you?

CUPCAKES: You know what's the matter with me, man ... I don't play that shit, man.

PACO: Don't play what?

CUPCAKES: You know what ... Don't push me, man.

PACO: Don't play what?

CUPCAKES: That faggot shit.

PACO: Man, cause I kiss you doesn't mean you're a faggot.

CUPCAKES: It means you're a faggot ... Don't do it again.

PACO: And if I do, what you gonna do.

CUPCAKES: Nothing ... I ain't saying I'm gonna do anything ...

PACO: Then why should I stop ... I dig it ...

CUPCAKES: I don't ... And I'm telling you to stop and don't ...

PACO: You're telling me? Boy, you don't tell me nothing.

CUPCAKES: Stop pushing on me ... Look, I'm asking you ...

PACO: Go on and ask me ... Ask me like a daddy should be asked ...

CUPCAKES: You're treading on me, man.

PACO: ¿Y qué? Oyeme, negrito ... déjame decirte algo ... Tú me tiene loco ... me desespera ... Nene, estoy enchulao contigo ... Yo quiero ser tuyo y quiero que tú sea mio ... ¿Y qué tu quiere que yo haga por tí?

CUPCAKES: Que me deje quieto ... Yo no soy un maricón ...

PACO: Papisito, yo no estoy diciendo que tú ere maricón ... Yo no pienso así ...

CUPCAKES: ¿Y que tú piensa?

PACO: Que te quiero y que te adoro ... nene.

CUPCAKES: No soy nene ...

PACO: Tú va a ser mio...mi nene lindo...Cupcakes, que dio bendiga la tierra que tú pise...

CUPCAKES: Hecha, que está caliente, Paco.

PACO: Pue ponme frio.

CUPCAKES: Paco, por favor, déjame ya. Cabrón.

PACO: Hijo la gran puta...punk, I ought to take you now.

CUPCAKES: Leave me alone...déjame.

PACO: Listen, little brother...I don't want nothing from you the hard way.

CUPCAKES: Well, that's all you gonna get out of me, a hard way to go ...and don't you ever call me brother...If you considered me your brother, would you be trying this shit...

PACO: Si mi hermano era tan lindo como tú...yeah...

CUPCAKES: You're sick...

PACO: I'm what? Sick—don't you say that to me...Sick...Shit, I'm sick cause I'm in love with you...

CUPCAKES: Love me...You use words that you don't even know the meaning of Brother...Love...Shit, there's a gringo...who does it to little girls...and you wanna mess with me...Why don't you hit on him ...why? Cause he's white...and you scared of the Whitey...But you'll fuck over your own kind...He's the one you should be cracking on... He's the one. Not me...But you're scared of him...

PACO: I fear nobody...or anything, man...God or spirits. Beside...I don't want him, I want you...

CUPCAKES: But you can't have me.

PACO: Push comes to shove, I'll take you. But I don't wanna do that cause I know I'm gonna have to hurt you in the doing. Look, man, I'll go both ways with you. Who you looking for? Juan is on the visit. And let me tell you this. Makes me no difference if he does have your back.

(BROWN *appears outside gate.*)

BROWN: On the gate.

(*Gate opens.* OMAR *enters.* BROWN *exits. Gate closes.*)

PACO: I'm going to have you...if I want you...right now...I'm gonna show you I ain't scared of nobody...cause you need to know that you gota man protecting you...I'm gonna take that honky and you're gonna help.

OMAR: What?

PACO: *(Crossing to gate.)* Hey, hey, officer, officer.

*(*BROWN *reappears at the gate.)*

BROWN: On the gate.

*(*BROWN *opens gate,* PACO *exits, gate closes,* BROWN *exits.)*

OMAR: Why you let that creep talk to you that way...All you gotta do is swing and keep swinging. Fuck it if you lose. Fuck it if you win. Makes no change either way. Just let him know you's a man. I ain't the smartest guy in the world...but I do know that some people you can talk to, some people you gotta fight.

CUPCAKES: I took a swing at him.

OMAR: Not hard enough...Not at the right place. You should wait till Juan is here.

CUPCAKES: I don't wanna use Juan.

OMAR: Bullshit. If you're drowning, you use anything. You's a fine mother fucker, Cupcakes. Like I said, I ain't the smartest guy in the place. But I get the feeling you like being a fine motherfucker. And maybe...

CUPCAKES: Look, look...we're gonna do it to the white freak.

OMAR: I'm down...either way.

CUPCAKES: What you mean, either way.

OMAR: I like you, Cupcakes. But if you're gonna give it up...with an excuse...I want some.

(Crossing above on catwalk, left to right, are LONGSHOE *and* ICE *.)*

LONGSHOE: Yeah...man, let me tell you, Ice, that old man put up one hell of a fight. He was about sixty years old. But he was hard as nails. Later in court I found out he was a merchant seaman.

(Exit above, LONGSHOE *and* ICE, BROWN *and* EL RAHEEM *appear at gate.)*

BROWN: On the gate. *(He opens gate.)*

EL RAHEEM: *(Ad-libs ending with)* Why don't you come on down to religious services sometime?

BROWN: No, I was born a Christian and I'll die a Christian.

(He leaves room, letting LONGSHOE *and* ICE *enter, closes gate and exits.)*

ICE: You think you got it beat

LONGSHOE: Oh yeah, no doubt about it...Like when we went to court ...He told the judge that I was Spanish...and that I spoke it when I was ripping him off. Cause the old man is South American. I told the judge I could hardly speak English, let alone some mira-mira language. The Legal Aid said we got one good chance behind that.

(PACO's voice comes offstage right. Ad-libs about drag queens that have just been arrested. BROWN and PACO appear at gate.)

BROWN: On the gate. *(Enter PACO.)*

OMAR: Hey, look, some fags . . . They bringing in some drag queens on the floor . . . Oy, baby . . . hey, sweet mama . . . Over here, check this out . . . ten inches.

(ICE joins OMAR to make some remarks to the "girls," or drag queens, offstage.)

ICE: Fuck that, check this out . . . Thirteen inches.

(Enter JUAN.)

JUAN: That belongs to Paco. Hey, what's happening, Ice . . . don't tell you are into that scene.

(BROWN closes gate and exits.)

ICE: Juan . . . a stiff dick knows no conscience . . . How was the visit?

JUAN: Beautiful . . . Told her to chalk the bail money up . . . just go for the lawyer. I think that's more important . . . don't you?

ICE: Yeah, it is . . . if I had somebody out there looking out for me, I'd do the same thing . . .

JUAN: She's not very pretty . . . not very bright . . . but she's all I have, man, and I burn her every night.

ICE: Damn, Juan, speaking of burning somebody, did I ever tell you about the first time I was upstate?—Clinton, to be exact.

OMAR: Yeah, I heard it before. The old Jane Fonda shit.

ICE: Well, Juan ain't heard it.

OMAR: Tell it to Juan.

JUAN: Go on, run it.

ICE: You know how hard it was to get short heist up in big-foot country before the riot.

LONGSHOE: What you mean before the riot—it still hard to cop short heist up there. People still making money renting the damn things out.

OMAR: Yeah, but it was harder then. Now they don't really give that much attention to short heist. Like before, they would keep-lock you. Now they just take them away.

JUAN: When I was in Cax—it was terrible up there. Man, I still hear tell they got the old track system running.

CUPCAKES: What's the track system?

JUAN: Segregation between inmates . . . Like black and white handball courts . . . water fountains, you know like . . .

ICE: If you're white you can't smoke after a black. Sit at the same table in the messhall, and if you do you can't eat your food. No taking anything from a black person. Like of you're a Whitey and you playing handball and your ball goes over on the black handball court and a black touches it, well you and the black have to fight. If you don't you go on the track and become a creep.

CUPCAKES: Break it down.

ICE: Break it down, Juan.

JUAN: For instance, the yard is broken in three sections.

ICE: Four. The track makes four.

JUAN: Yah, you're right. One white, one black, one Spanish-speaking.

ICE: Ricans, baby, Ricans.

PACO: Yah, there was Cubans up there.

JUAN: ...'n Mexicans 'n Dominicans 'n South Americans.

ICE: Same damn thing. They all eat rice 'n beans.

JUAN: You gotta lotta shit with you, Ice. But you're right. The track makes four. And if you're considered good people, you stay with your people and enjoy their protection. If you ain't good people and—like— go against the program your people set up...

ICE: Convicts' law of survival. The codes of crime.

JUAN: Well, anyway, you go to the track with the creeps...with no protection but your own two hands...dig.

ICE: Man, fuck that, he'll learn when he gets there...Dig this...I was in my cell...like this is where they have all those French Canadian bigots. Let me tell you I was raised in Georgia for a while, but like I swear to God I never seen anybody as racist as a French Canadian. Anyway, like I was in my cell about nine, dig. I was reading this short-heist book. Brother man, this was a smoker. S...M...O...K...E...R. Just after a few pages...I had to put down the damn book because my Johnson Ronson was ripping through my cheap underwears. So I put the book down...jumped out my bed...stick the mirrors out the cell ...to see if anybody was coming down the gallery...Coast clear...Like upstate you know ain't like down here. You ain't got no cellies,Cupcakes ...you be by yourself. So I would really stretch out in doing up my wood...I got this picture of Jane Fonda. Cause you can't have nothing on the walls. She's got this black silk satin bikini. Man, I could almost touch those fine white tits of hers. And that cute round butt sticking out and all. Dig, I strip naked...and started rolling. She was looking good on my mind.

OMAR: Why a white girl?

ICE: Cause, sucker, we weren't allow to have short-heist pictures . . . and how many black girls have taken short-heist flicks.

JUAN: Hundreds of them. And hundreds of Puerto Rican girls too.

ICE: Yeah, well . . . I guess I wanted a white girl.

EL RAHEEM: You wanted a girl so bad . . . made him no different if it was just imagination.

ICE: Hey, man, you guys gonna let me tell this thing or what?

OMAR: Ain't nobody stopping you. Run it. Juan's listenin'.

ICE: Yeah, she was sure looking good in my mind . . . Jesus . . . So I started calling out her name real softly . . . Jane . . . Jane . . . Janeeee . . . oooo Janeee baby. Ooooo Janeeee baby . . .

(LONGSHOE *shows short-heist book to* ICE. *Inmates gather around table.*)

OMAR: Goddamn! Will you look at the gash on that girl. That's pure polyunsaturated pussy.

ICE: Wesson Oil never had it so good. Oh, Jane baby. Oh Jane mama. Ooooo Jane. Come here, get a part of some reallll downnnn home gut-stomped black buck fucking . . . Man, I was really running. Wow. She was in front of me. Dancing, spreading her legs wider and wider . . . Till I could see her throatmmm. Them white thighs crushing me to death. Wiggling and crawling on the floor. Calling her name out, Janeee babyyyy . . . ooooo Janeeee baby . . . This is black power. Git honey, git honey, git git git . . . ununhahahaha . . . mmmmm, calling her name out faster, a little bit louder. A little bit faster, a little bit louder . . . And I'm whipping my Johnson to the bone . . . Soon everybody on the tier knew I was working out cause soon everybody's voices is with me. And we're all tryin' to get this one last big nut together. . . . Git it, git it. Janneeee . . . baby . . . Get it, get it, get it, get it, get it, get it, get it. I scream, my knees buckle . . . and I'm kneeling there, beat as a son of a bitch, because that's the way I felt, beat as a son of a bitch. I really burnt Jane that night. You know if I ever meet that broad, Jane Fonda . . .

(BROWN *and* CLARK *appear at gate.*)

BROWN: On the gate . . .

(CLARK *enters,* BROWN *closes gate,* BROWN *exits.*)

ICE: I'm going to ask her if she ever felt a strange sensation that night. Anyway, brother man . . . I turn my head and bang.

(CLARK *walks over to* JUAN.)

CLARK: Can I see you, please. I need to talk to you, please.

JUAN: Later.

CLARK: Please.

ICE: The man said later. You're interrupting me...creep.

PACO: Go to your place, maricón. You know...go on, man, bang, then what happened.

ICE: Oh yeah, bang. I happened to look up and there's these two redneck ...peckerwood big-foot country honkies...looking and grinning at me ...I don't know how they was there cause I had my eyes close all the time I was gitting my rocks off, better for the imagination. Helps the concentration, dig. They weren't saying a word, just standing there grinning...grinning these two big grins...these two real big grins on the faces that reach from one ear to the other. So I started grinning back. Grinning th—that old nigger grin we give to Charlie...We stood there grinning at each other for about five minutes...them grinning at my Johnson...me grinning at them grinning at my Johnson...just grinning...Hold it, no really, just grinning. It's weird. Freaky kinda thing. Somebody stops to watch you masturbate, then stands there grinning at you. I mean like what can you say. Really, what can you say to them. To anybody. All of a sudden the biggest one with the biggest grin gives out a groan. "Hey, Harry, this fucking face has been pulling his pecker on a white woman." So Harry comes over and said very intelligently, "Da...da...this ain't no white woman, Joey. I mean, no real white woman. She's a Communist, Joey, she really is, da...da...she's white trash, Joey. Take my word for it, she's white trash. The *Daily News* said so." So Joey runs this down on Harry: "Harry, I know what she is...I read the papers, too, you know. But she is a white woman. And this nigger has been thinking about...having screwed her. Now you know that's un-American. Harry, open up the dead lock." So Harry runs to open up the dead lock. Now Joey got the nigger knocker wrapped around his hand real tight, dig. I know he about to correct me on some honky rules. I know what's about to jump off...I'm in my cell...And I'm cool ...extra cool...That's my name...Ice...The lames roll in front of my cell and I go into my Antarctic frigid position...you can see the frost all over my cell. But before Harry could open the dead lock...I told him, Joey baby...now, I'm locking up on the third tier...I said, Joey baby...I sure hope you can fly. He said, What you talking about, nigger boy. I said fly like a bird. You know F-L-Y. Cause once you open this gate ...I ain't about to let you whip me with that stick. I stood up on my toes. Pointed over the rail and said both of us are going, Joey. He yelled out, Harry, don't up the gate. This nigger crazy. Now I'm a crazy nigger cause I wouldn't let them come in here and kick me in my ass.

CUPCAKES: So what happened after that?

ICE: What happen, they called in reinforcement and tear-gassed me out of the cell.

CUPCAKES: Tear-gas you in the cell?

ICE: Yeah, what you think they do, ask you pretty please, would you come out of your cell, we would like to break open your skull.

JUAN: Ain't nothing new about that . . . Happens all the time.

ICE: Anyway, when I comes out the hospital. I had to go see the psych . . .

CUPCAKES: For what.

ICE: For masturbating. And for not letting them crack my head willingly. You see only crazy people beat their meat.

CUPCAKES: I must be a lunatic.

PACO: The only lunatic is the freak.

(NETT appears at gate.)

NETT: On the gate. *(Opens gate.)* Sick call. Line up for sick call.

PACO: Come, I hear they got a brand-new nurse on.

(Exit LONGSHOE, PACO, CUPCAKES with various ad-libs.)

OMAR: Now what you got, the leg? Or is it the tooth?

ICE: Look, Jack, you had the leg last week.

OMAR: Fuck that, I'll take the tooth.

(Exit OMAR and ICE. NETT closes gate on EL RAHEEM and exits.)

EL RAHEEM: Mr. Brown, Mr. Brown—I want to go to sick call.

(BROWN appears outside gate.)

BROWN: On the gate.

(BROWN opens gate, lets EL RAHEEM out, closes gate, and both exit. CLARK and JUAN are left alone on stage.)

JUAN: What you want to see me about, Clark?

CLARK: Look, what I told you earlier . . . er . . . that between me and you . . . like, I don't know why I even said that, just . . . just that . . . man, like everything was just coming down on me . . . My wife . . . she was at the hospital . . . She . . . she didn't even look at me . . . once, not once . . . Please . . . don't let it out . . . please . . . I'll really go for help this time . . . I promise.

JUAN: What happened at the P.I. stand?

CLARK: Nothing . . . nothing . . . happened . . .

JUAN: Did she identify you? Did she?

CLARK: I don't know. I didn't see anybody. They put me next to a bunch of the other men about my size, weight . . . You—the whole line-up routine. I didn't see anybody or anything but the people there and this voice that kept asking me to turn around to say, "Hello, little girl." That's all.

JUAN: Nothing else?

CLARK: No.

JUAN: You mean they didn't make you sign some papers?

CLARK: No

JUAN: Was there a lawyer for you there? Somebody from the courts?

CLARK: Juan, I really don't know . . . I didn't see anybody . . . and they didn't let me speak to anyone at all . . . They hustled me in and hustled me right out . . .

JUAN: That means you have a chance to beat this case . . . Did they tell you what they are holding you for?

CLARK: No . . . no one told me anything.

JUAN: If they are rushing it—the P.I.—that could mean they only are waiting on the limitation to run out.

CLARK: What does that all mean?

JUAN: What it means is that you will get a chance to scar up some more little girls' minds.

CLARK: Don't say that, Juan. Please don't think like that. Believe me, if I thought I couldn't seek help after this ordeal, I would have never—I mean, I couldn't do that again.

JUAN: How many times you've said that in the street and wind up molesting some kid in the park.

CLARK: Believe me, Juan . . . please believe me. I wouldn't any more.

JUAN: Why should I?

CLARK: Cause I told you the truth before. I told you what I haven't told God.

JUAN: That's because God isn't in the House of Detention.

CLARK: Please, Juan, why are you being this way? What have I done to you?

JUAN: What have you done to me? What you've done to me? It's what you've done, period. It's the stand that you are forcing me to take.

CLARK: You hate me.

JUAN: I don't hate you. I hate what you've done. What you are capable of doing. What you might do again.

CLARK: You sound like a judge.

JUAN: In this time and place I am your judge.

CLARK: No ... no. You are not ... And I'm sick and tired of people judging me.

JUAN: Man, I don't give a fuck what you're sick and tired about. What you told about yourself was done because of the pressure. People say and do weird things under pressure.

CLARK: I'm not used to this.

JUAN: I don't care what you're used to. I got to make some kind of thing about you.

CLARK: No, you don't have to do anything. Just let me live.

JUAN: Let you live?

CLARK: I can't make this ... this kind of life. I'll die.

JUAN: Motherfucker, don't cry on me.

CLARK: Cry ... why shouldn't I cry ... why shouldn't I feel sorry for my-self ... I have a right to ... I have some rights ... and when these guys get back from the sick call ... I'm gonna tell them what the captain said to me, that if anybody bothers me to tell him ...

JUAN: Then you will die.

CLARK: I don't care one way or the other. Juan, when I came here I already had been abused by the police ... threatened by a mob the news-paper created ... Then the judge, for my benefit and the benefit of so-ciety, had me committed to observation. Placed in an isolated section of some nut ward ... viewed by interns and visitors like some abstract object, treated like a goddamn animal monster by a bunch of inhuman, incompetent, third-rate, unqualified, unfit psychopaths calling them-selves doctors.

JUAN: I know the scene.

CLARK: No, you don't know ... electros—sedatives—hypnosis—therapy— humiliated by some crank nurses who strapped me to my bed and played with my penis to see if it would get hard for "big girls like us."

JUAN: Did it?

CLARK: Yeah ... yes, it did.

JUAN: My father used to say he would fuck 'em from eight to eighty, blind, cripple, and/or crazy.

CLARK: Juan, you are the only human being I've met.

JUAN: Don't try to leap me up ... cause I don't know how much of a human being I would be if I let you make the sidewalk. But there's no way I could stop you short of taking you off the count.

(NETT *appears at gate.*)

NETT: On the gate.

(*He opens gate. The rest of the men enter. He closes gate and exits.*)

ICE: Juan ... come here for a second.

JUAN: Yeah, what is it, Ice?

ICE: Juan, if you remember what was said after the last riot here.

PACO: He should. He suggested it, didn't he?

JUAN: I remember everything that was said.

ICE: Anything that would affect the whole floor ... we would hold council on it, right? Well, he affects the whole floor.

JUAN: What's happening?

LONGSHOE: He white like I am ... And you ain't got no right according to the rules to take his back ... if he is stuff.

JUAN: Stuff? He ain't stuff.

LONGSHOE: Well, we say he is.

JUAN: Who says he is?

ALL: I say he is.

PACO: Anybody that has to rape little girls is a faggot. He's stuff ... squeeze.

JUAN: I say he ain't.

ICE: You got no say in this.

PACO: Oh, he's got a say, not that it means anything, but he's got a say.

LONGSHOE: Paco, be cool.

JUAN: Yeah, Paco, be very cool.

LONGSHOE: That ain't necessary. And neither is your getting in the way of the council.

JUAN: The council was set up to help, not to destroy.

PACO: The council was set up to help, not to destroy. Oh, would you listen to this ... Very ... very pretty ... He's fucking Cupcakes and now he's fucking the white freak.

CUPCAKES: Ain't nobody fucking me, Paco.

PACO: Maybe he's not yet, but he's setting you up. Giving you fatherly advice, my ass. He's just like El Raheem. He wants to fuck you too. Putting the wisdom in front of the knowledge. He's calling you a girl. That's what he means by that. And Omar playing exercises with you so that you can take showers together. Longshoe ... giving you short-heist books. Everybody wants you, Cupcakes. Cupcakes, Ice gave you that name, didn't he? Wasn't that your woman's name in the street, Ice? ... Nobody saying anything. Why? Cause I hit the truth. Pushed that little button ... Everybody on the whole floor is trying to cop ... but only Juan gets a share. Now he wants the white freak for himself, too.

JUAN: You're sick, man.

PACO: Tu madre ... tu madre, maricón ... hijo de la gran puta ... cabrón. *(He lunges toward* JUAN.*)*

ICE: Hold it ... hold it ... Man, why fight each other over some bullshit.

JUAN: Let the motherfucker go. Let him go.

PACO: All right ... all right, let me go. I'll be cool. O.K., Juan. Check this out. I want him. Longshoe is white. He gave the O.K. That means he wants him. Omar getting a share. So does El Raheem.

JUAN: El Raheem, you are in this too?

EL RAHEEM: He's a Whitey. A devil. Anything goes.

PACO: How about you, Cupcakes?

JUAN: Julio?

PACO: Well, it's either him or ... well, Cakes ... make up your choice, now. Which way? Who you stand with?

CUPCAKES: I go ... I go with you.

JUAN: You punk, you little punk. Everything I taught you just went in one ear and came out the other. You want to be an animal too ... You're letting this place destroy you.

PACO: Ice, which way?

ICE: Man, I ... I don't want no part of it.

PACO: You what? You want no part of it?

ICE: You heard what I said. Juan is right. This place makes animals out of us.

PACO: Man.

ICE: Man what? You think anybody here is good enough to take me.

JUAN: Take us.

PACO: That's the way you want it.

ICE: That the way it is.

EL RAHEEM: Ice, you don't have to take whole part.

OMAR: Ice, you my man ... but you sticking up for some honky is wrong ... You going upstate, you know that. Juan is likely to hit the street. He

got somebody out there. You don't. All you got is a plea to cop. I dig
you a whole lot. But you're wrong, Ice.

LONGSHOE: You don't have to take part, play chickie . . . that's all . . . play
chickie . . .

ICE: I . . . I . . . all right . . . I'll play chickie . . .

JUAN: You still got me to deal with . . .

(PACO grabs JUAN from behind.)

PACO: Hold him, Ice.

(ICE holds JUAN.)

JUAN: Let me go, Ice. Ice, don't do this to yourself. Ice, let me go.

CLARK: Mr. Nett. Mr. Nett . . .

(He runs to window ledge upstage center. OMAR jumps on ledge with him.)

*(NETT appears at gate, opens it, walks in, sees what's happening, and turns to go,
but remains.)*

CLARK: O.K. O.K. Don't hurt me anymore. Go 'head, do what you want.
Go 'head, you filthy bastards. Go 'head, Mr. Nett, don't think you can
walk away from this. I'll tell the captain. I'll bring you all before the
courts. You bastards. You too, you fat faggot.

JUAN: Shut up . . . shut up.

PACO: You gonna do what? *(He pulls out homemade knife.)*

LONGSHOE: He's gonna squeal. He's gonna rat us out.

(OMAR jumps off window ledge.)

JUAN: Ice, let him go.

EL RAHEEM: You're in this too, Ice. We'll all get more time.

CLARK: I'll make sure you get life, you son of a bitch.

MR. NETT: I'll lose my job.

(Opens gate to look down corridor.)

CLARK: I'll make sure you go to jail. My father has money . . . plenty
money.

JUAN: Shut up, Clark . . . shut up.

(PACO runs toward CLARK to kill him. EL RAHEEM restrains him.)

PACO: I ain't doing no more time than I have to.

OMAR: Paco, that murder.

CUPCAKES: What are we going to do?

LONGSHOE: Kill the motherfucking rat.

MR. NETT: Kill him—it's self-defense.

EL RAHEEM: Suicide...suicide...He did it to himself.

JUAN: It's murder. Ice, it's murder. you'll be a part of it, too.

PACO: Hold him, Ice.

CUPCAKES: I don't want to do more time.

LONGSHOE: Kill him...kill him...kill the sick motherfucker.

(He pulls CLARK *off window ledge.)*

PACO: Here, El...He's a devil...kill him...You said the devil is gonna die anyway.

(He gives the knife to EL RAHEEM.*)*

OMAR: Kill him, El...kill him.

EL RAHEEM: Hold him...hold him...

*(*CLARK *runs to downstage right corner.* OMAR *and* LONGSHOE *grab him and hold him.)*

PACO: Stab him.

MR. NETT: No, cut his throat.

EL RAHEEM: Cut his throat.

PACO: Do it, El...Do it, El.

(EL brings the knife down to CLARK's *neck.)*

LONGSHOE: Go on, nigger, kill him.

EL RAHEEM: I can't...I can't...I don't have the heart...I can't...do it.

LONGSHOE: What you mean? You can do it...You talk of killing Whitey every day.

EL RAHEEM: I can't do it. I just can't kill a man like that. Not that way. Get up and fight, honky. Let him up and I could do it.

LONGSHOE: Kill him...standing up...laying down...sitting...Either way, he's dead.

EL RAHEEM: It's not the same thing...I just can't do it.

LONGSHOE: Kill him...kill him.

PACO: He's a devil, El Raheem.

CUPCAKES: Oh, my God.

(He pushes EL RAHEEM *to shower and restrains him.)*

JUAN: Don't, El, don't do it. That's not the way a black god kills. That's a devil's way.

CLARK: Please...don't kill me...please, I didn't mean what I said. I didn't mean it. I won't tell anybody...please do what you want but don't kill me. I got a wife and kids. Please don't...please.

EL RAHEEM: *(Breaking loose from* CUPCAKES, *tries once more to kill* CLARK *.)* Allah Akbar, Allah Akbar, I can't do it—I just can't do it.

LONGSHOE: Give that knife, punk.

(Swings knife, cutting CLARK's *throat.)*

Scream, bastard...rat...Scream...monster...die...die...

(Everyone is silent.)

*(*NETT *closes gate and exits.)*

OMAR: El Raheem...black god...leader of the black nation... faggot...

EL RAHEEM: I'm not a faggot...I'm not a punk...Omar, believe me. It's just that I couldn't kill a man looking at me helpless.

LONGSHOE: You punk motherfucker you...You ain't nothing but a jive-ass nigger. I'm gonna cut your black ass until you turn white, nigger.

CUPCAKES: El...

ICE: Shoe...raise...or deal with me.

LONGSHOE: You want a part of this, too, Ice?...Nigger, you want a part of this?

ICE: Don't run it in the hole, Shoe.

LONGSHOE: You selling me a ticket, faggot?

ICE: That's right, honky. You feel you can cash it?

LONGSHOE: Come with it.

ICE: You bring it and bring your best.

*(*LONGSHOE *rushes* ICE, *swings the knife.* ICE *jumps out of the way.* PACO *throws chair to* ICE *.)*

LONGSHOE: Come, nigger. What's the matter, jig. You can't stand the sight of a knife. You bought this...now enjoy it. Come baby, don't run.

PACO: Ice.

LONGSHOE: Paco, you go against me?

ICE: Come, punk, now he stand on equal grounds.

LONGSHOE: You'll only get one shot, faggot.

ICE: That's all I need.

PACO: Don't look at me, Longshoe. You wanna kill each other, then go ahead. El que gane pierde.

LONGSHOE: Whoever wins loses.

ICE: Dirty cocksucker. Fuck it.

CUPCAKES: Stop it, goddamn it. Stop it ... Oh, my God ... is this really us.

BLACKOUT

Epilogue

(That evening. In dim light NETT *searches dayroom for remaining evidence, which he puts in shower. Closes shower curtain. Meanwhile, roll call is in progress.* BROWN *is on catwalk. As he calls out names, prisoners appear in their respective positions on the catwalk above.)*

BROWN: All right, listen up . . . When I call out your name . . . give me your cell location and your first name . . . Come out of your cell . . . Leave everything behind . . . Keep your mouth shut . . . eyes front . . . hands over your head. Blinker.

OMAR: Omar, upper D 9.

BROWN: Johnson.

JOHNSON: El Raheem, William, lower D 4.

BROWN: Pasqual.

PACO: Paco Pasqual, lower D 2.

BROWN: Wicker.

ICE: John, lower D 5.

BROWN: Murphy.

LONGSHOE: Charles, lower D 7.

BROWN: Otero.

JUAN: Juan, upper D 3.

BROWN: Mercado.

CUPCAKES: Julio, upper D 2.

BROWN: Put on your clothes and report to the dayroom . . .

*(*NETT *remains. Enter* ALLARD.*)*

ALLARD: Get the lights on in here.

NETT: On the lights.

(Lights on in dayroom.)

ALLARD: Get Merkaydo and Murphy.

NETT: Mercado, Murphy, in the dayroom.

BROWN: Mercado and Murphy.

*(*CUPCAKES *and* LONGSHOE *leave cells offstage and cross catwalk, left to right, led by* BROWN. *They appear at entrance to dayroom.)*

BROWN: Which one first?

NETT: Mercado.

(CUPCAKES and BROWN enter dayroom and BROWN searches CUPCAKES. BROWN leaves dayroom, closes gate, but remains outside it.)

ALLARD: Merkaydo, possession of drugs and sale of drugs.

CUPCAKES: Mi nombre es Mercado. Yo no hablo inglés.

ALLARD: You no what. Listen here, you little punk. I don't hear this speaka la english jazz. I'm not here to play games with you. That's why we give you recreation. The only game I'm going to play with you is to break your little Puerto Rican ass and slam you in the bing until you leave this place. Is this clear? Now you speak English, don't you?

CUPCAKES: Yes, sir, perfeckly.

ALLARD: Now, that's sales and possession of drugs, right?

CUPCAKES: Like, man ... Marijuana ain't no drug.

ALLARD: *(Almost shouting.)* My name is Captain Allard, my name is not man ... Do you understand that? Well, say so.

CUPCAKES: Yes, sir.

ALLARD: O.K. Let's see, your name is Merkaydo.

CUPCAKES: Mercado.

ALLARD: Jewleo.

CUPCAKES: Julio.

ALLARD: You are twenty-one years old and here for selling drugs. I wonder how many school kids you got hooked on this stuff.

CUPCAKES: I hooked no one onto anything, man.

ALLARD: What did you say?

CUPCAKES: I mean, sir.

ALLARD: You were in the dayroom when this happened, weren't you?

CUPCAKES: Yes, sir, he borrowed my towel, sir.

ALLARD: He borrowed your towel, went into the shower, and cut his throat? Why did you lend him your towel?

CUPCAKES: To dry himself.

ALLARD: What were you doing while he was in the shower?

CUPCAKES: I was watching TV and rapping to the fellas.

ALLARD: What program were you watching?

CUPCAKES: The Dating Game.

ALLARD: Did you know what Clark Davis was here for?

CUPCAKES: No, sir, it's none of my business.

ALLARD: Did he seemed depressed, uptight?

CUPCAKES: I didn't notice.

ALLARD: Merkaydo, this is your first time up on criminal charges, isn't it?

CUPCAKES: Yes, sir.

ALLARD: Come here, Merkaydo, sit down.

CUPCAKES: No, thank you, I'd rather stand. If you don't mind, Captain.

ALLARD: Well, I do mind . . . I ask you to sit down . . . I don't like looking up.

CUPCAKES: Yes, sir . . .

ALLARD: Merkaydo . . . I don't know if you are listening to any of these jailhouse lawyers. But you should take note that all the cooperation that is given to the Department is always taken into deep consideration by the courts. Why, I've known men who didn't stand a chance in a million to walk right out into the streets, all because of a letter of recommendation from the Department. And you know, of course, this is kept in the strictest of confidence. And who knows—maybe in the future, if you should ever get arrested again, it may go well with you. Now, think about this for a moment. Do you care to make a statement?

CUPCAKES: No, no statements . . .

ALLARD: All right, go back to your cell . . . Wait a minute, Merkaydo. Has anyone on this floor been hitting on you?

CUPCAKES: No, sir.

ALLARD: If anyone did approach you with a homosexual proposition, would you report it to the officer in charge, Mr. Nett?

CUPCAKES: No, sir, I'm no rat, I'm a man . . . I take care of myself . . .

ALLARD: O.K., mister . . . Get back to your cell.

BROWN: On the gate.

(BROWN *opens gate,* CUPCAKES *exits,* BROWN *closes gate.* CUPCAKES *crosses catwalk to his position above left.* BROWN *remains at entrance below, while* ALLARD *and* NETT *continue conversation.)*

ALLARD: Nett, how long has he been on your floor?

NETT: A little over a month, sir.

ALLARD: And no one has tried anything with him?

NETT: Not that I know of, sir.

ALLARD: Well, one thing's for sure, men ain't what they used to be . . .

NETT: Things have changed, sir.

ALLARD: Murphy—he's been around awhile . . .

NETT: Murphy's been in and out of these places since the day one, sir.

ALLARD: Call him in.

NETT: Yes, sir. On the gate. Murphy in the dayroom.

BROWN: Put your hands down.

(BROWN *opens gate,* LONGSHOE *enters,* BROWN *closes gate. During following dialogue,* CUPCAKES, *on catwalk above left, and* JUAN, *on catwalk above right, carry on a conversation in Spanish about the preceding interrogation.)*

ALLARD: Murphy . . . alias George Reagan . . . Michael Potter . . . Julian Berger . . . etc. . . . Drugs . . . burglary . . . assault . . . grand larceny . . . attempted murder . . . Now it's armed robbery, you got quite a record, Murphy.

LONGSHOE: Yes, sir.

ALLARD: Murphy . . . stand up straight . . . get that gum out of your mouth . . . and wipe that smirk off your face . . . You were in the dayroom when this happen?

LONGSHOE: Sir?

ALLARD: Were you in the dayroom when this incident concerning Clark Davis occurred. That's a very simple question, Murphy . . . And all I want is a simple answer, I'll try to keep my questions from being too profound for you.

LONGSHOE: I would appreciate it, Captain.

ALLARD: Yes, I'm sure you would . . . What were you doing while Clark Davis was bleeding to death in the shower?

(At this point PACO, *at entrance gate, joins Spanish conversation with* JUAN *and* CUPCAKES.)

LONGSHOE: I was sitting at the table reading a book and every once in a while I'd take a glance at the boob-tube.

ALLARD: At the what?

LONGSHOE: At the television, sir . . .

(At this point, ICE, *on catwalk above left, and* OMAR, *on catwalk above right, talk in "ism" language.)*

ALLARD: Well, say so, you're no Puerto Rican just off the banana boat. You speak English. What was the name of the book you were reading and what program did you every once in a while glance at?

LONGSHOE: The book was *Father's Little Girlfriend* and the name of the program was the Dating Game.

ALLARD: And I suppose everyone else on the floor was with you watching the Dating Game?

LONGSHOE: Yah, well, except those that were in court.

ALLARD: Nett, can't you keep those men quiet?

(NETT crosses to entrance gate. BROWN exits and reappears on catwalk.)

NETT: All right, pipe down.

(The inmates stop for a moment, then OMAR and ICE continue the "ism" talk.)

ALLARD: Sit down, Murphy, have a smoke . . .

LONGSHOE: No, thank you, Captain, I have my own . . .

ALLARD: Murphy, let me ask you a question . . . just between you and me . . . what do you know about this? Something isn't right . . . I can feel it . . . I think you know what I mean . . .

BROWN: *(On catwalk above, to* ICE *.)* Shut up, ol' simple ass nigger.

ICE: You mother's father is a simple ass nigger.

BROWN: What you say?

ICE: I didn't say nothing.

BROWN: *(Pulling* ICE *from catwalk above left.)* Come on out of there—shut up—shut up—I kick you in the ass, shut up, motherfucker.

(BROWN and ICE cross catwalk, left to right, and appear below at entrance gate.)

LONGSHOE: What's going on, Captain?

ALLARD: Murphy, I'm concerned about you . . . a lone white man among all these Puerto Ricans and Negros. You're not protecting these people, are you? . . . Do you realize that every offense that has been committed against a young white boy in this place has been perpetrated by the blacks and the Puerto Ricans. What do you owe these people . . . Look, you're an old-timer from the old school, I understand that . . . and I appreciate and respect your position—but we're in a different situation here . . . Murphy, I want you to make a statement to help out in this investigation.

LONGSHOE: I make no statements to anyone . . . I got nothing to say . . .

ALLARD: All right, go back to your cell. Just a moment. Murphy, what color was his hair?

LONGSHOE: I'm color-blind, sir.

ALLARD: Get out of here! I'm color-blind!

BROWN: On the gate

(Gate opens. BROWN enters, and LONGSHOE exits. Gate closes.)

NETT: Want me to write him up, sir?

ALLARD: Later.

NETT: You want to see anyone else, sir?

ALLARD: What for? . . . They'll all come in here with the same story about watching the Dating Game show, and they're all lying.

NETT: What makes you think they're lying, Captain?

ALLARD: What makes me think they're lying? Let me ask you. How can a man come on this floor . . . no one talk to him . . . no one notice him, no one remember a thing about him. Nett, I came here to get the facts . . . and you are not helping.

NETT: You have no right.

ALLARD: Don't raise your voice at me, Nett. I'm no inmate.

NETT: Captain, who are you investigating, these animals or a fellow officer?

ALLARD: Don't give me that fellow-officer routine, Nett. You are a disgrace to that uniform.

NETT: Captain, those gold bars don't give you the right to abuse.

ALLARD: Nett, did you send this TV repair order to the shop or not? This is your signature, isn't it? Then I can assume that the men were not watching TV, because the television was not working . . . And can I also assume that Clark Davis's death was not a suicide . . . Do you realize what you've gotten yourself into?

NET: Captain, he was—

ALLARD: Shut up, Nett . . . His parents are downstairs in the warden's office complaining about why he wasn't placed in a special unit . . . or given more protection. What are we supposed to say to this family? . . . I don't know if I'm doing the right thing, Nett . . . but I am going to tear up this repair order. It's the only thing that'll shake up their story, and yours as well . . .

NETT: Thank you, sir.

ALLARD: There's nothing to thank me for. I didn't do this for you, Nett, but for the Department. Do we understand each other?

NETT: Yes, sir.

ALLARD: I hope so. I'm going to recommend that these men be transferred to other floors, and I suggest that you make the same recommendation. Then you keep a tight rein on this floor and don't ever get involved with the inmates again.

NETT: Yes, sir.

ALLARD: I should demand your resignation, but I won't. I want you to take a sick leave early, like tomorrow. Write the reports first, get the men into the dayroom; I want to speak to them.

NETT: Captain, he was a child rapist...On the gate, everyone in the dayroom.

(BROWN opens gate.)

(ICE, EL RAHEEM, PACO enter and cross to table area. OMAR, CUPCAKES, LONGSHOE, and JUAN exit from catwalk and enter below. NETT stays on. BROWN leaves dayroom and closes gate.)

ALLARD: I'm Captain Allard, men. I'm here investigating the terrible tragedy that occurred here today...And I'm satisfied that it was a suicide...But I would like to state that I and Clark Davis's parents hold you all morally guilty...If you had taken some time out of your own problems to help this poor man that was placed in here because of a mistaken identity...

EL RAHEEM: What did you say? Mistaken identity? You mean he wasn't here because they caught him...

ICE: El.

ALLARD: Caught him doing what?

EL RAHEEM: With drugs...what else do people come to jail for?

ALLARD: No, Mr. Davis was not a drug addict. In fact, he was a very well liked and respected member of his community...a working man with a wife and child...We took him down for a positive-identification line-up...and the person that Mr. Davis was supposed to have assaulted was not in her right mind and had already pointed out two, maybe five other men, as the man who assaulted her...Mr. Davis was an innocent victim of circumstances...Innocent...Good night, men.

ALL: Good night.

BROWN: On the gate.

(BROWN opens gate, ALLARD and NETT exit, BROWN closes gate and BROWN exits.)

LONGSHOE: Man, he was guilty, I know, I could tell, I could see it in his eyes.

EL RAHEEM: Man, he was clean.

CUPCAKES: What have we done?

ICE: Ain't no use crying over it now, Cupcakes, be cool, don't blow your cool, kid.

PACO: Juan knows.

JUAN: I know nothing, I was watching the Dating Game.

VOICE: Mercado, on the bail.

ICE: Go on, boy, your pussy for the night has just come through ...

EL RAHEEM: Peace!

CUPCAKES: Juan, dime la verda del tipo ese, tú sabe.

JUAN: What's there to tell. You got it all under your belt, don't you?

PACO: Oye, y qué? What difference does it make? I took part? I saw him guilty. I feel nothing, mistake, it happens, eso pasa. Someday I'll be in the streets walking, minding my own business, and then boom-boom, I'll be shot down by a police, who will say it's a mistake, I accept it, as part of my destino ... Sí, es mi destino morir en la calle como un perro ...

LONGSHOE: That's right, what are you holding up to Juan so much for, will that bring him back?

CUPCAKES: You talk cause you did the killing.

EL RAHEEM: He talks cuz we did the killing.

CUPCAKES: I didn't take his head, I didn't swing the knife, he did.

ICE: Cupcakes, listen to me, you killed him just as much as I did.

CUPCAKES: You? You wasn't even there.

ICE: I was there ... I was there ... No, I didn't swing the knife ... and neither did you, but we're guilty by not stopping it ... We sanctioned it ... Only Juan is free ...

VOICE: Julio Mercado on the bail ...

ICE: Take it light, kid, cuz you take this place with you ...

OMAR: Cupcake, I mean Julio, do me a favor, little brother. Call this number when you get out ... Tell her to come up to see me ... fast ... Say that I need her, please, little brother, it's important.

CUPCAKES: Oye, Juan, por favor, tú sabe ...

ICE: What you want, kid? What is it? Oh shit, Juan, this kid think you're some kind of guru. Juan, if you don't tell him something, he's gonna go out there and run this thing on someone who shouldn' hear it. Can you dig it, Juan? Get his head straight ... Juan, can you dig where I'm coming from?

LONGSHOE: Cupcake, I've killed, and I'm not afraid to do it again, do you understand that?

JUAN: Shoe, if you run some shit on that kid again, I won't be afraid to kill, either.

EL RAHEEM: Neither would I.

JUAN: I'll give you something, a cheer, one last hooray, that's yours by law... cuz you're leaving this place... and only becuz of that, I can't give you no life-style pearls... no cues... becuz you, like the rest of us ... became a part of the walls... an extra bar in the gate... to remain a number for the rest of your life in the street world...

CUPCAKES: On the gate.

(BROWN *opens gate and walks away.*)

JUAN: Cupcake, you went past the money and blew it... yah, that's right, this is cop and blow... and you blew it becuz you placed yourself above understanding.

VOCIE: On the bail, Mercado... get your ass out here now.

JUAN: Oye, espera, no corra, just one thing, brother, your fear of this place stole your spirit... And this ain't no pawnshop.

BLACKOUT

Glossary of Slang

A train   Any depressant drug. They are readily available in most prisons—at a price; guards and prisoners bring them in from the outside; also, they have a way of disappearing from the shelves of prison clinics and pharmacies.

Back   As in "watch your back," meaning someone may attack you (usually with a knife) when you aren't looking. Prisoners attack each other from the front ("fronting") when they have some respect for their adversaries or when the attack constitutes some kind of showdown. Stabbing someone in the back is either an act of cowardice or signifies that the target isn't worth "fronting."

Bandido (or Bandit)   Someone who chases attractive young prisoners for sexual purposes.

Bing   Solitary confinement.

Break it down   Explain it.

Burn   To take a prisoner for something; also, to masturbate while looking at a provocative picture of a woman.

Cax   Coxsackie Correctional Facility, a prison in upstate New York.

Cellies   Cellmates.

Chickie   A lookout.

Coming out of your face wrong   Bullshitting; saying stupid things.

Coming out of the side of your neck   Same as Coming out of your face wrong.

Contract   An agreement between prisoners, such as a "contract" to wash another prisoner's clothes in exchange for a sandwich sneaked out of the kitchen by a prisoner who works there. Prison authorities tolerate such violations because this kind of crude barter helps make prison life more tolerable for inmates.

Count   The roll call of prisoners. A convict is "on the count" if he is present and accounted for; hence the expression "off the count," which means (since escapes from Sing Sing and other maximum-security prisons are so rare) that a prisoner is dead, usually murdered by fellow inmates.

Creep   Sexual offender; the lowest rung of the prison social hierarchy. Creeps never "get a hang-out card" (command enough respect to mingle and converse freely with other prisoners.)

Crimey   A fellow prisoner who was a member of one's gang or a partner in crime.

D   A felony.

Deuce   A couple of puffs on someone else's cigarette.

Don Gee   A big shot; "gee" is short for "gun."

Down   Willing.

Hack   A guard. Also known as a "roller."

Help   Prison job. To be "on the help" means to get a prison job.

Home piece   An inmate with whom one hung out before going to prison.

Homey   A fellow prisoner from one's neighborhood or home town.

"Ism" Language   A black version of pig Latin.

Some portions of this glossary originally appeared in an article by Howard A. Coffin in the *Philadelphia Inquirer.*

Jig   Derogatory term for a black man.

Johnson (or Johnson Ronson, Wood, or Swipe)   Terms for a phallus.

Keep-lock   Punish a prisoner by confining him to his cell.

Kick   Kick the habit.

Kitchen (as in "Don't go into my kitchen without permission")   One's private life. Stems from the custom among the poor of confining guests with whom they are not on intimate terms to the living room; only intimate friends are allowed into the kitchen, where fewer pretenses can be maintained.

Lame   Sucker; chump.

Leap someone up   Flatter someone; to "get leaped up" can also mean to get angry.

Locking   As in "Where are you locking?", meaning "Where's your cell?"

Longshoe   Someone who's hip, slick, and "has his act together."

Mellow-man   Close friend.

Pa'lante (short for "para adelante")   Forward and onward.

Parfait   A young male convict who is sexually desired by fellow prisoners.

Pingú   Big shot; literally, "big dick."

Plexes   Psychological complexes.

Program   The do's and don'ts of prison life. Programs are ethnically determined: they are different for whites, blacks, Puerto Ricans, etc. Programs are not enforced by prison authorities; they are determined by the prisoners themselves. The program for the whole prison population regulates the way in which members of different ethnic groups relate to one another in specific situations. It rigidly governs who sits with whom in the mess hall; where people sit in the auditorium; who smokes first; etc. It is the first thing a prisoner learns when he enters an institution. Failure to follow the program is a sure way to have trouble with fellow inmates and will result in physical reprisals—sometimes death.

Rub it on your chest   Forget about it.

Run it   Go ahead and tell your story.

Run it in the hole   Do something so many times that it becomes boring; needless repetition.

Salaam alaikum (from the Arabic)   Peace be with you.

Short Eyes   Child molester; according to prisoners, the lowest, most despicable kind of criminal.

Short heist   Any kind of pornography.

Snake   A homosexual.

Snake charmer   A "straight" prisoner who aggressively tries to get "snakes" to satisfy his sexual needs.

Squeeze   A blatant male homosexual; a queen.

Stuff   A male homosexual (not as blatant as "squeeze").

Tearoom   Men's room, especially in subways, where homosexuals seek sexual contact with each other. To "cruise the tearoom" is to go into a men's room for homosexual purposes.

Toasts   Long epic poems created and recited by prisoners for diversion. "Running toasts" is a favorite pastime of prisoners, and those who are good at it are likely to become popular with fellow inmates. "Standard" toasts are toasts that have been committed to memory and are still recited long after their creators are gone. Favorite standard toasts are "King Heroin," "The Ball of the Freaks," and "The Fall of the Pimp."

Vamp   Attack someone.

Wire (as in "to put out a wire on someone")   A false rumor or untrue story.

Yacoub   White man; honky; "devil."

David Rabe

Streamers

DAVID RABE was given his first professional production in the spring of 1971 by Joseph Papp at the New York Shakespeare Festival Public Theatre for his play *The Basic Training of Pavlo Hummel*, which was subsequently produced on Broadway starring Al Pacino. Since that time there have been professional productions of *Sticks and Bones* (also presented on television and cable), *The Orphans, In the Boom Boom Room, Streamers*, and *Hurlyburly*. Mr. Rabe's plays have won an Obie Award for Distinguished Playwrighting, a *Variety* Award, a Drama Desk Award, the Elizabeth Hull-Kate Warriner Drama Guild Award (twice), the John Gassner Outer Critics Circle Award, and a New York Drama Critics Citation. He has also won a New York Drama Critics Award for *Streamers* for Best American Play, 1976, and a Tony Award for *Sticks and Bones* for Best Play, 1972. In 1974 *Sticks and Bones* and *The Basic Training of Pavlo Hummel* were honored by the American Academy of Arts and Letters. Mr. Rabe wrote the screenplay for "I'm Dancing As Fast As I Can." He is currently working on a number of projects.

For stock and amateur production rights, contact: Samuel French, Inc., 25 West 45th Street, New York, NY 10036. For all other rights, contact: Ellen Neuwald, Inc., 905 West End Avenue, New York, NY 10025.

Original Production Notes

Streamers was produced by the Long Wharf Theater on January 30–February 27, 1976, under the direction of Mike Nichols, with the following cast:

MARTIN	Michael-Raymond O'Keefe
RICHIE	Peter Evans
CARLYLE	Joe Fields
BILLY	John Heard
ROGER	Herbert Jefferson, Jr.
COKES	Dolph Sweet
ROONEY	Kenneth McMillan
M.P. LIEUTENANT	Stephen Mendillo
PFC HINSON (M.P.)	Ron Siebert
PFC CLARK (M.P.)	Michael Kell

Produced by the Long Wharf Theater; set by Tony Walton; costumes by Bill Walker; lighting by Ronald Wallace; stage manager, Nina Seely.

Streamers was produced in New York by Joseph Papp on April 21, 1976 through June 5, 1977, at the Mitzi Newhouse Theater, Lincoln Center, under the direction of Mike Nichols, with the following cast:

MARTIN	Michael Kell
RICHIE	Peter Evans
CARLYLE	Dorian Harewood
BILLY	Paul Rudd
ROGER	Terry Alexander
COKES	Dolph Sweet
ROONEY	Kenneth McMillan
M.P. LIEUTENANT	Arlen Dean Snyder
PFC HINSON (M.P.)	Les Roberts
PFC CLARK (M.P.)	Mark Metcalf
FOURTH M.P.	Miklos Horvath

Associate producer, Bernard Gersten; set by Tony Walton; costumes by Bill Walker; lighting by Ronald Wallace; stage manager, Nina Seely.

Act One

(The time is 1965; the setting, an Army barracks in Virginia.)

(The set is a large cadre room thrusting angularly toward the audience. The floor is wooden and brown. Brightly waxed in places, it is worn and dull in other sections. The back wall is brown and angled. There are two lights at the center of the ceiling. They hang covered by green metal shades. Against the back wall and to the stage right side are three wall lockers, side by side. Stage center in the back wall is the door, the only entrance to the room. It opens onto a hallway that runs off to the latrines, showers, other cadre rooms and larger barracks room. There are three bunks. BILLY's bunk is parallel to ROGER's bunk. They are upstage and on either side of the room, and face downstage. RICHIE's bunk is downstage and at a right angle to BILLY's bunk. At the foot of each bunk is a green wooden footlocker. There is a floor outlet near ROGER's bunk. He uses it for his radio. A reading lamp is clamped on the metal piping at the head of RICHIE's bunk. A wooden chair stands beside the wall lockers. Two mops hang in the stage left corner near a trash can.)

(It is dusk as the lights rise on the room. RICHIE is seated and bowed forward wearily on his bunk. He wears his long-sleeved khaki summer dress uniform. Upstage behind him is MARTIN, a thin, dark young man, pacing, worried. A white towel stained red with blood is wrapped around his wrist. He paces several steps and falters, stops. He stands there.)

RICHIE: Honest to God, Martin, I don't know what to say anymore. I don't know what to tell you.

MARTIN: *(Beginning to pace again.)* I mean it. I just can't stand it. Look at me.

RICHIE: I know.

MARTIN: I hate it.

RICHIE: We've got to make up a story. They'll ask you a hundred questions.

MARTIN: Do you know how I hate it?

RICHIE: Everybody does. Don't you think I hate it too?

MARTIN: I enlisted, though. I enlisted and I hate it.

RICHIE: I enlisted, too.

MARTIN: I vomit every morning. I get the dry heaves. In the middle of every night. *(He flops down on the corner of BILLY's bed and sits there, slumped forward, shaking his head.)*

RICHIE: You can stop that. You can.

©1977 by David Rabe

MARTIN: No.

RICHIE: You're just scared. It's just fear.

MARTIN: They're all so mean; they're all so awful. I've got two years to go. Just thinking about it is going to make me sick. I thought it would be different from the way it is.

RICHIE: But you could have died, for God's sake. *(He has turned now; he is facing* MARTIN.*)*

MARTIN: I just wanted out.

RICHIE: I might not have found you, though. I might not have come up here.

MARTIN: I don't care. I'd be out.

(The door opens and a black man in filthy fatigues—they are grease-stained and dark with sweat—stands there. He is CARLYLE, *looking about.* RICHIE, *seeing him, rises and moves toward him.)*

RICHIE: No. Roger isn't here right now.

CARLYLE: Who isn't?

RICHIE: He isn't here.

CARLYLE: They tole me a black boy livin' in here. I don't see him. *(He looks suspiciously about the room.)*

RICHIE: That's what I'm saying. He isn't here. He'll be back later. You can come back later. His name is Roger.

MARTIN: I slit my wrist. *(Thrusting out the bloody, towel-wrapped wrist toward* CARLYLE.*)*

RICHIE: Martin! Jesus!

MARTIN: I did.

RICHIE: He's kidding. He's kidding.

CARLYLE: What was his name? Martin? *(He is confused and the confusion has made him angry. He moves toward* MARTIN.*)* You Martin?

MARTIN: Yes.

(As BILLY, *a white in his mid-twenties, blond and trim, appears in the door, whistling, carrying a slice of pie on a paper napkin. Sensing something, he falters, looks at* CARLYLE, *then* RICHIE.*)*

BILLY: Hey, what's goin' on?

CARLYLE: *(Turning, leaving.)* Nothin', man. Not a thing.

*(*BILLY *looks questioningly at* RICHIE. *Then, after placing the piece of pie on the chair beside the door, he crosses to his footlocker.)*

RICHIE: He came in looking for Roger, but he didn't even know his name.

BILLY: *(Sitting on his footlocker, he starts taking off his shoes.)* How come you weren't at dinner, Rich? I brought you a piece of pie. Hey, Martin.

(MARTIN thrusts out his towel-wrapped wrist.)

MARTIN: I cut my wrist, Billy.

RICHIE: Oh, for God's sake, Martin! *(He whirls away.)*

BILLY: Huh?

MARTIN: I did.

RICHIE: You are disgusting, Martin.

MARTIN: No. It's the truth. I did. I am not disgusting.

RICHIE: Well, maybe it isn't disgusting, but it certainly is disappointing.

BILLY: What are you guys talking about? *(Sitting there, he really doesn't know what is going on.)*

MARTIN: I cut my wrists, I slashed them, and Richie is pretending I didn't.

RICHIE: I am not. And you only cut one wrist and you didn't slash it.

MARTIN: I can't stand the Army anymore, Billy. *(He is moving now to petition BILLY, and RICHIE steps between them.)*

RICHIE: Billy, listen to me. This is between Martin and me.

MARTIN: It's between me and the Army, Richie.

RICHIE: *(Taking MARTIN by the shoulders as BILLY is now trying to get near MARTIN.)* Let's just go outside and talk, Martin. You don't know what you're saying.

BILLY: Can I see? I mean, did he really do it?

RICHIE: No!

MARTIN: I did.

BILLY: That's awful. Jesus. Maybe you should go to the infirmary.

RICHIE: I washed it with peroxide. It's not deep. Just let us be. Please. He just needs to straighten out his thinking a little, that's all.

BILLY: Well, maybe I could help him?

MARTIN: Maybe he could.

RICHIE: *(Suddenly pushing at MARTIN. RICHIE is angry and exasperated. He wants MARTIN out of the room.)* Get out of here, Martin. Billy, you do some push-ups or something.

(Having been pushed toward the door, MARTIN wanders out.)

BILLY: No.

RICHIE: I know what Martin needs. *(RICHIE whirls and rushes into the hall after MARTIN, leaving BILLY scrambling to get his shoes on.)*

BILLY: You're no doctor, are you? I just want to make sure he doesn't have to go to the infirmary, then I'll leave you alone. *(One shoe on, he grabs up the second and runs out the door into the hall after them.)* Martin! Martin, wait up!

(Silence. The door has been left open. Fifteen or twenty seconds pass. Then someone is heard coming down the hall. He is singing "Get a Job" and trying to do the voices and harmonies of a vocal group. ROGER, a tall, well-built black in long-sleeved khakis, comes in the door. He has a laundry bag over his shoulder, a pair of clean civilian trousers and a shirt on a hanger in his other hand. After dropping the bag on his bed, he goes to his wall locker where he carefully hangs up the civilian clothes. Returning to the bed, he picks up the laundry and then, as if struck, he throws the bag down on the bed, tears off his tie, and sits down angrily on the bed. For a moment, with his head in his hands, he sits there. Then, resolutely, he rises, takes up the position of attention, and simply topples forward, his hands leaping out to break his fall at the last instant and put him into the push-up position. Counting in a hissing, whispering voice, he does ten push-ups before giving up and flopping onto his belly. He simply doesn't have the will to do any more. Lying there, he counts rapidly on.)

ROGER: Fourteen, fifteen. Twenty. Twenty-five.

(BILLY, shuffling dejectedly back in, sees ROGER lying there. ROGER springs to his feet, heads toward his footlocker, out of which he takes an ashtray and a pack of cigarettes.)

ROGER: You come in this area, you come in here marchin', boy: standin' tall.

(BILLY, having gone to his wall locker, is tossing a Playboy magazine onto his bunk. He will also remove a towel, a Dopp kit, and a can of foot powder.)

BILLY: I was marchin'.

ROGER: You call that marchin'?

BILLY: I was as tall as I am; I was marchin'—what do you want?

ROGER: Outa here, man; outa this goddamn typin'-terrors outfit and into some kinda real army. Or else out and free.

BILLY: So go; who's stoppin' you; get out. Go on.

ROGER: Ain't you a bitch.

BILLY: You and me more regular Army than the goddamn sergeants around this place, you know that?

ROGER: I was you, Billy boy, I wouldn't be talkin' so sacrilegious so loud, or they be doin' you like they did the ole sarge.

BILLY: He'll get off.

ROGER: Shee-it, he'll get off. *(Sitting down on the side of his bed and facing* BILLY, ROGER *lights up a cigarette.* BILLY *has arranged the towel, Dopp kit and foot powder on his own bed.)* Don't you think L.B.J. want to have some sergeants in that Vietnam, man? In Disneyland, baby? Lord have mercy on the ole sarge. He goin' over there to be Mickey Mouse.

BILLY: Do him a lot of good. Make a man outa him.

ROGER: That's right, that's right. He said the same damn thing about himself and you, too, I do believe. You know what's the ole boy's MOS? His Military Occupation Specialty? Demolitions, baby. Expert is his name.

BILLY: *(Taking off his shoes and beginning to work on a sore toe,* BILLY *hardly looks up.)* You're kiddin' me.

ROGER: Do I jive?

BILLY: You mean that poor ole bastard who cannot light his own cigar for shakin' is supposed to go over there blowin' up bridges and shit? Do they wanna win this war or not, man?

ROGER: Ole sarge was over in Europe in the big one, Billy. Did all kinds of bad things.

BILLY: *(Swinging his feet up onto the bed,* BILLY *sits, cutting the cuticles on his toes, powdering his feet.)* Was he drinkin' since he got the word?

ROGER: Was he breathin', Billy? Was he breathin'?

BILLY: Well at least he ain't cuttin' his fuckin' wrists.

(Silence. ROGER *looks at* BILLY, *who keeps on working.)*

BILLY: Man, that's the real damn Army over there, ain't it? That ain't shinin' your belt buckle and standin' tall. And we might end up in it, man.

(Silence. ROGER, *rising, begins to sort his laundry.)*

BILLY: Roger . . . you ever ask yourself if you'd rather fight in a war where it was freezin' cold or one where there was awful snakes? You ever ask that question?

ROGER: Can't say I ever did.

BILLY: We used to ask it all the time. All the time. I mean, us kids sittin' out on the back porch tellin' ghost stories at night. 'Cause it was Korea time and the newspapers were fulla pictures of soldiers in snow with white frozen beards; they got these rags tied around their feet. And snakes. We hated snakes. Hated 'em. I mean, it's bad enough to be in the jungle duckin' bullets, but then you crawl right into a goddamn snake. That's awful. That's awful.

ROGER: It don't sound none too good.

BILLY: I got my draft notice, goddamn Vietnam didn't even exist. I mean, it existed, but not as in a war we might be in. I started crawlin' around the floor a this house where I was stayin' 'cause I'd dropped outa school, and I was goin' "Bang, bang," pretendin'. Jesus.

ROGER: *(Continuing with his laundry, he tries to joke.)* My first goddamn formation in basic, Billy, this NCO's up there jammin' away about how some a us are goin' to be dyin' in the war. I'm sayin', "What war? What that crazy man talkin' about?"

BILLY: Us, too. I couldn't believe it. I couldn't believe it. And now we got three people goin' from here.

ROGER: Five.

(They look at each other, and then turn away, each returning to his task.)

BILLY: It don't seem possible. I mean, people shootin' at you. Shootin' at you to kill you. *(Slight pause)* It's somethin'.

ROGER: What did you decide you preferred?

BILLY: Huh?

ROGER: Did you decide you would prefer the snakes or would you prefer the snow? 'Cause it look like it is going to be the snakes.

BILLY: I think I had pretty much made my mind up on the snow.

ROGER: Well, you just let 'em know that, Billy. Maybe they get one goin' special just for you up in Alaska. You can go to the Klondike. Fightin' some snowmen.

(RICHIE bounds into the room and shuts the door as if to keep out something dreadful. He looks at ROGER and BILLY and crosses to his wall locker, pulling off his tie as he moves. Tossing the tie into the locker, he begins unbuttoning the cuffs of his shirt.)

RICHIE: Hi, hi, hi, everybody. Billy, hello.

BILLY: Hey.

ROGER: What's happenin', Rich?

(Moving to the chair beside the door, RICHIE picks up the pie BILLY left there. He will place the pie atop the locker, and then, sitting, he will remove his shoes and socks.)

RICHIE: I simply did this rather wonderful thing for a friend of mine, helped him see himself in a clearer, more hopeful light—little room in his life for hope? And I feel very good. Didn't Billy tell you?

ROGER: About what?

RICHIE: About Martin.

ROGER: No.

BILLY: *(Looking up and speaking pointedly.)* No.

(RICHIE looks at BILLY and then at ROGER. RICHIE is truly confused.)

RICHIE: No? No?

BILLY: What do I wanna gossip about Martin for?

RICHIE: *(He really can't figure out what is going on with BILLY. Shoes and socks in hand, he heads for his wall locker.)* Who was planning to gossip? I mean, it did happen. We could talk about it. I mean, I wasn't hearing his goddamn confession. Oh, my sister told me Catholics were boring.

BILLY: Good thing I ain't one anymore.

RICHIE: *(Taking off his shirt, he moves toward ROGER.)* It really wasn't anything, Roger, except Martin made this rather desperate, pathetic gesture for attention that seems to have brought to the surface Billy's more humane and protective side. *(Reaching out, he tousles BILLY's hair.)*

BILLY: Man, I am gonna have to obliterate you.

RICHIE: *(Tossing his shirt into his locker.)* I don't know what you're so embarrassed about.

BILLY: I just think Martin's got enough trouble without me yappin' to everbody.

(RICHIE has moved nearer BILLY, his manner playful and teasing.)

RICHIE: "Obliterate"? "Obliterate," did you say? Oh, Billy, you better say "shit," "ain't" and "motherfucker" real quick now or we'll all know just how far beyond the fourth grade you went.

ROGER: *(Having moved to his locker, into which he is placing his folded clothes.)* You hear about the ole sarge, Richard?

BILLY: *(Grinning)* You ain't . . . shit . . . motherfucker.

ROGER: *(Laughing)* All right.

RICHIE: *(Moving center and beginning to remove his trousers.)* Billy, no, no. Wit is my domain. You're in charge of sweat and running around the block.

ROGER: You hear about the ole sarge?

RICHIE: What about the ole sarge? Oh, who cares? Let's go to a movie. Billy, wanna? Let's go. C'mon. *(Trousers off, he hurries to his locker.)*

BILLY: Sure. What's playin'?

RICHIE: I don't know. Can't remember. Something good, though.

(With a Playboy magazine he has taken from his locker, ROGER is settling down on his bunk, his back toward both BILLY and RICHIE.)

BILLY: You wanna go, Rog?

RICHIE: *(In mock irritation)* Don't ask Roger! How are we going to kiss and hug and stuff if he's there?

BILLY: That ain't funny, man. *(He is stretched out on his bunk, and* RICHIE *comes bounding over to flop down and lie beside him.)*

RICHIE: And what time will you pick me up?

BILLY: *(He pushes at* RICHIE, *knocking him off the bed and onto the floor.)* Well, you just fall down and wait, all right?

RICHIE: Can I help it if I love you? *(Leaping to his feet, he will head to his locker, remove his shorts, put on a robe.)*

ROGER: You gonna take a shower, Richard?

RICHIE: Cleanliness is nakedness, Roger.

ROGER: Is that right? I didn't know that. Not too many people know that. You may be the only person in the world who know that.

RICHIE: And godliness is in there somewhere, of course. *(Putting a towel around his neck, he is gathering toiletries to carry to the shower.)*

ROGER: You got your own way a lookin' at things, man. You cute.

RICHIE: That's right.

ROGER: You g'wan, have a good time in that shower.

RICHIE: Oh, I will.

BILLY: *(Without looking up from his feet, which he is powdering.)* And don't drop your soap.

RICHIE: I will if I want to. *(Already out the door, he slams it shut with a flourish.)*

BILLY: Can you imagine bein' in combat with Richie—people blastin' away at you—he'd probably want to hold your hand.

ROGER: Ain't he somethin'?

BILLY: Who's zat?

ROGER: He's all right.

BILLY: *(Rising, he heads toward his wall locker, where he will put the powder and Dopp kit.)* Sure he is, except he's livin' under water.

(Looking at BILLY, ROGER *senses something unnerving; it makes* ROGER *rise, and return his magazine to his footlocker.)*

ROGER: I think we oughta do this area, man. I think we oughta do our area. Mop and buff this floor.

BILLY: You really don't think he means that shit he talks, do you?

ROGER: Huh? Awwww, man...Billy, no.

BILLY: I'd put money on it, Roger, and I ain't got much money. *(He is trying to face* ROGER *with this, but* ROGER, *seated on his bed, has turned away. He is unbuttoning his shirt.)*

ROGER: Man, no, no. I'm tellin' you, lad, you listen to the ole Rog. You seen that picture a that little dolly he's got in his locker? He ain't swish, man, believe me—he's cool.

BILLY: It's just that ever since we been in this room, he's been different somehow. Somethin'.

ROGER: No, he ain't.

(BILLY turns to his bed, where he carefully starts folding the towel. Then he looks at ROGER.)

BILLY: You ever talk to any a these guys—queers, I mean? You ever sit down, just rap with one of 'em?

ROGER: Hell, no; what I wanna do that for? Shit, no.

BILLY: *(Crossing to the trash can in the corner, where he will shake the towel empty.)* I mean, some of 'em are okay guys, just way up this bad alley, and you say to 'em, "I'm straight, be cool," they go their own way. But then there's these other ones, these bitches, man, and they're so crazy they think anybody can be had. Because they been had themselves. So you tell 'em you're straight and they just nod and smile. You ain't real to 'em. They can't see nothin' but themselves and these goddamn games they're always playin'. *(Having returned to his bunk, he is putting on his shoes.)* I mean, you can be decent about anything, Roger, you see what I'm sayin'? We're all just people, man, and some of us are hardly that. That's all I'm sayin'. *(There is a slight pause as he sits there thinking. Then he gets to his feet.)* I'll go get some buckets and stuff so we can clean up, okay? This area's a mess. This area ain't standin' tall.

ROGER: That's good talk, lad; this area a midget you put it next to an area standin' tall.

BILLY: Got to be good fuckin' troopers.

ROGER: That's right, that's right. I know the meanin' of the words.

BILLY: I mean, I just think we all got to be honest with each other—you understand me?

ROGER: No, I don't understand you; one stupid fuckin' nigger like me—how's that gonna be?

BILLY: That's right; mock me, man. That's what I need. I'll go get the wax.

(Out he goes, talking to himself and leaving the door open. For a moment ROGER *sits, thinking, and then he looks at* RICHIE'S *locker and gets to his feet and walks to the locker which he opens and looks at the pinup hanging on the inside of the door. He takes a step backward, looking.)*

ROGER: Sheee-it.

(Through the open door comes CARLYLE. ROGER *doesn't see him. And* CARLYLE *stands there looking at* ROGER *and the picture in the locker.)*

CARLYLE: Boy . . . whose locker you lookin' into?

ROGER: *(He is startled, but recovers.)* Hey, baby, what's happenin'?

CARLYLE: That ain't your locker, is what I'm askin', nigger. I mean, you ain't got no white goddamn woman hangin' on your wall.

ROGER: Oh, no—no, no.

CARLYLE: You don't wanna be lyin' to me, 'cause I got to turn you in you lyin' and you do got the body a some white goddamn woman hangin' there for you to peek at nobody around but you—you can be thinkin' about that sweet wet pussy an' maybe it hot an' maybe it cool.

ROGER: I could be thinkin' all that, except I know the penalty for lyin'.

CARLYLE: Thank God for that. *(Extending his hand, palm up.)*

ROGER: That's right. This here the locker of a faggot. *(And* ROGER *slaps* CARLYLE'*s hand, palm to palm.)*

CARLYLE: Course it is; I see that; any damn body know that.

*(*ROGER *crosses toward his bunk and* CARLYLE *swaggers about, pulling a pint of whiskey from his hip pocket.)*

CARLYLE: You want a shot? Have you a little taste, my man.

ROGER: Naw.

CARLYLE: C'mon. C'mon. I think you a Tom you don't drink outa my bottle. *(He thrusts the bottle toward* ROGER *and wipes a sweat-and grease-stained sleeve across his mouth.)*

ROGER: *(Taking the bottle.)* Shit.

CARLYLE: That right. How do I know? I just got in. New boy in town. Somewhere over there; I dunno. They dump me in amongst a whole bunch a pale, boring motherfuckers. *(He is exploring the room. Finding* BILLY'*s* Playboy, *he edges onto* BILLY'*s bed and leafs nervously through the pages.)* I just come in from P Company, man, and I been all over this place, don't see too damn many of us. This outfit look like it a little short on soul. I been walkin' all around, I tell you, and the number is small. Like one hand you can tabulate the lot of 'em. We got few brothers I been able to see, is what I'm saying'. You and me and two cats down in the small bay. That's all I found. *(As* ROGER *is about to hand the bottle back,* CARLYLE, *almost angrily, waves him off.)* No, no, you take another; take you a real taste.

ROGER: It ain't so bad here. We do all right.

CARLYLE: *(He moves, shutting the door. Suspiciously, he approaches*

ROGER.) How about the white guys? They give you any sweat? What's the situation? No jive. I like to know what is goin' on within the situation before that situation get a chance to be closin' in on me.

ROGER: *(Putting the bottle on the footlocker, he sits down.)* Man, I'm tellin' you, it ain't bad. They're just pale, most of 'em, you know. They can't help it; how they gonna help it? Some of 'em got little bit a soul, couple real good boys around this way. Get 'em little bit of Coppertone, they be straight, man.

CARLYLE: How about the NCOs? We got any brother NCO watchin' out for us or they all white, like I goddamn well KNOW all the officers are? Fuckin' officers always white, man; fuckin' snow cones and cars everywhere you look. *(He cannot stay still. He moves to his right, his left, he sits, he stands.)*

ROGER: First sergeant's a black man.

CARLYLE: All right; good news. Hey, hey, you wanna go over the club with me, or maybe downtown? I got wheels. Let's be free. *(Now rushes at* ROGER.) Let's be free.

ROGER: Naw ...

CARLYLE: Ohhhh, baby ...! *(He is wildly pulling at* ROGER *to get him to the door.)*

ROGER: Some other time. I gotta get the area straight. Me and the guy sleeps in here too are gonna shape the place up a little.

*(*ROGER *has pulled free, and* CARLYLE *cannot understand. It hurts him, depresses him.)*

CARLYLE: You got a sweet deal here an' you wanna keep it, that right? *(He paces about the room, opens a footlocker, looks inside.)* How you rate you get a room like this for yourself—you and a couple guys?

ROGER: Spec 4. The three of us in here Spec 4.

CARLYLE: You get a room then, huh? *(And suddenly, without warning or transition, he is angry.)* Oh, man, I hate this goddamn Army. I hate this bastard Army. I mean, I just got outa basic—off leave—you know? Back on the block for two weeks—and now here. They don't pull any a that petty shit, now, do they—that goddamn petty basic training bullshit? They do and I'm gonna be bustin' some head—my hand is gonna be upside all kinds a heads, 'cause I ain't gonna be able to endure it, man, not that kinda crap—understand? *(And again, he is rushing at* ROGER.) Hey, hey, oh, c'mon, let's get my wheels and make it, man, do me the favor.

ROGER: How'm I gonna? I got my obligations.

*(*CARLYLE *spins away in anger.)*

CARLYLE: *Jesus, baby, can't you remember the outside? How long it been since you been on leave? It is so sweet out there, nigger; you got it all forgot. I had such a sweet, sweet time. They doin' dances, baby, make you wanna cry. I hate this damn Army. (The anger overwhelms him.)* All these mother-actin' jacks givin' you jive about what you gotta do and what you can't do. I had a bad scene in basic—up the hill and down the hill; it ain't somethin' I enjoyed even a little. So they do me wrong here, Jim, they gonna be sorry. Some-damn-body! And this whole Vietnam THING—I do not dig it. (He falls on his knees before ROGER. *It is a gesture that begins as a joke, a mockery. And then a real fear pulses through him to nearly fill the pose he has taken.)* Lord, Lord, don't let 'em touch me. Christ, what will I do, they do! Whoooooooooooooo! And they pullin' guys outa here, too, ain't they? Pullin' 'em like weeds, man; throwin' 'em into the fire. It's shit, man.

ROGER: They got this ole sarge sleeps down the hall—just today they got him.

CARLYLE: Which ole sarge?

ROGER: He sleeps just down the hall. Little guy.

CARLYLE: Wino, right?

ROGER: Booze hound.

CARLYLE: Yeh; I seen him. They got him, huh?

ROGER: He's goin'; gotta be packin' his bags. And three other guys two days ago. And two guys last week.

CARLYLE: *(Leaping up from* BILLY'*s bed.)* Ohhh, them bastards. And every-body just takes it. It ain't our war, brother. I'm tellin' you. That's what gets me, nigger. It ain't our war nohow because it ain't our country, and that's what burns my ass—that and everybody just sittin' and takin' it. They gonna be bustin' balls, man—kickin' and stompin'. Everybody here maybe one week from shippin' out to get blown clean away and, man, whata they doin'? They doin' what they told. That what they doin'. Like you? Shit! You gonna straighten up your goddamn area! Well, that ain't for me; I'm gettin' hat, and makin' it out where it's sweet and the people's livin'. I can't cut this jive here, man. I'm tellin' you. I can't cut it.

(He has moved toward ROGER, *and behind him now* RICHIE *enters, running, his hair wet, traces of shaving cream on his face. Toweling his hair, he falters, see-ing* CARLYLE. *Then he crosses to his locker.* CARLYLE *grins at* ROGER, *looks at* RICHIE, *steps toward him and gives a little bow.)*

CARLYLE: My name is Carlyle; what is yours?

RICHIE: Richie.

CARLYLE: *(He turns toward* ROGER *to share his joke.)* Hello. Where is Martin? That cute little Martin.

*(*RICHIE *has just taken off his robe as* CARLYLE *turns back.)*

CARLYLE: You cute, too, Richie.

RICHIE: Martin doesn't live here. *(Hurriedly putting on underpants to cover his nakedness.)*

CARLYLE: *(Watching* RICHIE, *he slowly turns toward* ROGER.*)* You ain't gonna make it with me, man?

ROGER: Naw... like I tole you. I'll catch you later.

CARLYLE: That's sad, man; make me cry in my heart.

ROGER: You g'wan get your head smokin'. Stop on back.

CARLYLE: Okay, okay. Got to be one man one more time. *(On the move for the door, his hand extended palm up behind him, demanding the appropriate response.)* Baby! Gimme! Gimme! *(Lunging.* ROGER *slaps the hand.)*

ROGER: G'wan home! G'wan home.

CARLYLE: You gonna hear from me. *(He is gone out the door and down the hallway.)*

ROGER: I can... and do... believe... that.

*(*RICHIE, *putting on his T-shirt, watches* ROGER, *who stubs out his cigarette, then crosses to the trash can to empty the ashtray.)*

RICHIE: Who was that?

ROGER: Man's new, Rich. Dunno his name more than that "Carlyle" he said. He's new—just outa basic.

RICHIE: *(Powdering his thighs and under his arms.)* Oh, my God...

(As BILLY *enters, pushing a mop bucket with a wringer attached and carrying a container of wax.)*

ROGER: Me and Billy's gonna straighten up the area. You wanna help?

RICHIE: Sure, sure; help, help.

BILLY: *(Talking to* ROGER, *but turning to look at* RICHIE, *who is still putting powder under his arms.)* I hadda steal the wax from Third Platoon.

ROGER: Good man.

BILLY: *(Moving to* RICHIE, *joking, yet really irritated in some strange way.)* What? Whata you doin', singin'? Look at that, Rog. He's got enough jazz there for an entire beauty parlor. *(Grabbing the can from* RICHIE's *hand.)* What is this? Baby Powder! BABY POWDER!

RICHIE: I get rashes.

BILLY: Okay, okay, you get rashes, so what? They got powder for rashes that isn't baby powder.

RICHIE: It doesn't work as good; I've tried it. Have you tried it? *(Grabbing BILLY's waist, RICHIE pulls him close. BILLY knocks RICHIE's hands away.)*

BILLY: Man, I wish you could get yourself straight. I'll mop, too, Roger—okay? Then I'll put down the wax and you can spread it? *(He has walked away from RICHIE.)*

RICHIE: What about buffing?

ROGER: In the morning. *(He is already busy mopping up near the door.)*

RICHIE: What do you want me to do?

BILLY: *(Grabbing up a mop, he heads downstage to work.)* Get inside your locker and shut the door and don't holler for help. Nobody'll know you're there; you'll stay there.

RICHIE: But I'm so pretty.

BILLY: NOW! *(Pointing to ROGER. He wants to get this clear.)* Tell that man you mean what you're sayin', Richie.

RICHIE: Mean what?

BILLY: That you really think you're pretty.

RICHIE: Of course I do; I am. Don't you think I am? Don't you think I am, Roger?

ROGER: I tole you—you fulla shit and you cute, man. Carlyle just tole you you cute, too.

RICHIE: Don't you think it's true, Billy?

BILLY: It's like I tole you, Rog.

RICHIE: What did you tell him?

BILLY: That you go down; that you go up and down like a Yo-Yo and you go blowin' all the trees like the wind.

(RICHIE is stunned. He looks at ROGER, and then he turns and stares into his own locker. The others keep mopping. RICHIE takes out a towel, and putting it around his neck, he walks to where BILLY is working. He stands there, hurt, looking at BILLY.)

RICHIE: What the hell made you tell him I been down, Billy?

BILLY: *(Still mopping)* It's in your eyes; I seen it.

RICHIE: What?

BILLY: You.

RICHIE: What is it, Billy, you think you're trying to say? You and all your wit and intelligence—your humanity.

BILLY: I said it, Rich; I said what I was tryin' to say.

RICHIE: Did you?

BILLY: I think I did.

RICHIE: Do you?

BILLY: Loud and clear, baby. *(Still mopping)*

ROGER: They got to put me in with the weirdos. Why is that, huh? How come the Army hate me, do this shit to me—know what to do. *(Whimsical and then suddenly loud, angered, violent.)* Now you guys put socks in your mouths, right now—get shut up—or I am gonna beat you to death with each other. Roger got work to do. To be doin' it!

RICHIE: *(Turning to his bed, he kneels upon it.)* Roger, I think you're so innocent sometimes. Honestly, it's not such a terrible thing. Is it, Billy?

BILLY: How would I know? *(He slams his mop into the bucket.)* Oh, go fuck yourself.

RICHIE: Well, I can give it a try, if that's what you want. Can I think of you as I do?

BILLY: *(Throwing down his mop)* GODDAMMIT! That's it! IT!

(He exits, rushing into the hall and slamming the door behind him. ROGER looks at RICHIE. Neither quite knows what is going on. Suddenly the door bursts open and BILLY storms straight over to RICHIE, who still kneels on the bed.)

BILLY: Now I am gonna level with you. Are you gonna listen? You gonna hear what I say, Rich, and not what you think I'm sayin'?

(RICHIE turns away as if to rise, his manner flippant, disdainful.)

BILLY: No! Don't get cute; don't turn away cute. I wanna say somethin' straight out to you and I want you to hear it!

RICHIE: I'm all ears, goddammit! For what, however, I do not know, except some boring evasion.

BILLY: At least wait the hell till you hear me!

RICHIE: *(In irritation)* Okay, okay! What?

BILLY: Now this is level, Rich; this is straight talk. *(He is quiet, intense. This is difficult for him. He seeks the exactly appropriate words of explanation.)* No b.s. No tricks. What you do on the side, that's your business and I don't care about it. But if you don't cut the cute shit with me, I'm gonna turn you off. Completely. You ain't gonna get a good mornin' outa me, you understand, because it's gettin' bad around here. I mean, I know how you think—how you keep lookin' out and seein' yourself, and that's what I'm tryin' to tell you because that's all that's happenin', Rich. That's all there is to it when you look out at me and think there's some kind of approval or whatever you see in my eyes—you're just seein' yourself. And I'm talkin' the simple quiet truth to you, Rich. I swear I am.

(BILLY looks away from RICHIE now and tries to go back to the mopping. It is embarrassing for them all. ROGER has watched, has tried to keep working. RICHIE has flopped back on his bunk. There is a silence.)

RICHIE: How . . . do . . . you want me to be? I don't know how else to be.

BILLY: Ohhh, man, that ain't any part of it. *(The mop is clenched in his hands.)*

RICHIE: Well, I don't come from the same kind of world as you do.

BILLY: Damn, Richie, you think Roger and I come off the same street?

ROGER: Shit . . .

RICHIE: All right. Okay. But I've just done what I wanted all of my life. If I wanted to do something, I just did it. Honestly, I've never had to work or anything like that and I've always had nice clothing and money for cab fare. Money for whatever I wanted. Always. I'm not like you are.

ROGER: You ain't sayin' you really done that stuff, though, Rich.

RICHIE: What?

ROGER: That fag stuff.

RICHIE: *(He continues looking at ROGER and then he looks away.)* Yes.

ROGER: Do you even know what you're sayin', Richie? Do you even know what it means to be a fag?

RICHIE: Roger, of course I know what it is. I just told you I've done it. I thought you black people were supposed to understand all about suffering and human strangeness. I thought you had depth and vision from all your suffering. Has someone been misleading me? I just told you I did it. I know all about it. Everything. All the various positions.

ROGER: Yeh, so maybe you think you've tried it, but that don't make you it. I mean, we used to . . . in the old neighborhood, man, we had a couple dudes swung that way. But they was weird, man. There was this one little fella, he was a screamin' goddamn faggot . . . uh . . . *(He considers RICHIE, wondering if perhaps he has offended him.)* Ohhh, ohhh, you ain't no screamin' goddamn faggot, Richie, no matter what you say. And the baddest man on the block was my boy Jerry Lemon. So one day Jerry's got the faggot in one a them ole deserted stairways and he's bouncin' him off the walls. I'm just a little fella, see, and I'm watchin' the baddest man on the block do his thing. So he come bouncin' back into me instead of Jerry, and just when he hit, he gave his ass this little twitch, man, like he thought he was gonna turn me on. I'd never a thought that was possible, man, for a man to be twitchin' his ass on me, just like he thought he was a broad. Scared me to death. I took off runnin'. Oh, oh, that ole neighborhood put me into all kinds a crap. I did some sufferin', just like Richie says. Like this once, I'm swingin' on up the street after school, and outa this phone booth comes this man with a goddamned knife stickin' outa his gut. So he sees me and starts tryin' to pull his motherfuckin' coat out over the handle, like he's worried about how he looks, man. "I didn't know this was gonna happen," he says. And then he falls over. He was just all of a sudden dead, man; just all of a sudden dead. You ever seen anything like that, Billy? Any crap like that?

BILLY, *sitting on* ROGER's *bunk, is staring at* ROGER.)

BILLY: You really seen that?

ROGER: Richie's a big-city boy.

RICHIE: Oh, no; never anything like that.

ROGER: "Momma, help me," I am screamin'. "Jesus, Momma, help me." Little fella, he don't know how to act, he sees somethin' like that.

(For a moment they are still, each thinking.)

BILLY: How long you think we got?

ROGER: What do you mean? *(He is hanging up the mops;* BILLY *is now kneeling on* ROGER's *bunk.)*

BILLY: Till they pack us up, man, ship us out.

ROGER: To the war, you mean? To Disneyland? Man, I dunno; that up to them IBM's. Them machines is figurin' that. Maybe tomorrow, maybe next week, maybe never. *(The war—the threat of it—is the one thing they share.)*

RICHIE: I was reading they're planning to build it all up to more than five hundred thousand men over there. Americans. And they're going to keep it that way until they win.

BILLY: Be a great place to come back from, man, you know? I keep thinkin' about that. To have gone there, to have been there, to have seen it and lived.

ROGER: *(Settling onto* BILLY's *bunk, he lights a cigarette.)* Well, what we got right here is a fool, gonna probably be one a them five hundred thousand, too. Do you know I cry at the goddamn anthem yet sometimes? The flag is flyin' at a ball game, the ole Roger gets all wet in the eye. After all the shit been done to his black ass. I don't know what I think about this war. I do not know.

BILLY: I'm tellin' you, Rog—I've been doin' a lot a readin' and I think it's right we go. I mean, it's just like when North Korea invaded South

Korea or when Hitler invaded Poland and all those other countries. He just kept testin' everybody and when nobody said no to him, he got so committed he couldn't back out even if he wanted. And that's what this Ho Chi Minh is doin'. And all these other Communists. If we let 'em know somebody is gonna stand up against 'em, they'll back off, just like Hitler would have.

ROGER: There is folks, you know, who are sayin' L.B.J. is the Hitler, and not ole Ho Chi Minh at all.

RICHIE: *(Talking as if this is the best news he's heard in years.)* Well, I don't know anything at all about all that, but I am certain I don't want to go—whatever is going on. I mean, those Vietcong don't just shoot you and blow you up, you know. My God, they've got these other awful things they do: putting elephant shit on these stakes in the ground and then you step on 'em and you got elephant shit in a wound in your foot. The infection is horrendous. And then there's these caves they hide in and when you go in after 'em, they've got these snakes that they've tied by their tails to the ceiling. So it's dark and the snake is furious from having been hung by its tail and you crawl right into them—your face. My God.

BILLY: They do not. *(He knows he has been caught; they all know it.)*

RICHIE: I read it, Billy. They do.

BILLY: *(Completely facetious, yet the fear is real.)* That's bullshit, Richie.

ROGER: That's right, Richie. They maybe do that stuff with the elephant shit, but nobody's gonna tie a snake by its tail, let ole Billy walk into it.

BILLY: That's disgusting, man.

ROGER: Guess you better get ready for the Klondike, my man.

BILLY: That is probably the most disgusting thing I ever heard of. I DO NOT WANT TO GO! NOT TO NOWHERE WHERE THAT KINDA SHIT IS GOIN' ON! L.B.J. is Hitler; suddenly I see it all very clearly.

ROGER: Billy got him a hatred for snakes.

RICHIE: I hate them, too. They're hideous.

BILLY: *(And now, as a kind of apology to RICHIE, BILLY continues his self-ridicule far into the extreme.)* I mean, that is one of the most awful things I ever heard of any person doing. I mean, any person who would hang a snake by its tail in the dark of a cave in the hope that some other person might crawl into it and get bitten to death, that first person is somebody who oughta be shot. And I hope the five hundred thousand other guys that get sent over there kill 'em all—all them gooks—get 'em all driven back into Germany, where they belong. And in the meantime, I'll be holding the northern border against the snowmen.

ROGER: *(Rising from* BILLY'*s bed.)* And in the meantime before that, we better be gettin' at the ole area there. Got to be strike troopers.

BILLY: Right.

RICHIE: Can I help?

ROGER: Sure. Be good. *(He crosses to his footlocker and takes out a radio.)* Think maybe I put on a little music, though it's gettin' late. We got time. Billy, you think?

BILLY: Sure. *(Getting nervously to his feet.)*

ROGER: Sure. All right. We can be doin' it to the music. *(He plugs the radio into the floor outlet as* BILLY *bolts for the door.)*

BILLY: I gotta go pee.

ROGER: You watch out for the snakes.

BILLY: It's the snowmen, man; the snowmen.

*(*BILLY *is gone and "Ruby," sung by Ray Charles, comes from the radio. For a moment, as the music plays,* ROGER *watches* RICHIE *wander about the room, pouring little splashes of wax onto the floor. Then* RICHIE *moves to his bed and lies down, and* ROGER*, shaking his head, starts leisurely to spread the wax, with* RICHIE *watching.)*

RICHIE: How come you and Billy take all this so seriously—you know.

ROGER: What?

RICHIE: This Army nonsense. You're always shining your brass and keeping your footlocker neat and your locker so neat. There's no point to any of it.

ROGER: We here, ain't we, Richie? We in the Army. *(Still working the wax)*

RICHIE: There's no point to any of it. And doing those push-ups, the two of you.

ROGER: We just see a lot a things the same way is all. Army ought to be a serious business, even if sometimes it ain't.

RICHIE: You're lucky, you know, the two of you. Having each other for friends the way you do. I never had that kind of friend ever. Not even when I was little.

ROGER: *(After a pause during which* ROGER*, working, sort of peeks at* RICHIE *every now and then.)* You ain't really inta that stuff, are you, Richie? *(It is a question that is a statement.)*

RICHIE: *(Coyly he looks at* ROGER.*)* What stuff is that, Roger?

ROGER: That fag stuff, man. You know. You ain't really into it, are you? You maybe messed in it a little is all—am I right?

RICHIE: I'm very weak, Roger. And by that I simply mean that if I have an impulse to do something, I don't know how to deny myself. If I feel like doing something, I just do it. I . . . will . . . admit to sometimes wishin' I . . . was a little more like you . . . and Billy, even, but not to any severe extent.

ROGER: But that's such a bad scene, Rich. You don't want that. Nobody wants that. Nobody wants to be a punk. Not nobody. You wanna know what I think it is? You just got in with the wrong bunch. Am I right? You just got in with a bad bunch. That can happen. And that's what I think happened to you. I bet you never had a chance to really run with the boys before. I mean, regular normal guys like Billy and me. How'd you come in the Army, huh, Richie? You get drafted?

RICHIE: No.

ROGER: That's my point, see. (He has stopped working. He stands, leaning on the mop, looking at RICHIE.)

RICHIE: About four years ago, I went to this party. I was very young, and I went to this party with a friend who was older and . . . this "fag stuff," as you call it, was going on . . . so I did it.

ROGER: And then you come in the Army to get away from it, right? Huh?

RICHIE: I don't know.

ROGER: Sure.

RICHIE: I don't know, Roger.

ROGER: Sure; sure. And now you're gettin' a chance to run with the boys for a little, you'll get yourself straightened around. I know it for a fact; I know that thing.

(From off there is a sudden loud bellowing sound of Sergeant ROONEY.)

ROONEY: THERE AIN'T BEEN NO SOLDIERS IN THIS CAMP BUT ME. I BEEN THE ONLY ONE—I BEEN THE ONLY ME!

(BILLY comes dashing into the room.)

BILLY: Oh, boy.

ROGER: Guess who?

ROONEY: FOR SO LONG I BEEN THE ONLY GODDAMN ONE!

BILLY: (Leaping onto his bed and covering his face with a Playboy magazine as RICHIE is trying to disappear under his sheets and blankets and ROGER is trying to get the wax put away so he can get into his own bunk.) Hut who hee whor—he's got some Yo-Yo with him, Rog!

ROGER: *Huh?*

(As COKES and ROONEY enter. Both are in fatigues and drunk and big-bellied. They are in their fifties, their hair whitish and cut short. Both men carry whiskey bottles, beer bottles. COKES is a little neater than ROONEY, his fatigue jacket tucked in and not so rumpled, and he wears canvas-sided jungle boots. ROONEY, very disheveled, chomps on the stub of a big cigar. They swagger in, looking for fun, and stand there side by side.)

ROONEY: What kinda platoon I got here? You buncha shit sacks. Everybody look sharp.

(The three boys lie there, unmoving.)

COKES: OFF AND ON! *(He seems barely conscious, wavering as he stands.)*

ROGER: What's happenin', Sergeant?

ROONEY: *(Shoving his bottle of whiskey at ROGER, who is sitting up.)* Shut up, Moore! You want a belt? *(Splashing whiskey on ROGER's chest.)*

ROGER: How can I say no?

COKES: My name is Cokes!

BILLY: *(Rising to sit on the side of his bed.)* How about me, too?

COKES: You wait your turn.

ROONEY: *(He looks at the three of them as if they are fools. Indicates COKES with a gesture.)* Don't you see what I got here?

BILLY: Who do I follow for my turn?

ROONEY: *(Suddenly, crazily petulant)* Don't you see what I got here? Everybody on their feet and at attention!

(BILLY and ROGER climb from their bunks and stand at attention. They don't know what ROONEY is mad at.)

ROONEY: I mean it!

(RICHIE bounds to the position of attention.)

ROONEY: This here is my friend, who in addition just come back from the war! The goddamn war! He been to it and he come back.

(ROONEY is patting COKES gently, proudly.)

ROONEY: The man's a fuckin' hero! *(He hugs COKES, almost kissing him on the cheek.)* He's always been a fuckin' hero.

(COKES, embarrassed in his stupor, kind of wobbles a little from side to side.)

COKES: No-o-o-o-o-o . . .

(ROONEY grabs him, starts pushing him toward BILLY's footlocker.)

ROONEY: Show 'em your boots, Cokes. Show 'em your jungle boots.

(With a long, clumsy step, COKES climbs onto the footlocker, ROONEY supporting

him from behind and then bending to lift one of COKES' *booted feet and display it for the boys.)*

ROONEY: Lookee that boot. That ain't no everyday goddamn Army boot. That is a goddamn jungle boot! That green canvas is a jungle boot 'cause a the heat, and them little holes in the bottom are so the water can run out when you been walkin' in a lotta water like in a jungle swamp. *(He is extremely proud of all this; he looks at them.)* The Army ain't no goddamn fool. You see a man wearin' boots like that, you might as well see he's got a chestful a medals, 'cause he been to the war. He don't have no boots like that unless he been to the war! Which is where I'm goin' and all you slaphappy motherfuckers, too. Got to go kill some gooks. *(He is nodding at them, smiling.)* That's right.

COKES: *(Bursting loudly from his stupor.)* Gonna piss on 'em. Old booze. 'At's what I did. Piss in the rivers. Goddamn GI's secret weapon is old booze and he's pissin' it in all their runnin' water. Makes 'em yellow. Ahhhha ha, ha, ha! *(He laughs and laughs, and* ROONEY *laughs, too, hugging* COKES.)

ROONEY: Me and Cokesy been in so much shit together we oughta be brown. *(And then he catches himself, looks at* ROGER.) Don't take no offense at that, Moore. We been swimmin' in it. One Hundred and First Airborne, together. One-oh-one. Screamin' goddamn Eagles! *(Looking at each other, face to face, eyes glinting, they make sudden loud screaming-eagle sounds.)* This ain't the Army; you punks ain't in the Army. You ain't ever seen the Army. The Army is Airborne! Airborne!

COKES: *(Beginning to stomp his feet.)* Airborne, Airborne! ALL THE WAY!

(As RICHIE, *amused and hoping for a drink, too, reaches out toward* ROONEY.)

RICHIE: Sergeant, Sergeant, I can have a little drink, too.

*(*ROONEY *looks at him and clutches the bottle.)*

ROONEY: Are you kiddin' me? You gotta be kiddin' me. *(He looks to* ROGER.) He's kiddin' me, ain't he, Moore? *(And then to* BILLY *and then to* COKES.) Ain't he, Cokesy?

*(*COKES *steps forward and down with a thump, taking charge for his bewildered friend.)*

COKES: Don't you know you are tryin' to take the booze from the hand a the future goddamn Congressional Honor Winner...Medal...? *(And he looks lovingly at* ROONEY. *He beams.)* Ole Rooney, Ole Rooney. *(He hugs* ROONEY's *head.)* He almost done it already.

*(*ROONEY, *overwhelmed, starts screaming "Agggggghhhhhhhhhh," a screaming-eagle sound, and making clawing eagle gestures at the air. He jumps up and down, stomping his feet.* COKES *instantly joins in, stomping and jumping and yelling.)*

ROONEY: Let's show these shit sacks how men are men jumpin' outa planes. Agggggghhhhhhhhhh. *(Stomping and yelling, they move in a circle,* ROONEY *followed by* COKES.*)* A plane fulla yellin' stompin' men!

COKES: All yellin' stompin' men!

(They yell and stomp, making eagle sounds, and then ROONEY *leaps up on* BILLY'S *bed and runs the length of it until he is on the footlocker,* COKES *still on the floor, stomping.* ROONEY *makes a gesture of hooking his rip cord to the line inside the plane. They yell louder and louder and* ROONEY *leaps high into the air, yelling, "GERONIMO-O-O-O!" as* COKES *leaps onto the locker and then high into the air, bellowing, "GERONIMO-O-O-O!" They stand side by side, their arms held up in the air as if grasping the shroud lines of open chutes. They seem to float there in silence.)*

COKES: What a feelin' . . .

ROONEY: Beautiful feelin' . . .

(For a moment more they float there, adrift in the room, the sky, their memory. COKES *smiles at* ROONEY.*)*

COKES: Remember that one guy, O'Flannigan . . . ?

ROONEY: *(Nodding, smiling, remembering)* O'Flannigan . . .

COKES: He was this one guy . . . O'Flannigan . . .

(He moves now toward the boys, BILLY, ROGER *and* RICHIE, *who have gathered on* ROGER'S *bed and footlocker.* ROONEY *follows several steps, then drifts backward onto* BILLY'S *bed, where he sits and then lies back, listening to* COKES.*)*

COKES: We was testing chutes where you could just pull a lever by your ribs here when you hit the ground—see—and the chute would come off you, because it was just after a whole bunch of guys had been dragged to death in an unexpected and terrible wind at Fort Bragg. So they wanted you to be able to release the chute when you hit if there was a bad wind when you hit. So O'Flannigan was this kinda joker who had the goddamn sense of humor of a clown and nerves, I tell you, of steel, and he says he's gonna release the lever midair, then reach up, grab the lines and float on down, hanging. *(His hand paws at the air, seeking a rope that isn't there.)* So I seen him pull the lever at five hundred feet and he reaches up to two fistfuls a air, the chute's twenty feet above him, and he went into the ground like a knife. *(The bottle, held high over his head, falls through the air to the bed, all watching it.)*

BILLY: Geezus.

ROONEY: *(Nodding gently.)* Didn't get to sing the song, I bet.

COKES: *(Standing, staring at the fallen bottle.)* No way.

RICHIE: What song?

ROONEY: *(He rises up, mysteriously angry.)* Shit sack! Shit sack!

RICHIE: What song, Sergeant Rooney?

ROONEY: "Beautiful Streamer," shit sack.

(COKES, *gone into another reverie, is staring skyward.*)

COKES: I saw this one guy—never forget it. Never.

BILLY: That's Richie, Sergeant Rooney. He's a beautiful screamer.

RICHIE: He said "streamer," not "screamer," asshole.

(COKES *is still in his reverie.*)

COKES: This guy with his chute goin' straight up above him in a streamer, like a tulip, only white, you know. All twisted and never gonna open. Like a big icicle sticking straight up above him. He went right by me. We met eyes, sort of. He was lookin' real puzzled. He looks right at me. Then he looks up in the air at the chute, then down at the ground.

ROONEY: Did *he* sing it?

COKES: He didn't sing it. He started going like this. (*He reaches desperately upward with both hands and begins to claw at the sky while his legs pump up and down.*) Like he was gonna climb right up the air.

RICHIE: Ohhhhh, Geezus.

BILLY: God

(ROONEY *has collapsed backward on* BILLY's *bed and he lies there and then he rises.*)

ROONEY: Cokes got the Silver Star for rollin' a barrel a oil down a hill in Korea into forty-seven chinky Chinese gooks who were climbin' up the hill and when he shot into it with his machine gun, it blew them all to grape jelly.

(COKES, *rocking a little on his feet, begins to hum and then sing "Beautiful Streamer," to the tune of Stephen Foster's "Beautiful Dreamer.")*

COKES: "Beautiful streamer, open for me . . . The sky is above me . . ." (*The singing stops.*) But the one I remember is this little guy in his spider hole, which is a hole in the ground with a lid over it. (*He is using* RICHIE's *footlocker before him as the spider hole. He has fixed on it, moving toward it.*) And he shot me in the ass as I was runnin' by, but the bullet hit me so hard— (*His body kind of jerks and he runs several steps.*) —it knocked me into this ditch where he couldn't see me. I got behind him. (*Now at the head of* RICHIE's *bed, he begins to creep along the side of the bed as if sneaking up on the footlocker.*) Crawlin'. And I dropped a grenade into his hole. (*He jams a whiskey bottle into the footlocker, then slams down the lid.*) Then sat on the lid, him bouncin' and yellin' under me. Bouncin' and yellin' under the lid. I could hear him. Feel him. I just sat there.

(*Silence.* ROONEY *waits, thinking, then leans forward.*)

ROONEY: He was probably singin' it.

COKES: *(Sitting there)* I think so.

ROONEY: You think we should let 'em hear it?

BILLY: We're good boys. We're good ole boys.

COKES: *(Jerking himself to his feet, he staggers sideways to join* ROONEY *on* BILLY'*s bed.)* I don't care who hears it, I just wanna be singin' it.

*(*ROONEY *rises; he goes to the boys on* ROGER'*s bed and speaks to them carefully, as if lecturing people on something of great importance.)*

ROONEY: You listen up; you just be listenin' up, 'cause if you hear it right you can maybe stop bein' shit sacks. This is what a man sings, he's goin' down through the air, his chute don't open.

(Flopping back down on the bunk beside COKES, ROONEY *looks at* COKES *and then at the boys. The two older men put their arms around each other and they begin to sing.)*

ROONEY and COKES: *(Singing)*
    Beautiful streamer,
    Open for me,
    The sky is above me,
    But no canopy.

BILLY: *(Murmuring)* I don't believe it.

ROONEY and COKES:
    Counted ten thousand,
    Pulled at the cord.
    My chute didn't open,
    I shouted, "Dear Lord."

    Beautiful streamer,
    This looks like the end,
    The earth is below me,
    My body won't bend.

    Just like a mother
    Watching o'er me,
    Beautiful streamer,
    Ohhhhh, open for me.

ROGER: Un-fuckin'-believable.

ROONEY: *(Beaming with pride)* Ain't that a beauty.

*(*COKES *topples forward onto his face and flops limply to his side. The three boys leap to their feet.* ROONEY *lunges toward* COKES.)*

RICHIE: Sergeant!

ROONEY: Cokie! Cokie!

BILLY: Jesus.

ROGER: Hey!

COKES: Huh? Huh?

(COKES sits up. ROONEY is kneeling beside him.)

ROONEY: Jesus, Cokie.

COKES: I been doin' that; I been doin' that. It don't mean nothin'.

ROONEY: No, no.

COKES: *(Pushing at ROONEY, who is trying to help him get back to the bed. ROONEY agrees with everything COKES is now saying and the noises he makes are little animal noises.)* I told 'em when they wanted to send me back I ain't got no leukemia; they wanna check it. They think I got it. I don't think I got it. Rooney? What you think?

ROONEY: No.

COKES: My mother had it. She had it. Just 'cause she did and I been fallin' down.

ROONEY: It don't mean nothin'.

COKES: *(He lunges back and up onto the bed.)* I tole 'em I fall down 'cause I'm drunk. I'm drunk all the time.

ROONEY: You'll be goin' back over there with me, is what I know, Cokie. *(He is patting COKES, nodding, dusting him off.)* That's what I know. *(As BILLY comes up to them, almost seeming to want to be a part of the intimacy they are sharing.)*

BILLY: That was somethin', Sergeant Cokes. Jesus. *(ROONEY whirls on him, ferocious, pushing him.)*

ROONEY: Get the fuck away, Wilson! Whata you know? Get the fuck away. You don't know shit. Get away! You don't know shit. *(He turns to COKES, who is standing up from the bed.)* Me and Cokes are goin' to the war zone like we oughta. Gonna blow it to shit. *(He is grabbing at COKES, who is laughing. They are both laughing. ROONEY whirls on the boys.)* Ohhh, I'm gonna be so happy to be away from you assholes; you pussies. Not one regular Army people among you possible. I swear it to my mother who is holy. You just be watchin' the papers for doin' darin' brave deeds. 'Cause we're old hands at it. Makin' shit disappear. Goddamn whooosh!

COKES: Whooosh!

ROONEY: Demnalitions. Me and . . . *(And then he knows he hasn't said it right.)* Me and Cokie . . . Demnal . . . Demnali . . .

RICHIE: *(Still sitting on ROGER's bed.)* You can do it, Sergeant.

BILLY: Get it. *(He stands by the lockers and* ROONEY *glares at him.)*

ROGER: 'Cause you're cool with dynamite, is what you're tryin' to say.

ROONEY: *(Charging at* ROGER, *bellowing.)* Shut the fuck up, that's what you can do; and go to goddamn sleep. You buncha shit . . . sacks. Buncha mothers—know-it-all motherin' shit sacks—that's what you are.

COKES: *(Shoulders back, he is taking charge.)* Just goin' to sleep is what you can do, 'cause Rooney and me fought it through two wars already and we can make it through this one more and leukemia that comes or doesn't come—who gives a shit? Not guys like us. We're goin' just pretty as pie. And it's lights-out time, ain't it, Rooney?

ROONEY: Past it, goddammit. So the lights are goin' out.

(There is fear in the room, and the three boys rush to their wall lockers, where they start to strip to their underwear, preparing for bed. ROONEY *paces the room, watching them, glaring.)*

ROONEY: Somebody's gotta teach you soldierin'. You hear me? Or you wanna go outside and march around awhile, huh? We can do that if you wanna. Huh? You tell me? Marchin' or sleepin'? What's it gonna be?

RICHIE: *(Rushing to get into bed.)* Flick out the ole lights, Sergeant; that's what we say.

BILLY: *(Climbing into bed.)* Put out the ole lights.

ROGER: *(In bed and pulling up the covers.)* Do it.

COKES: Shut up. *(He rocks forward and back, trying to stand at attention. He is saying good night.)* And that's an order. Just shut up. I got grenades down the hall. I got a pistol. I know where to get nitro. You don't shut up, I'll blow . . . you . . . to . . . fuck. *(Making a military left face, he stalks to the wall switch and turns the lights out.* ROONEY *is watching proudly, as* COKES *faces the boys again. He looks at them.)* That's right.

(In the dark, there is only a spill of light from the hall coming in the open door. COKES *and* ROONEY *put their arms around each other and go out the door, leaving it partly open.* RICHIE, ROGER *and* BILLY *lie in their bunks, staring. They do not move. They lie there. The sergeants seem to have vanished soundlessly once they went out the door. Light touches each of the boys as they lie there.)*

ROGER: *(He does not move.)* Lord have mercy, if that ain't a pair. If that ain't one pair a beauties.

BILLY: Oh, yeh. *(He does not move.)*

ROGER: Too much, man—too, too much.

RICHIE: They made me sad; but I loved them, sort of. Better than movies.

ROGER: Too much, Too, too much. *(Silence)*

BILLY: What time is it?

ROGER: Sleep time, men. Sleep time. *(Silence)*

BILLY: Right.

ROGER: They were somethin'. Too much.

BILLY: Too much.

RICHIE: Night.

ROGER: Night *(Silence)* Night, Billy.

BILLY: Night

(RICHIE stirs in his bed. ROGER turns onto his side. BILLY is motionless.)

BILLY: I . . . had a buddy, Rog—and this is the whole thing, this is the whole point—a kid I grew up with, played ball with in high school, and he was a tough little cat, a real bad man sometimes. Used to have gangster pictures up in his room. Anyway, we got into this deal where we'd drive on down to the big city, man, you know, hit the bad spots, let some queer pick us up . . . sort of . . . long enough to buy us some good stuff. It was kinda the thing to do for a while, and we all did it, the whole gang of us. So we'd let these cats pick us up, most of 'em old guys, and they were hurtin' and happy as hell to have us, and we'd get a lot of free booze, maybe a meal, and we'd turn 'em on. Then pretty soon they'd ask us did we want to go over to their place. Sure, we'd say, and order one more drink, and then when we hit the street, we'd tell 'em to kiss off. We'd call 'em fag and queer and jazz like that and tell 'em to kiss off. And Frankie, the kid I'm tellin' you about, he had a mean streak in him and if they gave us a bad time at all, he'd put 'em down. That's the way he was. So that kinda jazz went on and on for sort of a long time and it was a good deal if we were low on cash or needed a laugh and it went on for a while. And when Frankie—one day he come up to me—and he says he was goin' home with the guy he was with. He said, what the hell, what did it matter? And he's sayin'—Frankie's sayin'—why don't I tag along? What the hell, he's sayin', what does it matter who does it to you, some broad or some old guy, you close your eyes, a mouth's a mouth, it don't matter—that's what he's sayin'. I tried to talk him out of it, but he wasn't hearin' anything I was sayin'. So the next day, see, he calls me up to tell me about it. Okay, okay, he says, it was a cool scene, he says; they played poker, a buck minimum, and he made a fortune. Frankie was eatin' it up, man. It was a pretty way to live, he says. So he stayed at it, and he had this nice little girl he was goin' with at the time. You know the way a real bad cat can sometimes do that—have a good little girl who's crazy about him and he is for her, too, and he's a different cat when he's with her?

ROGER: Uh-huh. *(The hall light slants across* BILLY'*s face.)*

BILLY: Well, that was him and Linda, and then one day he dropped her, he cut her loose. He was hooked, man. He was into it, with no way he knew out—you understand what I'm sayin'? He had got his ass hooked. He had never thought he would and then one day he woke up and he was on it. He just hadn't been told, that's the way I figure it; somebody didn't tell him somethin' he shoulda been told and he come to me wailin' one day, man, all broke up and wailin', my boy Frankie, my main man, and he was a fag. He was a faggot, black Roger, and I'm not lyin', I am not lyin' to you.

ROGER: Damn.

BILLY: So that's the whole thing, man; that's the whole thing.

(Silence. They lie there.)

ROGER: Holy . . . Christ. Richie . . . you hear him? You hear what he said?

RICHIE: He's a storyteller.

ROGER: What you mean?

RICHIE: I mean, he's a storyteller, all right; he tells stories, all right.

ROGER: What are we into now? You wanna end up like that friend a his, or you don't believe what he said? Which are you sayin'?

(The door bursts open. The sounds of machine guns and cannon are being made by someone, and CARLYLE, *drunk and playing, comes crawling in.* ROGER, RICHIE *and* BILLY *all pop up, startled, to look at him.)*

ROGER: Hey, hey, what's happenin'?

BILLY: Who's happenin'?

ROGER: You attackin' or you retreatin', man?

CARLYLE: *(Looking up; big grin)* Hey, baby . . . ?

(Continues shooting, crawling. The three boys look at each other.)

ROGER: What's happenin', man? Whatcha doin'?

CARLYLE: I dunno, soul; I dunno. Practicin' my duties, my new abilities. *(Half sitting, he flops onto his side, starts to crawl.)* The low crawl, man; like I was taught in basic, that's what I'm doin'. You gotta know your shit, man, else you get your ass blown so far away you don't ever see it again. Oh, sure, you guys don't care. I know it. You got it made. You got it made. I don't got it made. You got a little home here, got friends, people to talk to. I got nothin'. You got jobs they probably ain't ever gonna ship you out, you got so important jobs. I got no job. They don't even wanna give me a job. I know it. They are gonna kill me. They are gonna send me over there to get me killed, goddammit. WHAT'S A MATTER WITH ALL YOU PEOPLE?

(The anger explodes out of the grieving and Roger *rushes to kneel beside* Carlyle. *He speaks gently, firmly.)*

Roger: Hey, man, get cool, get some cool; purchase some cool, man.

Carlyle: Awwwww ... *(Clumsily, he turns away.)*

Roger: Just hang in there.

Carlyle: I don't wanna be no DEAD man. I don't wanna be the one they all thinkin' is so stupid he's the one'll go, they tell him; they don't even have to give him a job. I got thoughts, man, in my head; alla time, burnin', burnin' thoughts a understandin'.

Roger: Don't you think we know that, man? It ain't the way you're sayin' it.

Carlyle: It is.

Roger: No. I mean, we all probably gonna go. We all probably gonna have to go.

Carlyle: No-o-o-o-o.

Roger: I mean it.

Carlyle: *(Suddenly he nearly topples over.)* I am very drunk. *(And he looks up at* Roger.) You think so?

Roger: I'm sayin' so. And I am sayin', "No sweat." No point.

*(*Carlyle *angrily pushes at* Roger, *knocking him backward.)*

Carlyle: Awwwww, dammit, dammit, mother ... shit ... it ... ohhh-hhhh. *(Sliding to the floor, the rage and anguish softening into only breathing)* I mean it. I mean it. *(Silence. He lies there.)*

Roger: What ... a you doin' ... ?

Carlyle: Huh?

Roger: I don't know what you're up to on our freshly mopped floor.

Carlyle: Gonna go sleep—okay? No sweat ... *(Suddenly very polite, he is looking up.)* Can I, soul? Izzit all right?

Roger: Sure, man, sure, if you wanna, but why don't you go where you got a bed? Don't you like beds?

Carlyle: Dunno where's zat. My bed. I can' fin' it. I can' fin' my own bed. I looked all over, but I can' fin' it anywhere. GONE! *(Slipping back down now, he squirms to make a nest. He hugs his bottle.)*

Roger: *(Moving to his bunk, where he grabs a blanket)* Okay, okay, man. But get on top a this, man. *(He is spreading the blanket on the floor, trying to help* Carlyle *get on it.)* Make it softer. C'mon, c'mon ... get on this.

*(*Billy *has risen with his own blanket, and is moving now to hand it to* Roger.)*

Billy: Cat's hurtin', Rog.

ROGER: Ohhhhh, yeh.

CARLYLE: Ohhhhh . . . it was so sweet at home . . . it was so sweet, baby;
so-o-o good. They doin' dances make you wanna cry . . . *(Hugging the
blankets now, he drifts in a kind of dream.)*

ROGER: I know, man.

CARLYLE: So sweet . . . !

(BILLY is moving back to his own bed, where, quietly, he sits.)

ROGER: I know, man.

CARLYLE: So sweet . . . !

ROGER: Yeh.

CARLYLE: How come I gotta be here?

*(On his way to the door to close it, ROGER falters, looks at CARLYLE, then moves
on toward the door.)*

ROGER: I dunno, Jim.

*(BILLY is sitting and watching, as ROGER goes on to the door, gently closes it and
returns to his bed.)*

BILLY: I know why he's gotta be here, Roger. You wanna know? Why
don't you ask me?

ROGER: Okay. How come he gotta be here?

BILLY: *(Smiling)* Freedom's frontier, man. That's why.

ROGER: *(Settled on the edge of his bed and about to lie back.)* Oh . . .
yeh . . .

*(As a distant bugle begins to play taps and RICHIE, carrying a blanket, is approaching
CARLYLE, ROGER settles back; BILLY is staring at RICHIE; CARLYLE does not stir;
the bugle plays.)*

ROGER: Bet that ole sarge don't live a year, Billy. Fuckin' blow his own
ass sky high.

*(RICHIE has covered CARLYLE. He pats CARLYLE's arm, and then straightens in order
to return to his bed.)*

BILLY: Richie . . . !

*(BILLY's hissing voice freezes RICHIE. He stands, and then he starts again to move,
and BILLY's voice comes again and RICHIE cannot move.)*

BILLY: Richie . . . how come you gotta keep doin' that stuff?

*(ROGER looks at BILLY, staring at RICHIE, who stands still as a stone over the
sleeping CARLYLE.)*

BILLY: How come?

ROGER: He dunno, man. Do you? You dunno, do you, Rich?

RICHIE: No.

CARLYLE: *(From deep in his sleep and grieving.)* It...was...so... pretty...!

RICHIE: No.

(The lights are fading with the last soft notes of taps.)

Act Two

Scene One

(Lights come up on the cadre room. It is late afternoon and BILLY *is lying on his stomach, his head at the foot of the bed, his chin resting on his hands. He wears gym shorts and sweat socks; his T-shirt lies on the bed and his sneakers are on the floor.* ROGER *is at his footlocker, taking out a pair of sweat socks. His sneakers and his basketball are on his bed. He is wearing his khakis.)*

(A silence passes, and then ROGER *closes his footlocker and sits on his bed, where he starts lacing his sneakers, holding them on his lap.)*

BILLY: Rog...you think I'm a busybody? In any way?

(Silence. ROGER *laces his sneakers.)*

BILLY: Roger?

ROGER: Huh? Uh-uh.

BILLY: Some people do. I mean, back home. *(He rolls slightly to look at* ROGER.*)* Or that I didn't know how to behave. Sort of.

ROGER: It's time we maybe get changed, don't you think? *(He rises and goes to his locker. He takes off his trousers, shoes, and socks.)*

BILLY: Yeh. I guess. I don't feel like it, though. I don't feel good, don't know why.

ROGER: Be good for you, man; be good for you. *(Pulling on his gym shorts, he returns to his bed, carrying his shoes and socks.)*

BILLY: Yeh. *(He sits up on the edge of his bed.* ROGER, *sitting, is bowed over, putting on his socks.)* I mean, a lot of people thought like I didn't know how to behave in a simple way. You know? That I overcomplicated everything. I didn't think so. Don't think so. I just thought I was seein' complications that were there but nobody else saw. *(He is struggling now to put on his T-shirt. He seems weary, almost weak.)* I mean, Wisconsin's a funny place. All those clear-eyed people sayin' "Hello" and lookin' you straight in the eye. Everybody's good, you think, and happy and honest. And then there's all of a sudden a neighbor who goes mad as a hatter. I had a neighbor who came out of his house one morning with axes in both hands. He started then attackin' the cars that were driving up and down in front of his house. An' we all knew why he did it, sorta. *(He pauses; he thinks.)* It made me wanna be a priest. I wanted to be a priest then. I was sixteen. Priests could help people. Could take away what hurt 'em. I wanted that, I thought. Somethin', huh?

ROGER: *(He has the basketball in his hands.)* Yeh. But everybody's got feelin's like that sometimes.

BILLY: I don't know.

ROGER: You know, you oughta work on a little jump shot, my man. Get you some kinda fall-away jumper to go with that beauty of a hook. Make you tough out there.

BILLY: Can't fuckin' do it. Not my game. I mean, like that bar we go to. You think I could get a job there bartendin', maybe? I could learn the ropes. *(He is watching* ROGER, *who has risen to walk to his locker.)* You think I could get a job there off-duty hours?

ROGER: *(Pulling his locker open to display the pinup on the inside of the door.)* You don't want no job. It's that little black-haired waitress you wantin' to know.

BILLY: No, man. Not really.

ROGER: It's okay. She tough, man. *(He begins to remove his uniform shirt. He will put on an O.D. T-shirt to go to the gym.)*

BILLY: I mean, not the way you're sayin' it, is all. Sure, there's somethin' about her. I don't know what. I ain't even spoke to her yet. But somethin'. I mean, what's she doin' there? When she's dancin', it's like she knows somethin'. She's degradin' herself, I sometimes feel. You think she is?

ROGER: Man, you don't even know the girl. She's workin'.

BILLY: I'd like to talk to her. Tell her stuff. Find out about her. Sometimes I'm thinkin' about her and it and I got a job there, I get to know her and she and I get to be real tight, man—close, you know. Maybe we screw, maybe we don't. It's nice . . . whatever.

ROGER: Sure. She a real fine-lookin' chippy, Billy. Got nice cakes. Nice little titties.

BILLY: I think she's smart, too.

*(*ROGER *starts laughing so hard he almost falls into his locker.)*

BILLY: Oh, all I do is talk. "Yabba-yabba." I mean, my mom and dad are really terrific people. How'd they ever end up with somebody so weird as me?

*(*ROGER *moves to him, jostles him.)*

ROGER: I'm tellin' you, the gym and a little ball is what you need. Little exercise. Little bumpin' into people. The soul is tellin' you.

*(*BILLY *rises and goes to his locker, where he starts putting on his sweat clothes.)*

BILLY: I mean, Roger, you remember how we met in P Company? Both of us brand-new. You started talkin' to me. You just started talkin' to me and you didn't stop.

ROGER: *(Hardly looking up)* Yeh.

BILLY: Did you see somethin' in me made you pick me?

ROGER: I was talkin' to everybody, man. For that whole day. Two whole days. You was just the first one to talk back friendly. Though you didn't say much, as I recall.

BILLY: The first white person, you mean. *(Wearing his sweat pants, he is now at his bed, putting on his sneakers.)*

ROGER: Yeh. I was tryin' to come outa myself a little. Do like the fuckin' head shrinker been tellin' me to stop them fuckin' headaches I was havin', you know. Now let us do fifteen or twenty push-ups and get over to that gymnasium, like I been sayin'. Then we can take our civvies with us—we can shower and change at the gym.

(ROGER crosses to BILLY, who flops down on his belly on the bed.)

BILLY: I don't know . . . I don't know what it is I'm feelin'. Sick like.

(ROGER forces BILLY up onto his feet and shoves him playfully downstage, where they both fall forward into the push-up position, side by side.)

ROGER: Do 'em, trooper. Do 'em. Get it.

(ROGER starts. BILLY joins in. After five, ROGER realizes that BILLY has his knees on the floor. They start again. This time, BILLY counts in double time. They start again. At about "seven," RICHIE enters. Neither BILLY nor ROGER sees him. They keep going.)

ROGER AND BILLY: . . . seven, eight, nine, ten . . .

RICHIE: No, no; no, no; no, no, no. That's not it; that's not it.

(They keep going, yelling the numbers louder and louder.)

ROGER AND BILLY: . . . eleven, twelve, thirteen . . .

(RICHIE crosses to his locker and gets his bottle of cologne, and then returning to the center of the room to stare at them, he stands there dabbing cologne on his face.)

ROGER AND BILLY: . . . fourteen, fifteen.

RICHIE: You'll never get it like that. You're so far apart and you're both humping at the same time. And all that counting. It's so unromantic.

ROGER: *(Rising and moving to his bed to pick up the basketball.)* We was exercisin', Richard. You heard a that?

RICHIE: Call it what you will, Roger.

(With a flick of his wrist, ROGER tosses the basketball to BILLY.)

RICHIE: Everybody has their own cute little pet names for it.

BILLY: Hey!

(He tosses the ball at RICHIE, hitting him in the chest, sending the cologne bottle flying. RICHIE yelps, as BILLY retrieves the ball and, grabbing up his sweat jacket from the bed, heads for the door. ROGER, at his own locker, has taken out his suit bag of civilian clothes.)

BILLY: You missed.

RICHIE: Billy, Billy, Billy, please, please, the ruffian approach will not work with me. It impresses me not even one tiny little bit. All you've done is spill my cologne. *(He bends to pick up the cologne from the floor.)*

BILLY: That was my aim.

ROGER: See you.

(BILLY is passing RICHIE. Suddenly RICHIE sprays BILLY with cologne, some of it getting on ROGER, as ROGER and BILLY, groaning and cursing at RICHIE, rush out the door.)

RICHIE: Try the more delicate approach next time, Bill.

(Having crossed to the door, he stands a moment, leaning against the frame. Then he bounces to BILLY's bed, sings "He's just my Bill," and squirts cologne on the pillow. At his locker, he deposits the cologne, takes off his shirt, shoes and socks. Removing a hard-cover copy of Pauline Kael's I Lost It at the Movies from the top shelf of the locker, he bounds to the center of the room and tosses the book the rest of the way to the bed. Quite pleased with himself, he fidgets, pats his stomach, then lowers himself into the push-up position, goes to his knees and stands up.)

RICHIE: Am I out of my fucking mind? Those two are crazy. I'm not crazy.

(RICHIE pivots and strides to his locker. With an ashtray, a pack of matches and a pack of cigarettes, he hurries to his bed and makes himself comfortable to read, his head propped up on a pillow. Settling himself, he opens the book, finds his place, thinks a little, starts to read. For a moment he lies there. And then CARLYLE steps into the room. He comes through the doorway looking to his left and right. He comes several steps into the room and looks at RICHIE. RICHIE sees him. They look at each other.)

CARLYLE: Ain't nobody here, man?

RICHIE: Hello, Carlyle. How are you today?

CARLYLE: Ain't nobody here? *(He is nervous and angrily disappointed.)*

RICHIE: Who do you want?

CARLYLE: Where's the black boy?

RICHIE: Roger? My God, why do you keep calling him that? Don't you know his name yet? Roger. Roger. *(He thickens his voice at this, imitating someone very stupid. CARLYLE stares at him.)*

CARLYLE: Yeh. Where is he?

RICHIE: I am not his keeper, you know. I am not his private secretary, you know.

CARLYLE: I do not know. I do not know. That is why I am asking. I come to see him. You are here. I ask you. I don't know. I mean, Carlyle made a fool outa himself comin' in here the other night, talkin' on and on like how he did. Lay on the floor. He remember. You remember? It all one hype, man; that all one hype. You know what I mean. That ain't the real Carlyle was in here. This one here and now the real Carlyle. Who the real Richie?

RICHIE: Well ... the real Richie ... has gone home. To Manhattan. I, however, am about to read this book. *(Which he again starts to try to do.)*

CARLYLE: Oh. Shit. Jus' you the only one here, then, huh?

RICHIE: So it would seem. *(He looks at the air and then under the bed as if to find someone.)* So it would seem. Did you hear about Martin?

CARLYLE: What happened to Martin? I ain't seen him.

RICHIE: They are shipping him home. Someone told about what he did to himself. I don't know who.

CARLYLE: Wasn't me. Not me. I keep that secret.

RICHIE: I'm sure you did. *(Rising, walking toward* CARLYLE *and the door, cigarette pack in hand.)* You want a cigarette? Or don't you smoke? Or do you have to go right away? *(Closing the door.)* There's a chill sometimes coming down the hall, I don't know from where. *(Crossing back to his bed and climbing in.)* And I think I've got the start of a little cold. Did you want the cigarette?

(CARLYLE is staring at him. Then he examines the door and looks again at RICHIE. He stares at RICHIE, thinking, and then he walks toward him.)

CARLYLE: You know what I bet? I been lookin' at you real close. It just a way I got about me. And I bet if I was to hang my boy out in front of you, my big boy, man, you'd start wantin' to touch him. Be beggin' and talkin' sweet to ole Carlyle. Am I right or wrong? *(He leans over to* RICHIE.*)* What do you say?

RICHIE: Pardon?

CARLYLE: You heard me. Ohhh. I am so restless, I don't even understand it. My big black boy is what I was talkin' about. My thing, man; my rope, Jim. HEY, RICHIE! *(He lunges, then moves his fingers through* RICHIE's *hair.)* How long you been a punk? Can you hear me? Am I clear? Do I talk funny? *(He is leaning close.)* Can you smell the gin on my mouth?

RICHIE: I mean, if you really came looking for Roger, he and Billy are gone to the gymnasium. They were—

CARLYLE: No. *(He slides down on the bed, his arm placed over* RICHIE's *legs.)* I got no athletic abilities. I got none. No moves. I don't know. HEY, RICHIE! *(Leaning close again.)* I just got this question I asked. I got no answer.

RICHIE: I don't know ... what ... you mean.

CARLYLE: I heard me. I understood me. "How long you been a punk?" is the question I asked. Have you got a reply?

RICHIE: *(Confused, irritated, but fascinated.)* Not to that question.

CARLYLE: Who do if you don't? I don't. How'm I gonna? *(Suddenly there is whistling in the hall, as if someone might enter, footsteps approaching, and* RICHIE *leaps to his feet and scurries away toward the door, tucking in his undershirt as he goes.)* Man, don't you wanna talk to me? Don't you wanna talk to ole Carlyle?

RICHIE: Not at the moment.

CARLYLE: *(He is rising, starting after* RICHIE, *who stands nervously near* ROGER's *bed.)* I want to talk to you, man; why don't you want to talk to me? We can be friends. Talkin' back and forth, sharin' thoughts and bein' happy.

RICHIE: I don't think that's what you want.

CARLYLE: *(He is very near to* RICHIE.) What do I want?

RICHIE: I mean, to talk to me. *(As if repulsed, he crosses away. But it is hard to tell if the move is genuine or coy.)*

CARLYLE: What am I doin'? I am talkin'. DON'T YOU TELL ME I AIN'T TALKIN' WHEN I AM TALKIN'! COURSE I AM. Bendin' over backwards. *(Pressing his hands against himself in his anger, he has touched the grease on his shirt, the filth of his clothing, and this ignites the anger.)* Do you know they still got me in that goddamn P Company? That goddamn transient company. It like they think I ain't got no notion what a home is. No nose for no home—like I ain't never had no home. I had a home. IT LIKE THEY THINK THERE AIN'T NO PLACE FOR ME IN THIS MOTHER ARMY BUT K.P. ALL SUDSY AND WRINKLED AND SWEATIN' EVERY DAY SINCE I GOT TO THIS SHIT HOUSE, MISTER! HOW MANY TIMES YOU BEEN ON K.P.? WHEN'S THE LAST TIME YOU PULLED K.P.? *(He has roared down to where* RICHIE *had moved, the rage possessing him.)*

RICHIE: I'm E.D.

CARLYLE: You E.D.? You E.D.? You Edie, are you? I didn't ask you what you friends call you, I asked you when's the last time you had K.P.?

RICHIE: *(Edging toward his bed. He will go there, get, and light a cigarette.)* E.D. is "Exempt from Duty."

CARLYLE: *(Moving after* RICHIE.) You ain't got no duties? What shit you talkin' about? Everybody in this fuckin' Army got duties. That what the fuckin' Army all about. You ain't got no duties, who got 'em?

RICHIE: Because of my job, Carlyle. I have a very special job. And my friends don't call me Edie. *(Big smile.)* They call me Irene.

CARLYLE: That mean what you sayin' is you kiss ass for somebody, don't it? Good for you. *(Seemingly relaxed and gentle, he settles down on* RICHIE's *bed. He seems playful and charming.)* You know the other night I was sleepin' there. You know.

RICHIE: Yes.

CARLYLE: *(Gleefully, enormously pleased)* You remember that? How come you remember that? You sweet.

RICHIE: We don't have people sleeping on our floor that often, Carlyle

CARLYLE: But the way you crawl over in the night, gimme a big kiss on my joint. That nice.

RICHIE: *(Shocked, he blinks.)* What?

CARLYLE: Or did I dream that?

RICHIE: *(Laughing in spite of himself.)* My God, you're outrageous!

CARLYLE: Maybe you dreamed it.

RICHIE: What...? No. I don't know.

CARLYLE: Maybe you did it, then; you didn't dream it.

RICHIE: How come you talk so much?

CARLYLE: I don't talk, man, who's gonna talk? YOU? *(He is laughing and amused, but there is anger near the surface now, an ugliness.)* That bore me to death. I don't like nobody's voice but my own. I am so pretty. Don't like nobody else face. *(And then viciously, he spits out at RICHIE.)* You goddamn face ugly fuckin' queer punk! *(And RICHIE jumps in confusion.)*

RICHIE: What's the matter with you?

CARLYLE: You goddamn ugly punk face. YOU UGLY!

RICHIE: Nice mouth.

CARLYLE: That's right. That's right. And you got a weird mouth. Like to suck joints.

(As RICHIE storms to his locker, throwing the book inside, he pivots, grabbing a towel, marching toward the door.)

CARLYLE: Hey, you gonna jus' walk out on me? Where you goin'? You c'mon back. Hear?

RICHIE: That's my bed, for chrissake. *(He lunges into the hall.)*

CARLYLE: You'd best. *(Lying there, he makes himself comfortable. He takes a pint bottle from his back pocket.)* You come back, Richie, I tell you a good joke. Make you laugh, make you cry. *(He takes a big drink.)* That's right. Ole Frank and Jesse, they got the stagecoach stopped, all the people lined up—Frank say, "All right, peoples, we gonna rape all the men and rob all the women." Jesse say, "Frank, no, no—that ain't it—

we gonna—" And this one little man yell real loud, "You shut up, Jesse; Frank knows what he's doin'."

(Loudly, he laughs and laughs. BILLY enters. Startled at the sight of CARLYLE there in RICHIE's bed, BILLY falters, as CARLYLE gestures toward him.)

CARLYLE: Hey, man ...! Hey, you know, they send me over to that Vietnam, I be cool, 'cause I been dodgin' bullets and shit since I been old enough to get on pussy make it happy to know me. I can get on, I can do my job.

(BILLY looks weary and depressed. Languidly he crosses to his bed. He still wears his sweat clothes. CARLYLE studies him, then stares at the ceiling.)

CARLYLE: Yeh. I was just layin' here thinkin' that and you come in and out it come, words to say my feelin'. That my problem. That the black man's problem altogether. You ever considered that? Too much feelin'. He too close to everthing. He is, man; too close to his blood, to his body. It ain't that he don't have no good mind, but he BELIEVE in his body. Is ... that Richie the only punk in this room, or is there more?

BILLY: What?

CARLYLE: The punk; is he the only punk? *(Carefully he takes one of RI-CHIE's cigarettes and lights it.)*

BILLY: He's all right.

CARLYLE: I ain't askin' about the quality of his talent, but is he the only one, is my question.

BILLY: *(He does not want to deal with this. He sits there.)* You get your orders yet?

CARLYLE: Orders for what?

BILLY: To tell you where to work.

CARLYLE: I'm P Company, man. I work P Company. I do K.P. That all. Don't deserve no more. Do you know I been in this army three months and ten days and everybody still doin' the same shit and sayin' the same shit and wearin' the same green shitty clothes? I ain't been happy one day, and that a lotta goddamn misery back to back in this ole boy. Is that Richie a good punk? Huh? Is he? He takes care of you and Roger— that how come you in this room, the three of you?

BILLY: What?

CARLYLE: *(Emphatically)* You and Roger are hittin' on Richie, right?

BILLY: He's not queer, if that's what you're sayin'. A little effeminate, but that's all, no more; if that's what you're sayin'.

CARLYLE: I'd like to get some of him myself if he a good punk, is what I'm sayin'. That's what I'm saying'! You don't got no understandin' how a man can maybe be a little diplomatic about what he's sayin' sorta sideways, do you? Jesus.

BILLY: He don't do that stuff.

CARLYLE: *(Lying there)* What stuff?

BILLY: Listen, man. I don't feel too good, you don't mind.

CARLYLE: What stuff?

BILLY: What you're thinkin'.

CARLYLE: What ... am I thinkin'?

BILLY: You ... know.

CARLYLE: Yes, I do. It in my head, that how come I know. But how do you know? I can see your heart, Billy boy, but you cannot see mine. I am unknown. You ... are known.

BILLY: *(As if he is about to vomit, and fighting it.)* You just ... talk fast and keep movin', don't you? Don't ever stay still.

CARLYLE: Words to say my feelin', Billy boy.

(RICHIE steps into the room. He sees BILLY and CARLYLE and freezes.)

CARLYLE: There he is. There he be.

(RICHIE moves to his locker to put away the towel.)

RICHIE: He's one of them who hasn't come down far out of the trees yet, Billy; believe me.

CARLYLE: You got rudeness in your voice, Richie—you got meanness I can hear about ole Carlyle. You tellin' me I oughta leave—is that what you think you're doin'? You don't want me here?

RICHIE: You come to see Roger, who isn't here, right? Man like you must have important matters to take care of all over the quad; I can't imagine a man like you not having extremely important things to do all over the world, as a matter of fact, Carlyle.

CARLYLE: *(He rises. He begins to smooth the sheets and straighten the pillow. He will put the pint bottle in his back pocket and cross near to RICHIE.)* Ohhhh, listen—don't mind all the shit I say. I just talk bad, is all I do; I don't do bad. I got to have friends just like anybody else. I'm just bored and restless, that all; takin' it out on you two. I mean, I know Richie here ain't really no punk, not really. I was just talkin', just jivin' and entertainin' my own self. Don't take me serious, not ever. I get on out and see you all later.

(He moves for the door, RICHIE right behind him, almost ushering him.)

CARLYLE: You be cool, hear? Man don't do the jivin', he the one gettin' jived. That what my little brother Henry tell me and tell me.

(Moving leisurely, he backs out the door and is gone. RICHIE *shuts the door. There is a silence as* RICHIE *stands by the door.* BILLY *looks at him and then looks away.)*

BILLY: I am gonna have to move myself outa here, Roger decides to adopt that sonofabitch.

RICHIE: He's an animal.

BILLY: Yeh, and on top a that, he's a rotten person.

RICHIE: *(He laughs nervously, crossing nearer to* BILLY.*)* I think you're probably right.

(Still laughing a little, he pats BILLY's *shoulder and* BILLY *freezes at the touch. Awkwardly* RICHIE *removes his hand and crosses to his bed. When he has lain down,* BILLY *bends to take off his sneakers, then lies back on his pillow staring, thinking, and there is a silence.* RICHIE *does not move. He lies there, struggling to prepare himself for something.)*

RICHIE: Hey . . . Billy? *(Very slight pause)* Billy?

BILLY: Yeh.

RICHIE: You know that story you told the other night?

BILLY: Yeh . . . ?

RICHIE: You know . . .

BILLY: What . . . about it?

RICHIE: Well, was it . . . about you? *(Pause)* I mean, was it . . . ABOUT you? Were you Frankie? *(This is difficult for him.)* Are . . . you Frankie? Billy?

*(*BILLY *is slowly sitting up.)*

BILLY: You sonofabitch . . . !

RICHIE: Or was it really about somebody you knew . . . ?

BILLY: *(Sitting, outraged and glaring)* You didn't hear me at all!

RICHIE: I'm just asking a simple question, Billy, that's all I'm doing.

BILLY: You are really sick. You know that? Your brain is really, truly rancid! Do you know there's a theory now it's genetic? That it's all a matter of genes and shit like that?

RICHIE: Everything is not so ungodly cryptic, Billy.

BILLY: You. You, man, and the rot it's makin' outa your feeble fuckin' brain.

*(*ROGER, *dressed in civilian clothes, bursts in and* BILLY *leaps to his feet.)*

ROGER: Hey, hey, anyone got a couple bucks he can loan me?

BILLY: Rog, where you been?

ROGER: *(Throwing the basketball and his sweat clothes into his locker.)* I need five. C'mon.

BILLY: Where you been? That asshole friend a yours was here.

ROGER: I know, I know. Can you gimme five?

RICHIE: *(He jumps to the floor and heads for his locker.)* You want five. I got it. You want ten or more, even?

(BILLY, watching RICHIE, turns, and nervously paces down right, where he moves about, worried.)

BILLY: I mean, we gotta talk about him, man; we gotta talk about him.

ROGER: *(As RICHIE is handing him two fives.)* 'Cause we goin' to town together. I jus' run into him out on the quad, man, and he was feelin' real bad 'bout the way he acted, how you guys done him, he was fallin' down apologizin' all over the place.

BILLY: *(As RICHIE marches back to his bed and sits down.)* I mean, he's got a lotta weird ideas about us; I'm tellin' you.

ROGER: He's just a little fucked up in his head is all, but he ain't trouble. *(He takes a pair of sunglasses from the locker and puts them on.)*

BILLY: Who needs him? I mean, we don't need him.

ROGER: You gettin' too nervous, man. Nobody said anything about anybody needin' anybody. I been on the street all my life; he brings back home. I played me a little ball, Billy; took me a shower. I'm feelin' good! *(He has moved down to BILLY.)*

BILLY: I'm tellin' you there's something wrong with him, though.

ROGER: *(Face to face with BILLY, ROGER is a little irritated.)* Every black man in the world ain't like me, man; you get used to that idea. You get to know him, and you gonna like him. I'm tellin' you. You get to be laughin' just like me to hear him talk his shit. But you gotta relax.

RICHIE: I agree with Billy, Roger.

ROGER: Well, you guys got it all worked out and that's good, but I am goin' to town with him. Man's got wheels. Got a good head. You got any sense, you'll come with us.

BILLY: What are you talkin' about—come with you? I just tole you he's crazy.

ROGER: And I tole you you're wrong.

RICHIE: We weren't invited.

ROGER: I'm invitin' you.

RICHIE: No, I don't wanna.

ROGER: *(He moves to RICHIE; it seems he really wants RICHIE to go.)* You sure, Richie? C'mon.

RICHIE: No.

ROGER: Billy? He got wheels, we goin' in drinkin', see if gettin' our heads real bad don't just make us feel real good. You know what I mean. I got him right; you got him wrong.

BILLY: But what if I'm right?

ROGER: Billy, Billy, the man is waitin' on me. You know you wanna. Jesus. Bad cat like that gotta know the way. He been to D.C. before. Got cousins here. Got wheels for the weekend. You always talkin' how you don't do nothin'—you just talk it. Let's do it tonight—stop talkin'. Be cruisin' up and down the strip, leanin' out the window, bad as we wanna be. True cool is a car. We can flip a cigarette out the window—we can watch it bounce. Get us some chippies. You know we can. And if we don't, he knows a cathouse, it fulla cats.

BILLY: You serious?

RICHIE: You mean you're going to a whorehouse? That's disgusting.

BILLY: Listen who's talkin'. What do you want me to do? Stay here with you?

RICHIE: We could go to a movie or something.

ROGER: I am done with this talkin'. You goin', you stayin'? (He crosses to his locker, pulls into view a wide-brimmed black and shiny hat, and puts it on, cocking it at a sharp angle.)

BILLY: I don't know.

ROGER: (Stepping for the door.) I am goin'.

BILLY: (Turning, BILLY sees the hat.) I'm going. Okay! I'm going! Going, going, going! (He runs to his locker.)

RICHIE: Oh, Billy, you'll be scared to death in a cathouse and you know it.

BILLY: BULLSHIT!(He is removing his sweat pants and putting on a pair of gray corduroy trousers.)

ROGER: Billy got him a lion-tamer 'tween his legs!

(The door bangs open and CARLYLE is there, still clad in his filthy fatigues, but wearing a going-to-town black knit cap on his head and carrying a bottle.)

CARLYLE: Man, what's goin' on? I been waitin' like throughout my fuckin' life.

ROGER: Billy's goin', too. He's gotta change.

CARLYLE: He goin', too! Hey! Beautiful! That beautiful! (His grin is large, his laugh is loud.)

ROGER: Didn't I tell you, Billy?

CARLYLE: That beautiful, man; we all goin' to be friends.

RICHIE: *(Sitting on his bed.)* What about me, Carlyle?

(CARLYLE looks at RICHIE, and then at ROGER and then he and ROGER begin to laugh. CARLYLE pokes ROGER and they laugh as they are leaving. BILLY, grabbing up his sneakers to follow, stops at the door, looking only briefly at RICHIE. Then BILLY goes and shuts the door. The lights are fading to black.)

Scene Two

(In the dark, taps begins to play. And then slowly the lights rise, but the room remains dim. Only the lamp attached to RICHIE's bed burns and there is the glow and spill of the hallway coming through the transom. BILLY, CARLYLE, ROGER and RICHIE are sprawled about the room. BILLY, lying on his stomach, has his head at the foot of his bed, a half-empty bottle of beer dangling in his hand. He wears a blue oxford-cloth shirt and his sneakers lie beside his bed. ROGER, collapsed in his own bed, lies upon his back, his head also at the foot, a Playboy magazine covering his face and a half-empty bottle of beer in his hands, folded on his belly. Having removed his civilian shirt, he wears a white T-shirt. CARLYLE is lying on his belly on RICHIE's bed, his head at the foot, and he is facing out. RICHIE is sitting on the floor, resting against ROGER's footlocker. He is wrapped in a blanket. Beside him is an unopened bottle of beer and a bottle opener.)

(They are all dreamy in the dimness as taps plays sadly on and then fades into silence. No one moves.)

RICHIE: I don't know where it was, but it wasn't here. And we were all in it—it felt like—but we all had different faces. After you guys left, I only dozed for a few minutes, so it couldn't have been long. Roger laughed a lot and Billy was taller. I don't remember all the details exactly, and even though we were the ones in it, I know it was about my father. He was a big man. I was six. He was a very big man when I was six and he went away, but I remember him. He started drinking and staying home making model airplanes and boats and paintings by the numbers. We had money from mom's family, so he was just home all the time. And then one day I was coming home from kindergarten, and as I was starting up the front walk he came out the door and he had these suitcases in his hands. He was leaving, see, sneaking out, and I'd caught him. We looked at each other and I just knew and I started crying. He yelled at me. "Don't you cry; don't you start crying." I tried to grab him and he pushed me down in the grass. And then he was gone. G-O-N-E.

BILLY: And that was it? That was it?

RICHIE: I remember hiding my eyes. I lay in the grass and hid my eyes and waited.

BILLY: He never came back?

RICHIE: No.

CARLYLE: Ain't that some shit. Now, I'm a jive-time street nigger. I knew where my daddy was all the while. He workin' in this butcher shop two blocks up the street. Ole Mom used to point him out. "There he go. That him—that your daddy." We'd see him on the street, "There he go."

ROGER: Man couldn't see his way to livin' with you—that what you're sayin'?

CARLYLE: Never saw the day.

ROGER: And still couldn't get his ass outa the neighborhood?

(RICHIE begins trying to open his bottle of beer.)

CARLYLE: Ain't that a bitch. Poor ole bastard just duck his head—Mom pointin' at him—he git this real goddamn hangdog look like he don't know who we talkin' about and he walk a little faster. Why the hell he never move away I don't know, unless he was crazy. But I don't think so. He come up to me once—I was playin'. "Boy," he says, "I ain't your daddy. I ain't. Your momma's crazy." "Don't you be callin' my momma crazy, Daddy," I tole him. Poor ole thing didn't know what to do.

RICHIE: *(Giving up; he can't get the beer open.)* Somebody open this for me? I can't get this open.

(BILLY seems about to move to help, but CARLYLE is quicker, rising a little on the bunk and reaching.)

CARLYLE: Ole Carlyle get it.

(RICHIE slides along the floor until he can place the bottle in CARLYLE's outstretched hand.)

RICHIE: Then there was this once—there was this TV documentary about these bums in San Francisco, this TV guy interviewing all these bums, and just for maybe ten seconds while he was talkin' . . . *(Smiling, CARLYLE hands RICHIE the opened bottle.)* . . . to this one bum, there was this other one in the background jumpin' around like he thought he was dancin' and wavin' his hat, and even though there wasn't anything about him like my father and I didn't really ever see his face at all, I just kept thinkin': That's him. My dad. He thinks he's dancin'.

(They lie there in silence and suddenly, softly, BILLY giggles, and then he giggles a little more and louder.)

BILLY: Jesus!

RICHIE: What?

BILLY: That's ridiculous, Richie; sayin' that, thinkin' that. If it didn't look like him, it wasn't him, but you gotta be makin' up a story.

CARLYLE: *(Shifting now for a more comfortable position, he moves his head to the pillow at the top of the bed.)* Richie first saw me, he didn't like me much nohow, but he thought it over now, he changed his way a thinkin'. I can see that clear. We gonna be one big happy family.

RICHIE: Carlyle likes me, Billy; he thinks I'm pretty.

CARLYLE: *(Sitting up a little to make his point clear.)* No, I don't think you pretty. A broad is pretty. Punks ain't pretty. Punk—if he good-lookin'—is cute. You cute.

RICHIE: He's gonna steal me right away, little Billy. You're so slow, Bill. I prefer a man who's decisive. *(He is lying down now on the floor at the foot of his bed.)*

BILLY: You just keep at it, you're gonna have us all believin' you are just what you say you are.

RICHIE: Which is more than we can say for you.

(Now ROGER rises on his elbow to light a cigarette.)

BILLY: Jive, jive.

RICHIE: You're arrogant, Billy. So arrogant.

BILLY: What are you—on the rag?

RICHIE: Wouldn't it just bang your little balls if I were!

ROGER: *(To RICHIE)* Hey man, What's with you?

RICHIE: Stupidity offends me; lies and ignorance offend me.

BILLY: You know where we was? The three of us? All three of us, earlier on? To the wrong side of the tracks, Richard. One good black upside-down whorehouse where you get what you buy, no jive along with it—so if it's a lay you want and need, you go! Or don't they have faggot whorehouses?

ROGER: IF YOU GUYS DON'T CUT THIS SHIT OUT I'M GONNA BUST SOMEBODY'S HEAD! *(Angrily he flops back on his bed. There is a silence as they all lie there.)*

RICHIE: "Where we was," he says. Listen to him. "Where we was." And he's got more school, Carlyle, than you have fingers and . . . *(He has lifted his foot onto the bed; it touches, presses, CARLYLE's foot.)* . . . toes. It's this pseudo-earthy quality he feigns—but inside he's all cashmere.

BILLY: That's a lie. *(Giggling, he is staring at the floor.)* I'm polyester, worsted and mohair.

RICHIE: You have a lot of school, Billy; don't say you don't.

BILLY: You said "fingers and toes"; you didn't say "a lot."

CARLYLE: I think people get dumber the more they put their butts into some schoolhouse door.

BILLY: It depends on what the hell you're talkin' about. *(Now he looks at CARLYLE, and sees the feet touching.)*

CARLYLE: I seen cats back on the block, they knew what was shakin'—

then they got into all this school jive and, man, every year they went, they come back they didn't know nothin'.

(BILLY *is staring at* RICHIE's *foot pressed and rubbing* CARLYLE's *foot.* RICHIE *sees* BILLY *looking.* BILLY *cannot believe what he is seeing. It fills him with fear. The silence goes on and on.*)

RICHIE: Billy, why don't you and Roger go for a walk?

BILLY: What? (*He bolts to his knees. He is frozen on his knees on the bed.*)

RICHIE: Roger asked you to go downtown, you went, you had fun.

ROGER: (*Having turned, he knows almost instantly what is going on.*) I asked you, too.

RICHIE: You asked me; you begged Billy. I said no. Billy said no. You took my ten dollars. You begged Billy. I'm asking you a favor now—go for a walk. Let Carlyle and me have some time. (*Silence*)

CARLYLE: (*He sits up, uneasy and wary.*) That how you work it?

ROGER: Work what?

CARLYLE: Whosever turn it be.

BILLY: No, no, that ain't the way we work it, because we don't work it.

CARLYLE: See? See? There it is—that goddamn education showin' through. All them years in school. Man, didn't we have a good time tonight? You rode in my car. I showed you a good cathouse, all that sweet black pussy. Ain't we friends? Richie likes me. How come you don't like me?

BILLY: 'Cause if you really are doin' what I think you're doin', you're a fuckin' animal!

(CARLYLE *leaps to his feet, hand snaking to his pocket to draw a weapon.*)

ROGER: Billy, no.

BILLY: NO, WHAT?!

ROGER: Relax, man; no need. (*He turns to* CARLYLE; *patiently, wearily, he speaks.*) Man, I tole you it ain't goin' on here. We both tole you it ain't goin' on here.

CARLYLE: Don't you jive me, nigger. You goin' for a walk like I'm askin', or not? I wanna get this clear.

ROGER: Man, we live here.

RICHIE: It's my house, too, Roger; I live here, too. (*He bounds to his feet, flinging the blanket that has been covering him so it flies and lands on the floor near* ROGER's *footlocker.*)

ROGER: Don't I know that? Did I say somethin' to make you think I didn't know that?

(Standing, RICHIE *is removing his trousers and throwing them down on his footlocker.)*

RICHIE: Carlyle is my guest.

(Sitting down on my side of his bed and facing out, he puts his arms around CARLYLE's *thigh.* ROGER *jumps to his feet and grabs the blanket from the foot of his bed. Shaking it open, he drops onto the bed, his head at the foot of the bed and facing off as he covers himself.)*

ROGER: Fine. He your friend. This your home. So that mean he can stay. It don't mean I gotta leave. I'll catch you all in the mornin'.

BILLY: Roger, what the hell are you doin'?

ROGER: What you better do, Billy. It's gettin' late. I'm goin' to sleep.

BILLY: What?

ROGER: Go to fucking bed, Billy. Get up in the rack, turn your back and look at the wall.

BILLY: You gotta be kiddin'.

ROGER: DO IT!

BILLY: Man . . . !

ROGER: Yeah . . . !

BILLY: You mean just . . .

ROGER: It been goin' on a long damn time, man. You ain't gonna put no stop to it.

CARLYLE: You . . . ain't . . . serious.

RICHIE: *(Both he and* CARLYLE *are staring at* ROGER *and then* BILLY, *who is staring at* ROGER.*)* Well, I don't believe it. Of all the childish . . . infantile . . .

CARLYLE: Hey! *(Silence)* HEY! Even I got to say this is a little weird, but if this the way you do it . . . *(And he turns toward* RICHIE *below him.)* . . . it the way I do it. I don't know.

RICHIE: With them right there? Are you kidding? My God, Carlyle, that'd be obscene. *(Pulling slightly away from* CARLYLE.*)*

CARLYLE: Ohhh, man . . . they backs turned.

RICHIE: No.

CARLYLE: What I'm gonna do? *(Silence. He looks at them, all three of them.)* Don't you got no feelin' for how a man feel? I don't understand you two boys. Unless'n you a pair of motherfuckers. That what you are, you a pair of motherfuckers? You slits, man. DON'T YOU HEAR ME!? I DON'T UNDERSTAND THIS SITUATION HERE. I THOUGHT WE MADE A DEAL!

(RICHIE rises, starts to pull on his trousers. CARLYLE grabs him.)

CARLYLE: YOU GET ON YOUR KNEES, YOU PUNK, I MEAN NOW, AND YOU GONNA BE ON MY JOINT FAST OR YOU GONNA BE ONE BUSTED PUNK. AM I UNDERSTOOD? *(He hurls RICHIE down to the floor.)*

BILLY: I ain't gonna have this going on here; Roger, I can't.

ROGER: I been turnin' my back on one thing or another all my life.

RICHIE: Jealous, Billy?

BILLY: *(Getting to his feet.)* Just go out that door, the two of you. Go. Go on out in the bushes or out in some field. See if I follow you. See if I care. I'll be right here and I'll be sleepin', but it ain't gonna be done in my house. I don't have much in this goddamn Army, but *here* is mine. *(He stands beside his bed.)*

CARLYLE: I WANT MY FUCKIN' NUT! HOW COME YOU SO UPTIGHT? HE WANTS ME! THIS BOY HERE WANTS ME! WHO YOU TO STOP IT?

ROGER: *(Spinning to face CARLYLE and RICHIE.)* That's right, Billy. Richie one a those people want to get fucked by niggers, man. It what he know was gonna happen all his life—can be his dream come true. Ain't that right, Richie!

(Jumping to his feet, RICHIE starts putting on his trousers.)

ROGER: Want to make it real in the world, how a nigger is an animal. Give 'em an inch, gonna take a mile. Ain't you some kinda fool, Richie? Hear me, Carlyle.

CARLYLE: Man, don't make me no nevermind what he think he's provin' an' shit, long as I get my nut. I KNOW I ain't no animal, don't have to prove it.

RICHIE: *(Pulling CARLYLE's arm, wanting to move him toward the door.)* Let's go. Let's go outside. The hell with it.

(But CARLYLE tears himself free; he squats furiously down on the bunk, his hands seizing it, his back to all of them.)

CARLYLE: Bull shit. Bullshit! I ain't goin' no-fuckin'-where—this jive ass ain't runnin' me. Is this you house or not? *(He doesn't know what is going on; he can hardly look at any of them.)*

ROGER: *(Bounding out of bed, hurling his pillow across the room.)* I'm goin' to the fuckin' john, Billy. Hang it up, man; let 'em be.

BILLY: No.

ROGER: I'm smarter than you—do like I'm sayin'.

BILLY: It ain't right.

ROGER: Who gives a big rat's ass!

CARLYLE: Right on, bro! That boy know; he do. *(He circles the bed toward them.)* Hear him. Look into his eyes.

BILLY: This fuckin' Army takin' everything else away from me, they ain't takin' more than they got. I see what I see—I don't run, don't hide.

ROGER: *(Turning away from* BILLY, *he stomps out the door, slamming it.)* You fuckin' well better learn.

CARLYLE: That right. Time for more schoolin'. Lesson number one. *(Stealthily he steps and snaps out the only light, the lamp clamped to* RICHIE's *bed.)* You don't see what you see so well in the dark. It dark in the night. Black man got a black body—he disappear.

(The darkness is so total they are all no more than shadows.)

RICHIE: Not to the hands; not to the fingers. *(Moving from across the room toward* CARLYLE.*)*

CARLYLE: You do like you talk, boy, you gonna make me happy.

(BILLY, nervously clutching his sneaker, is moving backward.)

BILLY: Who says the lights go out? Nobody goddamn asked me if the lights go out.

(BILLY, lunging to the wall switch, throws it. The overhead lights flash on, flooding the room with light. CARLYLE *is seated on the edge of* RICHIE's *bed,* RICHIE *kneeling before him.)*

CARLYLE: I DO, MOTHERFUCKER, I SAY! *(The switchblade seems to leap from his pocket to his hand.)* I SAY! CAN'T YOU LET PEOPLE BE?

(BILLY hurls his sneaker at the floor at CARLYLE's *feet. Instantly* CARLYLE *is across the room, blocking* BILLY's *escape out the door.)*

CARLYLE: Goddamn you, boy! I'm gonna cut your ass, just to show you how it feel—cuttin' can happen. This knife true.

RICHIE: Carlyle, now c'mon.

CARLYLE: Shut up, pussy.

RICHIE: Don't hurt him, for chrissake.

CARLYLE: Goddamn man throw a shoe at me, he don't walk around clean in the world thinkin' he can throw another. He get some shit come back at him.

(BILLY doesn't know which way to go, and then CARLYLE, *jabbing the knife at the air before* BILLY's *chest, has* BILLY *running backward, his eyes fixed on the moving blade. He stumbles, having run into* RICHIE's *bed. He sprawls backward and* CARLYLE *is over him.)*

CARLYLE: No, no; no, no. Put you hand out there. Put it out.

(Slight pause; BILLY *is terrified.)*

CARLYLE: DO THE THING I'M TELLIN'!

(BILLY lets his hand rise in the air and CARLYLE grabs it, holds it.)

CARLYLE: That's it. That's good. See? See?

(The knife flashes across BILLY's palm; the blood flows. BILLY winces, recoils, but CARLYLE's hand still clenches and holds.)

BILLY: Motherfucker.

(Again the knife darts, cutting, and BILLY yelps. RICHIE, on his knees beside them, turns away.)

RICHIE: Oh, my God, what are you—

CARLYLE: *(In his own sudden distress, CARLYLE flings the hand away.)* That you blood. The blood inside you, you don't ever see it there. Take a look how easy it come out—and enough of it come out, you in the middle of the worst goddamn trouble you ever gonna see. And know I'm the man can deal that kinda trouble, easy as I smile. And I smile...easy. Yeah.

(BILLY is curled in upon himself, holding the hand to his stomach as RICHIE now reaches tentatively and shyly out as if to console BILLY, who repulses the gesture. CARLYLE is angry and strangely depressed. Forlornly he slumps onto BILLY's footlocker as BILLY staggers up to his wall locker and takes out a towel.)

CARLYLE: Bastard ruin my mood, Richie. He ruin my mood. Fightin' and lovin' real different in the feelin's I got. I see blood come outa somebody like that, it don't make me feel good—hurt me—hurt on somebody I though was my friend. But I ain't supposed to see. One dumb nigger. No mind, he thinks, no heart, no feelings a gentleness. You see how that ain't true, Richie. Goddamn man threw a shoe at me. A lotta people woulda cut his heart out. I gotta make him know he throw shit, he get shit. But I don't hurt him bad, you see what I mean?

(BILLY's back is to them, as he stands hunched at his locker, and suddenly his voice, hissing, erupts.)

BILLY: Jesus...H...Christ...! Do you know what I'm doin'? Do you know what I'm standin' here doin'?

(He whirls now; he holds a straight razor in his hand. A bloody towel is wrapped around the hurt hand. CARLYLE tenses, rises, seeing the razor.)

BILLY: I'm a twenty-four-year-old goddamn college graduate—intellectual goddamn scholar type—and I got a razor in my hand. I'm thinkin' about comin' up behind one black human being and I'm thinkin' nigger this and nigger that—I wanna cut his throat. THAT IS RIDICULOUS. I NEVER FACED ANYBODY IN MY LIFE WITH ANYTHING TO KILL THEM. YOU UNDERSTAND ME? I DON'T HAVE A GODDAMN THING ON THE LINE HERE!

(The door opens and ROGER rushes in, having heard the yelling. BILLY flings the razor into his locker.)

BILLY: Look at me, Roger, look at me. I got a cut palm—I don't know what happened. Jesus Christ, I got sweat all over me when I think a what I was near to doin'. I swear it. I mean, do I think I need a reputation as a killer, a bad man with a knife?

(He is wild with the energy of feeling free and with the anger at what these others almost made him do. CARLYLE slumps down on the footlocker; he sits there.)

BILLY: Bullshit! I need shit! I got sweat all over me. I got the mile record in my hometown. I did four forty-two in high school and that's the goddamn record in Windsor County. I don't need approval from either one of the pair of you. *(He rushes at RICHIE.)* You wanna be a goddamn swish—a goddamn faggot-queer—GO! Suckin' cocks and takin' it in the ass, the thing of which you dream—GO! AND YOU— *(Whirling on CARLYLE.)* You wanna be a bad-assed animal, man, get it on—go—but I wash my hands. I am not human as you are. I put you down, I put you down— *(He almost hurls himself at RICHIE.)* —you gay little piece a shit cake—SHIT CAKE. AND YOU—

(Hurt, confused, RICHIE turns away, nearly pressing his face into the bed beside which he kneels, as BILLY has spun back to tower over the pulsing, weary CARLYLE.)

BILLY: —you are your own goddamn fault, SAMBO! SAMBO!

(The knife flashes up in CARLYLE's hand into BILLY's stomach, and BILLY yelps.)

BILLY: Ahhhhhhhhh. *(He pushes at the hand. RICHIE is still turned away.)*

RICHIE: Well, fuck you, Billy.

BILLY: *(He backs off the knife.)* Get away, get away.

RICHIE: *(As ROGER, who could not see because BILLY's back is to him, is approaching CARLYLE and BILLY goes walking up toward the lockers as if he knows where he is going, as if he is going to go out the door to a movie, his hands holding his belly.)* You're so-o messed up.

ROGER: *(To CARLYLE)* Man, what's the matter with you?

CARLYLE: Don't nobody talk that weird shit to me, you understand?

ROGER: You jive, man. That's all you do—jive!

(BILLY, striding swiftly, walks flat into the wall lockers; he bounces, turns. They are all looking at him.)

RICHIE: Billy! Oh, Billy!

(ROGER looks at RICHIE.)

BILLY: Ahhhhhhhh. Ahhhhhhhh.

(ROGER looks at CARLYLE as if he is about to scream, and beyond him, BILLY turns from the lockers, starts to walk again, now staggering and moving toward them.)

RICHIE: I think...he stabbed him. I think Carlyle stabbed Billy. Roger!

(ROGER *whirls to go to* BILLY, *who is staggering downstage and angled away, hands clenched over his belly.*)

BILLY: Shut up! It's just a cut, it's just a cut. He cut my hand, he cut gut. *(He collapses onto his knees just beyond* ROGER's *footlocker.)* It took the wind out of me, scared me, that's all. *(Fiercely he tries to hide the wound and remain calm.)*

ROGER: Man, are you all right?

(He moves to BILLY, *who turns to hide the wound. Till now no one is sure what happened.* RICHIE *only "thinks"* BILLY *has been stabbed.* BILLY *is pretending he isn't hurt. As* BILLY *turns from* ROGER, *he turns toward* RICHIE *and* RICHIE *sees the blood.* RICHIE *yelps and they all begin talking and yelling simultaneously.)*

CARLYLE: You know what I was learnin', he was learnin' to talk all that weird shit, cuttin', baby, cuttin', the ways and means a shit, man, razors.

ROGER: You all right? Or what? He slit you?

BILLY: Just took the wind outa me, scared me.

RICHIE: Carlyle, you stabbed him; you stabbed him.

CARLYLE: Ohhhh, pussy, pussy, pussy, Carlyle know what he do.

ROGER: *(Trying to lift* BILLY.*)* Get up, okay? Get up on the bed.

BILLY: *(Irritated, pulling free.)* I am on the bed.

ROGER: What?

RICHIE: No, Billy, no, you're not.

BILLY: Shut up!

RICHIE: You're on the floor.

BILLY: I'm on the bed. I'm on the bed. *(Emphatically. And then he looks at the floor.)* What?

ROGER: Let me see what he did.

(BILLY's hands are clenched on the wound.)

ROGER: Billy, let me see where he got you.

BILLY: *(Recoiling)* NO-O-O-O-O-O, you nigger!

ROGER: *(He leaps at* CARLYLE.*)* What did you do?

CARLYLE: *(Hunching his shoulders, ducking his head.)* Shut up.

ROGER: What did you do, nigger—you slit him or stick him? *(He then tries to get back to* BILLY.*)* Billy, let me see.

BILLY: *(Doubling over till his head hits the floor.)* NO-O-O-O-O-O! Shit, shit, shit.

RICHIE: *(Suddenly sobbing and yelling.)* Oh, my God, my God, ohhhh, ohhhh, ohhhh. *(Bouncing on his knees on the bed.)*

CARLYLE: FUCK IT, FUCK IT, I STUCK HIM. I TURNED IT. This mother Army break my heart. I can't be out there where it pretty, don't wanna live! Wash me clean, shit face!

RICHIE: Ohhhh, ohhhhh, ohhhhhhhhhhhh. Carlyle stabbed Billy, oh, ohhhh, I never saw such a thing in my life. Ohhhhhh.

(As ROGER *is trying gently, fearfully, to straighten* BILLY *up.)*

RICHIE: Don't die, Billy; don't die.

ROGER: Shut up and go find somebody to help. Richie, go!

RICHIE: Who? I'll go, I'll go. *(Scrambling off the bed.)*

ROGER: I don't know. JESUS CHRIST! DO IT!

RICHIE: Okay. Okay. Billy, don't die. Don't die. *(Backing for the door, he turns and runs.)*

ROGER: The sarge, or C.Q.

BILLY: *(Suddenly doubling over, vomiting blood.* RICHIE *is gone.)* Ohhhhhhhhhh. Blood. Blood.

ROGER: Be still, be still.

BILLY: *(Pulling at a blanket on the floor beside him.)* I want to stand up. I'm——vomiting—— *(Making no move to stand, only to cover himself.)* ——blood. What does that mean?

ROGER: *(Slowly standing.)* I don't know.

BILLY: Yes, yes, I want to stand up. Give me blanket, blanket. *(He rolls back and forth, fighting to get the blanket over him.)*

ROGER: RIICCHHHHIIIEEEE!

(As BILLY *is furiously grappling with the blanket.)*

ROGER: No, no. *(He looks at* CARLYLE, *who is slumped over, muttering to himself.* ROGER *runs for the door.)* Wait on, be tight, be cool.

BILLY: Cover me. Cover me.

(At last he gets the blanket over his face. The dark makes him grow still. He lies there beneath his blanket. Silence. No one moves. And then CARLYLE *senses the quiet; he turns, looks. Slowly, wearily, he rises and walks to where* BILLY *lies. He stand over him, the knife hanging loosely from his left hand as he reaches with his right to gently take the blanket and lift it slowly from* BILLY's *face. They look at each other.* BILLY *reaches up and pats* CARLYLE's *hand holding the blanket.)*

BILLY: I don't want to talk to you right now, Carlyle. All right? Where's Roger? Do you know where he is? *(Slight pause)* Don't stab me anymore, Carlyle, okay? I was dead wrong doin' what I did. I know that now. Carlyle, promise me you won't stab me anymore. I couldn't take it. Okay? I'm cold ... my blood ... is ... *(From off comes a voice.)*

ROONEY: Cokesy? Cokesy wokesy? *(He staggers into the doorway, very drunk, a beer bottle in his hand.)* Ollie-ollie oxen-freeee.

(He looks at them. CARLYLE *quickly, secretly, slips the knife into his pocket.)*

ROONEY: How you all doin'? Everybody drunk, huh? I los' my friend. *(He is staggering sideways toward* BILLY's *bunk, where he finally drops down, sitting.)* Who are you, soldier?

*(*CARLYLE *has straightened, his head ducked down as he is edging for the door.)*

ROONEY: Who are you, soldier?

*(*RICHIE, *running, comes roaring into the room. He looks at* ROONEY *and cannot understand what is going on.* CARLYLE *is standing.* ROONEY *is just sitting there. What is going on?* RICHIE *moves along the lockers, trying to get behind* ROONEY, *his eyes never off* CARLYLE.*)*

RICHIE: Ohhhhhh, Sergeant Rooney, I've been looking for you everywhere—where have you been? Carlyle stabbed Billy, he stabbed him.

ROONEY: *(Sitting there)* What?

RICHIE: Carlyle stabbed Billy.

ROONEY: Who's Carlyle?

RICHIE: He's Carlyle.

(As CARLYLE *seems about to advance, the knife again showing in his hand.)*

RICHIE: Carlyle, don't hurt anybody more!

ROONEY: *(On his feet, he is staggering toward the door.)* You got a knife there? What's with the knife? What's goin' on here?

*(*CARLYLE *steps as if to bolt for the door, but* ROONEY *is in the way, having inserted himself between* CARLYLE *and* RICHIE, *who has backed into the doorway.)*

ROONEY: Wait! Now wait!

RICHIE: *(As* CARLYLE *raises the knife.)* Carlyle, don't! *(He runs from the room.)*

ROONEY: You watch your step, you understand. You see what I got here? *(He lifts the beer bottle, waves it threateningly.)* You watch your step, motherfucker. Relax. I mean, we can straighten all this out. We— *(*CARLYLE *lunges at* ROONEY, *who tenses.)* I'm just askin' what's goin' on, that's all I'm doin'. No need to get all— *(*CARLYLE *swipes at the air again;* ROONEY *recoils.)* Motherfucker. Motherfucker. *(He seems to be tensing, his body gathering itself for some mighty effort. And he throws his head back and gives the eagle yell.)* Eeeeeeeeeeeeeaaaaaaaaaaaaaaaahhhhhh! Eeeeaaaaaaaaaaaaaahhhhhhhhhhhhhh!

*(*CARLYLE *jumps; he looks left and right.)*

ROONEY: Goddammit, I'll cut you good. *(He lunges to break the bottle on the edge of the wall lockers. The bottle shatters and he yelps, dropping everything.)* Ohhhhhhhh! Ohhhhhhhhhhhhhhhhhh!

(CARLYLE bolts, running from the room.)

ROONEY: I hurt myself, I cut myself. I hurt my hand. *(Holding the wounded hand, he scurries to BILLY's bed, where he sits on the edge, trying to wipe the blood away so he can see the wound.)* I cut—

(Hearing a noise, he whirls, looks; CARLYLE is plummeting in the door and toward him. ROONEY stands.)

ROONEY: I hurt my hand, goddammit! *(The knife goes into ROONEY's belly. He flails at CARLYLE.)* I HURT MY HAND! WHAT ARE YOU DOING? WHAT ARE YOU DOING? WAIT! WAIT! *(He turns away, falling to his knees, and the knife goes into him again and again.)* No fair. No fair!

(ROGER, running, skids into the room, headed for BILLY, and then he sees CARLYLE on ROONEY, the leaping knife. ROGER lunges, grabbing CARLYLE, pulling him to get him off ROONEY. CARLYLE leaps free of ROGER, sending ROGER flying backward. And then CARLYLE begins to circle ROGER's bed. He is whimpering, wiping at the blood on his shirt as if to wipe it away. ROGER backs away as CARLYLE keeps waving the knife at him. ROONEY is crawling along the floor under BILLY's bed and then stops crawling, lies there.)

CARLYLE: You don't tell nobody on me you saw me do this, I let you go, okay? Ohhhhhhhhh. *(Rubbing, rubbing at the shirt.)* Ohhhhhh, how'm I gonna get back to the world now, I got all this mess to—

ROGER: What happened? That you—I don't understand that you did this! That you did—

CARLYLE: YOU SHUT UP! Don't be talkin' all that weird shit to me— don't you go talkin' all that weird shit!

ROGER: Nooooooooooooo!

CARLYLE: I'm Carlyle, man. You know me. You know me.

(He turns, he flees out the door. ROGER, alone, looks about the room. BILLY is there. ROGER moves toward BILLY, who is shifting, undulating on his back.)

BILLY: Carlyle, no; oh, Christ, don't stab me anymore. I'll die. I will— I'll die. Don't make me die. I'll get my dog after you. I'LL GET MY DOG AFTER YOU!

(ROGER is saying, "Oh, Billy, man, Billy." He is trying to hold BILLY. Now he lifts BILLY into his arms.)

ROGER: Oh, Billy; oh, man. GODDAMMIT, BILLY!

(As a MILITARY POLICE LIEUTENANT comes running in the door, his .45 automatic drawn; he levels it at ROGER.)

LIEUTENANT: Freeze, soldier! Not a quick move out of you. Just real slow, straighten your ass up.

(ROGER has gone rigid; the LIEUTENANT is advancing on him. Tentatively ROGER turns, looks.)

ROGER: Huh? No.

LIEUTENANT: Get your ass against the lockers.

ROGER: Sir, no. I—

LIEUTENANT: *(Hurling ROGER away toward the wall lockers.)* MOVE!

(As another M.P., PFC HINSON, comes in, followed by RICHIE, flushed and breathless.)

LIEUTENANT: Hinson, cover this bastard.

HINSON: *(Drawing his .45 automatic, moving on ROGER.)* Yes, sir.

(The LIEUTENANT frisks ROGER, who is spread-eagled at the lockers.)

RICHIE: What? Oh, sir, no, no. Roger, what's going on?

LIEUTENANT: I'll straighten this shit out.

ROGER: Tell 'em to get the gun off me, Richie.

LIEUTENANT: SHUT UP!

RICHIE: But, sir, sir, he didn't do it. Not him.

LIEUTENANT: *(Fiercely he shoves RICHIE out of the way.)* I told you, all of you, to shut up. *(He moves to ROONEY's body.)* Jesus, God, this Sfc is cut to shit. He's cut to shit. *(He hurries to BILLY's body.)* This man is cut to shit.

(CARLYLE appears in the doorway, his hands cuffed behind him, a third M.P., PFC CLARK, shoving him forward. CARLYLE seems shocked and cunning, his mind whirring.)

CLARK: Sir, I got this guy on the street, runnin' like a streak a shit.

(He hurls the struggling CARLYLE forward and CARLYLE stumbles toward the head of RICHIE's bed as RICHIE, seeing him coming, hurries away along BILLY's bed and toward the wall lockers.)

RICHIE: He did it! Him, him!

CARLYLE: What is going on here? I don't know what is going on here!

CLARK: *(Club at the ready, he stations himself beside CARLYLE.)* He's got blood all over him, sir. All over him.

LIEUTENANT: What about the knife?

CLARK: No, sir, he must have thrown it away.

(As a fourth M.P. has entered to stand in the doorway, and HINSON, leaving ROGER, bends to examine ROONEY. He will also kneel and look for life in BILLY.)

LIEUTENANT: You throw it away, soldier?

CARLYLE: Oh, you thinkin' about how my sister got happened, too. Oh, you ain't so smart as you think you are! No way!

ROGER: Jesus God almighty.

LIEUTENANT: What happened here? I want to know what happened here.

HINSON: *(Rising from BILLY's body.)* They're both dead, sir. Both of them.

LIEUTENANT: *(Confidential, almost whispering.)* I know they're both dead. That's what I'm talkin' about.

CARLYLE: Chicken blood, sir. Chicken blood and chicken hearts is what all over me. I was goin' on my way, these people jump out the bushes be pourin' it all over me. Chicken blood and chicken hearts. *(Thrusting his hands out at CLARK.)* You goin' take these cuffs off me, boy?

LIEUTENANT: Sit him down, Clark. Sit him down and shut him up.

CARLYLE: This my house, sir. This my goddamn house. *(CLARK grabs him, begins to move him.)*

LIEUTENANT: I said to shut him up.

CLARK: Move it; move! *(Struggling to get CARLYLE over to ROGER's footlocker as HINSON and the other M.P. exit.)*

CARLYLE: I want these cuffs taken off my hands.

CLARK: You better do like you been told. You better sit and shut up!

CARLYLE: I'm gonna be thinkin' over here. I'm gonna be thinkin' it all over. I got plannin' to do. I'm gonna be thinkin' in my quietness; don't you be makin' no mistake.

(He slumps over, muttering to himself. HINSON and the other M.P. return, carrying a stretcher. They cross to BILLY, chatting with each other about how to go about the lift. They will lift him; they will carry him out.)

LIEUTENANT: *(To RICHIE)* You're Wilson?

RICHIE: No, sir. *(Indicating BILLY)* That's Wilson. I'm Douglas.

LIEUTENANT: *(To ROGER)* And you're Moore. And you sleep here.

ROGER: Yes, sir.

RICHIE: Yes, sir. And Billy slept here and Sergeant Rooney was our platoon sergeant and Carlyle was a transient, sir. He was a transient from P Company.

LIEUTENANT: *(Scrutinizing ROGER)* And you had nothing to do with this? *(To RICHIE)* He had nothing to do with this?

ROGER: No, sir, I didn't.

RICHIE: No, sir, he didn't. I didn't either. Carlyle went crazy and he got into a fight and it was awful. I didn't even know what it was about exactly.

Lieutenant: How'd the Sfc get involved?

Richie: Well, he came in, sir.

Roger: I had to run off to call you, sir. I wasn't here.

Richie: Sergeant Rooney just came in—I don't know why—he heard all the yelling, I guess—and Carlyle went after him. Billy was already stabbed.

Carlyle: *(Rising, his manner that of a man who is taking charge.)* All right now, you gotta be gettin' the fuck outa here. All of you. I have decided enough of the shit has been goin' on around here and I am tellin' you to be gettin' these motherfuckin' cuffs off me and you be gettin' me a bus ticket home. I am quittin' this jive-time Army.

Lieutenant: You are doin' what?

Carlyle: No, I ain't gonna be quiet. No way. I am quittin' this goddamn—

Lieutenant: You shut the hell up, soldier. I am ordering you.

Carlyle: I don't understand you people! Don't you people understand when a man be talkin' English at you to say his mind? I have quit the Army.

(Hinson returns.)

Lieutenant: Get him outa here!

Richie: What's the matter with him?

Lieutenant: Hinson! Clark!

(The move, grabbing Carlyle, and they drag him, struggling, toward the door.)

Carlyle: Oh, no. Oh, no. You ain't gonna be doin' me no more. I been tellin' you. To get away from me. I am stayin' here. This is my place, not your place. You take these cuffs off me like I been tellin' you! My poor little sister Lin Sue understood what was goin' on here! She tole me! She knew! *(He is howling in the hallway now.)* You better be gettin' these cuffs off me!

(Silence. Roger, Richie, and the Lieutenant are all staring at the door. The Lieutenant turns, crosses to the foot of Roger's bed.)

Lieutenant: All right now. I will be getting to the bottom of this. You know I will be getting to the bottom of this. *(He is taking two forms from his clipboard.)*

Richie: Yes, sir.

(Hinson and the fourth M.P. return with another stretcher. They walk to Rooney, talking to one another about how to lift him. They drag him from under the bed. They will roll him onto the stretcher, lift him and walk out. Roger moves, watching them, down along the edge of Billy's bed.)

LIEUTENANT: Fill out these forms. I want your serial number, rank, your MOS, the NCOIC of your work. Any leave coming up will be canceled. Tomorrow at 0800 you will report to my office at the provost marshal's headquarters. You know where that is?

ROGER: *(As the two M.P.'s are leaving with the stretcher and* ROONEY's *body.)* Yes, sir.

RICHIE: Yes, sir.

LIEUTENANT: *(Crossing to* ROGER, *he hands him two cards.)* Be prepared to do some talking. Two perfectly trained and primed strong pieces of U.S. Army property got cut to shit up here. We are going to find out how and why. Is that clear?

RICHIE: Yes, sir.

ROGER: Yes, sir.

(The LIEUTENANT *looks at each of them. He surveys the room. He marches out.)*

RICHIE: Oh, my God. Oh. Oh.

(He runs to his bed and collapses, sitting hunched down at the foot. He holds himself and rocks as if very cold.)

*(*ROGER, *quietly, is weeping. He stands and then walks to his bed. He puts down the two cards. He moves purposefully up to the mops hanging on the wall in the corner. He takes one down. He moves with the mop and the bucket to* BILLY's *bed, where* ROONEY's *blood stains the floor. He mops.* RICHIE, *in horror, is watching.)*

RICHIE: What . . . are you doing?

ROGER: This area a mess, man. *(Dragging the bucket, carrying the mop, he moves to the spot where* BILLY *had lain. He begins to mop.)*

RICHIE: That's Billy's blood, Roger. His blood.

ROGER: Is it?

RICHIE: I feel awful.

ROGER: *(He keeps mopping.)* How come you made me waste all that time talkin' shit to you, Richie? All my time talkin' shit, and all the time you was a faggot, man; you really was. You shoulda jus' tole ole Roger. He don't care. All you gotta do is tell me.

RICHIE: I've been telling you. I did.

ROGER: Jive, man, jive!

RICHIE: No!

ROGER: You did bullshit all over us! ALL OVER US!

RICHIE: I just wanted to hold his hand, Billy's hand, to talk to him, go to the movies hand in hand like he would with a girl or I would with someone back home.

ROGER: But he didn't wanna; he didn't wanna.

(Finished now, ROGER drags the mop and bucket back toward the corner. RICHIE is sobbing; he is at the edge of hysteria.)

RICHIE: He did.

ROGER: No, man.

RICHIE: He did. He did. It's not my fault.

(ROGER slams the bucket into the corner and rams the mop into the bucket. Furious, he marches down to RICHIE. Behind him SERGEANT COKES, grinning and lifting a wine bottle, appears in the doorway.)

COKES: Hey!

(RICHIE, in despair, rolls onto his belly. COKES is very, very happy.)

COKES: Hey! What a day, gen'l'men. How you all doin'?

ROGER: *(Crossing up near the head of his own bed.)* Hello, Sergeant Cokes.

COKES: *(Affectionate and casual, he moves near to ROGER.)* How you all doin'? Where's ole Rooney? I lost him.

ROGER: What?

COKES: We had a hell of a day, ole Rooney and me, lemme tell you. We been playin' hide-and-go-seek, and I was hidin', and now I think maybe he started hidin' without tellin' me he was gonna and I can't find him and I thought maybe he was hidin' up here.

RICHIE: Sergeant, he—

ROGER: No. No, we ain't seen him.

COKES: I gotta find him. He knows how to react in a tough situation. He didn't come up here looking for me?

(ROGER moves around to the far side of his bed, turning his back to COKES. Sitting, ROGER takes out a cigarette, but he does not light it.)

ROGER: We was goin' to sleep, Sarge. Got to get up early. You know the way this mother Army is.

COKES: *(Nodding, drifting backward, he sits down on BILLY's bed.)* You don't mind I sit here a little. Wait on him. Got a little wine. You can have some. *(Tilting his head way back, he takes a big drink and then, looking straight ahead, corks the bottle with a whack of his hand.)* We got back into the area—we had been downtown—he wanted to play hide-and-go-seek. I tole him okay, I was ready for that. He hid his eyes. So I run and hid in the bushes and then under this Jeep. 'Cause I thought it was better. I hid and I hid and I hid. He never did come. So finally, I got tired—I figured I'd give up, come lookin' for him. I was way over by the movie theater. I don't know how I got there. Anyway, I got back here and I figured maybe he come up here lookin' for me, figurin' I was hidin' up with you guys. You ain't seen him, huh?

ROGER: No, we ain't seen him. I tole you that, Sarge.

COKES: Oh.

RICHIE: Roger!

ROGER: He's drunk, Richie! He's blasted drunk, Got a brain turned to mush!

COKES: *(In deep agreement)* That ain't no lie.

ROGER: Let it be for the night, Richie. Let him be for the night.

COKES: I still know what's goin' on, though. Never no worry about that. I always know. Don't matter what I drink or how much I drink. I always still know what's goin' on. But . . . I'll be goin' maybe and look for Rooney. *(But rising, he wanders down center.)* But . . . I mean, we could be doin' that forever. Him and me. Me under the Jeep. He wants to find me, he goes to the Jeep. I'm over here. He comes here. I'm gone. You know, maybe I'll just wait a little while more I'm here. He'll find me then if he comes here. You guys want another drink. *(Turning, he goes to* BILLY's *footlocker, where he sits and takes another enormous guzzle of wine.)* Jesus, what a goddamn day we had. Me and Rooney started drivin' and we was comin' to this intersection and out comes this goddamn Chevy. I try to get around her, but no dice. BINGO! I hit her in the left rear. She was furious. I didn't care. I gave her my name and number. My car had a headlight out, the fender bashed in. Rooney wouldn't stop laughin'. I didn't know what to do. So we went to D.C. to this private club I know. Had ten or more snorts and decided to get back here after playin' some snooker. That was fun. On the way, we picked up this kid from the engineering unit, hitchhiking, I'm starting to feel real clear-headed now. So I'm comin' around this corner and all of a sudden there's this car stopped dead in front of me. He's not blinkin' to turn or anything. I slam on the brakes, but it's like puddin' the way I slide into him. There's a big noise and we yell. Rooney starts laughin' like crazy and the kid jumps outa the back and says he's gonna take a fuckin' bus. The guy from the other car is swearin' at me. My car's still workin' fine, so I move it off to the side and tell him to do the same, while we wait for the cops. He says he wants his car right where it is and he had the right of way 'cause he was makin' a legal turn. So we're waitin' for the cops. Some cars go by. The guy's car is this big fuckin' Buick. Around the corner comes this little red Triumph. The driver's this blond kid got this blond girl next to him. You can see what's gonna happen. There's this fuckin' car sittin' there, nobody in it. So the Triumph goes crashin' onto the back of the Buick with nobody in it. BIFF-BANG-BOOM. And everything stops. We're staring. It's all still. And then that fuckin' Buick kinda shudders and starts to move. With nobody in it. It starts to roll from the impact. And it rolls just far enough to get where the road starts a downgrade. It's driftin' to the right. It's driftin' to the shoulder and over it and onto this hill, where it's pickin' up speed 'cause the hill is steep and then it disappears over the side, and into the dark, just rollin' real quiet. Rooney falls over, he's laughin' so hard. I don't know what to do. In a minute the cops come and in another minute some guy comes runnin' up over the hill to tell us some other guy had got run over by this car with nobody in it. We didn't know what to think. This was fuckin' unbelieveable to us. But we found out later from the cops that this wasn't true and some guy had got hit over the head with a bottle in a bar and when he staggered out the door it was just at the instant that this fuckin' Buick with nobody in it went by. Seein' this, the guy stops cold and turns around and just goes back into the bar. Rooney is screamin' at me how we been in four goddamn accidents and fights and how we have got out clean. So then we got everything all straightened out and we come back here to play hide-and-seek 'cause that's what ole Rooney wanted. *(He is taking another drink, but finding the bottle empty.)* Only now I can't find him. *(Near RICHIE's footlocker stands a beer bottle and COKES begins to move toward it. Slowly he bends and grasps the bottle; he straightens, looking at it. He drinks. And settles down on RICHIE's footlocker.)* I'll just sit a little.

(RICHIE, lying on his belly, shudders. The sobs burst out of him. He is shaking. COKES, blinking, turns to study RICHIE.)

COKES: What's up? Hey, what're you cryin' about, soldier? Hey?

(RICHIE cannot help himself.)

COKES: What's he cryin' about?

ROGER: *(Disgustedly, he sits there.)* He's cryin' 'cause he's a queer.

COKES: Oh. You a queer, boy?

RICHIE: Yes, Sergeant.

COKES: Oh. *(Pause)* How long you been a queer?

ROGER: All his fuckin' life.

RICHIE: I don't know.

COKES: *(Turning to scold ROGER.)* Don't be yellin' mean at him. Boy, I tell you it's a real strange thing the way havin' leukemia gives you a lotta funny thoughts about things. Two months ago—or maybe even yesterday—I'da called a boy who was a queer a lotta awful names. But now I just wanna be figurin' things out. I mean, you ain't kiddin' me out about ole Rooney, are you, boys, 'cause of how I'm a sergeant and you're enlisted men, so you got some idea a vengeance on me? You ain't doin' that, are you, boys?

ROGER: No.

RICHIE: Ohhhh. Jesus. Ohhhh. I don't know what's hurtin' in me.

COKES: No, no, boy. You listen to me. You gonna be okay. There's a lotta worse things in this world than bein' a queer. I seen a lot of 'em, too. I mean, you could have leukemia. That's worse. That can kill you. I mean, it's okay. You listen to the ole sarge. I mean, maybe I was a queer, I wouldn't have leukemia. Who's to say? Lived a whole different life. Who's to say? I keep thinkin' there was maybe somethin' I coulda done different. Maybe not drunk so much. Or if I'd killed more gooks, or more Krauts or more dinks. I was kind-hearted sometimes. Or if I'd had a wife and I had some kids. Never had any. But my mother did and she died of it anyway. Gives you a whole funny different way a lookin' at things, I'll tell you. Ohhhhh, Rooney, Rooney.

(Slight pause.)

COKES: Or if I'd let that little gook outa that spider hole he was in, I was sittin' on it. I'd let him out now, he was in there. *(He rattles the footlocker lid under him.)* Oh, how'm I ever gonna forget it? That funny little guy. I'm runnin' along, he pops up outa that hole. I'm never gonna forget him—how'm I ever gonna forget him? I see him and dive, god-damn bullet hits me in the side, I'm midair, everything's turnin' around. I go over the edge of this ditch and I'm crawlin' real fast. I lost my rifle. Can't find it. Then I come up behind him. He's half out of the hole. I bang him on top of his head, stuff him back into the hole with a grenade for company. Then I'm sittin' on the lid and it's made outa steel. I can feel him in there, though, bangin' and yellin' under me, and his yelling I can hear is begging for me to let him out. It was like a goddamn Charlie Chaplin movie, everybody fallin' down and clumsy, and him in there yellin' and bangin' away, and I'm just sittin' there lookin' around. And he was Charlie Chaplin. I don't know who I was. And then he blew up. *(Pause)* Maybe I'll just get a little shut-eye sittin' right here while I'm waitin' for ole Rooney. We figure it out. All of it. You don't mind I just doze a little here, you boys?

ROGER: No.

RICHIE: No.

(ROGER rises and walks to the door. He switches off the light and gently closes the door. The transom glows. COKES sits in a flower of light. ROGER crosses back to his bunk and settles in, sitting.)

COKES: 'Night, boys.

RICHIE: 'Night, Sergeant.

(COKES sits there, fingers entwined, trying to sleep.)

COKES: I mean, he was like Charlie Chaplin. And then he blew up.

ROGER: *(Suddenly feeling very sad for this old man.)* Sergeant ... maybe you was Charlie Chaplin, too.

COKES: No. No. *(Pause)* No. I don't know who I was. 'Night.

ROGER: You think he was singin' it?

COKES: What?

ROGER: You think he was singin' it?

COKES: Oh yeah. Oh, yeah; he was singin' it.

(Slight pause. COKES, sitting on the footlocker, begins to sing a makeshift language imitating Korean, to the tune of "Beautiful Streamer." He begins with an angry, mocking energy that slowly becomes a dream, a lullaby, a farewell, a lament.)

COKES:
> Yo no som lo no
> Ung toe lo knee
> Ra so me la lo
> La see see oh doe.
> Doe no tee ta ta
> Too low see see
> Ra mae me lo lo
> Ah boo boo boo eee.
> Boo boo eee booo eeee
> La so lee lem
> Lem lo lee da ung
> Uhhh so ba booooo ohhh.
> Boo booo ee ung ba
> Eee eee la looo
> Lem lo lala la
> Eeee oohhh ohhh ohhh ohhhhh.

(In the silence, he makes the soft, whispering sound of a child imitating an explosion, and his entwined fingers come apart. The dark figures of RICHIE and ROGER are near. The lingering light fades.)

Dennis J. Reardon

The Leaf People

DENNIS J. REARDON is the author of half-a-dozen produced plays, a couple librettos for experimental musical pieces, and several screenplays and teleplays. Joseph Papp has produced three of Mr. Reardon's plays: *The Happiness Cage*, *Siamese Connections*, and *The Leaf People*. *The Happiness Cage* was released as a film starring Christopher Walken and Ronny Cox. Mr. Reardon's work has been performed both abroad and in regional and university theaters across America. He has served as Playwright-in-Residence at the University of Michigan, where he wrote and premiered *Siamese Connections*, and at Hartwick College in Oneonta, New York, where he taught playwriting and co-directed the premiere of his one-act, *The Incredible Standing Man and His Friends*.

Mr. Reardon is the recipient of numerous prizes and awards, the most recent of which include a two-year National Endowment for the Arts Playwright Fellowship (1986–87), the National Play Award (1985–86), and the Weissberger Foundation Award (1985), both for his full-length drama *Steeple Jack*; and a CAPS (Creative Artists Public Service) Award in 1984 for his evening of paired one-acts, *Unauthorized Entries*. He is presently affiliated with the State University of New York at Albany (SUNY Albany) where he is "pleased to be working alongside novelists William Kennedy and Toni Morrison." Mr. Reardon is the divorced father of a young daughter, Siobhan.

For stock and amateur production rights, contact: Broadway Play Publishing, Inc., 357 West 20th Street, New York, NY 10011. For all other rights, contact: Susan Schulman Agency, 454 West 44th Street, New York, N.Y. 10036

Original Production Notes

The Leaf People began previews at Broadway's Booth Theatre on September 3, 1975; it officially opened on October 20 and ran through October 26. The cast of that production included:

The Fishbellies

SHAUGHNESSY (SHAW), a compassionate man	Tom Aldredge
P. SIGMUND FURTH, a guide and adventurer	Lane Smith
MEATBALL, FURTH's apprentice	Ernesto Gonzalez
STEVEN, a musician	Ted LePlat
ANNA AMES, a missionary/pilot	Margaret Hall
1ST INTERPRETER	Grayson Hall
2ND INTERPRETER	Anthony Holland

The Leaf People

SUTREESHAY, a girl about 8 years old	Geanine-Michele Capozzoli
GITAUCHO, the Leader	Raymond J. Barry
THE SOUND, speaks for the Leader	Leon Morenzie
LEEBOH, a warrior	William Parry
MAYTEEMO, a warrior	James Sbano
MONKEY MAN, a shaman	Ernesto Gonzalez
KEERAH, GITAUCHO's sister	Denise Delapenha
YAWAHLAPEETEE, GITAUCHO's mother	Joanna Featherstone
KREETAHSHAY, THE SOUND's mother	Susan Batson
SHAY TAHNDOR, a cheerful pariah	Roy Brocksmith

The rest of the Tribe

JEESHOOM, a boy about 8 years old	Francisco Blackfeather
KAHLEEMSHOHT, a warrior	Ron Capozzoli
CHOOLKAHNOOR, a warrior	Jeffrey David-Owen
LAHBAYNEEZH, a warrior	Jelom Vieira
TREEKAH, a warrior	Josevaldo Machado
ZHAHBAHROOSH, a warrior	Ric Lavin
LOHZHOODISH, a squaw	Soni Moreno
LOHMOHEETET, a squaw	Jeannette Ertelt
MUSICIANS	Efstratios Vavagiakis, Ruben Rivera, Joel Kaye, Donald Hettinger, Michael Lamont

The production was directed by Tom O'Horgan and produced by Joseph Papp. Settings, John Conklin. Lighting, John McClain. Costumes and Makeup, Randy Barcelo.

The action takes place in the Amazon rain forest. The time is now. There is one intermission.

"In our modest opinion, the true defense of the Indian is to respect him and to guarantee his existence according to his own values."
Orlando and Claudio Villas Boas

"A White Man sneezes, and an Indian village dies."
Traditional Brazilian saying

This play is respectfully dedicated to the brothers Villas Boas.

Act One

(A portable tape recorder is visible on-stage as audience files in. Twenty-one minutes before the action begins, cue the overture. Six pieces of music are heard in succession: "Miles From Nowhere," Cat Stevens; "When I Paint My Masterpiece," Bob Dylan; "It's Only Rock N Roll," Rolling Stones; "A la mina no voy," traditional Colombian tune; "I Am A Pilgrim," traditional, recorded by Nitty Gritty Dirt Band; and concluding with Efrain Orozco's "Enigma," an Ecuadorian instrumental.)

(House to half at end of "I Am A Pilgrim." Dim to blackout two and a half minutes into "Enigma"; the last minute plays in Black. Strike the tape recorder.)

(SET: SHAUGHNESSY's tapiri. Lights up on SHAUGHNESSY's clearing. His lean-to hut, or tapiri, DSL, consists of a few vertical poles, some horizontal sticks, and rough thatching. He is dimly visible behind some mosquito netting fronting the structure; he is in his hammock and is in the process of waking up. Next to the hammock, affixed to one of the poles, is a compact bedside stand/shaving area complete with a small basin and a face mirror. Removed from the tapiri, perhaps near the SR wings, is a clothesline affair from which is suspended a variety of metal objects: pots, pans, kitchen knives, machetes, mashers, strainers, scissors, glass beads, fish-hooks—useful presents for any Indian who wishes to steal off with them. Finally, leaning against the tapiri is a seven-foot long wooden spear.)

(SHAUGHNESSY awakens to another day of waiting, pulling the netting back and peering out. He is not a healthy-looking man—fiftyish, thin, balding. Still, he moves pretty well—slowly, but with a sense of purpose and no wasted motion. He fumbles for a can of baby powder, then sprinkles it copiously on his feet and down his shorts as he surveys the sky and the jungle engulfing him.)

SHAUGHNESSY: Northern clouds. Ground mist. Sticky already. (*Slaps at a bug.*) The rains are coming back. (*Looks inside his boxer shorts.*) Hear that, Fungus? Monsoon time again. Six months of rain. By April I should look like a loaf of moldy bread . . . oh, God. (*Depressed, he flops back into his hammock.*) There'll be no April. Not if I stay. (*Broods a bit, then shouts:*) Discipline! (*Leaps from hammock, vigorously shakes out his boots and pulls them on as he lectures himself.*) Shave the beard! Brush the teeth! Powder the parasites! Look your best or you will quickly look your worst! (*Shouts sardonically toward jungle.*) Got to keep things tidy! Never know when I might have *visitors!* (*Laughs briefly, humorlessly*) . . . invisible bastards . . .

(At wash basin: flicks out a bug, splashes his face, towels off; puts on a pair of spectacles, lights a cigarette, and stares closely into the face mirror.)

Christ. No wonder they hide from me. I look contagious. (*Turns the mirror over.*) Verminous. Germy. Bugs inside and out.

(Searches clothesline area for evidence of visitors; counts the articles, enters it all in a pocket Diary.)

No tracks. No artifacts. And nothing stolen. (*Disgusted, he slaps Diary shut, crosses to hammock, muttering...*) Nothing. Three and a half years of Nothing...playing Hide and Seek with a bunch of xenophobic Indians...

(From within his tapiri *he seizes a cheerleader's megaphone he's constructed from broadleaf plants and twigs, then shouts invective from it.)*

Leaf People! Shaughnessy calls you *cowards!* You run from one old man dying from Athlete's Foot and Jock Rot! But now the game is over! I surrender! Shaughnessy is going home! And this time I *mean* it! (*Pauses to listen: silence*) You are fools of great stamina! Shaughnessy abandons you all to your fate! (*A sudden afterthought*) Which will be brief and conclusive!

(The phrase sobers him. He puts aside the megaphone. Hefts the spear leaning on the tapiri. *Studies it, talks quietly to it as if it were a person.)*

SHAUGHNESSY: If you don't like me, if you're really afraid of me, why haven't you killed me? Why am I *tolerated*? (*Walks toward jungle with spear, speaks without megaphone.*) Invisible Leader! The day I woke to find this spear, I wept. I ceased to fear for my life, and I rejoiced in yours. Now let me greet the man who left this gift! Let us congratulate each other on three and a half years of mutual stupidity...Show yourself, Leaf People! We are not eternal! *Leaf People!*

(SHAUGHNESSY suddenly grabs his head, tries to support himself with the spear.)

Oh Christ...fever, no more fever, not again, not now...

(He stumbles toward bedstand, fumbling for a bottle of pills.)

(Sound, faint at first, of HOVERCRAFT.)

(SHAUGHNESSY is unable to open the bottle before he collapses face down across his hammock. The hum of hovercraft now sounds like the droning of large insects.)

(As the lights dim, there is undefined movement in the US *jungle.)*

(BLACKOUT.)

(SET: FURTH's *Place. Lights up very bright on* FURTH's *domain. He lives near the bank of the Amazon River. His adobe hut may be suggested near the SL wings— a door, two small windows, a porch shielded by a ripply green plastic roof. But the functional part of* FURTH's *set consists of a circular metal table protected by a sun umbrella and two small rattan chairs. There is a rusty 55-gallon drum to one side with the words "Trespassers Will Be Prosecuted" painted on it. Greasy tools are scattered about, along with cases of empty Coke bottles and a decomposing fish. The ground is the texture of rocky sand, and the jungle US continues to dominate everything.)*

(MEATBALL squats by the rusted drum, indolently sharpening the blade on his machete. He wears tire-sole sandals, a torn and dirty T-shirt, and a dull, washed-out green pair of Bermuda shorts. A small, dark-skinned cafuso—*part black, part Indian—*MEATBALL *has gone to seed.)*

(Sound of hovercraft grows louder until P. Sigmund Furth *appears in the doorway SL holding two glasses full of a rum concoction. He's about 5'10" tall, very tacky looking, in his early forties. His eyes are protected against the glare by very dark sunglasses. He's dressed similarly to* Meatball *except that his Bermuda shorts are obscenely garish and look almost new. He carries an egg-shaped patch of scar tissue in the middle of his forehead. The roar of the hovercraft annoys him.)*

Furth: Meatball. Find out what's making that noise. Then make it stop.

*(*Meatball *grabs a pair of binoculars from the table and exits DSR;* Furth *sets down his two drinks, lights a cigarette, sits, and begins leafing idly through a pornographic magazine. He's in a genial mood today and sings to himself:)*

When the red red robin comes bob-bob-bobbin' along,
There'll be no more sobbin' when he starts throbbin'
His old sweet dong...

Meatball (OS): Eekendee mahlosh!

Furth: Eekendee mahlosh? *(Stands, mildly annoyed)* Don't believe I've ever seen a Roaring Turtle before.

*(*Meatball *re-enters, hands binocs to* Furth *at extreme DSR. He peers toward river. Sound of hovercraft cuts to half.)*

Furth: That's a hovercraft, Meatball. Cost *mucho dinero.* Look at that sucker move...uh oh...she's stopping here. *(Growing alarmed)* Only governments can afford boats like that. Have I sinned against any authorities lately?

Meatball: Maybe tahx mahn coom bahk?

Furth: Tax man! Coming back to padlock my fuel pumps!

Meatball: Get way-pon, Mr. Furth.

*(*Furth *tries to clear evidence that he's at home—gathering up magazines and drinks—as sound of hovercraft cuts out.)*

Furth: They touch my pumps, I'll make 'em bleed! *(In his haste to exit, he leaves a burning cigarette in the ash tray and a stray porn magazine under one chair.)* Stall 'em while I hide the accounts. *(He exits.)*

(Sound: Cue Dylan's "Watching the River Flow.")

*(*Steven *enters. Late twenties, about fifteen years younger than* Furth*. He wears huarache sandals, cut-off blue jeans, a thin drab shirt with no buttons left on it. A simple silver crucifix hangs from his neck. He wears a thin cloth headband to control his shoulder-length blond hair. He carries a small shoulder pouch which he keeps full of tape cassettes. Hanging from his other shoulder is the tape recorder that was pre-set at the top of the show and from which we hear the Dylan song.)*

SONG: "Watching the River Flow"
"What's the matter with me,
I don't have much to say..."

(STEVEN *is about* FURTH's *height and, though somewhat slender, he seems physically powerful. Perhaps out of deference to the heat, he moves slowly. When he speaks, his voice is calm, but with a thin, sardonic edge to it.*)

(*He eyes* MEATBALL *from behind sunglasses every bit as dark as* FURTH's. MEATBALL *squints back at him as he squats in the path to* FURTH's *hut, sharpening the machete. After the conclusion of the opening two lines of the song:*)

STEVEN: *Que lengua?*

(MEATBALL *says nothing, eyes* STEVEN's *tape recorder.*)

Es Los Cochinos?

(*When* MEATBALL *again ignores him,* STEVEN *starts toward* FURTH's *place.* MEATBALL *wordlessly stands to confront him, motions "No" with the machete, and points out the "Trespassers Will Be Prosecuted" sign.*)

I get it. I'm a Trespasser and you're the Prosecution.

(MEATBALL *shows no comprehension.*)

I'm looking for Dahku.

(MEATBALL *is surprised and angry.*)

Ring a bell? Good. Where's Dahku?

MEATBALL: No say him dat! Say Mista *Furth.*

STEVEN: (*Smiling*) Aha. You speak English, more or less. Tell Furth he's got a customer.

MEATBALL: He go way.

(STEVEN *picks up the still-burning cigarette.*)

STEVEN: He go way mucho pronto, verdad?

(MEATBALL *casually takes the cigarette and starts smoking it himself.* STEVEN *spots the porn mag and waves it at him.*)

This yours, too? You sly devil?

(MEATBALL *grins lasciviously.*)

Ah God, it's too hot to play Twenty Questions.

(*He sprawls on one of the rattan chairs and calls loudly toward hut:*)

When Dahku feels up to it, tell him I want fifty barrels!

(*He leafs through* FURTH's *magazine.* MEATBALL, *now satisfied* STEVEN *is harmless, turns his attention to acquiring the tape recorder. He squats close to Steven, who ignores him.*)

MEATBALL: From where you are?

STEVEN: (*Not looking up from magazine.*) Do you care deeply?

MEATBALL: Nord American hippie, you bet. You need green grass? Coom, I show.

(STEVEN abruptly hoots at a girlie picture, calls off toward FURTH's hut.)

STEVEN: A man must get pretty lonely living out here in the jungle!

MEATBALL: What you need, Hippie? You ask, I can. I know everything.

STEVEN: You know how to get lost?

MEATBALL: *(Puzzled but eager)* Lost? Lost?

STEVEN: There now, you see? You don't know how to get Furth, you don't know how to get lost ... what the hell good are you?

MEATBALL: *(Grinning)* I think you and me be good buddies, nay? *(Offering machete)* You like? Take!

STEVEN: Hmmm. A spontaneous outburst of international goodwill ...

MEATBALL: Keep!

(STEVEN accepts it, knowing he'll then have the drop on MEATBALL.)

STEVEN: I've sadly misjudged you. My heart is full. *(Edging toward FURTH's hut, smiling, but keeping the machete at the ready.)* Your land is beautiful, your people are handsome and gentle ...

(MEATBALL bluffs a move to detain him.)

MEATBALL: Stay!

(STEVEN laughs, fends him off. MEATBALL decides STEVEN is now far enough away. He whirls, grabs the tape recorder off the table, and heads for the bush.)

STEVEN: Hey!

FURTH: (OS) Meatball!

(MEATBALL is already OSR when he is halted by FURTH's weary reprimand. MEATBALL sullenly re-enters DSR as FURTH enters Left. FURTH is now wearing a holstered pistol.)

Meatball, you're being impetuous again.

(STEVEN takes back tape player, punches Off button. Sound: Kill "Watching the River Flow".)

Wait until he's sleeping, and *then* steal it.

STEVEN: *(To FURTH, indicating MEATBALL.)* You know this bandit?

FURTH: He's my vah-<u>lay</u>.

STEVEN: More likely your protégé.

FURTH: Something of that, too. *(Surveys STEVEN disapprovingly.)* Are you part of some sort of tour group?

STEVEN: A private expedition. I need to refuel my hovercraft.

FURTH: *Your* hovercraft? You *own* that thing?

STEVEN: Just leasing it for a while.

FURTH: Well, la-de-dah.... Look alive, Meatball: We are in the presence of great wealth.

MEATBALL: Mista Furth, he call you Dahku!

STEVEN: An Indian downriver said Dahku had gas, go find Dahku. Mean something dirty?

FURTH: Oh, just a nickname the Tupuias gave me. It means The Rapist.

STEVEN: (Laughing) Charming.

FURTH: One tribe's cheap opinion. Now the Jurunas, they call me The Jaguar.

STEVEN: A bit more dignified.

FURTH: I'm proud of both. Usually, though, I require white men to call me Mr. Furth.

(STEVEN pulls out a business card.)

STEVEN: As in "P. Sigmund Furth? Combat Photojournalist and Freelance Soldier?"

FURTH: That card is obsolete.

STEVEN: (Still reading) "Revolutions started. Revolutions halted. Bars cleared, enemies destroyed, Picassos authenticated."

FURTH: Cute, huh? But these days I just pump gas. Now you were hollering something about fifty barrels?

(STEVEN nods; FURTH calculates.)

That'll run you four thousand one hundred twenty-five U.S. dollars. Credit cards not accepted.

(STEVEN pulls a wad of bills from his shoulder pouch and counts as FURTH watches hungrily.)

You sure fifty barrels will do it? How far you heading?

STEVEN: Up the Rio Tapajós by hovercraft to Gifu. After that, I'm not sure.

FURTH: Not sure? Son, you had damn well better get sure. The Tapajós is not for day-trippers. Meatball, load that there eekendee mahlosh.

(MEATBALL exits DSR.)

Who you looking for?

STEVEN: A man called Shaughnessy.

FURTH: Shaughnessy!

STEVEN: Yes, Theophilus Shaughnessy. Know where I can find him?

FURTH: Sure. Take a left at the next bend in the river and start walking toward Bolivia.

STEVEN: Just give me some map coordinates.

FURTH: You can't get There from Here!

STEVEN: From Gifu. I've got a pilot lined up out of there, a missionary lady with a Cessna—

FURTH: Ole Anna Ames?

STEVEN: You know her, good.

FURTH: Nothing good about it. She's a royal pain in the ass. How come you're so hot to see Shaughnessy?

STEVEN: (*Somewhat thrown*) Well, he's ... he's a great man.

FURTH: (*Sneering*) The Schweitzer of the Amazon ...

STEVEN: The man has personally ensured the survival of entire tribes.

FURTH: Bullshit! Seventeen hundred straggly-assed refugees hiding out on his reservation ... what's the point? So they can die under his supervision?

STEVEN: (*Slamming the table*) They *don't* die! *That's* the point! Shaughnessy inoculates them and he—

FURTH: You can't inoculate an Indian against a white man!

STEVEN: Better that than nothing! What do *you* do? Sit back, slug down a drink, and let their goose cook?

FURTH: I *rape* 'em! Rape 'em before the next guy gets a chance! (*Quietly*) And I survive 'em. (*Takes a flask from pocket.*) Here's to History. (*He drinks.*)

STEVEN: I'll pay you ten thousand dollars to take me to Shaughnessy.

FURTH: Listen, kid ...

STEVEN: Steven.

FURTH: Shaughnessy's hanging around The Leaf People. You ain't gonna find *no*body to go in there, not for *no* kind of money.

STEVEN: You're out of touch, Furth. That region's opening up. The government's laying down a highway.

FURTH: Through Leaf People territory?

STEVEN: Surveyors already moving in.

FURTH: Then get *them* to take you. I don't want no part of it. (*Starting back toward hut*) Now if you'll excuse me, I have to go feed my lizard.

STEVEN: How come you're scared of The Leaf People and Shaughnessy isn't?

FURTH: Because Shaughnessy is (*Tapping his head*) ... *un poco loco en el coco. Sabe?* He thinks he's God's Annointed. Arrows will not pierce his flesh, et cetera. Personally, I got no use for the man.

STEVEN: I've heard rumors that he's dying.

FURTH: Of course he's dying! We're *all* dying, and Shaughnessy's been dying longer than anybody.

STEVEN: Fifteen thousand dollars, Furth.

(Enter MEATBALL DSR, carrying binoculars and motioning to FURTH.)

MEATBALL: Mista Furth...coom.

FURTH: Do yourself a favor. Send him a fan letter.

STEVEN: (*As FURTH crosses to MEATBALL.*) All right, I'm convinced. Your old calling card *is* obsolete. (*He tears it up.*) How 'bout I print you up a bunch saying "Dahku the Gas Jockey"?

FURTH: Yeah, do that. (MEATBALL *whispers something to* FURTH, *who peers through binoculars and is stunned.*) Merciful Jesus...

MEATBALL: Morena caba verde.

FURTH: Yep. My favorite type. (*Lowers the glasses, rubs his bleary eyes, peers again.*) That's enough to bring tears to the eyes of the dead. (*To* STEVEN) Who's your travelling companion?

STEVEN: Some girl from Caracas. She wanted to ride my boat.

FURTH: (*Laughing*) Did she now? And who can blame her, eh?

STEVEN: She didn't expect to go this far.

FURTH: That's what they all say.

STEVEN: Why don't you come with us as far as Gifu? We'll talk. Just you, me, and Michelle.

FURTH: Ah, Michelle! Lovely, lovely...(*Suddenly a bit self-conscious*) Think her and me might...get along? I mean if I shaved and got cleaned up a bit?

STEVEN: Furth, she's very put out with me, so she'll probably put out for you.

FURTH: (*Laughing again*) Well God bless her, yessir! I'm gonna have to give this some serious thought.

STEVEN: Think about this, too: twenty thousand dollars.

FURTH: Now you're getting dangerous.

(STEVEN fills and lights a small pipe.)

STEVEN: Half now, half when I see Shaughnessy. (*Puts a new cassette in recorder.*)

FURTH: God *damn*, it kills me to hear a kid like you toss around figures like these.

(STEVEN punches the Start button, then offers his pipe to FURTH.)

(Sound: Cue "On the Amazon" by New Riders of the Purple Sage.)

FURTH: How'd you get so rich?

STEVEN: Fate.

FURTH: You inherited it. Your old man is a prophylactic tycoon in Kansas City.

(STEVEN laughs. As he listens to the music, his hands simulate the piano line in the song. FURTH bemusedly smokes as he watches.)

SONG: "On the Amazon"
"Well I used to be a burglar,
rolled too many numbers,
now I am a smuggler on the Amazon . . ."

FURTH: You control the cocaine traffic out of Barranquilla?

STEVEN: I should live so long.

SONG: "On the Amazon" *(cont.)*
"Living on thrills down in Brazil,
got a big plantation
on the Amazon . . ."

(FURTH suddenly reaches over, turns down volume of song.)

FURTH: I know what you are.

STEVEN: And what am I, Mr. P. Sigmund Furth?

FURTH: You're a Rock Star. *(Pounds the table.) Aren't you?*

STEVEN: You could say that.

(STEVEN turns up volume of song. FURTH tries not to laugh as he smokes.)

FURTH: An honest to God rock shtar, out lookin for his fuggin guru—Shaughnessy! *(He laughs and coughs, clutching at the table as he momentarily loses his balance.)* My God, I'm dreamin . . .

STEVEN: I'll tell Michelle you're coming with us, o.k.?

FURTH: *(Disoriented, shuffling toward hut SL.)* Michelle . . . I'm coming, girl . . . Furth is on his way.

SONG: "On the Amazon" *(cont.)*
"Got a ton of acres,
Got a lot of land . . ."

(STEVEN watches intently as FURTH crosses to hut. STEVEN takes recorder, still playing, and exits DR toward river.)

FURTH: Just let me get clean...

(BLACKOUT. Music up loud during scene change.)

SONG: "On the Amazon" *(cont.)*
"Got a outlaw lady
who really understands
why her musician
is a South American man...."

(Sound of music fades during the instrumental bridge and goes out about a minute and a half into the song. The house remains in BLACKOUT during the complete silence that follows.)

(SET: A Dark Place. VERY DIM LIGHT spots SHAUGHNESSY. He is bound hand and foot, sprawled flat on the stage.)

SHAUGHNESSY: I must be calm. *(Silence)* I'm not injured. *(Silence)*. I think I'm alone. But I could be wrong. *(He twists around, strains to listen.)* Can't listen, everything slips away, no! No, it will not slip away, I will not let it. *(Silence)* What is this place? This dark place? *(Silence)* My hands are bound. And my feet.

(Sound, faint and muffled, of dog barking.)

A dog! I'm in a village. Oh God. Oh dear God. Can it be possible? Am I with The Leaf People?

(A hot red spot slams down on SHAUGHNESSY, and he groans. He is delirious throughout this scene.)

Ohhh... it's a lie. A fever dream... *(Laughs, then sings)* "Sleepy Time Gal..." How many days we been shacked up this time? Three? Four? I can't move. Does that mean more than four? *Water! Give me water!*

(Green spot up near SHAUGHNESSY's feet. A little girl walks slowly into the Spot. She is about eight years old, and her name is SUTREESHAY. Her hair is black and straight down her back. Her skin is distinctly green. SUTREESHAY stares at SHAUGHNESSY—not wildly curious, but detached, relaxed. SHAUGHNESSY does not trust his vision.)

SHAUGHNESSY: If you're real, bring water. Agua, por favor, *agua.*

(SUTREESHAY turns and, glancing back once at SHAUGHNESSY, walks slowly ou: of the Spot. Take out green spot. SHAUGHNESSY begins to tremble. Through chattering teeth he peevishly demands:)

Where's my Diary? And my spectacles? How am I to see without my glasses? Nothing is ever where I put it in this house! Take this entry, take it down: The Leaf People have come. They sent their mightiest warrior, and she was green.

(He croaks out a laugh and struggles to his knees before collapsing.)

(Kill red spot. Lights up UC on GITAUCHO, the Leader of The Leaf People. His skin

is reddish bronze. His body is elaborately painted in red and black geometric pat-
terns. Unlike the rest of his tribe, GITAUCHO's *hair is very long, straight, and black;*
his warriors wear it cropped, sort of in bangs. He wears a headpiece of some ten
brilliant yellow feathers. A strip of cloth is wrapped round his waist and through
his crotch. He is cloaked from shoulders to feet in a robe that simulates fresh-cut
green leaves.* The Leaf Robe functions as his power token and, more practically,
as his raincoat. He carries a sturdy seven-foot spear. He leans on it, right foot
placed on left knee, and impassively observes SHAUGHNESSY. *He is deciding whether*
or not to let him die.)

*(*THE SOUND *(or* KEET*) appears behind* GITAUCHO. *He wears a loin cloth and a*
smaller leaf garment, a cape that betokens his rank as second-in-command in the
tribe's dual chieftain structure. His function is literally to speak for GITAUCHO *when*
a command is given. At such moments THE SOUND *assumes a ritual position in*
front of GITAUCHO—*an open-kneed half-squat that brings his head below* GITAU-
CHO's *face, arms extended palms out and parallel to his thighs. His headpiece*
features the feathers and open beak of a squawking jungle bird. As might be expected
of such an official, his voice is resonant and strong. THE SOUND *regards* GITAUCHO
as his older brother, perhaps at times even as his father, although both are in their
early twenties.)

(A third man appears off to one side—the MONKEY MAN (MUTUTAHSH), *the tribe's*
shaman. He's a strange, withered creature, apparently quite old. His authority
symbol is the upper half of a monkey skull adorned with long, brilliant turquoise
and yellow feathers; he wears it like a hat. He also has tufts of monkey fur wrapped
around his wrists and knees. One thigh is greased jet black, and half his chest is
smeared red. He takes everything in with peripheral glances, holding himself aloof,
immersed in his own thoughts.)

(See the Production Notes on the Interpreters, located at the end of the play. In this
version it is suggested that the Interpreters not be seen. They should be seated where
they have a view of the action and they should be miked. 1ST INTERPRETER *is a*
woman, 2ND INTERPRETER *is a man. Their work is detached and efficient.)*

(When Leafish appears at the left margin, the words are meant to stand clear of the
translation. When Leafish appears in the right column alongside the left column
English, it indicates a simultaneous translation—again, see the Production Notes.
Above the Leafish, within parentheses, is a literal word-for-word translation of
Leafish designed entirely as an aid for the actors.)

*(*SHAUGHNESSY *becomes aware of the Indians.)*

SHAUGHNESSY: Leader . . .

(He weakly mimes the concepts of thirst and drinking as GITAUCHO *watches,*
unmoved.)

1ST INTERP: He dies.   GITAUCHO: (He dies.) Koh noor.

**Authenticity suggests the use of waxy-textured broadleaf succulents matted with*
twine.

2ND INTERP: It's so.   THE SOUND: (It's so.) Shem.

(THE SOUND turns to leave. GITAUCHO remains a moment longer, then also turns to walk off.)

SHAUGHNESSY: Wait!

(GITAUCHO looks back)

You ... bring water.

2ND INTERP: Let him die.   THE SOUND:(Allow him death.)
                                       Ga<u>het</u>'ee noor.

SHAUGHNESSY: *(Pleading for his life.)* I have come ... to *help* you.

(THE SOUND has been holding an innocent-looking wooden object resembling a flute. He now holds it to his mouth as if to play and does a slow, sweeping dance around SHAUGHNESSY. Suddenly he pulls the object apart, and it becomes an unsheathed six-inch dagger. He lunges for SHAUGHNESSY's heart, stopping short by inches. The MONKEY MAN yelps in shock, which causes THE SOUND to laugh jeeringly at him. GITAUCHO has not even blinked, and now he, too, laughs curtly at the MONKEY MAN for being so foolish as to believe THE SOUND would act without GITAUCHO's authorization. The MONKEY MAN snarls at THE SOUND.)

1ST INTERP: Demon.   MONKEY MAN: (Danger spirit.)
                                       Kah<u>leem</u>!

(THE SOUND is now down on his knees. SHAUGHNESSY's head rests on THE SOUND's thigh, and THE SOUND's knife is poised at his throat. THE SOUND looks to GITAUCHO for permission to kill.)

2ND INTERP: BETTER   THE SOUND: (Better.) H<u>yee</u>nish!

(GITAUCHO glances at the MONKEY MAN, who shakes his head dubiously, muttering:)

1ST INTERP: He is a mighty   MONKEY MAN:
mystery.   (He is like-trees danger-shadow.)
                                       Koh she <u>goh</u>jee kah<u>naht</u>.

(SHAUGHNESSY has never taken his eyes off GITAUCHO, not even at THE SOUND's lunge—a point which is not lost on THE SOUND.)

SHAUGHNESSY: *(Feebly, to* Gitaucho) You were not born ... to let me die.

(GITAUCHO crosses to him, reaches down, puts his hand on SHAUGHNESSY's cheek. He leaves it there for some time, staring hard at SHAUGHNESSY all the while. Finally he stands and murmurs ...)

                                       GITAUCHO: (Water)
                                       <u>Lah</u>bay.

(Instantly THE SOUND assumes the command position in front of GITAUCHO, adding the force and majesty of his voice to the command.)

BOTH INTERPRETERS: *(In Unison)*   THE SOUND: (Water) LAH-bay!
Water.

(A young woman runs on stage carrying a small bladder-skin water bag and a

drinking gourd. She wears a yellow feather in her black hair, a feathered necklace and ankle bracelets. She's clothed from the waist down in a sarong-like cloth garment. Her forehead has a small, geometric tatoo. This is KEERAH, GITAUCHO*'s sister, and she is beautiful. Though her brother's skin is the conventional reddish-bronze,* KEERAH—*like the little girl* SUTREESHAY—*is a delicate shade of green.* KEERAH *helps* SHAUGHNESSY *drink.)*

(Upstage several more members of The Leaf People edge curiously into view, waiting to see what will happen to this odd-looking, helpless creature. Notable among them are two important warriors, MAYTEEMO *and* LEEBOH. *Peering from behind them are two children,* SUTREESHAY *and a boy about her age,* JEESHOOM. *Jeeshoom is the same reddish-bronze color as the other males.)*

(When SHAUGHNESSY *has his fill, he falls back to the floor.* KEERAH *starts to exit, but* SHAUGHNESSY *desperately grabs her ankle.* KEERAH *yelps in surprise and* THE SOUND *moves protectively, but relaxes when* GITAUCHO *laughs.)*

SHAUGHNESSY: Tetrex...red   and   yellow   capsules...(*He squirms around like a caterpillar, still clutching* KEERAH*'s ankle. He spots his fever pills.)* There! Please bring.

(When he is sure KEERAH *sees what he's after, he lets go of her ankle. She grabs the kit bag, hands it to* SHAUGHNESSY, *who shakes out his pill bottle.)*

Oh sweet angel, sweet mercy...

(He gulps a killing dose of four pills as KEERAH *again assists with the water. He calms himself, stretches out on the floor, and begins to nod off, muttering...)*

Thank you, God, thank you, thank you...

1ST INTERP: Why have you come?	GITAUCHO: (Why have you come?) Kee<u>shahsh</u> ahn doh <u>seent</u>?
2ND INTERP: Why have you come?	THE SOUND: (*Assuming ritual stance*) Kee<u>shahsh</u> ahn doh <u>seent</u>?

(As SHAUGHNESSY *drifts into a profound sleep, he murmurs...)*

SHAUGHNESSY: To save you...
*(*GITAUCHO *leaps beside* SHAUGHNESSY, *straining to hear any further noises he might make. But all he hears is a gentle snore.* THE SOUND *laughs at* GITAUCHO*'s reaction.* GITAUCHO *turns to him and painstakingly enunciates...)*

	GITAUCHO: Tu. Zave. Yu.
	THE SOUND: Tu. Zave. Yu.
	GITAUCHO: (Not forget that, my
1ST INTERP: Do not forget that,	Sound.) Tet <u>men</u>doh nay, ree
my Sound.	Keet.

(THE SOUND performs a gesture of obedience called "pohahlaj" by dropping to one knee and kissing the thigh of his Leader. GITAUCHO stares at SHAUGHNESSY.)

1ST INTERP: For now, he lives.   GITAUCHO: (For now, he lives.
Come.   Come.) Eence, koh moor. Hetch.

(GITAUCHO hands his spear to THE SOUND and exits. THE SOUND gestures to MAYTEEMO and LEEBOH.)

THE SOUND: Hetch!

(THE SOUND hands them the seven-foot long spear and supervises as they pass it through SHAUGHNESSY's hand and foot ties. MAYTEEMO and LEEBOH each takes an end of the stake. Easily they lift SHAUGHNESSY off the ground and smoothly, even gently, carry him off like a dressed sheep.)

(SOUND. Cue "The Yellow Snake" by The Incredible String Band.)

(THE LIGHTS ARE FADING.)

SONG: "The Yellow Snake"
"Someone you saw stretched sleeping on the sand,
Five withered violets cradled in his hand.
His dreams are so loud, calling in your ear . . .
The yellow snake coils from the water
And all is refreshed far and near. . . . "

(BLACKOUT)

(SET: Inside Anna's Airplane. Still in BLACKOUT, the sound of a light airplane begins to be heard under the instrumental bridge following the above line. Crossfade the two sounds during the conclusion of the song, then fade the sound of the airplane and play it under the following scene.)

(Lights up on a mockup of the cockpit of a Cessna 150 or similar small aircraft. Pilot is Miss ANNA AMES, Missionary for the Second Evangelical Church of God United—a perky woman in her early fifties.)

(STEVEN is seated to her right in the co-pilot's seat; he studies the ground out to his right through binoculars. FURTH sits between them and to their rear, and he trains his binoculars out the left side of the aircraft.)

(The tape recorder sits between ANNA and STEVEN. She glances at it mistrustfully every so often. The sound of the song continues to conclusion.)

SONG: "The Yellow Snake" (*concluded*)
"The yellow snake coils from the water
and all is refreshed far and near."

ANNA: Furth tells me you're a musician, Steven.

STEVEN: (*Still peering through binocs.*) Sometimes.

ANNA: What instrument, guitar?

STEVEN: Keys.

ANNA: Keys? You mean piano?

STEVEN: Synthesizers. Yamaha DX's, Fairlight CMI, Kurzweil 250—
that stuff.

ANNA: Heavens, how esoteric. (*Sighs*) Whatever happened to clarinets?

(STEVEN *rummages in his bag, selects a new tape.*)

Is Shaughnessy a friend of yours?

STEVEN: No. I just read about him. I like what he's doing.

(STEVEN *starts tape. Sound of song:* "Someday Never Comes," *Creedence Clearwater Revival.*)

ANNA: The admiration I have for that man! The courage, the dedication!

FURTH: Spare me, Anna. I'm already feeling airsick.

(STEVEN *is again surveying terrain through binoculars, but he unconsciously sings along with the opening lines.* ANNA *listens with interest, glancing at him.*)

SONG: "Someday Never Comes."
"First thing I remember was asking Papa 'Why?'
For there were many things I didn't know ... "

ANNA: Is that one of your songs?

(STEVEN *shakes No.*)

SONG: (*cont.*)
"Daddy always smiled, took me by the hand,
Saying 'Someday you'll understand.' "

ANNA: (*Shouting to* FURTH) Furth, did you bring baby powder?

FURTH: Yeah.

ANNA: (*To* STEVEN) Shaughnessy suffers from prickly heat. We *all* do.

SONG: (*cont.; chorus*)
"Well I'm here to tell you now
Each and every Mother's Son,
You better learn it fast,
You better learn it young,
Cause Someday never comes ... "

(ANNA *reaches over and punches tape off: kill sound of song. Out at 1:37.* STEVEN's *irritated, glares at her.*)

ANNA: You have quite a nice voice. (*Staring intently at him.*) And you look very much like old pictures I've seen of Shaughnessy.

STEVEN: (*Coldly*) Is that so?

ANNA: Yes, it is. Speaking of pictures ... (*Flips a packet on his lap*) ... did Furth show you these?

(FURTH *leans forward, peers suspiciously as* STEVEN *pulls out photos.*)

STEVEN: Oh my God.

ANNA: No, I didn't think he had. The Leaf People did that four months ago.

STEVEN: Furth, have you seen these?

ANNA: *Seen* them? He *took* them.

FURTH: God damn it, Anna, why drag these things out?

ANNA: Because I am burdened by something you have been spared, Mister Furth—a conscience!

STEVEN: You have any shots of The Leaf People themselves?

ANNA: No, only their victims.

STEVEN: Jesus. Look what they did to this one. They *skinned* him.

ANNA: Yes, they do that with a drug. Inject it subcutaneously, and the skin can be removed intact.

STEVEN: (*Looking ill*) But why? Why do something like that at all?

(FURTH *grabs pictures away.*)

FURTH: Because they're *savages*, you idiot! Dirty fucking wild men!

ANNA: They are children of the jungle, and no doubt reasonably clean.

FURTH: Anna's gonna put them all in her Sunday School class, aren't you, Anna. Sing hymns to each other! (*He rips the photos in half.*)

ANNA: It is criminal for this young man to go waltzing into that jungle without knowing precisely *what is in there*. He has no experience whatever!

(STEVEN *is again surveying terrain.*)

FURTH: He's got me.

ANNA: You! You're just grabbing his money! You don't care two cents for his welfare!

FURTH: Yeah? Well, I care about *mine*! I plan to come back out with my skin on, and if I do, so will he.

STEVEN: There's a structure down there. Crescent roof, tin...

(FURTH *and* ANNA *check it out.*)

FURTH: Yeah. Got it. That's one of Shaughnessy's *tapiri*. Nothin movin'.

ANNA: May be an old camp, one he abandoned.

FURTH: Can you put us down there?

ANNA: Not without a helicopter.

STEVEN: There's some kind of plateau out this way.

ANNA: I see it. That's a four-day march, if you're lucky.

FURTH: Take it down.

ANNA: Steven, I can turn this around, and it won't cost you a penny.

FURTH: Leave the kid alone!

STEVEN: (*To* FURTH) It's all right. (*To* ANNA) Shaughnessy needs help. He may be dying.

ANNA: Yes, I've heard those rumors. I knew he'd broken contact, but ...as bad as that, you think?

FURTH: *I* think the man is dead meat. (*To* STEVEN) You're aware of that possibility?

STEVEN: Don't worry, you'll still get your twenty grand.

ANNA: Twenty-thousand dollars? You'd pay that much to see Shaughnessy?

FURTH: He's getting a bargain, believe me.

ANNA: Well, that clinches it. He's your father, isn't he?

FURTH: True?

(STEVEN hesitates, then nods.)

Damn.

ANNA: Oh dear, then there's no hope for it.

FURTH: Uh, you know those things I was saying about Shaughnessy ...

STEVEN: Forget it. I know you meant every syllable.

ANNA: When did you last see him?

STEVEN: Five years ago, briefly. Letters very occasionally.

(FURTH hands STEVEN a small pouch)

What's this?

FURTH: Your pharmacy. Salt tablets, chloroquine for Vivax malaria, Fansidar for Falciperum malaria, Tetrex, of course—good all-purpose antibiotic—

STEVEN: Gotcha.

ANNA: (*To* FURTH) Did you remember clothespins?

FURTH: Yeah.

ANNA: (*To* STEVEN) Uncommonly useful, clothespins.

STEVEN: You'll be back in two weeks?

ANNA: On the dot. Now remember, Steven. This is the end of the dry season. You'll find shallow pools of water everywhere, stranded by the run-off. Stay away from them! They'll be alive with starving piranha. Furth, did you warn him about the *Tocandeira* ants?

STEVEN: *Stop it, please!*

FURTH: (*After a beat*) He'll be o.k., Anna. Just take us down.

(Fade to BLACKOUT.)

(Sound of light plane banking and landing.)

*(In the BLACKOUT we hear a woman's voice—*KEERAH*—and then* SHAUGHNESSY.*)*

                                        KEERAH: (Hair.) Meez.

1ST INTERP: Hair.   SHAUGHNESSY: <u>Meez</u>.

(SET: Inside GITAUCHO's *Tukul. Lights up on the inside of* GITAUCHO's *tukul, a hut made from sticks and leaves.* GITAUCHO *is squatting UR, smiling and relaxed, looking younger than in his last scene. His Leaf Robe hangs from the side of the tukul.)*

*(*GITAUCHO's *mother, a chubby woman named* YA-<u>WAH</u>-LA-<u>PEE</u>-TEE *(Rubber Ball), sits on the dirt floor weaving another Leaf Robe for her son. She is wrapped in a loose hide garment which doubles as a blanket. Her pigmentation is the same as* GITAUCHO's. *She laughs animatedly at the language lesson being conducted by her daughter* KEERAH.*)*

*(*KEERAH *is dressed as before with her sarong-like skirt. She is having a wonderful time, holding her long black hair out as far as it will go. For his part,* SHAUGHNESSY *is not fully recovered from his fever but is reclining comfortably on hide pillows, revelling in the culmination of his 3½-year ordeal in the rain forest.)*

                                        KEERAH: Hee-yair.

                                        SHAUGHNESSY: (*Jots in his note-book.*) <u>Meez</u>.

                                        GITAUCHO: (Beautiful hair) Ten-<u>dah</u>mosh meez.

BOTH INTERPRETERS: Beautiful   YAWAHLAPEETEE: (*Laughing*) Ten-
hair.   <u>dah</u>mosh meez.

                                        SHAUGHNESSY: Ten<u>dah</u>mosh
                                        meez.

2ND INTERP: Do you like my   GITAUCHO: (You my sister like?)
sister?   Doh ree <u>ohmoh</u> <u>een</u>drah?

1ST INTERP: Stop it. Shut up.   KEERAH: (*Turns and slaps at him,
                                        yelling:*) (Not-not-not-not-not)
                                        Tet-tet-tet-tet-tet!

SHAUGHNESSY:
(Beautiful sister ... beautiful
Keerah)
Ten_dah_mosh ohmoh ... tendah-
_mosh Keerah.

*(YAWAHLAPEETEE goes 'aaahhh?' and looks quite pleased, as does GITAUCHO.
KEERAH is embarrassed.)*

1ST INTERP: Beautiful sister. Beautiful Keerah.

2ND INTERP: Amazing. He likes   GITAUCHO:
you, you ugly flea.   (Amazing. He you like, you
                                       Noh_shin_tay! Koh doh _een_drah,
                                       doh

                                       ugly flea.)
                                       ek_beesh_ cheet.

                                       YAWAHLAPEETEE:
                                       (Rolling to her feet) (And I him
                                       like.)
                                       Jah moh t'_eendrah_!

(She hugs the debilitated man, a limp rag in her massive arms.)

2ND INTERP: And I like him.   YAWAHLAPEETEE:
                                       (Little white wrinkle)
                                       Zheet noom peetah ...

2ND INTERP: Little white wrinkle.

*(KEERAH breaks free from GITAUCHO, who's been harassing her, and charges over
to protect SHAUGHNESSY from her mother's emphatic caresses.)*

                                       KEERAH:
                                       (not-not-not)
                                       Tet-tet-tet!

(YAWAHLAPEETEE whacks KEERAH's shoulder, mocking her.)

                                       YAWAHLAPEETEE:
                                       (Not-not-not. Not-not-not!)
                                       Tet-tet-tet! Tet-tet-tet!

(GITAUCHO laughs.)

                                       KEERAH:
                                       (Rubber Ball! Still he is weak
                                       Yawahlapeetee! _Eentah_ _koh_ she
                                       _ah_lahm

                                       like baby, and you him crush.)
                                       goh _lahm_, jah _doh_ tee _noorku_.

1ST INTERP: Yawahlapeetee! Still
he is weak as a baby, and you
crush him.

(YAWAHLAPEETEE *does a knowing waddle away from* KEERAH, *grinning at*
GITAUCHO.)

YAWAHLAPEETEE:
(Little hen begins to squat and
tremble.)
Zheet boontu bah gahsh jah root.

2ND INTERP: The little hen begins
to squat and tremble.

1ST INTERP: Little hen? But hens
do not wear clothes. Do they, my
Mother?

GITAUCHO:
(Little hen?   But hen
Zheet boontu? Mah boontu
wear not clothes.
pishah tet raleem.

Is it so, my mother?)
Shemish, ree Jeetah?

2ND INTERP: You are right, my
son. Hens never wear a thing, especially in front of the rooster.

YAWAHLAPEETEE:
(It's so, my son.
Shem, ree Tohndor.
Hens wear never a thing,
Boontu pishah tedish ahm,
especially before rooster.)
kutet say kite.

KEERAH:
(Shaw not in front!)
Shaw tet say!

1ST INTERP: Not in front of Shaw.

YAWAHLAPEETEE:
(Shaw not in front?)
Shaw tet say?

2ND INTERP: Not in front of Shaw?

KEERAH:
(He wear thing.)
Koh pishah'm.

1ST INTERP: He wears things.

2ND INTERP: Because he is
strange, must you be? You begin
to offend me. Take off that garb.

GITAUCHO:
(He not-Leaf, and you is it so?
Koh hiwahtet, jah doh shemish?

You begin to offend me.
Doh bah   yagah moh.

Wear not that clothes.)
Pishatet nay raleem.
KEERAH:
Tet!

(GITAUCHO looks like he's been slapped. He angrily grabs for his Leaf Robe: When he wears it, his will is the will of the tribe. But KEERAH darts out through the opening in the tukul. YAWAHLAPEETEE tries to pacify GITAUCHO.)

1ST INTERP: Gitaucho, she is a little hen, but she is still just a *silly*
little hen.

YAWAHLAPEETEE:
(Gitaucho, she is chicken
 Gitaucho, loh she boontu

little, but she is still
zheet, mah loh sh'eentah

silly chicken little.)
poobish boontu zheet.

GITAUCHO:*(Shouting out the opening)* (She will be plucked!)

2ND INTERP: She will be plucked!   Loh rahn geet!

(SHAUGHNESSY laughs. GITAUCHO looks over in surprise.)

GITAUCHO:
(You that understand?)

2ND INTERP: You understood that?   Doh nay kusht?

SHAUGHNESSY: I think I picked
up the punch line.

(GITAUCHO doesn't understand exactly, but he whispers conspiratorially off to one side with YAWAHLAPEETEE.)

2ND INTERP: Take note. He understands much. He understands
fast.

GITAUCHO:
(Be aware. He much understands.
 Hasheem. Koh roh kusht.

He soon understands.)
Koh eeshee kusht.

1ST INTERP: He is a clever monkey.   YAWAHLAPEETEE:
(He is clever monkey.)
Koh she purah mutu.

2ND INTERP: So. You must not talk so much in front of him.

GITAUCHO:
(So. Talk not much
Jum. Hyahba tet roh

in front of him.)
say tee.

YAWAHLAPEETEE:
(Why?   He is my little
Keeshahsh? Koh she ree zheet
white wrinkle.)
noom peetah.

1ST INTERP: Why? He is my little white wrinkle.

2ND INTERP: He is something much bigger than a wrinkle. I do not know how yet, but that man changes everything.

GITAUCHO:
(He is something bigger wrinkle.
Koh she ahm roh yahdish peetah.

I even now know not how,   but
Moh eentah kush'tet nabah, mah

that man changes everything.)
nay tahsh keensay mohm.

1ST INTERP: He is as harmless as a soft raindrop.

YAWAHLAPEETEE:
(He is harmless
Koh she ahlem

as soft raindrop.)
goh lahshoom.

2ND INTERP: Why has he come?

GITAUCHO:
(Why   has he come?)
Keeshahsh ahn koh seent?

1ST INTERP: Because you are the best Leader the Leaf People ever had.

YAWAHLAPEETEE:
(Because you is much better
 Pah doh she roh hyeenish

Leader had Leaf People ever)
Meesho ahn Hiwahtoh saymohm!

2ND INTERP: That must be it. He has come to reward my Leadership.

GITAUCHO (laughing):
(That must is. Has he come
Nah toom she. Ahn koh seent

reward my Leadership.
tahloom ree Meeshotum.

YAWAHLAPEETEE: *Shem!*

(GITAUCHO stares at SHAUGHNESSY, then murmurs...)

GITAUCHO: Tu. Zave. Yu. Tu. Zave. Yu.

1ST INTERP: What are you saying?

SHAUGHNESSY: (What you say?) Teesh doh hyahba?

GITAUCHO:

2ND INTERP: What does that mean, Shaw?

(What that mean?) Tu. Zave. Yu. Teesh nay bah-kusht, Shaw?

1ST INTERP: Where did you hear that, my Leader?

SHAUGHNESSY: (Where you hear, my Leader?) Nabu doh keetroo, ree Meesho?

2ND INTERP: From you, my Captive.

GITAUCHO: (From you, my Captive.) Bu doh, ree Ootoh.

1ST INTERP: I must learn more words.

SHAUGHNESSY: (I must begin-to-know Moh toom bahkusht roh

many man-sounds.) kee'tahsh.

2ND INTERP: So must I. Soon, Shaw.

GITAUCHO: (I too must. Soon, Shaw.) Shem'oh toom. Eeshee, Shaw.

(Sound of light plane, followed almost immediately by a shout.)

THE SOUND: Ree Meesho!

(GITAUCHO, already in his Leaf Robe, ducks out of the tukul. SHAUGHNESSY and YAWAHLAPEETEE stare at each other somberly; then both smile.)

1ST INTERP: What's that noise?

YAWAHLAPEETEE: (What that sound?) Teesh nay keet?

2ND INTERP: It's an airplane. Do you know what an airplane is?

SHAUGHNESSY: (It is Nah she airplane.

You know?) Doh kusht airplane?

1ST INTERP: Some kind of Tree Devil?

YAWAHLAPEETEE: (Thing tree devil?) Hyee-yair-pain. Ahm jee kahleem?

(THE SOUND *bursts into the* tukul. *He points a dagger at* SHAUGHNESSY *and doesn't put it down till he's finished.)*

2ND INTERP: I am cursed for not killing you four long rains ago. Now they come for you from the sky. The buzzards circle over the carcass of the Leaf People. So they think. They are deceived. We are mighty. We are holy. The Others will all be killed. And then I myself will rip out your heart.

THE SOUND:
(I is curse for you
Moh she <u>doom</u> pah doh

crush-spirit
noorku<u>leem</u>

not four long-rains ago.
tet min <u>soom</u>lahsh'ay.

Now Dangermen
Tah Kah<u>tahsh</u>

come for you from sky. Buzzard
<u>seent</u> pah doh bu <u>lohm</u>.
<u>Chohmoosh</u>

circle over carcass of Leaf People.
klee boo'<u>tohm</u> na Hi<u>wah</u>toh.

They   think.
Kahtahsh <u>keent</u>!

Others   lie-to-shadow.
Kahtahsh oomee<u>naht</u>!

We are like-tree. We
Toh she <u>goh</u>jee! Toh

are holy.   Will Others
she <u>zhoo</u>dish! Rahn Kah<u>tahsh</u>

crush-spirit all. And soon
noorkulee'<u>mohm</u>.   Jah <u>ee</u>shee

I-my   heart will rip out.
mohree <u>moosh</u> rahn <u>choht</u>!

(THE SOUND *ducks out of the* tukul. *BLACKOUT.)*

(SET: The Jungle. Hacking, slashing noises are heard in the BLACKOUT—machetes clearing jungle. When the lights come up, STEVEN *staggers onstage. He's a mess. His shirt is torn and sticks to his torso with sweat. He bleeds from a variety of cuts and scratches, and his breath comes in great gasps.)*

*(*FURTH *enters carrying a pack. He is wearing long pants now; other than that, he looks the same as usual. He isn't breathing particularly hard, but he, too, is drenched in sweat.)*

FURTH: Take five, Steven.

*(*STEVEN *drops in his tracks like he's been shot.* FURTH *pulls a small fold-up cloth chair out of his pack and composedly sits down.)*

Get off the ground and find your salt pills.

(STEVEN *doesn't budge.*)

Suit yourself.

(FURTH *takes several tablets, swills them down with canteen water, makes a face.*)

Canteen water's enough to make you gag.

(STEVEN *suddenly leaps up, yelling and slapping himself.* FURTH *watches a bit distinterestedly.* STEVEN *finally rids himself of the biting insects and takes an exhausted look around.*)

STEVEN: We're always so shut in. Can't see shit beyond ten feet.

FURTH: What's to see? This goes on for three thousand miles.

STEVEN: How'my doin' today, Furth? Better than yesterday, huh?

FURTH: Great, kid.

STEVEN: Yeah, I think I'm hitting my stride. Can I take off my boots?

FURTH: Can't get too comfortable.

STEVEN: O.K.

FURTH: Feet are really sore, huh?

(STEVEN *shrugs.*)

Take 'em off.

(STEVEN *does. He looks disgusted.*)

STEVEN: Hey Furth . . . look at my skin. It's all white and saggy.

FURTH: The moisture does it—that and your lousy boots. Too bad.

(STEVEN *again looks all around.*)

STEVEN: How can a human being live in a place like this?

FURTH: Your father did. Years at a time, all by himself. Crazy.

STEVEN: Or something. Hey Furth, I been meaning to ask you—what's the 'P' stand for in your name? "P. Sigmund Furth?"

FURTH: Are you gonna laugh?

STEVEN: Naw, just curious.

FURTH: Percival.

STEVEN: Oh no . . . Percy Furth? (*He bursts out laughing.*)

FURTH: See? I knew you were gonna laugh. Now you've gone and hurt me. (*He spots something up in the trees.*) Hey, look up there.

STEVEN: Butterflies! That tree's all full of butterflies! *Thousands* of 'em! Huge! Look at 'em all, Furth, rippling like waves!

(As STEVEN *and* FURTH *stare DS, The Leaf People silently encircle them from behind, gigantic bows and spears poised to kill. NOTE: In the Broadway production, the Indians descended in waves from above, clambering over tiered shot-cord as if dropping out of trees.)*

(When FURTH turns and sees them, he doesn't change expression or tone.)

FURTH: Steven, keep your face a blank and make no sudden movements.

STEVEN: Oh shit.

FURTH: Gimme your tape recorder. Slowly.

STEVEN: *(Does so)* Got a plan?

FURTH: Yeah. I'm gonna try to surrender. Then I'm gonna beg for my life.

STEVEN: Sounds good to me. (FURTH *holds out the tape recorder.)*

FURTH: First we give them some presents. Play 'em a little music. *(Slowly places recorder on ground, punches Start button.)*

(Sound: Cue Leon Russell's "Out in the Woods.")

(The Leaf People leap back apprehensively. FURTH goes through the same routine with his pistol, laying that on the ground beside the tape. FURTH then moves away slowly, palms out.)

| 2ND INTERP: Monkey Man. They surrender. As you have willed. | GITAUCHO: (Monkey Man. Others surrender. Mu<u>tu</u>tahsh! Kah<u>tahsh</u> <u>ya</u>h<u>l</u>ah. Have you willed it.) Ahn dom <u>shem</u>. |

(GITAUCHO, THE SOUND, and MONKEY MAN advance, covered by the other warriors. THE SOUND is attracted to the pistol. He holds it awkwardly.)

SONG: "Out in the Woods"
"People make me crazy
I can hardly sing my song . . . "

(At this line GITAUCHO stomps on the tape recorder like he's squishing a snake— Kill sound of song—and then kicks it ten feet US.)

FURTH: We got trouble.

GITAUCHO: Kohsh tee.

THE SOUND: <u>Kohsh</u> tee!

(WARRIORS grab FURTH and STEVEN and tie them up as THE SOUND supervises.)

STEVEN: Say something, Furth.

FURTH: I don't know their language—nobody does.

STEVEN: *Shaughnessy!* Where's *Shaughnessy?*

(He sees MONKEY MAN'S startled reaction)

You! You know Shaughnessy? Is Shaughnessy alive?

(THE SOUND seizes MAYTEEMO's bow and butts the lower end of it between STEVEN's legs—STEVEN drops to the ground. MONKEY MAN screams at SOUND.)

1ST INTERP: Childish fool!	MONKEY MAN: (Like a pre-initiate boy fool.) Goh<u>toh</u>doh <u>chum</u>ish!
2ND INTERP: Don't hit them, my Sound.	GITAUCHO: (Hit nothing more, my Sound) <u>Bu</u>mah te<u>dahm</u> roh, ree Keet.
1ST INTERP: Ancient Monkey Man. You demand to lick their living flesh. Here!	THE SOUND: (Ancient Monkey Man. You demand <u>Moo</u>droh <u>Mu</u>tutahsh! Doh <u>dee</u>cho to lick breathe flesh. Here.) bu<u>shoht</u> roosh <u>moo</u>ru. <u>Hyoh</u>!

(THE SOUND grabs STEVEN by his hair and holds his head ready for MUTUTAHSH.)

2ND INTERP: Come, Monkey Man. Fulfill your decree so we may kill them.	GITAUCHO: (Come, Monkey Man. Hetch, Mututahsh. Fulfill your <u>Pah</u>moh dohna decree and we crush-spirit.) kee<u>tah</u>zhee jah toh noorku<u>leem</u>.
1ST INTERP: It feels unborn.	MONKEY MAN: (It feels unborn.) Nah <u>moo</u>jee bah<u>roosh</u>tet.
2ND INTERP: Unborn!	THE SOUND: (Unborn!) Bah<u>roosh</u>tet!
1ST INTERP: It needs prayer.	MONKEY MAN: (Prayer this desires.) Oo<u>teel</u> nah <u>deet</u>.
2ND INTERP: The old man grows feeble. He will be our destruction.	THE SOUND: (Old man approaches weakness. Moo'tahsh <u>hoo</u>lee <u>ah</u>lahm! Will be our corpse.) Rahn <u>pah</u>moh tohna <u>tohm</u>!

Four rains ago he seized my bow
when Shaw was meant to die.

(Before four rains seized my
 Say <u>min</u> lahsh <u>koht</u> ree

death-bringer when right-
moment
<u>noor</u>poosh koo <u>zhoh</u>tah'n <u>seent</u>

came for death of Shaw.)
pah <u>noor</u> na Shaw.

1ST INTERP: If these die, who will
come after them?

MONKEY MAN:
(When these die, who will come
 Koo rah'<u>noor</u>, naboh rahn <u>seent</u>

next?)
<u>bah</u>zhah?

2ND INTERP: If they live, the Others
will leave their arrows by our
bones!

THE SOUND:
(When they live, Others will
 Koo rah'<u>moor</u>, Kah<u>tahsh</u> rahn

leave arrows near our bones!)
hee'<u>treek</u> bee tohna noo<u>mahm</u>!

1ST INTERP: It needs thought, my
Leader, not fearsome words. These
men have come for Shaw. Shaw is
a mighty mystery.

MONKEY MAN:
(It needs study, my Leader,
 Nah <u>deet</u> bah<u>kusht</u>, ree Meesho,

not man-sounds of fear.
tet kee<u>tahsh</u> na kah<u>mool</u>.

Men come for Shaw.
Tahsh <u>seent</u> pah Shaw.

Shaw is mighty mystery.)
Shaw she <u>goh</u>jee kah<u>naht</u>.

2ND INTERP: Shaw is an old
Fishbelly!

THE SOUND:
(Shaw is old Fishbelly!)
<u>Shaw</u> she mood <u>Chum</u>leet!

1ST INTERP: You are childish!

GITAUCHO:
(You are like-a-pre-initiate-boy)
Doh she goh<u>tohdoh</u>!

(THE SOUND is stung into silence. FURTH seizes the moment.)

FURTH: Leaf People, take us to Shaughnessy, we bring gifts for you *all*!

*(THE SOUND lashes out at FURTH, smashing him in the back of the head. A tense
silence follows with the outraged MONKEY MAN barely containing himself until
GITAUCHO's softly-spoken reprimand:)*

2ND INTERP: You disobey me, my
Sound.

GITAUCHO:
(You wish-refuse, my Sound.)
Doh deegah<u>tet</u>, ree Keet.

1ST INTERP: Abase yourself!   MONKEY MAN:
                                     (Show love)
                                     Pohah<u>laj</u>!

(THE SOUND is angry and sullen, but moves toward GITAUCHO for the ritual thigh-kiss of deference and respect. GITAUCHO refuses to let him perform it; takes THE SOUND's shoulders and glares into his eyes.)

2ND INTERP: From this moment,   GITAUCHO:
my Sound, my Brother, I trust   (From right-moment until,
you less.   Bu <u>zhoh</u>tah een<u>tu</u>,

                                     my Sound, my Brother,
                                     ree Keet, ree <u>Toh</u>moh,

                                     I trust you much weak.)
                                     moh doh <u>keent</u> roh <u>ah</u>lahm.

1ST INTERP: I beg your forgiveness. THE SOUND:
                                     (I pray   your happy-light)
                                     Moh oo<u>teel</u> dohna <u>zhoo</u>leesh.

2ND INTERP: You will have it in   GITAUCHO:
time.   (It will be yours again.)
                                     Nah rahn dohna <u>bah</u>zhah.

(GITAUCHO takes the MONKEY MAN's totem—a carved stick surmounted by the dried, clawlike hand of a monkey—and shakes it over the "Fishbellies," exorcising them, then motions for the warriors to pull them to their feet and march off with them.)

FURTH: We live longer today, Steven.

(GITAUCHO returns to solemn conference with MONKEY MAN as THE SOUND hovers suspiciously nearby.)

1ST INTERP: You have studied   GITAUCHO:
Shaw. What does he mean?   (You Shaw have studied.
                                     Doh Shaw ahn bah<u>kusht</u>.

                                     Why   he breathe?)
                                     Kee<u>shahsh</u> koh <u>roosh</u>?

2ND INTERP: I hesitate. But I will   MONKEY MAN:
tell you my prayer thoughts: I   (I hesitate. But tell you
begin to believe Shaw has been   Moh lek. Mah <u>hyah</u>ba doh
sent by the Invisible.
                                     my prayer thoughts:
                                     ree oo<u>teel</u> keent:

                                     Begin I to know Shaw has
                                     Bah moh <u>kusht</u> Shaw ahn

                                     come from Invisible.)
                                     <u>seent</u> bu <u>Hyai</u>rsu.

1ST INTERP: Is this so?

GITAUCHO:
(Is it so?)
Shemish?

2ND INTERP: He is without doubt a most holy man. And for now I am reluctant to kill Shaw's emissaries.

MONKEY MAN:
(Not hesitate he is much
Tet <u>lek</u> koh she roh

holy man.
<u>zhoo</u>dish tahsh.

And for now I hesitate
Jah eence moh <u>lek</u>

to kill guest of Shaw.)
noorkulee<u>m oo</u>ta na Shaw.

1ST INTERP: So be it. But I will expect you to pray very hard on this matter. I want counsel, not mysteries. Soon Fishbellies will be dropping on our heads out of trees.

GITAUCHO:
(So be it. But you must
Shem.   Mah doh toom

pray much strength on this.
oo<u>teel</u> roh ek<u>cho</u> yoh nah.

Want I direction, not mysteries.
Deet moh <u>meent</u>, tet kah<u>naht</u>!

Soon will Fishbellies
<u>Ee</u>shee rahn <u>Chum</u>leet

drop upon our heads from trees.)
ga<u>hoom</u> yoh tohna <u>reesh</u> bu <u>jee</u>!

(*As they exit,* THE SOUND *spitefully grabs the tape recorder from the* MONKEY MAN.)
(*BLACKOUT.*)

(*SET: In Front of the* Maloca. *Lights up on a space in front of the* maloca, *which is a structure equal parts city hall, community center, and church. It uses the same pole and thatch construction as the* tapiri *and* tukul—*only the facade need be indicated US.*)

(*The women of the tribe are settled on the cleared ground, going about their daily work—some pounding and straining manioc, others weaving hammocks and garments. All of them wear the minimum raiment of tropical Indians. The Boy* JEE-SHOOM *practises with a small bow and arrow; the Girl* SUTREESHAY *hangs around teasing the placid* YAWAHLAPEETEE.)

(THE SOUND'S *mother enters, a wiry little woman named* KREETAHSHAY. *She balefully regards* YAWAHLAPEETEE. SUTREESHAY, *sensing trouble, edges away.* KREE-TAHSHAY *speaks in a voice filled with venomous insinuation.*)

1ST INTERP: Look at Yawahlapeetee, the Great Sow. Weaving,
weaving, weaving, always weaving Leaf Robes for her precious
boy Gitaucho.

KREETAHSHAY:
(Look upon
Ha<u>sheem</u> yoh

Yawahlapeetee, mighty
Yawahla<u>pee</u>tee, gohjee

pig mother. Weaving, weaving,
<u>kun</u>du jeetah. <u>Yoo</u>koo, <u>yoo</u>koo,

weaving—always weaving Leaf
Robes
<u>yoo</u>koo—loo<u>mohm</u> yookoo huah-
<u>hi</u>wah

for her
pah lohna

holy   boy)
<u>zhoo</u>dish <u>toh</u>doh Gi<u>tau</u>cho.

2ND INTERP: That's true, Kreetahshay, I weave more than you. I
have to. My son's Leaf Robe is so
much longer than your Sound's
cape.

YAWAHLAPEETEE:
(This is true,
Nah she <u>gaht</u>,

Kreetahshay, I
Kree<u>tah</u>shay, moh

weave more than you. I must.
<u>yoo</u>koo roh tu doh. Moh <u>toom</u>.

Leaf Robe   of my   son   is
Huah-<u>hi</u>wah na ree <u>Tohn</u>dor she

longer than Cape of your Sound.)
<u>soom</u>-roh tu <u>yah</u> na dohna <u>Keet</u>.

1ST INTERP: My son is still growing. Soon he will have to toss off
his Cape like a child's blanket!

KREETAHSHAY:
(My Son
Ree <u>Tohn</u>dor

grows   even now.
gah<u>yah</u>dish <u>she'en</u>tah!

Soon will toss of his Cape like
<u>Ee</u>shee rahn <u>yo</u>ho kohna <u>yah</u> goh

garb of baby)
ra<u>leem</u> na <u>lahm</u>!

*(These are more than fighting words; it's an insurrection. YAWAHLAPEETEE struggles
to her feet and the women attack each other.)*

2ND INTERP: Devil! Witch!

YAWAHLAPEETEE:
(Danger-spirit.
Kah<u>leem</u>!

Curse-bringer.)
Doo<u>moosh</u>!

1ST INTERP: Stupid Not-Leaf
woman!

KREETAHSHAY:
(Clever-not
<u>Pu</u>rahtet

leaf-not woman)*
<u>hi</u>wahtet <u>ee</u>moh!

(The conflict ends abruptly when JEESHOOM sees the WARRIORS returning.)

JEESHOOM:
(Look.   Look.)
Ha<u>sheem</u>! Ha<u>sheem</u>!

(Enter WARRIORS with STEVEN and FURTH, who provoke a flurry of excitement, humor, fear, and revulsion among the women and children. KREETAHSHAY goes to THE SOUND and YAWAHLAPEETEE greets GITAUCHO. After the initial flurry of interest over the new Fishbellies, STEVEN and FURTH are tied US and the TRIBE disperses as MAYTEEMO and LEEBOH shoo them away. GITAUCHO orders THE SOUND:)

2ND INTERP: Hide them from
Shaw until their truth is revealed. Monkey Man, we talk
further.

GITAUCHO:
(Hide them
Shee<u>toom</u> tee

from Shaw until truth is
revealed.
bu <u>Shaw</u> eentu <u>gaht</u> na<u>heet</u>-ahn.

Monkey Man, we talk more.)
<u>Mu</u>tutahsh, toh <u>hyah</u>ba roh.

(GITAUCHO exits with MONKEY MAN as KREETAHSHAY and THE SOUND stare after them. The stage is clear now except for the captives and the guards, MAYTEEMO and LEEBOH. KREETAHSHAY advances on them.)

1ST INTERP: Leave us.

KREETAHSHAY: (Leave us)
Hee'<u>toh</u>!

(MAYTEEMO and LEEBOH look dubiously to THE SOUND. He impatiently motions them off.)

2ND INTERP: Be gone!

THE SOUND:
(Be gone)
<u>Heesht</u>!

---

* *"<u>hi</u>wahtet"*: Kreetahshay is taunting Yawahlapeetee by reminding her that she's not a blood-member of the tribe, that she arrived as a prisoner-of-war, a captive.

(LEEBOH and MAYTEEMO drift off. As THE SOUND inspects FURTH's pistol, KREE-TAHSHAY studies the Fishbellies with scorn and repugnance before sharply dismissing them.)

1ST INTERP: Why are these things still breathing?

KREETAHSHAY:
(Why breathe
Kee<u>sh</u>ahsh
still these things?)
roo<u>sh ee</u>ntah n'ahm?

2ND INTERP: The weakness of the Monkey Man, my Mother.

THE SOUND:
(Weakness
A<u>h</u>lahm
of Monkey Man, my Mother.)
na <u>M</u>ututahsh, ree <u>J</u>eetah.

1ST INTERP: The weakness of Gitaucho!

KREETAHSHAY:
(Weakness
A<u>h</u>lahm
of Gitaucho.)
na Gi<u>tau</u>cho!

2ND INTERP: Silence! Where do Fishbellies find things that feel like this?

THE SOUND:
(Silence)
A<u>h</u>sh!

(Examining the pistol)

(Where Fishbelly find that
Na<u>bu</u> Chumleet bah<u>roo</u> nay
thing feel like this?)
ah'<u>moo</u>jee goh nah?

1ST INTERP: I don't know. Even Fishbelly skin feels not-Leaf.

KREETAHSHAY:
(I know not.
Moh kush'<u>tet</u>.
Even Fishbelly skin
Een Chumleet <u>moo</u>ru
feels not-Leaf.)
moojee <u>Hi</u>wahtet.

2ND INTERP: Is this a toy?

THE SOUND:
(Is this toy?)
She nah <u>lah</u>lish?

(His curiosity overcoming him, THE SOUND crosses US to FURTH and STEVEN; he waves the gun in STEVEN's face as STEVEN tries to squirm out of the line of fire.)

Fishbelly. What means this not-Leaf thing?

(Fishbelly. What means this Chumleet! Teesh bahkusht nah not-leaf thing?)
Hiwahtet ahm?

STEVEN: Get that out of my face!

FURTH: Easy does it, Steven.

(THE SOUND *is fascinated by the reaction he's provoked.)*

2ND INTERP: This brings fear?

THE SOUND:
(This brings
Nah poosh
danger-poison?)
kahmool?

(KREETAHSHAY *laughs as* THE SOUND *waves the pistol at* FURTH.)

1ST INTERP: They look like they have no blood.

KREETAHSHAY:
(Is like
She goh

they are without blood.)
kahtahsh'ee mahtet deesht!

FURTH: He doesn't understand the trigger yet.

STEVEN: Is the safety on?

FURTH: No.

(THE SOUND *becomes momentarily diverted by* STEVEN's *long blond hair; he tastes it.)*

2ND INTERP: This is hair like the sun.

THE SOUND:
(This is
Nah she

hair like sun.)
meez goh deezh.

FURTH: If he wants you to pucker up, pucker.

(THE SOUND *recognizes something he does not like in* FURTH's *voice. He begins to lecture them, working himself into a fury.)*

2ND INTERP: Why have you come?
Do you not already have land?
Are there no rivers near your vil-
lages? Or have you come to take
away our green women? Will you
cage them like monkeys?

THE SOUND:
(Why
Keeshahsh
have you come? Not
ahn doh seent? Tet
already stand upon land? Not
saytah keesh yoh kohlohm? Tet
river is   near where you live?
lahneesh'ee bee nabu doh moor?

Or have you come
Oo ahn doh seent

steal our women green?
yekah tohna eemoh shay?

Will cage she like monkey?)
Rahn kohtoo'loh goh mutu?

STEVEN: I wish I was my father. He can talk to you, can't he? He's alive
because he has the gift of tongues.

(THE SOUND angrily waves the gun about as he rants at the captives.)

2ND INTERP: My Blood will not be
destroyed while I live. Flow over
us like the sand by the river. We
will become Invisible like rain.
We will wash you off the land.

THE SOUND:
My Blood
Ree Deesht

not will be killed
tet rahn noorkuleem

I while live. Us flow like
moh loo moor! Toh yuchee goh

sand   near river.   We will
mahleezh bee lahneesh. Toh rahn

invisible like rain. We will
hyairsu goh lahsh. Toh rahn

wash   you from Land.)
yahlahbay doh bu Kohlohm!

(THE SOUND accidentally pulls the trigger. Sound of pistol. The shot goes up, and
the pistol leaps from THE SOUND's hand on the recoil. The jungle explodes with
noise—pia birds, howler monkeys, Indians—a cacophony of shock and outrage.)

FURTH: Steven? You all right?

STEVEN: Yeah!

(THE SOUND stares at the gun on the ground, overwhelmed by what he's done.
GITAUCHO bursts onto the scene and quickly and silently sizes things up as MONKEY
MAN, MAYTEEMO, and LEEBOH rush to join him.)

2ND INTERP: My Leader, a Fishbelly Deathbringer! I know the
magic of it. It is mighty!

THE SOUND:
(My Leader,
Ree Meesho,

Fishbelly Deathbringer.)
Chumleet noorpoosh!

I know   magic   of it. It
Moh kusht nah'kusht n'ah! Nah

is mighty.)
she gohjee!

1ST INTERP: We kill like Warriors,
not like Devils. Destroy it.

GITAUCHO:
(We kill
Toh noorkuleem

like Warriors, not Devils.
goh Kahndor, tet Kahleem.

Crush it.)
Noorku nah.

2ND INTERP: But there is much
power here.

THE SOUND:
(But is
Mah she

here much power.)
hyoh roh ekcho!

1ST INTERP: How many deathbringers do you see?

GITAUCHO:
(How many
Nabah roh

Deathbringers you see?)
noorpoosh doh roo?

2ND INTERP: One, my Leader.

THE SOUND:
(One, my Leader.)
Tay, ree Meesho.

1ST INTERP: How many do the
Fishbellies have?

GITAUCHO:
(Are
She

how many with Fishbellies?)
nabah roh sah Chumleet?

(THE SOUND is silent.)

Can this thing have babies?

(Will this give babies?)
Rah'nah dzoo lahm?

(Again, silence.)

The Tribe must not know of this. It will make them weak with fear.

(Tribe must know-not of this.
Toh <u>toom</u> kush'<u>tet</u> n'ah.

(Will make us
Rahn <u>pah</u>moh Toh

weak with danger-poison)
<u>ah</u>lahm sah kah<u>mool</u>.

2ND INTERP: But if we learn their magic, victory is ours.

THE SOUND:
(But when
Mah <u>koo</u>

Tribe learns their magic,
Toh bah<u>kush</u>'tee nah'<u>kusht</u>,

victory is ours.)
zhah<u>lem</u> she <u>Toh</u>na!

1ST INTERP: The noise offends me thoroughly. Destroy it.

GITAUCHO:
(Sound offends
Keet <u>y</u>agah

inside and out. Crush it.)
<u>y</u>oha   Noorku nah.

(THE SOUND angrily assumes the command posture.)

2ND INTERP: Destroy it!

THE SOUND:
(Crush it)
<u>Noor</u>ku nah!

(LEEBOH moves to obey, but the MONKEY MAN intercedes to remove the curse on the gun. GITAUCHO instructs LEEBOH.)

1ST INTERP: Leeboh, don't touch it with your hands. It is poison. It is not-Leaf.

GITAUCHO:
(Leeboh,
Leeboh,

touch-not with hands.
moojee-<u>tet</u> sah <u>hee</u>mu.

It is poison. It is not-Leaf.)
Nah she <u>mool</u>. Nah she <u>H</u>iwahtet.

(LEEBOH carefully passes twine through the trigger housing. He exits with gun.)

1ST INTERP: You like the feel of things not-Leaf, don't you, my Sound?

GITAUCHO:
(You like
Doh <u>ee</u>ndrah

feel of-things not-Leaf,
<u>moo</u>jee n'ahm <u>H</u>iwahtet,

is it so, my Sound?)
<u>shem</u>ish, ree Keet?

(THE SOUND angrily jumps US, grabs STEVEN by the hair and shouts—)

2ND INTERP: This is not-Leaf! I
hate the feel of it. Will you destroy this?

THE SOUND:
(This is
Nah she

not-Leaf. I hate feel
Hiwahtet! Moh tek moojee

of it. Will crush this?)
n'ah! Rahn noorku nah?

1ST INTERP: I don't answer to you!
Why have you not concealed the
captives? Must I say everything
twice for you? Hide them.

GITAUCHO:
(I proclaim
Moh keetahzhee

not for you.   Why   not
tet pah doh! Keeshahsh tet

hide   captives?
sheetoom ahn ootoh?

Must I speak twice all
Too'moh hyahba zhah mohm

for you? Hide   them.)
pah doh? Sheetoom tee!

THE SOUND: Sheetoom tee!

(MAYTEEMO and CHOOLKAHNOOR shove FURTH and STEVEN offstage. GITAUCHO
glares angrily at THE SOUND, then exits briskly with the MONKEY MAN. KREETAH-
SHAY is seething.)

1ST INTERP: Are you not a man?
Are you not a Warrior? Gitaucho
speaks to you like a foolish little
boy.

KREETAHSHAY:
(Not is man?
Tet she tahsh?

Not is Warrior?
Tet she Kahndor?

Gitaucho speak you
Gitaucho hyahba doh

like-little-boy foolish.)
gohtohdoh   chumish.

2ND INTERP: Do not mock me, my
mother.

THE SOUND:
(Laugh
Leeshay

not me, my Mother.
tet yee, ree Jeetah.

(Confused, thinking it out.)

I am filled with thoughts of danger. Why does Gitaucho allow them life?

(I am filled with thoughts
  Moh gah<u>leet</u> sah <u>keent</u>

of danger.   Why
na <u>kah</u>. Kee<u>shahsh</u>

Gitaucho allow them life?)
Gitaucho ga<u>het</u>'ee <u>moor</u>?

1ST INTERP: Gitaucho is bewitched by Shaughnessy.

KREETAHSHAY:
(Gitaucho
Gi<u>tau</u>cho

is bewitched by Shaw.)
ahn doo<u>moosh</u> pah <u>Shaw</u>.

2ND INTERP: Yes, my Mother, you speak truth.

THE SOUND:
(Yes, my Mother,
<u>Shem</u>, ree Jeetah,

you speak truth.)
doh <u>hyah</u>ba <u>gaht</u>!

1ST INTERP: Shaw is the Fishbelly Devil.

KREETAHSHAY:
(Shaw
Shaw

is Fishbelly Devil.)
she <u>Chum</u>leet Kah<u>leem</u>!

2ND INTERP: He feeds on Gitaucho's heart. Shaw must die.

THE SOUND:
(He eats   heart
Koh <u>chohtoh</u>'<u>moosh</u>

of Gitaucho. Shaw die must.)
na Gi<u>tau</u>cho! Shaw noor <u>toom</u>!

(*A brief pause, then:*)

1ST INTERP: Gitaucho protects Shaw.

KREETAHSHAY:
(Gitaucho
Gitaucho

protects Shaw.
zhee<u>tahm</u> Shaw.

(*Very gently*)

Gitaucho must die.

Gitaucho die must.)
Gitaucho noor <u>toom</u>.

2ND INTERP: You speak of my
Brother.

THE SOUND:
(You speak
Doh <u>hyah</u>ba

of my Brother.)
na ree <u>Toh</u>moh!

1ST INTERP: Your Brother betrays
us to the Fishbellies.

KREETAHSHAY:
(Your Brother
Dohna <u>Toh</u>moh

betrays us to Fishbellies.)
ta<u>hool</u> Toh <u>Chum</u>leet.

2ND INTERP: These words are
poison.

THE SOUND:
(These
Nah

man-sounds are poison.)
kee<u>tahsh</u>'ee <u>mool</u>.

(THE SOUND exits. exits. KREETAHSHAY stares after him as if he were a vision of undiminishing glory. She says her dream.)

1ST INTERP: My Son. Soon I will
weave you the longest Leaf Robe
any woman ever wove. It will
trail behind you on the ground,
and Warriors will hold their
breath when you pass by.

KREETAHSHAY:
(My Son.
Ree <u>Tohn</u>dor.

Soon I will weave
<u>Eence</u> moh rahn <u>yoo</u>koo

longest Leaf Robe woman weave
<u>soom</u>-roh huah-<u>Hi</u>wah eemoh
<u>yoo</u>koo

ever.   It will follow
say<u>mohm</u>. Nah rahn ga<u>heet</u>

you below on ground,
doh <u>baht</u> yoh koh<u>lohm</u>,

and Warriors will hold
jah <u>Kahn</u>dor rahn koht

breath when you approach.)
<u>roosh</u> koo doh <u>hoo</u>lee.

(BLACKOUT.)

(From the Blackout, the sound of crying is heard . . . sporadic groans and soft, muffled sobs.)

(SET: Inside Gitaucho's Tukul. Lights up very dim on two slightly raked areas. In one location KEERAH and SUTREESHAY are sleeping on either side of YAWAHLAPEE-

TEE, *who snores lightly. Isolated in another area,* SHAUGHNESSY *is awake and listening to the muffled whimpering. He strikes a match, lights a taper, which gives off a faint but constant glow.)*

SHAUGHNESSY:
Keerah?

KEERAH:
(What?)
Teesh?

SHAUGHNESSY:
(Someone breaths-tears—i.e., cries.)
<u>Boh</u>koh roo<u>shoom</u>.

*(*KEERAH *silently moves over to join him.)*

2ND INTERP: Someone cries.

1ST INTERP: Green Father. Sometimes he cries while sleeping.	KEERAH: (Green Father. Shay <u>Tahn</u>dor.
	Sometimes he cries Boh<u>say</u>tah koh roo<u>shoom</u>
	while spirit-lives = sleeping.) loo lee<u>moor</u>.
2ND INTERP: Is he sad?	SHAUGHNESSY: (Is he sad?) <u>She</u> koh <u>oom</u>roh?
1ST INTERP: Not when awake.	KEERAH: (Not when awake.) <u>Tet</u> koo zhee<u>reet</u>.
2ND INTERP: Why is he called the Green Father?	SHAUGHNESSY: (Why Kee<u>shahsh</u>
	he named Green Father?) koh <u>tah</u>zhee Shay <u>Tahn</u>dor?
1ST INTERP: Because he was the first to turn green.	KEERAH: (For he Pah koh
	was altered first green.) ahn <u>keen</u>say tay <u>shay</u>.

2ND INTERP: He's green like you?

SHAUGHNESSY:
(He is
<u>Koh</u> she

like you green?)
<u>goh</u> doh <u>shay</u>?

1ST INTERP: Yes. Before him, everyone was brown like Gitaucho.

KEERAH:
(It's so.
Shem.

Him before us was brown
Tee <u>say</u> toh ah<u>n</u> <u>or</u>u

like Gitaucho.)
goh Gitaucho.

2ND INTERP: Why haven't I seen him yet?

SHAUGHNESSY:
(Why
Kee<u>shahsh</u>

I not see him-still?)
moh tet roo <u>tee'n</u>tah?

1ST INTERP: He is not allowed in the living place.

KEERAH:
(He is not
<u>Koh</u> she <u>tet</u>

allowed where-we-live.)
ga<u>het</u>'a toh<u>moor</u>.

SHAUGHNESSY:
(Why?)
Kee<u>shahsh</u>?

1ST INTERP: He makes green baby girls.

KEERAH:
(He makes
<u>Koh</u> <u>pah</u>moh

green baby girls.)
shay lahm <u>loh</u>moh.

SHAUGHNESSY: (*Increasingly intrigued*) Just females . . .

2ND INTERP: Keerah, take me to him.

SHAUGHNESSY:
(Keerah,
Keerah,

take me before him.)
<u>poosh</u> yee <u>say</u> tee.

1ST INTERP: Shaw ... in the   KEERAH: (Shaw ...
morning.   Shaw ...

                                      when morning.)
                                      koo <u>zhoo</u>loh.

2ND INTERP: How can I sleep with   SHAUGHNESSY: (How I sleep
the Green Father crying?   <u>Na</u>bah moh

                                      because Green Father cries?)
                                      lee<u>moor</u> pah Shay <u>Tahn</u>dor
                                      roo<u>shoom</u>?

(KEERAH starts to massage his shoulders and chest.)

1ST INTERP: (I will help you.   KEERAH: (I will
                                             Moh rahn

                                      help you.)
                                      jee<u>mu</u> doh.

2ND INTERP: I'll go myself.   SHAUGHNESSY: (I myself will go.)
                                             Mohree hee<u>trahn</u>.

(Concerned he'll exert himself, she makes him recline again.)

                                      KEERAH: Tet-tet-tet.
2ND INTERP: Take me to the man   SHAUGHNESSY: (Take me
who weeps.   <u>Poosh</u> yee

                                      before man   who   weeps.)
                                      say <u>tahsh</u> naboh roo<u>shoom</u>.

1ST INTERP: Green Father must   KEERAH: (Green
wait.   Shay

                                      Father must wait.)
                                      <u>Tahn</u>dor too'<u>moht</u>!

*(YAWAHLAPEETEE stirs and groans softly in her sleep. KEERAH checks with a glance
to make sure her mother is still sleeping. Then she opens the thin garment she is
wearing, shows herself to SHAUGHNESSY, takes his hand and presses it to her.)*

2ND INTERP: Your brother will   SHAUGHNESSY: (Your brother
beat you if you give yourself to   Dohna <u>toh</u>moh
me.
                                      will beat you when me give up.)
                                      rahn <u>bu</u>mah doh koo'ee <u>yah</u>lah.

(KEERAH flips his hand away.)

1ST INTERP: You think I'm ugly. You don't like my skin.

KEERAH: (You think
            Doh keent

I am ugly. You
moh she ekbeesh. Doh

like   not my skin.)
eendrah tet ree mooru.

(YAWAHLAPEETEE awakens and asks sleepily:)

2ND INTERP: Are you all right, Keerah?

YAWAHLAPEETEE: (Safe
                        Ahlem

are, Keerah?)
she, Keerah?

1ST INTERP: Yes. Sleep.

KEERAH: (Yes. Sleep.)
            Shem. Leemoor.

(She lays her head on SHAUGHNESSY's chest, and he holds her tenderly.)

SHAUGHNESSY: Ree tendahmosh Keerah ...*(Takes her shoulders)* Look at me.

2ND INTERP: I'm ugly, not you. And I'm old and sick.

SHAUGHNESSY: (I am
                    Moh she

ugly,   not you. And   I
ekbeesh, tet doh. Jah moh

am old   and-sick.)
she mood jah'laht.

1ST INTERP: You are a holy man.

KEERAH: (You are holy man.)
Doh she zhoodish tahsh.

2ND INTERP: Who tells you this?

SHAUGHNESSY: (Who
                    Naboh

you speaks this?)
doh hyahba nah?

1ST INTERP: The Monkey Man.

KEERAH: (Monkey Man.)
            Mututahsh.

2ND INTERP: He is self-deceived.

SHAUGHNESSY: (He
                    Koh

lies-to-shadow.)
oomeenaht!

1ST INTERP: He speaks truth. I see it.

KEERAH: (Speaks truth.
            Hyahba gaht.

I   see it.)
Moh roo nah.

(SHAUGHNESSY is truly displeased. He forces her away from him.)

2ND INTERP: The Sound calls me Ancient Fishbelly. He is closer to the truth.

SHAUGHNESSY: (Sound me Keet yee call ancient Fishbelly. tahzhee moodroh Chumleet! He-approaches truth.) Ko'hoolee gaht.

1ST INTERP: Beware, Shaw. The Sound thirsts to kill you.

KEERAH: (Danger-comes, Shaw. Kahseent, Shaw! Sound thirsts you crush-spirit.) Keet lahdek doh noorkuleem!

2ND INTERP: I know. I am careful. I go to the Green Father. Will you come?

SHAUGHNESSY: (I know. Moh kusht. I am aware. I-go Moh she hasheem. Mo'heet Green Father. Will come?) Shay Tahndor. Rahn'etch?

1ST INTERP: Why do you make me cry? I don't like to cry.

KEERAH: (Why you Keeshahsh bring-tears? I like doh pooshoom? Moh eendrah not breathe-tears.) tet rooshoom.

SHAUGHNESSY: I'm sorry.

(He struggles to his feet, takes the taper and stumbles through the dimness out of the tukul. KEERAH puts her head on the floor and weeps softly. YAWAHLAPEETEE rolls over lazily and pulls KEERAH to her. She goes back to sleep with the sobbing KEERAH trapped beneath her massive arms.)

(Blackout . . . except for SHAUGHNESSY's taper.)

(A campfire appears in the Blackout.)

(SET: Green Father's Camp. Lights up dim. The GREEN FATHER is concealed beneath a blanket of leaves. SHAUGHNESSY falteringly makes his way toward the light of the fire.)

SHAUGHNESSY: Shay Tahndor!

(GREEN FATHER sits up abruptly, and the leaf blanket drops away to reveal an enormous man, hairless and corpulent as a Buddha. And green, of course.)

1ST INTERP: You must be Fishbelly.

SHAY TAHNDOR: (You Doh must be Fishbelly.) toom she Chumleet.

(SHAUGHNESSY laughs a bit hysterically. He is once again being wasted by fever.)

2ND INTERP: Yes, yes, how do you do, Green Father?

SHAUGHNESSY: (Yes, yes. Shem, shem! How are you, Green Father?) Nabah she doh, Shay Tahndor?

(SHAY TAHNDOR, *now fully awake, becomes a generous host.*)

1ST INTERP: Better than you, I see. Lie down.

SHAY TAHNDOR: (Better than you, Hyeenish tu doh, I see. Lie down.) moh roo. Gahzheb.

(He eases SHAUGHNESSY *onto his bed.)*

SHAUGHNESSY: Thank you, thank you ...

SHAY TAHNDOR: (Water?) Lahbay?

SHAUGHNESSY: Yes, yes please ...

*(*SHAY TAHNDOR *helps him drink from gourd, then* SHAUGHNESSY *falls back.)*

1ST INTERP: Tell me what else I can do to help you.

SHAY TAHNDOR: (Tell what Hyahba teesh will you assist?) rahn doh jeemu?

2ND INTERP: Nothing. You are kind, but I'm dying. Soon.

SHAUGHNESSY: (Nothing. Tedahm. Me you are, but I Yee doh she, mah moh die. Soon.) noor. Eeshee.

SHAY TAHNDOR: (Is this so?) Shemish?

SHAUGHNESSY: My pills don't touch this stuff.

1ST INTERP: How old are you, Fishbelly?

SHAY TAHNDOR: (How much Nabah roh life, Fishbelly?) moor, Chumleet?

2ND INTERP: Fifty-eight.

SHAUGHNESSY: (Five-ten-eight) Pekreksool.

1ST INTERP: You have seen 58 long rains?

SHAY TAHNDOR: (You have Doh ahn seen 58 long rains?) roo pekreksool soomlahsh?

SHAUGHNESSY: I feel much older right now.

1ST INTERP: I am very ancient, and I have only 47 rains.

SHAY TAHNDOR: (I am Moh she much ancient, and I have roh moodroh, jah moh ahn only four-ten-seven.) nee minrekyem.

(SHAY TAHNDOR laughs.)

No wonder you are dying. You should have died long ago.

(Not amazing you die. Should Tet nohshintay doh noor. Toom have died long before.) ah'noor soom say!

(Pulls SHAUGHNESSY toward him, props him up, saying as he does so:)

Come. I will give up my strength to you.

(Come. I will you give up Hetch. Mon rahn doh yahlah my force.) ree ekcho.

2ND INTERP: I am one with you, and with the beautiful night.

SHAUGHNESSY: (I am one with Moh she tay sah you and with beautiful night.) doh, jah sah tendahmosh kaht.

1ST INTERP: Beautiful night? The night is hideous! I must burn the fire all night long. If it dies, I will be eaten by animals. And the firewood is always wet. Oh, don't tell me of the beauties of the night.

SHAY TAHNDOR:
(Beautiful night?
Tendahmosh kaht?
Night is hideous.
Kaht she moolkahchoh!
I must burn fire night
Moh tom huahteel heezh kaht
long-all. When this dies, me
soo'mohm. Koo nah noor, yee
wild animals will devour.
kahdek rahn chohtohm.
And firewood all is wet.
Jah heezhee mohm she pishlah.
Oh, tell not of
Um, hyahba tet na
beauties of night.)
tendahsh na kaht.

(Momentary silence)

Talk of the dew in the morning and listen to the birds greet the sun. Did you know that, one by one, every morning women of the tribe come to see me? They say "Give me green girls, Holy Father!" And I do. Only I can do this.

(Talk of dew of morning and Hyahba na sulah na zhooloh, jah sound-see birds praise sun. keetroo lohzh tahloom deezh. Know you this, one by one, Kusht doh nah, tay pah tay, morning every, women of Tribe zhooloh mohm, eemoh na Toh come me to see? Say "Me give seent yee roo? Hyahba "Yee dzoo girl   green, holy father." lohmoh shay, zhoodish tahndor!" And   do. Only-I-my can do.) Jah pahmoh. Neemohree pahmoh.

2ND INTERP: Keerah is your daughter?

SHAUGHNESSY: (Keerah
               Keerah
is your girl baby?)
she dohna lohmohlahm?

1ST INTERP: Yes, Keerah is my first. Then Lohzhoodish and Sutreeshay ... soon there will be many. Gitaucho likes green girls.

SHAY TAHNDOR:
(Yes, Keerah is
Shem, Keerah she
my first. Next Bird-holy
ree tay. Bahzhah Lohzhoodish
and Flower-green and soon more
jah Sutreeshay jah eeshee roh
there will be. Gitaucho
soot rahn. Gitaucho
likes   girls green.)
eendrah lohmoh shay!

2ND INTERP: Because they're so beautiful?

SHAUGHNESSY:
(For are beautiful?)
Pah she tendahmosh?

1ST INTERP: Because they are invisible in the jungle.

SHAY TAHNDOR: (For are
               Pah she
invisible in land.)
Hyairsu ha Kohlohm!

Gitaucho says when the Tribe is green like leaves, our enemies will not see us. We will be safe. We will live like trees.

Gitaucho says when we are green Gitaucho <u>hyah</u>ba koo <u>Toh</u> she shay

like leaves, our enemies will be goh <u>hi</u>wah, tohna <u>tek</u>ah rahn

blind. Tribe will be safe. Tribe roo<u>tet</u>.   Toh rahn ah<u>lem</u>   Toh

will live like trees.) rahn <u>moor</u> goh <u>jee</u>.

2ND INTERP: Do you believe that?

SHAUGHNESSY: (You believe that?) Doh <u>keent</u> nay?

1ST INTERP: Without doubt.

SHAY TAHNDOR: (Not hesitate.) Tet lek.

(Pause)

I am happy you have come, Fishbelly. But isn't this a strange time to visit?

(I am happy you have come, Moh she <u>leesh</u> ahn doh <u>seent</u>,

Fishbelly. But is it Chumleet. Mah <u>shem</u>ish

not-Leaf come-now?) <u>hi</u>wahtet seent'ah?

2ND INTERP: I couldn't sleep. Your weeping troubled me.

SHAUGHNESSY: (Not sleep.   <u>Tet</u> lee<u>moor</u>.

Your crying   me awakened.) Dohna roo<u>shoom</u> yee zhee<u>reet</u>.

1ST INTERP: Why do you say that? I do not cry.

SHAY TAHNDOR: (Why you   Kee<u>shahsh</u> doh

say   that? Not cry.) <u>hyah</u>ba nay? <u>Tet</u> roo<u>shoom</u>!

2ND INTERP: But Keerah heard you, too.

SHAUGHNESSY: (But Keerah heard.) Mah Keerah'n kee<u>troo</u>.

1ST INTERP: That was not me. It was my other self.

SHAY TAHNDOR: (Me that   Yee <u>nay</u>

was not. It was my other-life.) ahn <u>tet</u>! Nah'n <u>ree</u>shee!

SHAUGHNESSY: Reeshee?

1ST INTERP: A night-bird that married my soul.

SHAY TAHNDOR:
(Bird-night
Lohzh<u>kaht</u>

that married my spirit.)
n'ahn jee<u>lah</u> ree <u>leem</u>.

I hear her, too, sometimes.

Even I hear   her sometime.)
Een moh kee<u>troo</u> loh boh<u>sav</u>tah.

2ND INTERP: Green Father, all men weep.

SHAUGHNESSY: (Green Father,
                    Shay <u>Tahn</u>dor,
all men breathe-tears.)
mohm <u>tahsh</u> roo<u>shoom</u>.

1ST INTERP: I don't cry! I am the happiest man alive. I have been happy for seven long rains. Ever since power came to Gitaucho. He lets me live near the People. He protects me.

SHAY TAHNDOR: (Not cry.
                    <u>Tet</u> roo<u>shoom</u>!
   I am man   alive much
happy.
Moh she tahsh <u>moor</u> roh <u>leesh</u>!

   I am happy now from seven
Moh she <u>leesh</u> tah bu   <u>yem</u>

long-rains. From when power
<u>soom</u>lahsh. Bu koo ek<u>cho</u>

    came   Gitaucho. He me
allows
seen<u>t ahn</u> Gi<u>tau</u>cho. Koh yee
ga<u>het</u>

near People. He me protects.)
bee <u>Toh</u>.   Koh yee zhee<u>tahm</u>.

2ND INTERP: And before him?

SHAUGHNESSY: (And before him?)
                    Jah <u>say</u> tee?·

1ST INTERP: Before Gitaucho, no one loved my skin. Tribe made me live all alone in the jungle. For twenty long rains I was filled with fear and sorrow. That was when I learned to hate the night.

SHAY TAHNDOR:
(Before Gitaucho,
 Say Gi<u>tau</u>cho,

    no one liked my skin.
te<u>dahm</u> <u>een</u>drah ree <u>moor</u>u.

Tribe demand only-I-my live
Toh <u>dee</u>cho neemohree <u>moor</u>

upon Land.　For twenty
yoh Kohlohm. Pah zhah<u>rek</u>

long-rains　I　　　filled
<u>soom</u>lahsh moh gahlee<u>t ahn</u>

with fear　and sorrow. That was
sah kah<u>mool</u> jah <u>oom</u>roh. Nay
<u>ahn</u>

when I learned hate-night.)
koo moh bah<u>kush</u>' te'<u>kaht</u>.

(Brief pause)

But I *lived*. And now I am the Green Father.	(But lived.　And now,　I am Mah moo<u>r ahn</u>! Jah <u>tah</u>, moh she Green Father.) Shay <u>Tahn</u>dor!

(He laughs as he revels in his present glory.)

2ND INTERP: Green Father, may I sleep here?	SHAUGHNESSY: (Green Father, 　　　　　　　Shay <u>Tahn</u>dor, will me spirit-live?) rahn yee lee<u>moor</u>?

SHAY TAHNDOR: Shem, shem . . .

(SHAUGHNESSY wins a brief moment of repose in the arms of Shay Tahndor.)
(BLACKOUT.)
(Sound of Indian Music. Sound of a rattle wielded by MONKEY MAN.)
(SET: Same. Lights up full on SHAY TAHNDOR and SHAUGHNESSY as before. After a moment ENTER MONKEY MAN and GITAUCHO.)

1ST INTERP: We greet you, my Leader.	SHAY TAHNDOR: (We 　　　　　　　Toh you speak, my Leader.) doh <u>hyah</u>ba, ree Meesho.

(SHAY TAHNDOR makes an effort to rise for the 'pohahlaj' but GITAUCHO's hand on his head stays him.)

SHAUGHNESSY: Ree Meesho. Mututahsh.

2ND INTERP: I have come to learn more words.	GITAUCHO: (I come 　　　　Moh <u>seent</u>

have to study more words.)
ahn bah<u>kusht</u> roh kee<u>tahsh</u>.

1ST INTERP: I will try.

SHAUGHNESSY: (Will try)
Pah<u>b</u>ahmoh.

GITAUCHO: Tu. Zave. Yu.

SHAUGHNESSY: (To save you.)
Pah<u>lem</u> doh.

(The MONKEY MAN*'s worst fears are confirmed, and he is terrified. He shakes his rattle, makes a keening noise.* GITAUCHO *seems merely irritated.)*

2ND INTERP: And from what can
you save me, Shaw?

GITAUCHO: (And from
     Jah bu

what you save me, Shaw?)
<u>teesh</u> doh pah<u>lem</u> yee, Shaw?

From jaguars? I have killed seventeen. From the Kreen Akorore?
Or the Caibi? They live in terror
of my Sound.

From jaguars? Seventeen have I
Bu ahsee<u>lah</u>til? Rek<u>yem</u> ahn
killed.   From Kreen Akorore?
noorku<u>leem</u>. Bu K<u>reen</u> Ako<u>rore</u>?

Or Caibi? Live danger-men under
Oo Ca<u>i</u>bi? Moor kah<u>tahsh</u> baht

fear   of my Sound.)
kah<u>mool</u> na ree <u>Keet</u>.

1ST INTERP: I will save you from
the Fishbellies.

SHAUGHNESSY: (I will
       Moh rahn

save   you from Fishbellies.)
pah<u>lem</u> doh bu <u>Chum</u>leet.

2ND INTERP: The Fishbellies plan
to make war on me?

GITAUCHO: (Fishbellies
       <u>Chum</u>leet

want many-deaths with me?)
deet roh<u>noor</u> sah yee?

1ST INTERP: They draw near.
Where once the Suyah Indians
lived, now there live Fishbellies.

SHAUGHNESSY: (They
     Kah<u>tahsh</u>

draw near. Where before live
gah<u>oo</u>lee. Na<u>bu</u> say moor

Suia, now live Fishbellies.)
<u>Su</u>yah, tah moor <u>Chum</u>leet.

2ND INTERP: The Suyah have been
destroyed?

1ST INTERP: They are no more.

2ND INTERP: The Suyah live only
twelve mornings from my People.

1ST INTERP: Now you must be a
great Leader, Gitaucho.

2ND INTERP: Will you bring me
weapons?

1ST INTERP: No weapon will save
you from the Fishbellies. They
will kill you with fire and with
loud noises. They will poison you
with insects too small to see.
They destroy with things for
which you have no words. If you
stay here, you will not even be
able to stand and fight. You must
flee, or you will die.

GITAUCHO: (Suia crushed?)
       Suyah'noorku?

SHAUGHNESSY:
(They are nothing.)
Kahtahsh'ee tedahm.

GITAUCHO: (Suia live only
       Suyah moor nee

mornings twelve from my Tribe.)
zhooloh rekzhah bu ree Toh.

SHAUGHNESSY: (Now you must
            Tah doh toom

be mighty Leader, Gitaucho.)
she gohjee Meesho, Gitaucho.

GITAUCHO: (You bring
       Doh poosh

will weapons?)
rahn noorahm?

SHAUGHNESSY: (No weapon
            Ted noorahm

save you from Fishbellies.
pahlem doh bu Chumleet.

Will destroy with fire and big
Rah'noorku sah beezh jah
yahdish

noise. Will you poison with
insects
keet. Rahn doh mool sah beet

much small see. Destroy with-
things
roh zheet roo. Noorku sah' mah-

lacking words. When you remain,
tet kee'tahsh. Koo doh hee'tet,

not will permit you stand and
tet rahn gahet doh keesh jah

fight.   You must flee,
choolkah. Doh toom kaheesht,

or you will die.)
oo doh rah'noor.

2ND INTERP: There is nothing to fear but the Invisible!

GITAUCHO: (Nothing is Tedahm she to fear but the Invisible.) kahmool mah Hyairsu!

1ST INTERP: *Greed* is invisible.

SHAUGHNESSY: (Greed is invisible.) Sheemoosh'ee hyairsu!

(The MONKEY MAN and GITAUCHO are both shaken by the force of SHAW's words. He continues more gently.)

You and your Tribe are skilled in concealment. You must let me hide you on *my* land. It is vast and as beautiful almost as this. And it is safe. Fishbellies do not go there. Only . . . Indians.

(You and your Tribe are smart in Doh jah dohna Toh she purah ha hiding.   You must me allow to sheetoom. Doh toom yee gahet hide   you upon my land. sheetoom doh yoh ree kohlohm.

Is big   and beautiful near She yahdish jah tendahmosh bee like this. And it is safe. goh nah.   Jah nah she ahlem.

Fishbellies not allow there. Chumleet tet gahet soot.

Only . . . Indians.) Nee . . . Indians.

2ND INTERP: Enemy Others?

GITAUCHO: (Enemy Danger-men?) Tekah Kahtahsh?

SHAUGHNESSY: Tupuias, Yamatari, many Karawetari . . .

2ND INTERP: Enemies! I live with the Leaf People. I do not live with murdering devils!

GITAUCHO: (Enemy. Tekah! With Leaf People I live. Sah Hiwahtoh moh moor!

Live not with murderer   devils.) Moor tet sah noorkutahsh kahleem!

1ST INTERP: Then soon you will all die.

SHAUGHNESSY: (Quickly you Eeshee doh will die   all.) rah'noorkulee'mohm!

2ND INTERP: If willed by the Invisible, yes. So be it.

GITAUCHO: (When Invisible
Koo <u>Hy</u>airsu
wills it, yes. So be it.)
<u>deet</u> nah, <u>shem</u>! <u>SHEM</u>!

(He pauses, composes himself, continues with grace and strength.)

But we will not die. Fishbellies do not know the Land. They drown in the leaves.

(But Tribe not will die.
Mah Toh <u>tet</u> rah'noorku<u>leem</u>.

Fishbellies know not the Land.
<u>Chum</u>leet kush'<u>tet</u> Koh<u>lohm</u>.

Suffocate under leaves.)
<u>Pool</u>kah baht <u>hi</u>wah.

(Spreads his Leaf Robe.)

But we *are* the leaves. We move like sunlight through the trees. We strike as suddenly as the rain, and our arrows are poisoned raindrops.

(But we are leaves. Tribe
Mah <u>Toh</u> she <u>hi</u>wah! Toh
moves   as sunlight under trees.
ga<u>hoo</u>lee goh dee<u>zhoo</u> baht <u>jee</u>.

We strike quickly as rain,
Toh <u>bu</u>mah <u>ee</u>shee goh <u>lahsh</u>,

and our arrows are
jah tohna <u>treek</u> she

poison rain-darts.)
<u>mool</u> lahsheek!

(Wraps Robe about him, continues more gently—even a bit lyrically.)

And then we are gone. Our Warriors become leaves once more, and we are one with the Invisible. Soon even our women will all be as green as flowers, and no devil will ever be able to see them.

(And soon Tribe is gone. Our
Jah <u>ee</u>shee Toh heet ahn. Tohna

Warriors are leaves again, and
<u>Kahn</u>dor she <u>hi</u>wah <u>bah</u>zhah, jah

we are Invisible. Soon even
<u>Toh</u> she <u>Hy</u>airsu. <u>Ee</u>shee een

our   women will be all green
<u>toh</u>na <u>ee</u>moh rahn mohm <u>shay</u>
goh

as flowers, and no   devil   will
<u>su</u>treesh, jah <u>ted</u> kah<u>leem</u> rahn

ever   them see.)
say<u>mohm</u> loh <u>roo</u>.

1ST INTERP: Fishbellies will find them. Fishbellies kill even flowers.

SHAUGHNESSY: (Fishbellies
         Chum<u>l</u>eet
will find them.
rahn bah<u>roo</u> loh.

Fishbellies kill   even flowers.)
<u>Chum</u>leet noorku<u>leem</u> een
<u>s</u>utreesh.

2nd Interp: I will hear no more fearsome words. You speak as if my People were all as weak as you.

GITAUCHO: (Not hear
         Tet kee<u>troo</u>
nothing words   of fear.
tedahm kee<u>tahsh</u> na kah<u>mool</u>!

You speak like my People
Doh <u>hyah</u>ba goh ree <u>Toh</u>

are weak   like you.)
she <u>ah</u>lahm goh <u>doh</u>!

1ST INTERP: My Leader, this man is holy. You must show respect.

MONKEY MAN: (My Leader,
         Ree <u>Mee</u>sho,
this man is holy.
nah <u>tahsh</u> she <u>zhoo</u>dish.

You must show respect.)
Doh <u>toom</u> poh tay<u>huah</u>.

2ND INTERP: He shows no respect for the Leaf People. Our smallest child is brave and junglesmart. Our women, our children, we are all Warriors. Shaw asks us to run like deer.

GITAUCHO: (He shows not
         Koh poh <u>tet</u>
respect for Leaf People.
tay<u>huah</u> pah Hi<u>wah</u>toh!

Our much little boy   is brave
<u>Toh</u>na roh zheet <u>toh</u>doh she
doh<u>keel</u>

and smart-Land.   Our
women,
jah <u>p</u>urah-Koh<u>lohm</u>. Tohna
<u>ee</u>moh

our   children,   we are all
tohna <u>toh</u>mohlahm, Toh she
<u>mohm</u>

Warriors. Shaw wants us to run
<u>Kahn</u>dor! <u>Shaw</u> dee'Toh ka<u>heesh</u>t

like deer.)
goh <u>pee</u>tu!

1ST INTERP: I ask you to lead your
Tribe to safety. I ask you to be
wise.

SHAUGHNESSY: (I want
                    Moh <u>deet</u>
you to lead your Tribe
doh <u>mee</u>shoht dohna Toh

safe.   I want you
ah<u>lem</u>. Moh <u>deet</u> doh

to be much smart.)
she roh <u>pu</u>rah.

2ND INTERP: My Leader, when this
man came to us, he did not know
us. He knew only that when the
Fishbellies come, we kill them.
But he came. He followed us
where we went, and he gave
many gifts. Even when the children shot darts at him for sport,
he gave us presents. Is this not
holy?

MONKEY MAN: (My Leader
                    Ree <u>Mee</u>sho,
when this man   came   Tribe,
koo nah <u>tahsh</u> seent <u>ahn</u> Toh,

he know not us. Know only
koh kush'tet Toh. <u>Kusht</u> nee

when Fishbellies come, we kill.
koo <u>Chum</u>leet <u>seent</u>, Toh
noorku<u>leem</u>.

But he came.   He us
followed
Mah koh seent <u>ahn</u>! Koh Toh
ga<u>heet</u>

    where we went   and gave
ahn na<u>bu</u> Toh heet <u>ahn</u>, j'ahn
dzoo

gifts many. Even when boys for
<u>loom</u> roh. Een koo <u>toh</u>doh pah

entertainment dart-spit, he us
<u>een</u>dreesh eek kah<u>choh</u>, koh Toh

    gave   gifts. Is it not holy?)
ahn dzoo <u>loom</u>. <u>Shem</u>ish
<u>zhoo</u>dish?

1ST INTERP: It is powerful.

GITAUCHO: (It is strong.)
                    Nah she ek<u>cho</u>.

2ND INTERP: And for four long-
rains, he slept without a woman.
For four long-rains he chose to
live like the Green Father, alone
in the Jungle. Why? Ask him, my
Leader.

MONKEY MAN: (And for four
                    Jah pah <u>min</u>
long-rains, he slept lacking
soomlahsh, koh lee<u>moor</u> mahtet

woman. For four long-rains he

eemoh. Pah <u>min</u> soomlahsh, koh

willed like to live Green Father,
 dee<u>t ahn</u> goh <u>moor</u> Shay
 <u>Tahn</u>dor,

alone   upon   Land.
neekoh<u>ree</u> yoh Koh<u>lohm</u>.

  Why?
Kee<u>shahsh</u>?

Discover of him, my Leader.)
Bah<u>roo</u> na tee, ree Meesho.

(GITAUCHO smiles bleakly.)

1ST INTERP: I know why, Monkey Man.	GITAUCHO: (I know already, Moh <u>kusht</u> saytah,

Monkey Man.)
Mututahsh.
"Tu. Zave. Yu."

(During MONKEY MAN's argument, the tribe begins to filter onstage, assuming a semicircular ring around the principals. They watch curiously as GITAUCHO performs a pohahlaj *with* SHAUGHNESSY, *kneeling and kissing his thigh in a gesture of submission. As he does so,* MONKEY MAN *ecstatically shouts:)*

2ND INTERP: I understand the Mystery of Shaw. It is revealed. Shaw is the Sound of the Invisible.	MONKEY MAN: (I know Moh <u>kusht</u>

mystery of Shaw. It is revealed.
kah<u>naht</u> na <u>Shaw</u>! Nah'n na<u>heet</u>!

Shaw is Sound of Invisible)
<u>Shaw</u> she <u>Keet</u> na <u>Hyairsu</u>!

(GITAUCHO assumes his declamatory stance with THE SOUND *half-crouched before him in his official posture.)*

The Proclamation:

2ND INTERP: Leaf People, my Blood! We are cursed and we are blessed!	GITAUCHO: (Leaf People, Hi<u>wah</u>toh,

my Blood. We are
ree <u>Deesht</u>! Toh she

cursed and we are holy.)
<u>doom</u> jah Toh she <u>zhoo</u>dish!

THE SOUND: Hiwahtoh, ree Deesht! Toh she doom jah Toh she zhoodish!

2ND INTERP: The Fishbellies approach. The Invisible has told me this through the tongue of Shaw.

GITAUCHO: (Fishbellies Chumleet approach. Invisible me has hoolee. Hyairsu y'ahn told for tongue of Shaw.) hyahba pah bushoh na Shaw.

THE SOUND: Chumleet hoolee! Hyairsu y'ahn hyahba pah bushoh na Shaw!

2ND INTERP: There is great evil in the Fishbellies. Much of it can be seen, but most of it lies hidden like poison in the fangs of a snake.

GITAUCHO: (Is mighty She gohjee danger in-and-out of Kah yoha na Fishbellies. Of much this we see, Chumleet. Na roh nah toh roo, but of most this hide like mah na beemohm nah sheetoom goh poison of fang of snake.) mool na drahk na neezh.

THE SOUND: She gohjee Kah yoha na Chumleet! Na roh nah toh roo, mah na beemohm nah sheetoom goh mool na drahk na neezh.

(There is great tension throughout the tribe during the Proclamation; occasional whimpering-like noises escape some of the women.)

2ND INTERP: But do not fear, my Blood. The Invisible is our Lover. It gives us Shaw.

GITAUCHO: (But not fear, Mah tet kahmool, my Blood. Invisible is our ree Deesht. Hyairsu she Tohna Lover. Gives us Shaw.) ahlajahm. Dzoo Toh Shaw.

(THE SOUND does not like the ring of that. He shows some displeasure, but repeats it.)

THE SOUND: Mah tet kahmool, ree Deesht! Hyairsu she Tohna ahlajahm! Dzoo Toh Shaw!

2ND INTERP: Leaf People, my Blood! Shaw is the Sound of the Invisible. While I breathe, it is true.

GITAUCHO:
(Leaf People, my Blood.
Hiwahtoh, ree Deesht!

Shaw is Sound of Invisible.
Shaw she Keet na Hyairsu!

While I breathe, it is true.)
Loo moh roosh,   nah she gaht!

(THE SOUND can't bring himself to say the words. The TRIBE is instantly tense to the point of confusion. KREETAHSHAY, his mother, is thunderstruck: events have outstripped her plans.)

GITAUCHO: Loo moh roosh, nah she gaht.

(THE SOUND angrily relents.)

THE SOUND: Hiwahtoh, ree Deesht! Shaw she Keet na Hyairsu! Loo moh roosh, nah she gaht!

(The tribe remains in a state of incipient panic. They sense THE SOUND will balk at any moment.)

| 2ND INTERP: It has been revealed. We must follow Shaw to a hidden place away from the Fishbellies. There we must live with the different Others. | GITAUCHO: (It has been revealed.
         N'ahn   naheet.

  We must Shaw way   follow
Toh toom Shaw meent gaheet

where hide   from Fishbellies.
nabu sheetoom   bu Chumleet.

There must join   us
   Soo'toom jeelah Toh

and different Others.)
jah gohtet Kahtahsh. |

(The tribe is appalled by these words. THE SOUND lets the adverse reaction sink in, then booms out only the last sentence.)

THE SOUND: Soo'toom jeelah Toh jah gohtet Kahtahsh!

| 2ND INTERP: When we do this, the Invisible allows life for the Leaf People. But if we remain on our land and fight . . . | GITAUCHO: (When we this do,
         Koo Toh nah
         pahmoh,

Invisible allows life for
Hyairsu gahet moor pah

Leaf People. But when we remain
Hiwahtoh.   Mah koo Toh
hee'tet

on our land and
yoh tohna kohlohm jah

fight . . .)
choolkah . . . |

(GITAUCHO deliberately stops, waits for THE SOUND to repeat his uncompleted thought. THE SOUND does so, suspiciously.)

THE SOUND: Koo Toh nah pahmoh, Hyairsu gahet moor pah Hiwahtoh! Mah koo Toh hee'tet yoh tohna kohlohm jah choolkah ...

2ND INTERP: ... the Invisible has told me we will all die.	GITAUCHO: (Invisible me has ...Hyairsu y'ahn
	told we will die all.)
	hyahba Toh rah'noor mohm!

(The tribe looks as one to THE SOUND. Slowly he leaves the ritual stance and faces GITAUCHO. THE SOUND takes off his Cape and holds it out.)

1ST INTERP: My tongue cannot speak treason.	THE SOUND: (My tongue Ree bushoh
	speaks not treason.)
	hyahba tet keetahool.

(THE SOUND drops his Cape to the ground. Chaos breaks loose in the TRIBE. Many weep, others plead with THE LEADER and THE SOUND. THE SOUND trumpets above it all:)

1ST INTERP: Shaw is not the Sound of the Invisible! He is the Fishbelly Devil!	THE SOUND: (Shaw not is Sound of Invisible. Shaw tet she Keet na Hyairsu!
	He is Fishbelly Danger-spirit.)
	Koh she Chumleet Kahleem!
2ND INTERP: Those who would fight, fight by our side!	KREETAHSHAY: (You for Doh pah
	fight, fight with us.)
	choolkah, choolkah sah toh!
1ST INTERP: Leaf People, my Blood! I must kill Gitaucho so my Blood can live. Pray for me, Leaf People.	THE SOUND: (Leaf People, my Blood. Hiwahtoh, ree Deesht!
	I must Gitaucho kill
	Moh toom Gitaucho noorkuleem
	so my Blood will live.
	pah ree Deesht moo'rahn!
	Pray for me, Leaf People.)
	Ooteel pah yee, Hiwahtoh!

(THE SOUND and KREETAHSHAY exit defiantly. The tribe becomes hushed as they stare at GITAUCHO. For his part SHAUGHNESSY wants desperately to address the Tribe, but his training inhibits him from intervening in a profoundly tribal matter.)

(In the hush, GITAUCHO *imagines himself preparing for combat with* THE SOUND.*)*

2ND INTERP: I am sad, my
Brother. The Fishbellies came,
and now I must kill you.

GITAUCHO: (Feel I many tears,
    Moojee moh oomroh,

my Brother. Fishbellies came,
ree Tohmoh. Chumleet
seent ahn,

and now I
must   kill   you.)
jah tah moh toom noorkuleem
doh.

(He moves into a semi-slow motion pre-enactment of his coming duel with THE
SOUND.*)*

My Brother. Let us fight well.
Come. Dance. Dance with me.
But you're clumsy, yes. Catch
me, Fat Fish. Fight better. Ah,
much better. Don't get too good
now, my Brother, yes.

(My Brother. Power fight.
Ree Tohmoh! Ekcho choolkah!

Come.   Dance.   Me with
Hetch! Leemshoht! Yee sah

dance.   But you are clumsy,
leemshoht! Mah doh she dahah,

  yes. Catch, Fat Fish. Fight
shem! Hoosht, Tucunare!
Choolkah

better.   Um, better much.
hyeenish! Um, hyeenish roh.

Learn not   much, my Brother,
Bahkush'tet roh, ree Tohmoh,

yes.)
shem.

(Moving now with a powerful, controlled frenzy.)

I am cursed, my Brother. But you
will die!

(I am cursed, my Brother.
Moh she doom, ree Tohmoh!

But you will die.)
Mah doh rah'noor!

*(He finishes off the imaginary Sound with a devastatingly varied final attack of
kicks, blows, and bites.)*

And I will *rule!*

(And I   will rule.)
Jah moh rahn tohkeel!
GITAUCHO!

(The tribe jubilantly echoes his name as the curtain falls.)

End of Act One

*(During Intermission two songs are played. The first is "*All Along the Watchtower,*" using the live version recorded by Dylan and The Band. Follow immediately with a plangent instrumental called "*The End of the World,*" performed by the Nitty Gritty Dirt Band. Lights up for Act Two at conclusion of songs.)*

Act Two

(SET: THE SOUND's Tukul. It is the night before the Fight for Leadership. THE SOUND is brooding over the tape recorder, trying to fathom the source of its power.)

(KREETAHSHAY stares with pride at him. She begins talking softly. He doesn't pay any attention to her.)

1ST INTERP: My son, today you were a beauty of a man. *More than a man, a jaguar. I saw you move toward power like the sun over the trees, and my body filled with love.*

KREETAHSHAY: (My Son,
          Ree <u>Tohn</u>dor,

today   were you beauty   of man.
loo<u>zhoo</u> ahn doh ten<u>dahsh</u> na <u>tahsh</u>.

More than man, jaguar.
<u>Roh</u> tu tahsh, ahsee<u>lah</u>til!

I   saw move toward power
Moh <u>roo</u>-ahn ga<u>hoo</u>lee ek<u>cho</u>

like Sun over trees, and my
goh <u>deezh</u> boot <u>jee</u>, jah ree

body filled with-love.)
<u>tohm</u> gah<u>leet</u> sah'<u>laj</u>.

2ND INTERP: This is powerful magic for a toy. But I will come to understand it. I will steal this power.

THE SOUND: (This is power
          Nah she ek<u>cho</u>

magic   for toy.   But will
nah'<u>kusht</u> pah <u>lah</u>lish. Mah rahn

know it.   I will steal
<u>kusht</u> nah. Moh rahn <u>ye</u>kah

this power.)
nah ek<u>cho</u>.

KREETAHSHAY: Ree Tohndor. Ha<u>sheem</u>.

(She removes a shield and reveals a speaking platform.)

2ND INTERP: What's that thing?

THE SOUND: (What that thing?)
          <u>Teesh</u> nay ahm?

1ST INTERP: It's a speaking platform. After you kill Gitaucho, you will speak to the Tribe on top of this.

KREETAHSHAY:
(Speaking platform.
Tahzheeahm.

When you   kill   Gitaucho,
Koo doh noorku<u>leem</u> Gi<u>tau</u>cho,

you will speak Tribe on this)
doh rahn <u>hyah</u>ba Toh yoh nah.

2ND INTERP: Stupid Mother. The Tribe will laugh at me when I stand on that.

THE SOUND: (Mother-silly.
                    Jeetah-poobish!

Tribe will laugh me
    Toh rahn leeshay'ee

when I stand   on that.)
koo moh keesh yoh nay.

1ST INTERP: They will stop laughing. They will come to demand it.

KREETAHSHAY: (Not will
                    Tet rahn

laugh. Tribe will demand it.)
leeshay! Toh rahn deecho nah!

2ND INTERP: You talk like Gitaucho already lies dead.

THE SOUND: (You speak like
                    Doh hyahba goh

Gitaucho already dies.)
Gitaucho saytah noor.

1ST INTERP: He is dead. Today, when you turned to face him, his eyes were filled with fear. Did you not see?

KREETAHSHAY: (He is dead.
                    Koh she noor!

Today, when you turn, his
Loozhoo, koo doh hoht, kohna

eyes   filled   with fear.
hyahdee gahleet-ahn sah
kahmool.

You not see?)
Doh tet roo?

(THE SOUND laughs curtly.)

2ND INTERP: By morning you will see Gitaucho on fire with life.

THE SOUND:
(By morning will you see
Pah zhooloh rahn doh roo

Gitaucho aflame with life.)
Gitaucho gaheezh sah moor.

1ST INTERP: Piss on fire and it will die. So will Gitaucho.

KREETAHSHAY: (Piss   on fire
                    Yahlahbay yoh
                    heezh

and will die. Like will Gitaucho.)
jah rah'noor! Goh rahn Gitaucho!

2ND INTERP: Maybe we'd do better if *you* fight him.

THE SOUND: (Perhaps better
                    Shem'uted hyeenish

when you fight him.)
koo doh choolkahtee.

1ST INTERP: My Son. I see things
hidden from you. I see how all
things have brought us to this
moment. And I see Gitaucho
dead.

KREETAHSHAY: (My Son.
         Ree Toh̲n̲dor.

  I see things hide from you.
Moh r̲o̲o̲ ahm shee̲t̲o̲o̲m̲ bu doh.

  I see how everything comes
Moh r̲o̲o̲ nabah moh̲m̲ seent

to right moment. And   I
zho̲h̲tah.   Jah moh

see Gitaucho dead.)
r̲o̲o̲ Gitaucho n̲o̲o̲r̲!

2ND INTERP: Why do I have to
fight Gitaucho anyway?

THE SOUND: (Why   I
        Kee̲s̲h̲a̲h̲s̲h̲ moh

must even Gitaucho fight?)
t̲o̲o̲m̲ een Git̲a̲u̲cho cho̲o̲l̲kah?

KREETAHSHAY: Teesh?

2ND INTERP: I hate being The
Sound. I will be a good Warrior
instead.

THE SOUND: (I hate being
        Moh t̲e̲k̲ she

the Sound. Still I   will
K̲e̲e̲t̲.   Eentah moh r̲a̲h̲n̲

be mighty Warrior.)
gohjee K̲a̲h̲n̲dor.

1ST INTERP: Don't say boyish
things.

KREETAHSHAY: (Speak
        Hyahba

not like boy.)
t̲e̲t̲ goh t̲o̲h̲doh.

2ND INTERP: But I love Gitaucho.
What joy is there for me in his
death?

THE SOUND: (But Gitaucho I
        Mah Git̲a̲u̲cho moh

love. What happy for me
ahl̲a̲j̲. Teesh l̲e̲e̲s̲h̲ pah y̲e̲e̲

in him death?)
ha tee n̲o̲o̲r̲?

(KREETAHSHAY *studies him thoughtfully. She speaks quite gently.*)

1ST INTERP: You have worked
hard today. Your head is tired.

KREETAHSHAY: (Today
        Loo̲z̲h̲o̲o̲

have you learned much.
ahn doh bah̲k̲u̲s̲h̲t̲ roh.

Your   head-is tired.)
Dohna r̲e̲e̲s̲h̲'ee z̲h̲ebah.

2ND INTERP: It's the Fishbellies I
hate. Why can't I just kill them?

THE SOUND: (It is Fishbellies
                    Nah she Chumleet

I hate. Why   not
moh tek. Keeshahsh tet

    kill   only them?)
noorkuleem nee tee?

1ST INTERP: Come. No more talking for a while. No more thinking. Just sit and I will sharpen
your teeth.

KREETAHSHAY: (Come. For now,
                    Hetch. Eence,

speak not. And think not.
hyahba tet. Jah keen'tet.

    Sit only and I   will
Gahsh nee jah moh rahn

sharpen your teeth.)
kahtreek dohna dek.

(She sits in front of him and pulls a small object from her wrist. THE SOUND *submits docilely as she files his upper and lower incisors and canines. It seems to relax him, like a monkey being groomed.* KREETAHSHAY *talks gently to him as if he were a child whose hair was being combed.)*

After you kill Gitaucho and the
Fishbellies, you must kill Yawahlapeetee and Keerah.

(When have killed   Gitaucho
  Koo ahn noorkuleem Gitaucho

and Fishbellies, must   kill
jah Chumleet,   toom
noorkuleem

Yawahlapeetee and Keerah.)
Yawahlapeetee jah Keerah.

THE SOUND: (*Protesting despite
the file in his mouth.*)
(Not Keerah.)
Tet Keerah.

1ST INTERP: I believe the Monkey
Man can be put to use. He may
live so long as he is needed.

KREETAHSHAY: (I believe
                    Moh keent

Monkey Man will help us.
Breath
Mututahsh rahn jeemu toh.
Roosh

allow until he has helped.)
gahet eentu koh ahn jeemu.

(THE SOUND *pulls the file out.*)

2ND INTERP: Not Keerah. Keerah   THE SOUND: (Not Keerah.
will marry me.   Tet Keerah!

                                   Keerah will-me marry.)
                                   Keerah <u>rahn</u>'ee jee<u>lah</u>!

1ST INTERP: Marry you?   KREETAHSHAY: (Marry you?)
                                                   Jee<u>lah</u> doh?

(KREETAHSHAY *thinks it over, decides it's not a bad idea.*)

1ST INTERP: All right. But only   KREETAHSHAY:
after Yawahlapeetee is dead.   (It's so. But only when
                                     Shem.   Mah <u>nee</u> koo

                                   Yawahlapeetee is dead.)
                                   Yawahla<u>pee</u>tee ah'<u>noor</u>.

(*She returns to filing his teeth.*)

(*A brief blackout.*)

(SET: *Inside* GITAUCHO'S *Tukul.* YAWAHLAPEETEE *is busy sharpening* GITAUCHO'S
teeth, when he permits her. He is extremely edgy and can scarcely sit still.)

(FURTH *and* STEVEN *have now been placed in his lodging, tied together to a beam
off in a corner.* FURTH *is sleeping, but* STEVEN *is wide awake though it is well past
dark.*)

(GITAUCHO *specifies a tooth and says:*)

2ND INTERP: Sharpen.   GITAUCHO: (Sharpen.)
                                              Kah<u>treek</u>.

(YAWAHLAPEETEE *attempts to do so, but* GITAUCHO *impatiently pushes away the
file.*)

Where is the ugly flea? Why does   (Where is ugly   flea?
she take so long? Do they wait   Na<u>bu</u> she ek<u>beesh</u> cheet?
for power to fall from me?
                                   Why   gone   still?
                                   Kee<u>shahsh</u> heet_ahn <u>een</u>tah?

                                   She wait for power fall
                                   Loh <u>moht</u> pah ek<u>cho</u> ga<u>hoom</u>

                                   from me?)
                                    bu yee?

1ST INTERP: Keerah hasn't been gone that long. And Shaw is very sick and slow afoot.

YAWAHLAPEETEE: (Keerah not Keerah tet long gone.   And Shaw is much soom heet-ahn. Jah Shaw she roh sick   and walk-toward ahlaht, jah gahoolee sloth-like.) yorkoozhgoh.

(GITAUCHO feels his teeth with his thumb. One does not pass muster, and he files it himself.)

Would you like some dahbish, my Son?

(Want some dahbish, my Son?) Deet boh dahbish, ree Tohndor?

(GITAUCHO nods. She gets a short hollow reed and a small bowl containing a reddish-brown powdery substance. She sucks a quantity of powder into the tube, and GITAUCHO assists her in placing it in one of his nostrils. She blows the contents into his nose. He holds his breath for a moment, then expels it slowly. Almost immediately he seems to relax.)

(STEVEN observes all this with fascination.)

STEVEN: Uh . . . excuse me?

(GITAUCHO and YAWAHLAPEETEE look his way as STEVEN indicates the reed.)

Mind if I join you?

GITAUCHO: (*Holding out reed*) Dahbish?

(STEVEN nods, smiling. GITAUCHO brings over the bowl and the reed and assists STEVEN in the same fashion YAWAHLAPEETEE did for him. Only when STEVEN has ingested the substance does he inspect the contents of the bowl.)

STEVEN: That doesn't look like anything I've ever done. What's it . . . s'posed . . . to . . .

(GITAUCHO and YAWAHLAPEETEE catch STEVEN as he sags forward from the waist, stone-cold unconscious. They laugh and pat his head and stroke his face.)

2ND INTERP: His head dances on his body.

GITAUCHO: (His head Tee reesh dances   on his body.) leemshoht yoh tee tohm.

1ST INTERP: While his Other-Self sings.

YAWAHLAPEETEE: (While his Loo tee alter-ego sings.) reeshee leempoor.

(Enter SHAUGHNESSY assisted by LEEBOH and MAYTEEMO. SHAY TAHNDOR, KEERAH

and MONKEY MAN *bring up the rear. During the remainder of this scene, several other warriors and squaws filter in to observe.)*

2ND INTERP: Finally.

GITAUCHO: (Finally.)
       Jah<u>tah</u>.

1ST INTERP: You must not fight The Sound. You must not risk dying!

SHAUGHNESSY: (Sound must
      <u>Keet</u> toom

fight   not. Must approach
choo<u>lkah tet</u>! Toom <u>hoo</u>lee

not death.)
tet <u>noor</u>!

2ND INTERP: Don't talk, Shaw. I see how much it hurts you.

GITAUCHO: (Soft, Shaw,
      Ah<u>loom</u>, Shaw,

talk
hyahba

not.   I see you sick   much.)
<u>tet</u>. Moh <u>roo</u> doh <u>ah</u>lahm roh.

(In fact, SHAUGHNESSY *has never looked worse. The commotion has awakened* FURTH, *but* STEVEN *remains in a stupor.)*

FURTH: Hello, Shaughnessy. How's your Messiah Complex?

*(*SHAUGHNESSY *looks over toward them for the first time but still does not recognize* STEVEN, *whose head rests on the ground away from him. But* SHAUGHNESSY *knows* FURTH.*)*

SHAUGHNESSY: Furth.

FURTH: That's good, the way you contain your joy.

2ND INTERP: You know the captives?

GITAUCHO: (You captives know?)
      Doh <u>oo</u>toh kusht?

1ST INTERP: One of them. I can't see the other.

SHAUGHNESSY: (One of him.
      <u>Tay</u> na tee.

Not see other.)
Tet roo kah<u>tahsh</u>.

(Without an order LEEBOH *and* MAYTEEMO *help* SHAUGHNESSY *over to the prisoners, then lift Steven's head.* SHAUGHNESSY *stares incredulously, and* STEVEN *gazes helplessly back, his mouth agape.)*

SHAUGHNESSY: Steven! Are you all right?

STEVEN: *(Badly slurred)* Hi . . . Pop . . .

*(*SHAUGHNESSY *looks accusingly at* GITAUCHO.*)*

1ST INTERP: Did you give him dah̲bish?

SHAUGHNESSY: (Give you
Dzoo doh

him dahbish?)
tee dah̲bish?

(GITAUCHO *smiles down at Steven.*)

2ND INTERP: He is such a baby warrior. Do you know him?

GITAUCHO: (He is-still
Koh she'entah

baby warrior. You him know?)
lahm kah̲ndor. Doh tee kush̲t?

1ST INTERP: Yes. He is my son.

SHAUGHNESSY: (It's so.
Shem.

He is my son.)
Koh she ree Toh̲ndor.

(SHAUGHNESSY's *answer causes consternation and wonder in all but* GITAUCHO, FURTH, *and the bedrugged* STEVEN. *The first distinct sentence that can be heard is from* YAWAHLAPEETEE.)

The Sound of the Invisible and the Son of the Sound of the Invisible. In my dwelling, all at once.

YAWAHLAPEETEE: (Sound of
Keet na

Invisible and son   of Sound
Hyairsu   jah Toh̲ndor na Keet

of Invisible. In my tukul.
na Hyairsu! Ha ree tukul!

Now all.
Tah mohm!

(She embrances GITAUCHO.)

We are blessed. Victory is yours.

We are blessed.
Toh she gahzhoodish!

Victory is yours.)
Zhahl̲em she doh̲na!

GITAUCHO: (It's so. It's so)
Shem! SHEM!

(KEERAH *joins him and his mother in a three-way embrace, then* GITAUCHO *breaks away to issue a decree.*)

2ND INTERP: I rule: Free the Son of the Sound of the Invisible.

GITAUCHO: (I rule: Bind
Moh tohkeel: Kohsh

not Son of Sound of Invisible.)
tet Toh̲ndor na Keet na Hyairsu.

(LEEBOH *undoes* STEVEN's *bonds. He falls face forward onto floor.*)

And the other one? What is he,
Shaw?

(And other.   What-is
Jah kah<u>tahsh</u>. <u>Teesh</u>'ee
he, Shaw?)
koh, Shaw?

1ST INTERP: He is my enemy.

SHAUGHNESSY:
(He is my enemy.)
<u>Koh</u> she ree <u>te</u>kah.

2ND INTERP: So. We kill him now.

GITAUCHO: (So. He
                                Um. Tee

kill   now.)
noorku<u>leem</u> tah.

(Several warriors leap for FURTH, *stopping only after* GITAUCHO *backs up* SHAUGH-
NESSY's *objection.)*

1ST INTERP: No! I don't want his
blood on my hands.

SHAUGHNESSY: (No. No want
                                Ted! Te'<u>deet</u>

his blood on my hands.)
kohna <u>deesht</u> yoh ree <u>hee</u>mu.

GITAUCHO: Shem. Mayteemo? Leeboh?

MAYTEEMO and LEEBOH: Ree <u>Mee</u>sho?

2ND INTERP: Do you want to play
Jaguars and Tapir?

GITAUCHO: (You want to do
                                Doh deet <u>pah</u>moh

Jaguar   -   Tapir?)
ahsee<u>lah</u>til-kun<u>dah</u>bu?

1ST INTERP: Much yes. Great fun.

MAYTEEMO: (Much it's so.
                                <u>Roh</u> <u>shem</u>!

Mighty entertainment.)
<u>Gohjee</u> <u>eendreesh</u>!

A wise decision, my Leader.

LEEBOH: (Much better
                                Roh <u>hyee</u>nish

decree,   my Leader.)
kee<u>tah</u>zhee, ree <u>Mee</u>sho!

2ND INTERP: I rule: He is a tapir.

GITAUCHO: (I rule:
                                Moh toh<u>keel</u>:

He is tapir.)
Koh she kun<u>dah</u>bu.

(General amusement from tribe. MAYTEEMO *and* LEEBOH *enthusiastically unbind*
FURTH *and drag him to his feet.)*

FURTH: What's happening here, Shaughnessy?

SHAUGHNESSY: It seems to be a game called Jaguars and Tapir.

FURTH: Uh-oh, I think I know that one. I get to be the tapir, right?

(GITAUCHO leads YAWAHLAPEETEE and KEERAH off to one side where they again embrace and stroke each other's faces with great tenderness.)

SHAUGHNESSY: As I understand it, these two will take you to the edge of the jungle and release you. They'll wait till they can't hear you anymore, and then they'll come after you.

FURTH: And if they catch me?

> SHAUGHNESSY: *(To* MAYTEEMO *and* LEEBOH)
> (When caught, what you will do?)
> Koo <u>koht</u>,   <u>teesh</u> doh rahn <u>pah</u>moh?

(MAYTEEMO and LEEBOH share a laugh.)

> MAYTEEMO: (What we want.)
> <u>Teesh</u> toh <u>deet</u>!

SHAUGHNESSY: (To FURTH) Don't get caught.

FURTH: Fun-loving little bastards, aren't they? Wait a minute, wait a *minute*! First I want my money. Steven's giving me twenty grand for finding you. I'll bet that burns your ass, don't it?

> SHAUGHNESSY: (Hold not)
> Koht<u>'et</u>.

(Warriors allow FURTH to rifle STEVEN's day-pack till he finds the money.)

FURTH: Please certify I take only my fee.

SHAUGHNESSY: Take what you want, take it all. Steven couldn't care less.

FURTH: Yeah? Well, a hazardous duty bonus does seem to be in order.

(He stuffs it all into his pockets. MAYTEEMO and LEEBOH again begin to shove him out.)

SHAUGHNESSY: I hope you make it, Furth.

FURTH: You're all heart, Shaughnessy. You gonna throw your kid to these dogs, too?

(They push him out. GITAUCHO finishes saying goodbye to KEERAH and YAWAHLAPEETEE.)

2ND INTERP: Monkey Man. We go to pray.

> GITAUCHO: (Monkey Man.
> <u>Mu</u>tutahsh.
>
> We go pray.)
> Toh heet oo<u>teel</u>.

MONKEY MAN: Shem, ree Meesho.

1ST INTERP: Don't fight the Sound. SHAUGHNESSY:
Only you can persuade the Leaf   (Fight   not Sound.
People to come to my land. Lis-   Choolkah tet Keet!
ten: When I die, you must follow
the river north, then east until Only you-self will teach
you see my people. Maybe ten   Needohree   rahn jeemu
days. Give them this and they   Leaf People come my land.
will save you and your Blood.   Hiwahtoh   heet ree kohlohm.

                                  Listen: When   I die,
                                  Keetroo: Koo moh noor,

                                  must you follow river
                                  toom doh gaheet lahneesh

                                  north and east until you see
                                  tutah jah tutoh eentu doh roo

                                  my people. Maybe   ten
                                  ree toh. Shem'uted rek

                                  mornings. Give them
                                  zhooloh. Dzoo tee

(Presses an envelope upon GITAUCHO.)

                                  this and they   will save
                                  nah, jah kahtahsh rahn pahlem

                                  you and your Blood.)
                                  doh jah dohna Deesh't.

2ND INTERP: First I must kill The GITAUCHO: (First I
Sound.   Tay moh

                                   must Sound . kill.)
                                   toom Keet noorkuleem.

1ST INTERP: He's too strong.   SHAUGHNESSY: (He is
                                               Koh she

                                   power-much.)
                                   ekcho-roh!

2ND INTERP: I am not weak. I am   GITAUCHO: (I am not weak.
fast. I am smart.   Moh she tet ahlahm!

                                     I am fast. I   am smart.)
                                   Moh she hueet! Moh she purah!

(Pauses, then calmly)

You must not talk of weakness.   (You must talk   not of-
You must bless me.   weakness.
                                   Doh <u>toom</u> hyahba <u>tet</u> n'ahlahm.

                                   You must bless-me.)
                                   Doh <u>toom</u> gah<u>zhoo</u>dish'ee.

(SHAUGHNESSY is defeated by the humility in GITAUCHO's request. He surrenders both the argument and all further hope of saving the Tribe. He bows to the imperatives of ritual.)

1ST INTERP: You are right. Come.   SHAUGHNESSY: (You are
                                                       Doh she
                                     true. Come.)
                                     <u>gaht</u>. Hetch.

(SHAUGHNESSY kisses GITAUCHO's left thigh.)

The Invisible is your Lover.   (Invisible is your Lover.)
                                     <u>Hyairsu</u> she dohna ah<u>lajahm</u>.

(GITAUCHO is deeply moved by this gesture. After a moment, he touches SHAUGHNESSY's face and murmurs . . .)

2ND INTERP: Breathe softly, Shaw.   GITAUCHO: (Breathe
                                                  Roo<u>shoom</u>
                                     soft, Shaw.)
                                     ah<u>loom</u>, Shaw.

(Takes YAWAHLAPEETEE by her shoulders.)

Tonight, my Mother, you must   (This night my Mother you must
sleep in the camp of the Green   Nah <u>kaht</u>, ree <u>Jee</u>tah, doh <u>toom</u>
Father. And Keerah . . .
                                     sleep   near fire of
                                     lee<u>moor</u> bee <u>heezh</u> na

                                     Green Father. And Keerah . . .)
                                     Shay <u>Tahn</u>dor. Jah Keerah . . .

1ST INTERP: I stay with Shaw.   KEERAH: (I remain
Here.   Moh hee'<u>tet</u>
                                     Shaw with. Here.)
                                     Shaw sah. Hyoh.

2ND INTERP: As you will it, my   GITAUCHO: (As you will it,
Sister.   Doh <u>shem</u>,
                                     my Sister.)
                                     ree <u>Ohmoh</u>.

(He is helped into his Leaf Robe)

I will return to you with one less
Brother.

(I will return minus
Moh rahn hoh<u>teet</u> mah<u>tet</u>

one Brother.)
tay <u>Toh</u>moh.

(The other members of the Tribe slowly exit. SHAY TAHNDOR *remains to comfort*
YAWAHLAPEETEE. SHAUGHNESSY *stares at* STEVEN *until* KEERAH *joins him and*
persuades him to lie down upon a leafy 'bed' area on floor.)

(Lights dim to Blackout.)

(Sound of Indian music, low.)

(SET: A Clearing in the Jungle. Blue light up on MONKEY MAN *and* GITAUCHO. *They*
stand back to back, separated by a few feet, and they stare up at the night sky
through a hole in the roof of the jungle. At no time do they touch or even look at
one another. They sing the prayer in an alternating chant as the MONKEY MAN
mimes climbing a tree. He lifts first one leg, then an arm; repeats. He freezes whenever
he sings his part. GITAUCHO *holds his arms out to his side, palms up, head back.)*

2ND INTERP: Monkey Man climb
to the tallest tree.

GITAUCHO: (Monkey Man-climb
          Mu<u>tu</u>tah'<u>shoom</u>

on much tall tree.)
yoh roh hee <u>jee</u>.

1ST INTERP: Monkey Man climbs,
Monkey Man climbs...

MONKEY MAN: (Monkey Man-
            climb,
            Mu<u>tu</u>tah'<u>shoom</u>,

Monkey Man-climb)
Mu<u>tu</u>tah'<u>shoom</u>...

2ND INTERP: I am blind down on
the ground.

GITAUCHO: (I am
          <u>Moh</u> she

blind upon ground.)
roo<u>tet</u> yoh koh<u>lohm</u>.

1ST INTERP: I can see, from the
tree, Monkey Man climbs, Monkey Man climbs...

MONKEY MAN: (I see from tree
            <u>Moh</u> roo bu <u>jee</u>,

Monkey Man-climb,
Mu<u>tu</u>tah'<u>shoom</u>,

Monkey Man-climb...)
Mu<u>tu</u>tah'<u>shoom</u>...

2ND INTERP: Climb until you see
the stars.

GITAUCHO: (Climb until you
          <u>Shoom</u> een<u>tu</u> doh

see stars.)
<u>roo</u> kah<u>tahm</u>.

1ST INTERP: Taller than the tallest tree ...

MONKEY MAN: (Much tall tree
                     Roh hee jee

much big all ...)
roh yahdish mohm ...

1ND INTERP: Open wide your eyes.

GITAUCHO: (Open
                    Zheemosh

big   your eyes.)
yahdish dohna hyahdee.

1ST INTERP: Like the lemur, there is no night ...

MONKEY MAN: (Like lemur
Goh mutukaht

is night-not ...)
she kah'tet ...

2ND INTERP: Turn your head around one time.

GITAUCHO: (Turn your
                    Hoht dohna

head until circle.)
reesh eentu klee.

1ST INTERP: Like the lemur I can see.

MONKEY MAN: (Like lemur
                    Goh mutukaht

myself see!)
mohree roo!

1ST INTERP: See the Invisible.

GITAUCHO:
(Invisible be aware!)
Hyairsu hasheem!

2ND INTERP: See the Invisible.

MONKEY MAN: (Invisible be
                    aware!)
                    Hyairsu
                    hasheem!

2ND INTERP: My Blood sings.

GITAUCHO: (Sing   my Blood!)
                    Leempoor ree Deesht!

(There is silence. The MONKEY MAN is frozen in a trancelike state, his head thrown back to the sky. Suddenly a star explodes and falls earthward like a used flash bulb.)

(Sound of Indian music out.)

2ND INTERP: A star dies.

GITAUCHO: (Dies star)
                    Noor kahtahm!

1ST INTERP: The Sound dies.

MONKEY MAN: (Dies Sound)
                    Noor Keet!

(Another shooting star spurts up and out.)

2ND INTERP: And another.

GITAUCHO: (And again)
            Jah bahzhah!

MONKEY MAN: Shaw!

(Lights flare up and out all over the stage.)

2ND INTERP: This cannot be.
There. And there. All over. The
sky is full of corpses.

GITAUCHO: (This is not. There.
            Nah she tet! Soot!

And there. All over.
Jah soot! Mohm boot!

Sky full   of corpses.)
Lohm gahleet na tohm!

*(Silence from the MONKEY MAN, who is overwhelmed by the meteor shower. GI-
TAUCHO watches the display until a deep calm comes over him.)*

This speaks of war with the Fishbellies, Monkey Man.

(This speak of many-death from
Nah hyahba na rohnoor bu

Fishbellies, Monkey Man.)
Chumleet, Mututahsh.

MONKEY MAN: Shem.

(The MONKEY MAN whirls and embraces GITAUCHO. They cling to one another.)

GITAUCHO:
(Bigger danger awake   than I dreamed.)
Roh yahdish kah zheereet tu moh leemoor-ahn.

2ND INTERP:
There is more evil loose than I
dreamed.

(GITAUCHO presses SHAW's letter into the MONKEY MAN's hands.)

2ND INTERP: Get this to the Green
Father. He must flee tonight with
my mother. By morning it is
buzzards.

GITAUCHO:
(Take this Green Father.
Poosh nah Shay Tahndor.

    He escape   tonight-must with
Koh kaheesht nahkah'toom sah

my Mother. By morning
ree Jeetah. Pah zhooloh

it is buzzards.)
nah she chohmoosh.

1ST INTERP: What of Keerah?

MONKEY MAN: (What of Keerah?)
                Teesh na Keerah?

2ND INTERP: She is in no danger. She must only endure a few long-rains of sadness. Go, Monkey Man. I must be alone now.

GITAUCHO: (She is danger not.
        Loh she kah tet.
She must only live few long-rains
Loh toom nee moor boh soomlahsh

of sadness. Go,   Monkey Man.
na oomroh. Heet, Mututahsh.

    I be must alone   now.)
Moh she toom neemohree tah.

(The MONKEY MAN *kisses* GITAUCHO'*s thigh in a final* pohahlaj, *then exits quickly.* GITAUCHO *raises his arms. He sings a brief dirge.)*

2ND INTERP: From women come Warriors. From the newly born come women. From the Invisible come the newly born. Only the Invisible lives.

GITAUCHO: (From women come
        Bu eemoh seent
Warriors. From newly born
Kahndor. Bu bahzhah bahroosh

come women. From Invisible come
seent eemoh. Bu Hyairsu seent

newly born.   Only
bahzhah bahroosh. Nee

Invisible lives.)
Hyairsu moor.

(BLACKOUT)

(SET: Inside GITAUCHO'*s* Tukul. *Interpreters offstage.* KEERAH *is washing the fever-wracked* SHAUGHNESSY *as his son* STEVEN *begins to groan and shake off the effects of the* dahbish.*)*

SHAUGHNESSY: Steven? Are you o.k.?

STEVEN: Pop? Gimme glatha wotta . . .

                        KEERAH: (Water?)
                                Lahbay?

2ND INTERP (*OS*): You must sleep.

SHAUGHNESSY: (You must sleep.)
                Doh toom
                leemoor.

1ST INTERP (o.s.): I can't sleep. I'm afraid to close my eyes.

KEERAH: (Not sleep.   I
        Tet leemoor. Moh

fear   to hide my eyes.)
kahmool sheetoom ree hyahdee.

(KEERAH exits briefly.)

SHAUGHNESSY: She's bringing it, son.

STEVEN: What happened to me?

SHAUGHNESSY: They gave you <u>dah</u>bish. It's a powerful muscle relaxant. Steven, what in God's name are you doing here?

STEVEN: I came to get you.

SHAUGHNESSY: That was ... unnecessary.

(KEERAH re-enters, takes water to STEVEN, who drinks.)

STEVEN: How do you say "Thank you"?

SHAUGHNESSY: You can't. They have no word for that.

(STEVEN crawls over to his father.)

STEVEN: I got a cable from the Foundation. They said you were sick, but they couldn't get you to pack it in.

SHAUGHNESSY: Those idiots, what do they know? Sitting on their butts in their offices ...

(STEVEN spots a 'light-cup' and holds it up to SHAUGHNESSY's face.)

STEVEN: Jesus, look at you. Your face is like a hatchet.

SHAUGHNESSY: Fightin' trim, Stevie.

STEVEN: (Touching SHAW's face.) You're burning up inside, Pop.

SHAUGHNESSY: Oh hell, I get this every year around this time.

(They stare at one another for a moment and then embrace.)

SHAUGHNESSY: I've missed you, Stevie. God, I've missed you all.

STEVEN: I brought you a present. (Hands him the silver crucifix.) Don't know what good a crucifix is gonna do us, but Mother wanted me to get it to you.

SHAUGHNESSY: (Moved, remorseful) How has she ever forgiven me? You tell her ... I think it's beautiful.

STEVEN: Tell her yourself. I'm taking you back with me. I met this doctor in New Orleans, a specialist in tropical medicine—

SHAUGHNESSY: No, Stevie ...

STEVEN: He knows all about you! We'll see him first thing.

SHAUGHNESSY: It's too late for all that! Oh God, Steven, a terrible joke has been played. You've strolled into my own nightmare, and you must get out! Tonight, Steven, right away!

STEVEN: Easy, easy now. Just tell me how tight it is. Do these people really want to kill me?

SHAUGHNESSY: It all comes down to Gitaucho. If he can kill The Sound ...

STEVEN: He'll take him o.k.

SHAUGHNESSY: You can't risk that! You've got to run, like Furth!

STEVEN: I'm not Furth, and I'm not gonna crash around in that jungle at night. That's just a nasty kind of suicide.

SHAUGHNESSY: You're right. They'd find you easily, just like they will Furth. (*Grows calmer, reflective*) I see now. I'm being punished. For my vanity.

STEVEN: Pop, what're you saying?

SHAUGHNESSY: I left *you* for *them*. Not because I didn't love you, but . . .

(*He is momentarily overcome.* STEVEN *hugs him.*)

STEVEN: It's all right, Pop.

SHAUGHNESSY: (*Breaking away, furious with himself*) But because I felt more *important* down here! I felt that I *mattered*!

STEVEN: You're damn right you mattered! Look at the lives you've saved—entire cultures! If you don't matter, who does?

SHAUGHNESSY: (*Numbly*) They're all going to die. Furth is right.

STEVEN: Don't talk like this, Pop, don't diminish yourself. (*He hugs him again.*)

SHAUGHNESSY: I'm glad you were my son, and I'm sorry I was your father. Please don't be embarrassed by what I'm going to do.

(SHAUGHNESSY *crosses himself, kisses the silver crucifix, and quietly recites a Catholic prayer of contrition.*)

(*Sound: Cue "If" by Pink Floyd. It plays softly over* SHAUGHNESSY's *murmured prayer.*)

(*Dim light UL on an elevated area in which* THE SOUND *is reclining peacefully in the arms of* KREETAHSHAY.)

SHAUGHNESSY: Domine, vehementer dolemus quod adversus te peccavimus, nam tu es infinite bonus et infinite amandus, et peccatum abominaris . . . (*He is unable to finish.*) . . . Amen.

(STEVEN *holds his head in his lap as* KEERAH *hovers anxiously near.*)

SONG: "If"
"If I were a swan,
  I'd be gone.
  If I were a train,
  I'd be late.
  If I were a good man,
  I'd talk with you
  more often than I do . . ."

STEVEN: Pop, don't just ... don't just lie back and die, Pop, please. ...
(But he does.)

KEERAH: Shaw!

STEVEN: *(Gasping)* No, I can't ... something ... in me ... doesn't want ...
to *breathe.*

(The lights dim on KEERAH, STEVEN, and SHAUGHNESSY, but they remain visible during the scene which follows SR in the camp of SHAY TAHNDOR. Dim light remains on THE SOUND and KREETAHSHAY until the song fades out at 1:25 into it.)

(Set: SHAY TAHNDOR's Camp. By the glow of the CAMPFIRE, SHAY TAHNDOR and YAWAHLAPEETEE can be seen sleeping close together.)

(The MONKEY MAN bursts onto the scene. Before he can even speak, SHAY TAHNDOR is standing over YAWAHLAPEETEE, machete in hand. He moves shockingly fast for such a corpulent man.)

2ND INTERP: No, Green Father, it's me.	MONKEY MAN: (No, Green Father. <u>Ted</u>, Shay Tahndor! Me is it.) <u>Yee</u> she nah!
1ST INTERP: Why do you jump out of the night at me?	SHAY TAHNDOR: (Why Kee<u>shahsh</u> drop ga<u>hoom</u> from night on me?) bu <u>kaht</u> yoh yee?
2ND INTERP: You must flee. Now. You and Yawahlapeetee. It is revealed.	MONKEY MAN: (Must flee. Toom ka<u>heesht.</u> Now. Tah. You and Yawahlapeetee. Doh jah Yawahla<u>pee</u>tee. It revealed is.) Nahee<u>t-ahn</u> she.

(SHAY TAHNDOR accepts without a word. Quickly he gathers his most precious and necessary possessions. But YAWAHLAPEETEE is distraught.)

1ST INTERP: But they haven't fought yet.	YAWAHLAPEETEE: (But Mah'n have they fought not.) kah<u>tahsh</u> choolkah <u>tet.</u>

2ND INTERP: I come from Gitaucho. This is his dream and his
wish. You must obey.

MONKEY MAN: (Come from
                    Seent bu

Gitaucho.
Gitaucho.

This is dream and wish.
Nah she leemoor jah deet.

Must wish-permit.)
Toom deegahet.

1ST INTERP: Where? Where can a
fat old woman run?

YAWAHLAPEETEE: (Where? Where
                    Nabu? Nabu

flee
kaheesht

fat old woman?)
choo mood eemoh?

2ND INTERP: Take.

MONKEY MAN: (Take.)
Poosh.

(Hands her SHAW's *paper.)*

With this, you have the protection of the Sound of the Invisible.
Ten mornings up the great river
you will find Shaw's men. And
you will be alive for many long-
rains. Now run.

(With this you protect by
  Sah nah, doh zheetahm pah

Sound of Invisible. Over ten
  Keet na Hyairsu.   Boot rek

mornings great river   you
zhooloh gohjee lahneesh doh

will find   men   of Shaw.
rahn bahroo tahsh na Shaw.

And you will live for many
Jah doh rahn moor pah roh

long-rains. Now run away.)
soomlahsh. Tah kaheesht!

1ST INTERP: I hope I am killed
and eaten by the jaguar.

YAWAHLAPEETEE: (Wish is
                    Deet she

killed   and
noorkuleem-ahn jah

devoured by jaguar.)
chohtohm p'ahseelahtil!

*(*SHAY TAHNDOR *moves to comfort her.)*

2ND INTERP: No, Yawahlapeetee.
The Sun will be up soon, and I
will show you the great river.
Think how happy you'll be with
me.

SHAY TAHNDOR: (No,
            Yawahlapeetee.
            Ted,
            Yawahlapeetee.

Soon   sun   will again   come
Eeshee <u>deezh</u> rahn bahzhah
<u>seent</u>,

and will you show great
jah rahn doh <u>poh</u> gohjee

river.   Think how   happy you
lah<u>neesh</u>. <u>Keent</u> nabah <u>leesh</u> doh

will be with me.)
rahn sah <u>yee</u>!

1ST INTERP: Run.

MONKEY MAN: (Escape.)
            Kah<u>eesht</u>!

2ND INTERP: Monkey Man, old
friend. I carry you with me.

SHAY TAHNDOR: (Monkey Man.
            Mututahsh!

Old Brother.   I you
Mood <u>Toh</u>moh! Moh doh

carry with me.)
<u>poosh</u> sah yee!

1ST INTERP: I go willingly.

MONKEY MAN: (I go with wish.)
            Moh <u>heet</u> sah
            <u>deet</u>.

*(As SHAY TAHNDOR and YAWAHLAPEETEE escape into the jungle, KEERAH begins to
sing a dirge for SHAUGHNESSY.)*

1ST INTERP: When I was small, I
did not cry . . .

KEERAH: (When I little-was
        Koo <u>moh</u> zhee<u>t ahn</u>,

I   not   cried)
Moh tet roo<u>shoom</u>-ahn . . .

*(The MONKEY MAN crouches DR. He pulls a curare-tipped dart from his quiver,
kisses it, and then pokes his thumb on it as if giving a blood sample. The MONKEY
MAN dies.)*

*(Set: Inside GITAUCHO's Tukul. Lights crossfade from campfire to dawn light on
KEERAH, STEVEN, SHAUGHNESSY.)*

1ST INTERP: And when I did,

KEERAH: (And when I did,
        Jah <u>koo</u> moh ahn,

you dried my eyes.

You dried   eyes.
Doh <u>lah</u>dish <u>hyah</u>dee.

Your hands are rain upon my
skin.

Your hands are rain upon
Dohna heemu she lahsh yoh

my skin.)
ree mooru.

(Sound of sharp drum raps indicates beginning of music for the Fight for Lead-ership—"Choolkah pah Meeshohtum." Words appear at the end of the play text.)

(KEERAH is startled back to a sense of present dangers. She immediately tries to enlist STEVEN's aid in hiding SHAUGHNESSY's corpse, but he has withdrawn com-pletely within his grief and fails to understand her pulling and tugging.)

(The Fight itself can be handled in two ways—either completely offstage or as a shadowy combat behind scrim with the participants moving like ghosts in slow motion.)

1ST INTERP: We must bury Shaw
now. Come.

KEERAH: (We must Shaw
               Toh toom Shaw

bury   now. Come.)
zhetohm tah! Hetch!

STEVEN: Leave him alone. Go away.

1ST INTERP: We must bury him
before the fight. They must not
get the body. Help me.

KEERAH: (We must him bury
               Toh toom tee zhetohm

before fight. Must   they   not
say choolkah. Toom kahtahsh tet

take body. Me help.)
poosh tohm! Yee jeemu!

(Offstage noises—scuffling, some laughing—precede the entrance of FURTH, MAY-TEEMO, and LEEBOH. KEERAH protects SHAUGHNESSY's body by pretending they are asleep.)

(FURTH and MAYTEEMO are getting on genially. MAYTEEMO is even trying to pour some kind of fermented drink down FURTH; LEEBOH is more sullen and shoves FURTH roughly into the tukul.)

MAYTEEMO: (Drink, drink)
                    Shoht, shoht!

(Some liquor gets inside FURTH, though most is spilt.)

FURTH: Get away with that turkey piss!

1ST INTERP: You hesitate like a
baby. Why not kill him?

LEEBOH: (You hesitate like baby.
               Doh lek   goh lahm!

Why   not   kill   him?)
Keeshahsh tet noorkuleem tee?

2ND INTERP: He ran well. Very amusing. We'll do it again, then kill him.

MAYTEEMO: (He ran clever. Much sport. We will do again, then kill him.)
Koh kaheesht-ahn purah! Roh eendreesh! Toh rahn pahmoh bahzhah, tu noorkuleem tee.

FURTH: Morning, Steven! Boy, I gave 'em a helluva chase, kid, you shoulda seen me! I had my night vision working like infrared, coulda choked a jaguar if I had to.

(The warriors re-tie STEVEN *and* FURTH. KEERAH's *deceit works; she and* SHAUGHNESSY *are ignored.)*

1ST INTERP: Fishbelly-lover.

LEEBOH: (Lover of Fishbellies.)
Ahlajahm na Chumleet!

2ND INTERP: Shut up and tie. The fight begins.

MAYTEEMO: (Speak not and tie. Fight begins.)
Hyahba tet jah kohsh! Choolkah bah!

FURTH: (*Indicating* LEEBOH) This joker here wants to cut me into little bitty pieces, but the other guy just keeps buying me drinks. How do you figure it? (*To* MAYTEEMO) Want some fish hooks? How bout some stick matches, strike even when wet. Let us walk and I'll make you rich, whadaya say?

*(*LEEBOH *grabs his face.)*

1ST INTERP: Be a quiet captive until The Sound can kill you.

LEEBOH: (Be captive silent until Sound you kill.)
She ootoh ahsh eentu Keet doh noorkuleem.

(They exit. Noise from fight increases sharply.)

STEVEN: Jesus.

FURTH: The noise? Yeah, not very pretty. I caught a glimpse of those two horses going at each other out there. Makes you want to be someplace else. (*Pause*) Steven? How you holding up?

STEVEN: My father is gone.

FURTH: (*Glances at* SHAUGHNESSY.) Oh . . . is that it.

STEVEN: I didn't finish talking to him.

FURTH: Yeah. No one ever finishes that conversation, Steven.

STEVEN: Furth? You know what he told me. He said if that Taucho guy loses, the other one will kill us.

FURTH: Yeah? Well ... he might be right.

STEVEN: I was born in Massillon, Ohio. It don't make sense I'm gonna die in the Amazon.

FURTH: Sense? I was born in San Francisco. I got laid for the first time in Oregon. I got married in London and divorced in Tijuana. I killed my first man in Burma, and in Yokohama some drunken prick scarred my forehead. I could have died in any of those places. I didn't. So if I end up dying here, well, tough shit.

STEVEN: Furth. Too much is coming down on me. I don't want to act shameful.

FURTH: Listen, it sounds funny, but if you can get yourself to throw up, sometimes that helps.

STEVEN: Nothing down there. Just a big hollow.

FURTH: Well, Steven ... there is no one here to see how bravely you comport yourself. Just a bunch of Stone Age natives who think you come from Mars. And me. And I've seen every fear reaction in the book. I've lived them all. And you know something? It's all way over-rated, this bravery horse shit. It's all body chemistry.

(The noise stops. Silence.)

(KEERAH freezes toward the tukul opening, and FURTH cranes around to see better.)

(THE SOUND stoops through the entrance. He is smeared slippery with blood in several places. Some of it is his own, but most of it is GITAUCHO's. He is utterly exhausted, and his pained movements suggest a back injury of some type has been sustained.)

(He takes GITAUCHO's Leaf Robe off the wall of the tukul. As he puts it on, KEERAH begins to grieve—sustained shrill whistling intakes of breath, released in prolonged moans.)

(THE SOUND notices SHAUGHNESSY's corpse. He bats KEERAH away and removes the crucifix from the body, placing it around his own neck. Then he leans outside the tukul and speaks so softly that it's scarcely audible.)

THE SOUND: (Come.)
Hetch.

(MAYTEEMO and LEEBOH enter. THE SOUND points to SHAUGHNESSY's corpse.)

(Take that my dwelling.)
Poosh nay tee tukul.

2ND INTERP: Take that to my dwelling.

(KEERAH *lunges for the body and fights bitterly, but she is driven back by the* WARRIORS. *She finally sprawls on the floor sobbing, and the* WARRIORS *exit with* SHAUGHNESSY'S *body.* STEVEN *looks on helplessly, first confused, then appalled.)*

STEVEN: Furth, what are they doing? (*Silence*) Furth? They fightin' for ...for my Pop's body?

FURTH: Hang on, Steven.

STEVEN: Oh God no...why? What's he gonna do? Huh? *Tell me!*

FURTH: I don't know, Steven.

STEVEN: (*Screaming at* SOUND) *YOU ASSHOLE! YOU MOTHER-FUCKER!*

(THE SOUND *stares back at him with no expression except weariness.)*

FURTH: *Steven!* That's not your father. Your father is gone. You told me so yourself.

(STEVEN *fights back wracking sobs as* THE SOUND *continues to stare at him impassively.)*

2ND INTERP: The Leaf People will mourn for one day. Tomorrow The Leaf People will judge you. Then you will be punished for the murder of Gitaucho.

THE SOUND: (Leaf People will Hiwahtoh rahn sorrow for one sun. oomroh pah tay deezh. Next morning Leaf People Bahzhah zhooloh Hiwahtoh will judge on you. And soon rahn tohkeel yoh doh. Jah eeshee you will be punished for doh rahn pahmohzhoh pah death of Gitaucho.) noorkuleem na Gitaucho.

(THE SOUND *exits.)*

(*BLACKOUT.*)

(SET: *In Front of the* Maloca. *The clearing in front of the* maloca *is the public area where all speeches and executions take place.)*

(*Far DS lights come up on* MAYTEEMO. *He is in the surly stages of a drunk. A brown pot dangles from his hand. His friend* LEEBOH *is expected to become the new Sound as the result of Gitaucho's death and the present Sound's ascension, and* MAYTEEMO *doesn't like it.* LEEBOH *strolls over to him, smiling benignly.)*

2ND INTERP: A fine morning for killing, eh Leeboh?

MAYTEEMO: (Morning of beauty Zhooloh na tendahsh for death, eh Leeboh?) pah noor, um Leeboh?

1ST INTERP: Cheer up, Mayteemo, you drunken toad.

LEEBOH: (Be amused,
      Sh'eendreesh,
Mayteemo, drunken   toad.)
Mayteemo, shohtahlaht poot.!

2ND INTERP: How quickly the new Sound shows his smile today.

MAYTEEMO: (How quickly Sound
      Nabah eeshee Keet
born   shows teeth today.)
bahroosh poh dek loozhoo.

1ST INTERP: How quickly my brother shows his jealousy.

LEEBOH: (How quickly my
      Nabah eeshee ree
brother
tohmoh
shows him greed.)
poh tee   sheemoosh.

2ND INTERP: You're too young to be the Sound.

MAYTEEMO: (You are
      Doh she
young to be Sound.)
lahmish she Keet!

1ST INTERP: Gitaucho had only seventeen rains when he became the Leader.

LEEBOH: (Gitaucho seventeen
      rains
      Gitaucho rekyemlahsh
only was when came to rule.)
nee ahn koo seent tohkeel!

MAYTEEMO: (Gitaucho
      Gitaucho
was Warrior.)
ahn Kahndor!

2ND INTERP: Gitaucho was a Warrior.

MAYTEEMO: (*Takes a long drink, then:*)
(Tribe water breathes.)

We are drowning.

Toh lahbay roosh.

1ST INTERP: Look. Here come the Fishbellies.

LEEBOH: (Observe.
      Hasheem!
Come Fishbellies.)
Seent Chumleet!

(THE SOUND *enters with* FURTH *and* STEVEN. KREETAHSHAY *trails behind, carrying her speaking platform.*)

2ND INTERP: And here comes Chicken Mother. Look. What's that stupid thing the hag carries?

MAYTEEMO: (And comes Jah seent Chicken Mother. Observe. That Boontu-Jeetah. Hasheem! Nay what-is silly-thing hag carries?) teesh'ee poobish-ahm moodoopoosh?

(THE SOUND stands on the platform.)

May I be dumped in pig shit. What's he doing?

(Bury   under pig turds... Zhetohm baht kundu yush... what's going on?) pahmish?

1ST INTERP: He wants to see better.

LEEBOH: (He wants see better.) Koh deet roo hyeenish.

(MAYTEEMO falls over in drunken laughter. THE SOUND glares at him.)

Sit up, sit up. He looks this way.

(Sit, sit. Looks this way.) Gahsh, gahsh! Roo nah meent!

(MAYTEEMO straightens up, quickly.)

2ND INTERP: He sees like a buzzard. Beware of him, Leeboh.

MAYTEEMO: (He sees like buzzard. Koh roo goh chohmoosh. Beware of him, Leeboh.) Hasheem na tee, Leeboh.

THE SOUND: (Leaf People, my Blood. Gitaucho is dead because Hiwahtoh, ree Deesht! Gitaucho she noor pah Fishbellies came.) Chumleet ahn seent!

1ST INTERP: Leaf People, my Blood! Gitaucho is dead because these Fishbellies came.

2ND INTERP: Gitaucho is dead because our Tall Leader bit through his neck.

MAYTEEMO: (Gitaucho is dead Gitaucho she noor because our tall Leader pah tohna hee Meesho bit   him neck.) ahn chohdek tee bahtreesh.

1ST INTERP: Do not speak of that.
Only The Sound can save us from
the Fishbellies.

LEEBOH: (Speak not that.
        Hyahba tet nay!

Sound only will save Tribe
Keet nee   rahn pahlem Toh

from Fishbellies.)
bu Chumleet.

2ND INTERP: The Invisible demands to make right.

THE SOUND: (Invisible
           Hyairsu

demands to-make-right.)
deecho pahmohzhoh!

(THE SOUND grabs STEVEN by the hair.)

How shall we kill the Yellow
Hair?

(How we will
Nabah toh rahn

   kill   Yellow Hair?)
noorkuleem Mohtil-meez?

1ST INTERP: Bite his neck. Like
you did to Gitaucho.

MAYTEEMO: (Bite   neck.
          Chohdek bahtreesh!

Like you did Gitaucho.)
Goh doh ahn Gitaucho!

(There is a nervous titter that runs through the tribe. Then the little girl, SUTREESHAY,
shouts:)

2ND INTERP: The Yellow Hair can
sing. I heard him.

SUTREESHAY: (Yellow-hair
            Mohtil-meez

sings.   I   heard   him.)
leempoor. Moh ahn keetroo tee.

1ST INTERP: Did you hear that?
Sing. Amuse us.

LEEBOH: (Hear that?
        Keetroo nay?

Sing.   Tribe amuse.)
Leempoor! Toh eendreesh!

(The demand to "Leempoor" is taken up throughout the Tribe. MAYTEEMO shouts
over it:)

2ND INTERP: Amuse me. Take off
your clothes.

MAYTEEMO: (Me amuse.
          Y'eendreesh!

Toss off clothes.)
Yoho raleem!

(KREETAHSHAY confidentially advises THE SOUND.)

1ST INTERP: Let him sing, if he can. On the platform.

KREETAHSHAY: (Him allow
Tee ga<u>het</u>
sing,   when do.
leem<u>poor</u>, koo <u>pah</u>moh.
On speaking platform.)
Yoh <u>tahz</u>heeahm.

2ND INTERP: So my Blood. Have you ever heard a Fishbelly sing? That alone will condemn him.

THE SOUND: (So my Blood.
Jum, ree Deesht.
Ever   heard Fishbelly
Say<u>mohm</u> ahn kee<u>troo</u> Chumleet
sing?   That-alone will
leem<u>poor</u>? Neenay<u>ree</u> rahn
him curse.
tee <u>doom</u>.

(THE SOUND shoves STEVEN onto platform.)

Sing, Fishbelly.)
Leem<u>poor</u>, Chumleet!

1ST INTERP: Sing a pretty song.

SUTREESHAY: (Sing
Leempoor
sound beauty.)
<u>keet</u> ten<u>dahsh</u>!

(The Tribe points to their mouths, making "ahh" sounds to STEVEN.)

STEVEN: Furth? They want me to sing? Now?

FURTH: Command performance, Steven. Show me why you're so rich.

STEVEN: I play the keys! I never even do back-up vocals.

FURTH: Sing a goddam song! Something that sounds good *a capella.* You know what that means?

STEVEN: All alone?

(STEVEN presses the palms of his hands against his ears and shuts his eyes till he captures a feeling of complete isolation. He begins to sing, weakly at first, provoking titters among the Indians, but he finishes powerfully. The song he picks is Dylan's "I Shall Be Released.")

"They say ev'ry man needs protection,
They say ev'ry man must fall.
Yet I swear I see my reflection
Some place so high above this wall.

I see my light come shining
From the west unto the east.

Any day now, any day now,
I shall be released.

Standing next to me in this lonely crowd,
Is a man who swears he's not to blame.
All day long I hear him shout so loud,
Crying out that he was framed.

I see my light come shining
From the west unto the east.
Any day now, any day now,
I shall be released."

(No one makes a sound at first. Finally, SUTREESHAY *gets up and walks slowly over to* STEVEN. *She hugs him. Suddenly* MAYTEEMO *shouts:)*

| 2ND INTERP: Free him. | MAYTEEMO: (Him tie   not.) |
| | Tee kohsh tet! |

(Several others in the Tribe begin to shout the same thing. KREETAHSHAY, *ever alert to the whims of the constituency, whispers to* THE SOUND:*)*

| 1ST INTERP: You must. | KREETAHSHAY: (You must.) |
| | Doh toom. |

2ND INTERP: The Leaf People do not execute birds.	THE SOUND: (Leaf People Hiwahtoh
	not execute birds.)
	tet pahmonzhoh lohzh.

(The Tribe makes sound of approval as THE SOUND *shoves* STEVEN *off the platform.)*

FURTH: Congratulations, Steven.

2ND INTERP: Annoying Bug. Tell us why you should not die.	THE SOUND: (Annoy-bug. Yagah-beet!
	Tell Tribe why
	Hyahba Toh keeshahsh
	you must not die.)
	doh toom tet noor.

*(*FURTH *is dragged to the platform.)*

FURTH: Shit. What am I supposed to do? The old soft shoe?

STEVEN: Talk to them, Furth. Most of these people don't want to hurt you.

FURTH: You're a tough act to follow, kid. (*Clears his throat.*) My Fellow Savages. Unaccustomed as I am to pleading for my life—Steven, this is one hell of a note, I swear to God.

STEVEN: You're doing great, Furth.

(FURTH *breaks into laughter*)

That's it, laugh. They understand that.

(MAYTEEMO *joins with* FURTH's *laughter.*)

2ND INTERP: Leeboh, I like that Fishbelly. He gave us a wonderful chase.

MAYTEEMO: (Leeboh, I Leeboh, moh like that Fishbelly. eendrah nay Chumleet. Gave us amazing chase.) Dzoo toh nohshintay zhookuah.

FURTH: Brothers and Sisters. As you may have noticed, we are confronted with something of a language barrier. But I got nothing against you Indians, for what that's worth. Hell, in five years you'll all be begging pennies from tourists, right? I can't think of any reason for you not to kill me except that I like living, but that don't mean shit. So. (*Turns to* THE SOUND) I place myself in the tender mercy of this fine-looking young Headhunter.

(FURTH *bows. An inconclusive silence follows, broken by* MAYTEEMO's *yell:*)

2ND INTERP: Free him.

MAYTEEMO: (Him tie not.) Tee kohsh tet!

(STEVEN *has figured out that phrase and, since no one seconds* MAYTEEMO, *he yells it himself.*)

STEVEN: Tee kohsh tet! Tee kohsh tet!

(*Several in Tribe laugh*)

1ST INTERP: He dies. And so does anyone who disputes me.

THE SOUND: (He dies. Koh noor! And all me challenge.) Jah mohm yee huahkeel!

STEVEN: Leaf People! We're just like you, we want to live, everybody should be allowed that!

THE SOUND: (Not speak.) TET HYAHBA!

STEVEN: We're all each other! All of us is God!

(THE SOUND *brutally smashes him down.* FURTH *is enraged, leaps at* SOUND *but is quickly restrained by warriors.*)

FURTH: Try *me*! Try *ME*, you ugly fucking cannibal!

2ND INTERP: The Fishbelly wants to fight. Let him fight, I say.

MAYTEEMO: (Fishbelly Chumleet want fight. Permit deet choolkah! Gahet fight,   I proclaim.) choolkah, moh tahzhee!

(The Tribe begins to mutter "Choolkah")

1ST INTERP: You're tired. Fight tomorrow.

KREETAHSHAY: (You tired. Doh zhebah. Fight   next   morning.) Choolkah bahzhah zhooloh.

2ND INTERP: I fight now.

THE SOUND: (I fight   now.) Moh choolkah tah!

(The tribe falls silent with anticipation. STEVEN is only now shaking off the effects of THE SOUND's blow, and he's upset to see FURTH preparing for combat.)

STEVEN: Jesus, Furth, what are you doing?

2ND INTERP: Come, Fishbelly. We dance.

THE SOUND: (Come, Hetch, Fishbelly. We dance.) Chumleet. Toh leemshoht.

FURTH: I can take him. Gitaucho hurt him. Cracked ribs, maybe. It's my only chance, god damn it!

STEVEN: O.K., Furth, o.k. Use your legs. Keep him away.

(THE SOUND, snarling and baring his teeth like a jaguar, moves in on FURTH.)

FURTH: Fucker's got teeth like a shark.

(THE SOUND and FURTH fight. FURTH's strategy is to attack the ribs and avoid the teeth. He is physically overmatched but fights with a filthy imagination and gives THE SOUND more than he ever wanted. Yet the moment comes when FURTH is wrestled to his hands and knees, and in the next instant THE SOUND bites through FURTH's neck. FURTH dies instantly, without a cry. THE SOUND rolls over on the ground, gasping for breath and staring at STEVEN. When he can talk...)

THE SOUND: Leeboh.

(LEEBOH leaps to his side.)

2ND INTERP: Chew some seebayloh.*

THE SOUND: (Eat Chohtohm some seebayloh.) boh seebayloh.

---

* *"seebayloh": A plant used as a local anesthetic and cauterizing agent.*

(LEEBOH *pops some small, crumpled leaves into his mouth and chews vigorously.*
THE SOUND *staggers to his feet, takes a large shield, and places it gently over* FURTH's
corpse. He turns his attention to MAYTEEMO.)

I don't like drunks, Mayteemo.	(I like not Moh <u>ee</u>ndrah <u>tet</u> drunk, Mayteemo.) shohtah<u>laht</u>, May<u>tee</u>mo.
1ST INTERP: Yes, my Leader.	MAYTEEMO: (It's so, my Leader.) Shem, ree <u>Mee</u>sho.
2ND INTERP: Listen closely: Never say the name of Gitaucho again. Ever.	THE SOUND: (Listen much aware: Kee<u>troo</u> roh ha<u>sheem</u>: Never speak word of <u>Ted</u>ish <u>hyah</u>ba kee<u>tahsh</u> na Gitaucho again. Ever.) Gi<u>tau</u>cho <u>bah</u>zhah. Say<u>mohm</u>.
1ST INTERP: Yes, my Leader.	MAYTEEMO: (It's so, my Leader.) <u>Shem</u>, ree <u>Mee</u>sho.
2ND INTERP: Yellow-hair.	THE SOUND: (Yellow-hair.) <u>Moh</u>til-meez.!

(LEEBOH *drags* STEVEN *over to* THE SOUND. *Though* THE SOUND *seems to be talking
to* STEVEN, *his speech is really to the Tribe.*)

And so you leave us, Fishbelly.	(And now you us Jah <u>tah</u> doh toh leave, Fishbelly. <u>heet</u>, Chumleet.
You will to back to the others and Tell many fine stories of	You will go back the Others and Doh rahn hoh<u>teet</u> Kah<u>tahsh</u> jah speak many amazing <u>hyah</u>ba roh noh<u>shin</u>tay stories of <u>tah</u>moosh na
the Leaf People. They will all be amused.	Leaf People. Others Hi<u>wah</u>toh. Kah<u>tahsh</u> will amuse rahn <u>een</u>dreesh
And soon it will come to seem like a	all. And soon mohm. Jah <u>ee</u>shee it will be like nah <u>rahn</u> goh

dream to you. Leeboh. Spit.   you dreamed.
                                        doh lee<u>moor</u>-ahn.
                                        Leeboh. Spit.)
                                        Leeboh! Kah<u>choh</u>.

*(*LEEBOH *spits a glob of* see<u>bay</u>loh *into* THE SOUND'*s cupped hands.* THE SOUND *rubs it into his palms as he continues to talk thoughtfully to* STEVEN *and the Tribe. Then he begins to rub the green matter into* STEVEN'*s thumb.)*

After a while no one will want to   (After none
hear   Loo-ahn te<u>dahm</u>

                                 will want to hear
                                 rahn deet kee<u>troo</u>

your stories. They will not sound   your stories.
true.   dohna <u>tah</u>moosh.

                                 Truth will believe not
                                   <u>Gaht</u> rahn keen'<u>tet</u>

And more Fishbellies will stum-   and many Fishbellies
ble on to us,   jah <u>roh</u> Chumleet

                                 on us will find,
                                 yoh <u>Toh</u> rahn bah<u>roo</u>,

and more, and no one will   and many, and none will
                               jah <u>roh</u>, jah te<u>dahm</u> rahn

heed your warnings.   hear   your warning.)
                               kee<u>troo</u> dohna kah<u>moht</u>.

STEVEN: What are you doing? Oh God . . .

1ST INTERP: Even you will no   THE SOUND: (Even you will
longer believe I ever existed.   Een doh <u>rahn</u>

                               believe not I   born-was.)
                               keen'<u>tet</u> moh bah<u>roosh</u>-ahn.

STEVEN: My hand's turning numb, oh Jesus!

1ST INTERP: This must not hap-   THE SOUND: (This must happen
pen, Fishbelly. Hold him.   Nah <u>toom</u> pahmoh

                               not, Fishbelly. Hold him.)
                             <u>tet</u>, Chumleet.   <u>Koh</u>'tee.

*(*LEEBOH *and* MAYTEEMO *grab* STEVEN. THE SOUND *bites off* STEVEN'*s thumb.* STEVEN'*s face explodes with horror and he makes a rasping, choking noise but doesn't scream.* THE SOUND *calmly inspects the thumb.)*

Now when you speak of the Leaf People, the Danger-men will listen. Mayteemo.

(When now you speak of
  Koo <u>tah</u> doh <u>hya</u>hba na
Leaf People, Danger-men will
Hi<u>wa</u>htoh,   Kah<u>tahsh</u> rahn
hear.   Mayteemo.
keе<u>troo</u>. Mayteemo!

Return the Yellow-hair to his tribe.

Return Yellow-hair his tribe.
Hoh<u>teet</u> <u>Moh</u>til-meez kohna <u>toh</u>.

Try to keep him alive.

Try to   save   him life.
<u>Pah</u>bahmon pah<u>lem</u> tee <u>moor</u>.

He is my messenger

He is my messenger
she ree tah<u>poosh</u>

to the Danger-men.

for Danger-men.)
pah Kah<u>tahsh</u>.

2ND INTERP: It is done, my Leader.

MAYTEEMO: (It is done,
                  Shem<u>pahn</u>,
my Leader.)
ree Meesho.

(As STEVEN and MAYTEEMO exit.)

1ST INTERP: Escape with your breath, Fishbelly.

THE SOUND: (Escape with
                  Ka<u>heesht</u> sah
your breath, Fishbelly.)
dohna <u>roosh</u>, Chumleet.

(STEVEN, clutching his right wrist, is in shock. His voice is like a croak and his eyes are wide.)

STEVEN: I play keys.

(Exit MAYTEEMO and STEVEN. THE SOUND ascends the platform.)

The Investiture:

2ND INTERP: Leaf People, my Blood. Keerah is mine.

THE SOUND: (Leaf People,
                  Hi<u>wa</u>htoh,
my Blood. Keerah is for me.)
ree Deesht! <u>Kee</u>rah she pah <u>yee</u>.

(KREETAHSHAY, stage-managing this event, leads KEERAH into position. KEERAH is wearing red mourning ribbons. KREETAHSHAY then motions LEEBOH into THE SOUND position.)

1ST INTERP: Leeboh. Proclaim.

KREETAHSHAY: (Leeboh.
                  Proclaim.)
Leeboh. <u>Tah</u>zhee.

2ND INTERP: And I am your
Leader. Me!

THE SOUND: (And I am
Jah <u>moh</u> she

your Leader. Me.)
she dohna <u>Mee</u>sho! <u>YEE</u>!

1ST INTERP: And I am your
Leader—

LEEBOH: (And I
    Jah <u>moh</u>

am your Leader—)
she dohna <u>Mee</u>sho—

(THE SOUND knocks him away.)

2ND INTERP. Be gone! No one will
speak for me. I am my own
Sound. While I breathe, it is true.

THE SOUND: (Be gone.
    <u>Hee</u>sht!

None   will speak for me.
Te<u>dahm</u> rahn <u>hyah</u>ba pah <u>yee</u>!

I   am my only Sound. While I
Moh she <u>ree</u> <u>nee</u> <u>Keet</u>! Loo moh

breathe, it is true.)
<u>roosh</u>, nah she <u>gaht</u>!

TRIBE: Loo moh <u>roosh</u>, nah she <u>gaht</u>.

(KREETAHSHAY is taken by surprise at this move, but approves. LEEBOH most reluctantly accepts demotion. KREETAHSHAY now places "the longest Leaf Robe any woman ever wove" on the shoulders of her son.)

1ST INTERP: And no one will pray
for me.

THE SOUND: (And none
    Jah te<u>dahm</u>

will pray   for me.
rahn oo<u>teel</u> pah yee.

I am my own Monkey Man.

I   am my only Monkey Man.)
Moh she <u>ree</u> nee <u>Mututahsh</u>.

(KREETAHSHAY hands him the MONKEY MAN's headpiece, and he places it over his head. SUTREESHAY, the little girl, has never seen anyone other than the old MONKEY MAN wear the object. She thinks THE SOUND looks funny in it, and she laughs.)

1ST INTERP: All who laugh at the
Leader will die. It is so. I proclaim it. While I breathe, it is
true.

THE SOUND: (All   who
    <u>Mohm</u> naboh

  laugh
<u>lee</u>shay

on Leader will die. It's so.
yoh <u>Mee</u>sho rah'<u>noor</u>! <u>Shem</u>!

I proclaim it. While I
Moh <u>tahz</u>hee nah. Loo moh

breathe, it is true.)
<u>roosh</u>, nah she <u>gaht</u>!

TRIBE: Loo moh <u>roosh</u>, nah she <u>gaht</u>.

(KREETAHSHAY *is taken by surprise at this move, but approves.* LEEBOH *most reluctantly accepts demotion.* KREETAHSHAY *now places "the longest Leaf Robe any woman ever wove" on the shoulders of her son.*)

1ST INTERP: And no one will pray   THE SOUND: (And none
for me.   Jah te<u>dahm</u>

                                     will pray   for me.
                                     rahn oo<u>teel</u> pah yee.

I am my own Monkey Man.   I am my only Monkey Man.)
                                     Moh she <u>ree</u> nee <u>Mu</u>tutahs.

(KREETAHSHAY *hands him the* MONKEY MAN'*s headpiece, and he places it over his head.* SUTREESHAY, *the little girl, has never seen anyone other than the old* MONKEY MAN *wear the object. She thinks* THE SOUND *looks funny in it, and she laughs.*)

1ST INTERP: All who laugh at the   THE SOUND: (All   who
Leader will die. It is so. I pro-   <u>Mohm</u> naboh
claim it. While I breathe, it is
true.   laugh
                                     <u>lee</u>shay

                                     on Leader will die. It's so.
                                     yoh <u>Mee</u>sho rah'<u>noor</u>! <u>Shem</u>!

                                         I proclaim it. While I
                                     Moh <u>tahzhee</u> nah. Loo moh

                                     breathe, it is true.)
                                     <u>roosh</u>, nah she <u>gaht</u>!

TRIBE: Loo moh <u>roosh</u>, nah she <u>gaht</u>.

2ND INTERP: You have heard the   THE SOUND: (You have
Fishbellies possess   Doh ahn

                                     heard Fishbellies do
                                     kee<u>troo</u> Chumleet <u>pah</u>moh
powerful magic. It is so. But you   power magic.
                                     ek<u>cho</u> nah'<u>kusht</u>.

                                     It's so. But you
                                        Shem. Mah doh
have a powerful Leader now,   now follow power Leader, much
                                     tah ga<u>heet</u> ekcho <u>Mee</u>sho, roh
more powerful than Fishbelly   power than Fishbelly devil.
deviltry.   ek<u>cho</u> tu   Chumleet Kah<u>leem</u>.
Leaf People, my Blood. I am the   Leaf People, my Blood. I am
Sound of the Invisible.   Hi<u>wah</u>toh, ree Deesht! Moh she

                                     Sound of Invisible.)
                                     <u>Keet</u> na <u>Hya</u>irsu!

(KREETAHSHAY *enlists the aid of* LEEBOH *and other warriors in displaying a grisly new totem of power: the complete head and body skin of* SHAUGHNESSY, *held up in front of* THE SOUND *like the hide of a steer. The rest of the Tribe moves in to touch it, making little "ooo" sounds.)*

1ST INTERP: My Warriors! We must become	THE SOUND: (My Warriors. Ree <u>Kahn</u>dor!
	We must be much Toh <u>toom</u> she roh
mightier than the River. Leaves will	mighty than river. Leaves will <u>goh</u>jee tu lah<u>neesh</u>. <u>Hi</u>wah rahn
tremble with fear when we approach and wither	tremble with fear when <u>root</u> pah kah<u>mool</u> koo approach we, and wither <u>hoo</u>lee Toh, jah kah<u>lah</u>noor
at our touch. Do not	when touch. Not fear koo <u>moo</u>jee. Tet kah<u>mool</u>
fear the Fishbellies. I understand	fear Fishbellies. I understand kah<u>mool</u> Chumleet. Moh <u>kusht</u>
their magic. Listen.	their magic. Listen. teenah'<u>kusht</u>. Kee<u>troo</u>.
The Fishbellies sing	Fishbellies sing Chum<u>leet leempoor</u>
at my command.	upon my desire.) yoh ree <u>deet</u>!

*(*KREETAHSHAY *hands him* STEVEN's *tape recorder; he punches Start button.)*

(Sound: Cue The Byrds' "Farther Along.")

SONG: "Farther Along"
"Farther along we'll know all about it
Farther along we'll understand why . . . "

BOTH INTERPS: Leaf People, my Blood! We are Holy! We live like trees!	THE SOUND: (Leaf People, Hi<u>wah</u>toh,
	my Blood. We are holy. ree Deesht! Toh she <u>zhoo</u>dish!
	We live like trees.) Toh <u>moor</u> goh <u>jee</u>!

(Freeze as music plays.)

SONG: "Farther Along"
" . . . Cheer up my brothers
Live in the sunshine
We'll understand it all by and by . . . "

(The INTERPRETERS *begin the* Epilogue. *In slow motion the Tribe begins to disintegrate and* THE SOUND *is divested piece by piece of all his authority symbols.)*

1ST INTERP: Twelve days after The Sound assumes total control of The Leaf People, the little boy, Jee<u>shoom</u>, succumbs to a virus transmitted by Shaughnessy.

(JEESHOOM *is cleared from stage.*)

2ND INTERP: Green Father and Yawahlapeetee succeed in finding Shaughnessy's reservation. Yawahlapeetee gains acceptance among the Juruna Indians, but Green Father is driven away. He is believed to be living alone in the jungle.

1ST INTERP: After helping Steven reach the town of Barra do Garcas, Mayteemo disappears. He never returns.

(Sound over music: construction noises, heavy machinery.)

2ND INTERP: The new highway reaching from Brasilia to Cuiaba touches the eastern frontier of The Leaf People. A civil engineer named Melendez shoots and kills Choolkahnoor.

(CHOOLKAHNOOR slumps to stage.)

1ST INTERP: The Leaf People attempt to flee from the highway. As they migrate north, they are attacked by their ancient enemies, the Kreen Akorore. Leeboh, Kreetahshay, Treekah, and Zhahbahroosh are all killed.

(They fall. One or two attempt to crawl offstage; the others lie where they drop.)

Keerah, Lohzhoodish, and Lomoheetet are all taken captive.

(The women disappear.)

2ND INTERP: Lahbayneezh is bitten by a snake and dies.

(He drops.)

(Enter ANNA AMES. She puts a dress on SUTREESHAY as KAHLEEMSHOHT hides his face.)

1ST INTERP: Kahleemshoht and the little girl, Sutreeshay, make their way to the mission run by Anna Ames. Kahleemshoht dies four days later from an allergic reaction to a penicillin shot.

(He falls. Exit ANNA AMES. SUTREESHAY remains standing silently in her dress.)

The girl is kept in seclusion to avoid publicity over her pigmentation. She is studied. She wears dresses and speaks to no one.

(THE SOUND has by now divested himself of everything. He pulls on a pair of dirty Bermuda shorts like MEATBALL wore earlier.)

2ND INTERP: After months of wandering in the jungle, The Sound appears at the highway construction site. He is hired to kill birds for the workers. He is considered sullen and untrustworthy and is thought to drink too much. Occasionally he is punished for begging.

1ST INTERP: By the end of this year, Señor Alfredo Soto expects to finish burning off the trees on his 130,000 acre *fazenda*. Within three years he confidently predicts his investment will be worth 2½ million dollars more than he paid for it. Señor Soto says there are no Indians for miles around. He says he has never heard of any tribe called The Leaf People.

(THE LIGHTS FADE TO BLACKOUT.)

End of The Leaf People

Choolkah Pah Meeshotum
(Fight for Leadership)

A deep *drum* (ideally fashioned from a hollow tree trunk) starts it off with an insistent beat. After two bars, it is joined with a *hoof rattle*. Two more bars and

A *baritone male chorus* begins to chant: "POWER"

ek-CHO ek-CHO ek-CHO ek-CHO ...

A *mixed chorus* sings in variations of the "ek-CHO" rhythm:

> (Fight   for breath
> CHOOLKAH PAH ROOSH
>
> Fight   with Fate
> CHOOLKAH SAH ROOSH
>
> Mighty Warriors
> GOHJEE KAHNDOR
>
> Fight   for me.)
> CHOOLKAH PAH YEEeeeeee ...

A *female chorus* breaks in:
> (Victory is with-lover of Eye of the Invisible)
> ZHAHLEM SHE SAH'LAJ NA HYAHDEENA HYAIRSUuuuu ...

Mixed Chorus now sings alternate lines by gender:

	(Fight for breath
Males:	CHOOLKAH PAH ROOSH
	Fight with Fate
Females:	CHOOLKAH SAH ROOSH
	Mighty Warriors
Males:	GOHJEE KAHNDOR
	Fight for me.)
All:	CHOOLKAH PAH YEEeeeeee ...

A *Woman* screams in a high-pitched, falling wail.

Repeat entire sequence as above.

Afterword

I have been loathe to write so much as a one-paragraph Program Note for any of my other plays, reasoning that explaining a play is like explaining a joke: If the thing works, you shouldn't have to do it. But I've never written a play like *The Leaf People*. To tell the truth, I'm not sure anybody has, or ever will again. I make no claims to its greatness—there are hordes of people whose job is to make such assessments. But my studies of dramatic literature compel me to assert its uniqueness. It demands to be discussed. Steeling myself, I'll tackle the most *angst*-filled aspect of it first, then move on to subjects of more practical value in mounting productions.

Historical Context of the Broadway Production and Notes on Its Critical Reception

After seeing an early draft of THE LEAF PEOPLE, Joseph Papp put together a reading of it down in his Public Theatre. It was attended by about thirty theatre professionals, including some highly-gifted playwrights such as Michael Weller. The reading was a smash, perhaps the pleasantest experience the theatre has yet bestowed upon me.

Five months later in September 1975 I found myself crouched in the Booth Theatre on Broadway watching this strange beast of a play unfold. After that opening preview, director Tom O'Horgan dropped a bomb: "We got to lose an hour, babe." The show was running about three hours. They wanted it down to two. I was to perform these massive amputations in full view of the theater-going public under a brighter glare of publicity than I ever wish to be exposed to again. Thus began six weeks of twenty-hour work days, all culminating the morning of October 21st in a series of utterly savage reviews. Other far more complimentary pieces were to appear over the next couple weeks, but by then the issue was moot. The dailies had done their duty, and *The Leaf People* closed before the end of the month.

What went wrong between that glorious April reading and that ignominious October trashing? Perhaps fifty things, almost all of which will go unrecorded here and many of which had nothing whatever to do with the production itself. Let me shoulder my share of the blame right now. Despite repeated assurances from a variety of interested parties during rehearsals that no cuts were necessary, I should never have allowed myself to lumber onto the Great White Way with a 180-minute marathon. (This was 42nd Street, not Germany.) The svelter version now printed may not have fared any better, given the peculiar circumstances surrounding the production. But I certainly would have spared myself the evil word-of-mouth generated by the prolonged agony of the cutting process. *Mea culpa*, and I am a wiser man for it.

Now about those "peculiar circumstances." Here I must speak of a man to whom I owe everything—good, bad, and mixed—that the theatre has bequeathed me to date: Joseph Papp. In 1975 Joe bestrode the back-biting world of American theatre like a pugnacious Colossus. He was the acknowledged Lord of Off-Broadway, and I guess he still is. He was also the Keeper of the Keys for Lincoln Center, that woebegone Culture Emporium-in-waiting. In fact, while I was cranking out *The Leaf People*, I had visions of filling the intimidating spaces of the Vivian Beaumont Theatre with it. Broadway? Perish the thought. The notion literally never entered my mind.

But it entered Joe's. Sometime after the reading at the Public, he conceived a startling idea. He would rent the Booth Theatre for the entire 1975–76 season and fill it with new American plays by Mike Weller, Tom Babe, John Ford Noonan, Miguel Piñero, and yours truly. In fact, I was to be the lead-off hitter.

The publicity machine chugged to life. The five playwrights were gathered together in Shubert Alley* in our native costumes—Miguel in his beret and dashiki, Noonan in his pirate's turban and bib overalls, me in my headband restraining scapula-length hair, and so on. Our pictures were taken and duly published in full-page spreads in *The New York Times*, repeatedly. Gone forever was the image of playwrights as effete turtlenecked and betweeded wraiths. Together we looked like escapees from a heavy-metal rock group—scruffy and, well, *radical* for God's sake. The Ad Men ran the picture in the form of a Wanted poster, calling us desperadoes and generally wallowing in our various alternative-culture postures. And they told an appalled world that, ready or not, we were all coming to Broadway.

I dwell on this seemingly puerile irrelevancy because I believe it set the tone for everything which was to follow. Joe Papp barging directly onto Broadway with five untried dramas was regarded as overweening, to say the least, by the territorially obsessed Broadway establishment. But this picture was a goddam *provocation*. Months after it ran Mel Gussow was still fulminating in *The New York Times Magazine*: "The new playwrights are in varying degrees radical, not just in what they write but even in their life-styles. A ragtag bunch of young men, they were not only outlaws on Broadway, they were not the kind of people the average Broadway theater-goer would ask home to dinner." It's true. In my two months on Broadway, I never got a single dinner invitation. Not that I would have had time to accept. I was too busy trying to save my ass.

The attacks were not long in coming. About two months before we even opened, the *Times* published an outrageous assault on Papp by Charles Marowitz, the gist of which was that Papp and everything he had ever done was not worth the powder to blow it all to hell. I leave it to the reader to surmise the effect this diatribe had upon my actors as they struggled to memorize their Leafish lines. The sound of pistols being cocked filled the rehearsal hall.

Things got worse. No sooner had Joe's all-time monster hit, *A Chorus Line*, opened to unprecedented reviews than the Musicians Union went on strike, short-circuiting Papp's money machine. We plowed onward, shutting out so far as was possible the bad vibes crackling through the turbulent world outside. The opening was postponed. Then it was postponed again as I frantically re-

---

I remember the phone call summoning me to this rendezvous very well. My wife hailed me to descend from the top of an apple tree in need of pruning to field a call from Bernie Gersten, then Joe's righthand man. He told me where to be and when to be there, but never mentioned pictures were to be taken. He did mention Broadway and seemed astonished and embarrassed that that was the first I'd heard of it. Joe is often not given to prior consultations.

wrote. (Re-writing in *two* languages is no joke.) Anticipatory cackling among the critics was deafening. But damn if the show wasn't coming together at last in its sleek two-hour format. The general feeling within the company was, by gosh, we've got a chance. Myself, I was beyond caring, or so I thought. Terminal exhaustion had set in, and I just wanted to be done with the whole business.

The final, irrefutable, inexorable Opening Day arrived on October 20th. One last blow still awaited us, the most shocking one of all. A scant two hours before the tuxedoed critics waltzed into the Booth (some, I am certain, with their reviews already tucked within their cummerbunds), Joe called a press conference. The Booth Theatre Season of New American Plays was history. Over. *Finis. The Leaf People* would be the first and the last in the series.

The reason he cited was the financial crunch imposed upon his empire by the strike-necessitated temporary closing of *A Chorus Line.* I don't know if anyone believed him. I know a now-departed critic for the *New York Post* named Martin Gottfried didn't. His lead-line in the next morning's tabloid read, "Dennis J. Reardon's THE LEAF PEOPLE may not have killed the New York Shakespeare Festival's projected season of five new plays all by itself. After all, Japan didn't surrender the Second World War until a few weeks after the atom bomb was dropped."

I've always secretly thought (Joe and I never discussed it) that he called that news conference when he did precisely to spare me such cruelties, that he was bowing to the accumulating weight of establishment resentment over his "presumptuous arrogance" in foisting serious American drama into the domain of the multimillion-dollar musical, and that he wished to salvage what was left of my battered psyche. Unfortunately, the immediate effect of his timing was to tell the critics they were only going to get one shot at the whole deal, and *The Leaf People* was it.

I hope I do not come off like LBJ baring his tummy scar when I say that it was three years before I could bring myself to set foot in a theater again, let alone write for it. I am now fully recovered, thank you, writing prolifically and (I hope) better than ever. But I do not yearn to return to Broadway, no more than I ever yearned to go there in the first place.

What the Play is About

I have described *The Leaf People* elsewhere as "a fantasia on the theme of genocide," and that is true enough as far as it goes. But it does not go far enough. It makes the piece sound like a "thesis" play, a righteous broadside arguing a sad case no serious person would dispute in the first place. Is there *anyone* who wants whole tribes exterminated? Perhaps a rogue Nazi holed up in Asunción, Paraguay.

The play is concerned with a variety of subjects. It is about culture and the smashing force of history. It is about the futility of good intentions. It is about saying goodbye to your father before he dies. It is about power and ritual and kingship. (Indeed, having already suffered the consequences of *hubris* in permitting this strange play to go to Broadway, I am free to admit that among my models for it was Shakespeare—the history plays and *Macbeth.*) *The Leaf People* is also about two philosophies of self-preservation: Gitaucho's, which may be summed up as "Be silent, be cunning, be Invisible," and The Sound's, a far less subtle code which dictates "I'm the Boss, and I say if it moves, kill it."

I confess that I am fascinated by the ironies of the story. A truly saintly man intent only upon the salvation of a people nevertheless precipitates a deadly, disintegrating civil conflict among them. The Redeemer bestows upon them a terminal virus.

Above all, *The Leaf People* is a *yarn*, an adventure story cut from the same cloth as *The African Queen*. It is not meant to argue a case nearly so much as it is meant to be thoroughly entertaining.

On The Noble Savage

Anybody who writes anything about Indians which does not totally demean them runs the risk of being harpooned upon the critical cliché of The Noble Savage. Nobility is a scarce enough commodity in this beleaguered world, but it does still exist, cropping up now and again when the combination of circumstances and personality are in proper alignment. Even among Indians. Is not Peter Shaffer's Atahuallpa noble in *The Royal Hunt of the Sun*? Of course. He is, in fact, a God.

Gitaucho is not a god, nor is his usurper, The Sound. Yet they are both possessed of dignity and courage and powerful strength of will. And if there is something inherently noble in the blind struggle of a foredoomed people to survive, who am I to gainsay it? Shall we reduce all men everywhere to the prevailing American standards of crassness, cynicism, and mediocrity? Not on *my* stage. *The Leaf People* seeks to reveal our fundamentally shared humanity in all its aspects—good and evil, noble and base, comic and tragic.

I shall let Ross Wetzsteon have the last word on this subject. Writing in *The Village Voice*, he described *The Leaf People* as "an evocative contrast not between modern sophistication and prehistoric barbarism on the one hand, or 20th-century oppression and noble natives on the other, but between two complex and ambiguous civilizations."

The Interpreters and the Problem of Language

One of my goals in writing *The Leaf People* was to create a full-blown Amazonian Indian culture based upon (but not limited to) known anthropological data. After agonizing over a variety of safer theatrical choices, I concluded that culture cannot exist apart from language. I could not have my Indians wandering around saying "Ugh." Nor was I willing to master one of the known Amazonian languages—one of the Tupi dialects, for instance. For one thing, those languages are invariably highly polysyllabic with orthographic constructions that would gag most actors. What to do? Leave it to the actors to invent some impromptu gibberish? Unfair to them and sure to result in glaring tonal inconsistencies.

The problem was moot when I realized I literally could not *conceive* of this tribe without knowing what ideas they were capable of expressing linguistically. What do they call white-skinned people and what does their choice of word say about their concept of Self and Other? How important is the Sun in their lives? Rain? Bloodlines and relatives? What scares them? How do they express what we know as Love? How do they talk about death, if at all? What *sounds* do they make? If no one had ever used the word "flower," what pure noise would best convey the feeling that object inspires within the observer? There was no way out of it. I had to invent a language.

I did so quite laboriously and very thoughtfully. I averaged about seven new words a day. I built them from a series of what I came to think of as "primary vocables" or Prime Roots—amoebas of structured noise such as the sound "kah." By carefully limiting myself to a sound pool of about 140 noises, I hoped to create a flexible, highly euphonious language that actors could speak "trippingly on the tongue" yet which sounded utterly unlike any language known to Western ears. The result was Leafish. (For a closer examination of all this, read "Notes on the Leaf Language.") My efforts were rewarded in one of the unkinder critical cuts administered by Clive Barnes, then writing for *The New York Times*, when he blithely dismissed Leafish as "gibberish." He of all reviewers should have known better since he had access to the text prior to his review.

Having gone through the outrageous labor of building this lingo, I was confronted with the next problem: How to make it intelligible to my audiences. Again, various solutions presented themselves. Rear screen projections of the English as the Indians spoke? I dismissed that as too distracting visually. Translations piped into rented head sets worn by the audience? Economically prohibitive, obstructive to the sound of Leafish, and incapable of obviating what I came to regard as a necessity: Interpreters, two of them, male and female.

Where to put them, onstage or off? And should they be miked? These details were resolved by the physical possibilities afforded us by the Booth Theatre—and, I should add, by the visual inventiveness of director Tom O'Horgan. We chose to encase The Interpreters within clear plastic bullet-shaped capsules suspended high above the stage. Not only were they miked, they were lit, they were comfortably seated, and they were even air-conditioned. Imagistically I found it a superb choice. Throughout the play they functioned visually as representatives of Western technology, hovering like gods about my Stone Age tribe, at once civilized, omnipotent, omniscient, and dangerous—twin Damoclean swords suspended menacingly above the heads of Gitaucho, The Sound, and their Blood.

But as fond of that solution as I am, I am also fully aware that not every producer can be as munificent as Joseph Papp. Nor does every theater possess the magnificent vertical sightlines of the Booth. Other directors will be forced to make other choices, such as placing two podiums extreme down right and left. In every case where The Interpreters are used, however, they must be miked. Great care should be taken to provide an aural balance throughout the house so that those farthest from the stage are not blasted with the English to the detriment of the Leafish.

I personally regard the roles of The Interpreters as the most important, the most difficult, and probably the most thankless in the play. Their task is nothing less than to render the text comprehensible. And yet, while they must be responsive to the different levels of intensity from scene to scene, they must somehow refrain from "acting the words." Their personas should be those of U.N. translators—detached, efficient, precise. Except where indicated (see notes, "Typing and Orthography"), their translations are simultaneous with the Leafish but must not blot it out. The trick is to find the natural breaks in the longer

Leafish sentences and to fill those caesuras with translation. Above all, 1ST INTERPRETER must be a woman and 2ND INTERPRETER must be a man, and there should be no playing around with who translates what.

We come now to the question of "free" translations versus "literal." When The Sound abases himself before Gitaucho and says, "Moh ooteel dohna zhooleesh," he is literally saying "I pray your happy-light." It is translated by the rather bland, though correct, "I beg your forgiveness." And if Shaughnessy's "Moh toom bahkusht roh kee'tahsh" were to be conveyed precisely as a member of the tribe hears it, the translation would have to read "I must begin-to-know many man-sounds" rather than the more direct free translation "I must learn more words." Time and again I have been forced to opt for immediate accessibility in lieu of fresher, even evocative literal translations which would ultimately only serve to put a further strain on an audience already working pretty hard to cope with two languages.

Yet in other instances there are certain words and idioms so completely Leafish in their nature that a free rendering makes them senseless. For instance, it's clearly established that these Indians have never before seen a pistol. But they understand its purpose: It is a noorpoosh, a death-bringer, and I go with that literal rendering. Similarly they have no concept for "year." The closest word is "soomlahsh," which means "long-rain." Time for them is measured by the number of monsoon seasons they have endured. Nor does "God" mean anything to them. They revere "Hyairsu," the Invisible.

Naturally, out of these hundreds, probably thousands, of judgment calls, a few were truly up for grabs. Two that come to mind are "Pah zhooloh nah she chohmoosh" ("By morning it is buzzards") and Mayteemo's despairingly succinct "Toh lahbay roosh"—literally, "Tribe water-breathes" but freely rendered as "We are drowning." The "buzzards" line may puzzle a few people or make a few others giggle, but I like it and no good equivalents came to mind. On the other hand, "Tribe water-breathes," for all its freshness, was overruled on the all-important principle of immediate accessibility.

And so it went, line by line, word by word—all options weighed with excruciating care. Undoubtedly there will still be instances where a particular director or reader will dispute a given choice. Fine. But I stand by my decisions even as a voice within me screams, "But this is madness! Who will know? Who will care? Don't you realize all this painstaking pedantry is going to be dismissed as gibberish?"

Yes, I do so realize.

On Fact vs. Imagination

The stage is not the proper place for anthropological disquisitions. Film serves that purpose to much greater advantage, and it was a BBC documentary called *The Tribe That Hides From Man* which initially stoked up my imagination and got me thinking of *The Leaf People*. (I believe the chief creative force behind the film was a man named Adrian Cowell.) It depicted the Brazilian *sertanista* Claudio Villas Boas ensconced month after month in a rain forest, endlessly enduring the grossest deprivations in hopes of making contact with a tribe called the Kreen

Akorore. I was staggered by Villas Boas' self-imposed isolation, and yes, by the nobility of his purpose: to save a culture. He became my model for Shaughnessy.

About that time (the autumn of 1974) I received an invitation to journey to Ethiopia, and I leaped at it. For a month I travelled that ancient land, flying from one dirt air strip to another in a painfully unpressurized DC-3. The bloody revolution to oust Haillie Selassie and his nepotistic hordes was in full swing, as was the interminable civil war for Eritrean independence.

Starvation was not the central issue in the country at that time, though starvation was there in abundance. The issue was power, and the tool to achieve it was murder. Everywhere hand was turned against hand. Endless factions played out centuries-old fantasies of vengeance. It was a country coming apart at the seams.

In Addis Ababa I met Gitaucho. That was his name. He was a young man from the country working as a houseboy for my rather nefarious host. I listened to him bow out intricate melodies on a single-stringed violinlike instrument. I went hunting for hyena with him in the hills above the city. And I found in him all the characteristics I sought for the leader of the Indian tribe forming in my mind.

The name and character of Gitaucho was not all I brought back from Ethiopia. I carried with me a dysentery I ignored for months until the first draft of *The Leaf People* was completed, by which time I discovered that my strength was gone, I weighed less than at any time since junior high school, and my skin was nearly as green as Keerah's. Other souvenirs of Ethiopia: part of the composite that became Furth; the notion of The Sound (the Proclaimer for the Emperor was a time-honored Ethiopian functionary); and a very strong feeling for a troubled people living on the brink of existence. It hardly mattered that Ethiopia was arid and the country I chose to write about periodically inundated. What mattered was the scrabbling to survive and the murderous path to power.

Since then, more than ten years now, my research on the Amazon and its cultures has never stopped. In 1977–78 I spent six months traversing South America from Ecuador to the tip of Tierra del Fuego. I now know far more about the place than when I initially created *The Leaf People*, but nothing I've read or seen since then has in any way invalidated anything in that original draft. (There have subsequently been five more drafts of, which *this*, I swear it, is the very last ever.)

Highway crews are still slicing through the jungles like *sauba* ants. Tribes are still disappearing *en masse* off the face of the earth. (The pre-Columbian estimates of Amazon Indians run as high as six million. There are now 80–250,000 left in Brazil, only 20–50,000 of them still isolated in the Amazon. Alex Shoumatoff in his invaluable *The Rivers Amazon* writes, "Of the 260 Amazonian tribal groups known to have existed in 1900 only 143 are left. Perhaps another forty groups remain to be contacted.") The jungle itself is putting up a terrific fight, but the soil is astonishingly infertile. The entire ecosystem depends upon trillions of fungal filaments called mycorrhizae, which act like a giant sponge in the three shallow inches of topsoil , soaking up nutrients and feeding them back into plants before they can leach away.

But once the trees are taken down the system collapses like a punctured tire. The mycorrhizae shrivel, rain washes away the soil, wind blows away the sand, and the red clay hardens into a brick-solid hard-pan called laterite, in which few seeds can germinate. The process, 'green hell to red desert,' is irreversible. In five to ten years most of the cleared land will be no good, for pasture or anything else.

(Shoumatoff, p. 20)

And so, sadly, the essence of *The Leaf People* remains inviolate to the passing of time. Perhaps as much as anyone, I wish the dilemmas it confronts could be gloriously resolved and my play rendered a curious, dated period piece.

But if the essence of the play remains intact, how many of the specific details stand up to anthropological scrutiny? How much is poetic license? Let's get down to cases, insofar as my still highly-limited knowledge will permit.

Drugs: Various drugs are mentioned in the course of the play. See<u>bay</u>loh is described as a local anesthetic and cauterizing agent. <u>Dah</u>bish is used as a tranquilizer/muscle relaxant. These are purely Leafish words adopted in accordance with the linguistic rules I set for myself. That such plants with such properties actually exist under arcane Latinate names is indisputable, and you may be sure that the Indians—masters of their environments that they are— are well aware of them and make use of them.

What is even more certain is that there is a widespread addiction among Amazonian Indians to a hallucinogen extracted from the bark of the *Virola elongata* tree. The substance is called by various names from tribe to tribe— *washaharua, epena, yupa, yecuana, niopo*. We know it as DMT, and the active ingredient is triptamine. In addition to its recreational uses (ingested in the manner I've described for <u>dah</u>bish), it is used as an arrow poison for killing birds and monkeys. (" . . . the eyes take on a special brilliance. One feels a sense of freedom from time and a desire to scream and move around as the drug has a contracting effect on the lungs." Shoumatoff, pp. 173–4)

I mention one other drug in *The Leaf People*, something injected within corpses to assist in the removal of their skins. This is not a flight of fancy. My source is Branston's *The Last Great Journey on Earth*. He describes the use of such a skin-stripper so that the Indian can wear his enemy's skin "like a glove or a fine rubber suit, covering him in front from head to foot and tied down the back with little apron bows." (p. 123) The Atroaris apparently made use of this substance following the massacre (not unprovoked) of the Father Calleri expedition in 1968.

> *O Globo* had a full page of the most tragic and horrifying photographs I have ever seen. The first showed a pile of bones on the leafy forest floor with a human skull resting on top. This was all the physical remains of one of the party. It seems that the Atroari Indians strip the entire fleshy covering from their victims and burn it; but how they could have produced, in so sort a time, a broken skeleton of polished bones and shining skull was to me a puzzle. Not a shred of skin or tissue or muscle and hardly a hair remained and the bones looked as if they had lain a thousand years to be burnished by nature and time. Why the Atroaris do this is another puzzle. My guess would be to lay the spirit of the dead man and prevent his haunting them by walking again in the flesh.
>
> (Branston, p. 49)

Later Branston learns of the pharmacological tool which assists the Indians in such grisly chores. Since I'm quoting Branston, let me now offer his gloomy assessment of the Villas Boas brothers' famous Xingú reservation.

But what is sacrosanct about a reserve, whether it is for animals or men, when the pressure of rapidly changing events associated with so-called "civilization" begins to crowd the barriers? Unless the Indians can assimilate themselves into the culture of the whites they will be wiped out as their forest is cleared away. In any case, even if they do assimilate, they will become but a strain in the new population of Brazil and Venezuela: it is inevitable that, in time, the way of life of the jungle Indians of South America must be lost for ever.

(Ibid.)

"*Reeshee*: Shay Tahndor tells Shaughnessy that *he* was not weeping, that it was his reeshee, a night-bird that married his spirit. And when Steven passes out from dahbish, Yawahlapeetee says that Steven's reeshee is singing. Again, not an invention. From Shoumatoff: "The Aika also believe that each person has a rishi or alterego—perhaps a hawk, a jaguar, a tortoise, or a rock—living an existence parallel to his own." (p. 169) See also repeated references to this from the books of Carlos Castaneda.

Leadership and social structures: I have already indicated that the model for my dual-chieftain tribal structure comes not from the Amazon but from the Ethiopian Emperor-Proclaimer relationship. (And, to some extent, from our own President-Vice President system.) The normative pattern for the Amazon, insofar as such generalizaitons can be made for so many diverse Indian nations (including many not yet contacted and studied), suggests that the leadership roles are far less structured, that there are individual cliques within most tribes, and that the Indians do pretty much what they want to do when they want to do it. Decisions tend to be made along informal group consensus lines. The Chief as such is usually a ceremonial position, often falling to an old fellow with a good memory and a nice way with a story. For instance, among the Aika the chief is called *touchaua*, and as Shoumatoff has it, his role "was not to tell anyone what to do...rather, it was to be a good orator and to have a deep knowledge of Aika culture." All of which is inherently nondramatic and blurred. I chose to assign clear leadership chores to Gitaucho, orator duties to The Sound, and shamanistic culture-bearing to the Monkey Man. Finally, in contrast to our American notion of the Strong Silent Brave, Amazonian Indians tend to be extremely verbose, given to long, long tales in whcih they describe in minute detail patterns of light on the trees, motions of the wind and clouds, and virtually anything else that comes into their remarkably all-inclusive and observant minds. This, of course, is dramatic suicide, and I've made my Indians keep to the point and make it fast.

Among The Leaf People a certain measure of privacy is described, often along nuclear family lines. (Gitaucho has his tukul, shared with sister and mother, as does The Sound with his mother.) This was done, again, primarily for dramatic reasons. By far the more common arrangement calls for segregation between the sexes with the men all living in a large communal structure like the maloca and the women off in their own. Although some tribes seem obsessed with genealogies (not only within their own tribe, but within neighboring tribes as well), an utter disregard for such matters seems more comonplace. Fathers often totally ignore not only their offspring but their "wives." Always, though, the roles of women and of men are universally comprehended and beyond dispute; they simply tend to co-exist separately but equally. The *tribe* is the family. But like all families everywhere, tensions and squabbles are endemic, and a blood-feud such as that between Kreetahshay and Yawahlapeetee is unremarkable.

Physical stature and games: Amazonian Indians tend to be short. About 5'5" is considered normal. (No Masai warriors in South America.) I dispense with this fact, of course. Our eyes are accustomed to professional athletes, and we like our leaders tall in the saddle. So both Gitaucho and The Sound should have magnificent bodies—tall, lean, and powerful—physically well matched so that the outcome of their *mano-a-mano* possesses some suspense. Wrestling is the primary athletic endeavor among Amazonian Indians. No tribe comes to visit another tribe without gift-giving, story-telling, *epena*-snorting, and long hours of awesomely energetic wrestling. The sport frequently gets out of hand, and when it does, clubs appear. If bashing each other over the head and on the limbs fails to satisfy, things escalate until they become truly deadly. (See a blood-curdling anthropological film entitled *A Man Called Bee*.) So when Furth badgers The Sound into fighting, he is effectively giving his opponent his preferred choice of weapon. Wrestling an Amazonian Indian is inadvisable.

Teeth filing: Tobias Schneebaum, in his decidedly bizarre memoir of life among the Indians of the Oriente in Peru (*Keep the River On Your Right*), speaks of a native whose teeth had been filed down from too much gnawing on raw stalks of sugar cane. Beyond that, my description of teeth filing within *The Leaf People* is an undocumented invention. Yet it seems to me to be entirely within the bounds of what is known of these cultures. People that smash each other over the head for sport and then proudly shave their scalps to display the scars acquired in such games, people who happily mutilate their ears, their lips, their noses, and their genitalia in the name of ornamentation—are not such people capable of investigating and improving upon the killing potential within their mandibles?

Animal teeth are a ubiquitous ornamental material in Amazonia. And human teeth are routinely made to perform feats that would seriously incapacitate most "civilized" jaws. I stand by this logical extrapolation of the known lore.

Green skin: Here, of course, we come to an intuitive imaginative incursion—poetic license of the purest sort. One of the chief principles of defense available to the Indians is to hide. Again, from Alex Shoumatoff in *The Rivers Amazon*: "The overriding mimetic theme, and the most effective strategy for survival in the rain forest, is to keep a low profile, to remain indistinguishable from the green welter of life." (p. 121) Plants have evolved astonishingly complex inter-relationships with insects (see Shoumatoff on the symbiosis of *Heliconius* butterflies with passionflower vines). I permitted myself to imagine a mutant—Shay Tahndor, the Green Father—possessed of a highly desirable genetic character-istic transmittable only to females: green pigmentation. It is part of Gitaucho's wisdom that he comes to see the advantage of this startling deviation from the norm.

But this invention need not be defended on any terms other than the poetic. Green women and green children (see *The Green Child* by Herbert Read) is my evocation of the inherent fertility of a nonetheless doomed people, part of my fantasia on the theme of genocide. It is one of the things that makes *The Leaf People* a creature of the Theatre rather than an excerpt from Anthropology 101.

Finally, for those directors wishing to ground themselves firmly in the ways of South American Indians, I must mention an altogether remarkable book by Ettore Biocca called *Yanoáma*. It recounts in fascinating detail the harrowing story of Helena Valero, a white woman who was captured in 1939 at the age of 11 and who was shunted from tribe to tribe for 22 years.

The Use of Music

The Leaf People was somewhat naively conceived as a sort of prerecorded musical. It was first written during what seems now to have been the final magnificent flowering of rock music, a time when the Beatles were a fresh memory, when Mick Jagger and Bob Dylan were not old men, a time when albums sold like hotcakes in December without benefit of glitzy TV videos. Where are the snows of yesteryear? All melted, a vast slag heap of polyvinyl chloride.

Time marches on. Music and plays themselves, with very few exceptions, are ephemera. The smatterings of songs I selected could in some cases be called "classics," though others ("The Yellow Snake," for instance) were esoteric choices even in 1974. Now, of course, the songs are positively hoary. No single element dates the play more than their inclusion.

And yet . . . for me, they still work. They still do what they were supposed to do. Each makes its own particular comment in the telling of the story. This may be an egocentric judgment call, but I don't feel a single selection is hard to listen to for either the most conservative or the hippest members of an audience. To substitute more *au courant* pieces is merely to delay the inevitable aging process the inclusion of contemporary music invites. And so I bow before the relentless onslaught of history: the original songs stay.

That said and done, and with great trepidation, I hereby promise not to sue or yank my show if a director absolutely insists upon substituting my musical choices with his own *if* said director does not tamper with the *placement* of the songs or with their *duration*. In any case, Western music *must be present* in *The Leaf People*. It is part of the interchange of alienation which passes back and forth between the Indians and the Whites, as vital a part of the "cultures in collision" theme as the juxtaposed languages. Steven, after all, plies the trade of Orpheus: he is a musician. (I have updated the models of synthesizers to which he claims expertise. Those, too, shall date and should be revised accordingly in subsequent productions.) And of course the tape recorder he carries with him into the jungle is more important in and of itself than some of the characters (I will not disclose which ones).

As for the Indian music, Tom O'Horgan composed some of his own which for copyright reasons cannot be included in this text. He also incorporated five on-stage musicians who played on reconstructions of authentic Amazonian instruments in addition to increasing in visual impact the sheer weight of numbers of the Tribe. (*Historical footnote*: As a result of *The Leaf People*, the powerful

Musicians Union now specifies higher salaries for members required to wear body makeup.) But I'm sure few productions will be able to afford such extravagancies, however desirable. So I advise the use of prerecorded Indian music. There is considerable latitude available in the selection of it, but like the Western music, it is a vital part of the cultural equations at the heart of the play, and it must be there. The following albums may provide some of the cues: *Pre-Columbian Instruments* (Folkways FE4177); *Anthology of Brazilian Indian Music* (FE4311); and *Maori Songs of New Zealand* (FE4433). Minimal research will undoubtedly unearth other relevant albums.

Typography and Orthography

The Leaf People, of course, is a typist's nightmare, and I speak from the frazzled soul of one who has been through six drafts of it. The format in this version preponderantly employs The Interpreters' speeches in the left column and the Leafish in the right with a word-for-word literal translation above the Leafish— a maddening device I grant as a courtesy to the actors, who find it beneficial in memorizing. In this configuration a *simultaneous* translation is indicated. There are other places where the Leafish is typed *above* The Interpreters' lines, and these indicate Leafish lines that I wish to stand clear, unbroken by The Interpreters' translations. In a very few cases no translation whatever is called for.

I underscore all stressed syllables as a guide not only to the pronunciation of the Leafish but to its proper cadences. Occasionally there are gaps in the Leafish:

> (You hesitate like baby.)
> Doh <u>lek</u>   goh <u>lahm</u>!

These are necessitated by nothing more mysterious than English words containing more letters than the corresponding Leafish word, and the actor should read the speech exactly as if it were unbroken.

Pronunciation is purely phonetic—it sounds the way it looks. If I may anticipate what few stumbling blocks there are ...

"ch" as in <u>choh</u> is always soft

"tau" as in Gi<u>tau</u>cho is pronounced like <u>tow</u>el

"hy" words such as <u>hyah</u>ba are run-together sounds; it's not pronounced "hy-ah-ba" but rather as two syllables: hyah-ba

The convoluted format *The Leaf People* requires, together with the various supporting materials I've seen fit to supply, leads the uninitiated to presume that it's a monstrously long show. It's not, not anymore. It should run the usual two hours, certainly no longer than 2:15. And yes, it plays much more smoothly than it reads.

Technical Production Elements

Costumes and makeup: There are two basic problems in this area. One has to do with the way Amazonian Indians dress, which is to say, barely. Exposed breasts are *de rigueur*. Beyond that, there need be no frontal nudity in a production, though simple geographical logic dictates large expanses of naked flesh.

Which brings us to the second problem: body makeup. There are three acceptable skin colors in this play—white, reddish-brown, and green. The Broadway cast employed blacks, whites, latinos, and Indians. Remarkably, they all ended up looking like they came from the same tribe. Geometric designs are painted over the basic body makeup. Black and red pigments are by far the most prevalent, though yellow and white are also used.

Indians, though confining themselves to a few strips of cloth, should not be regarded as naked. They are masters of adornment. Bracelets, arm bands, headpieces, anklets, necklaces—they lavish their considerable imaginations upon such accessories. Feathers, bones, seeds, and teeth are their raw materials. A visit to Randy Barcelo's costume shop during preparations for the Broadway production was an awesome and exhilirating experience. One nearly drowned in magnificently colored feathers. I will never forget nor cease to be grateful for the mind-numbing work Randy and his crew unleashed in the creation of Leaf Robes, Leaf Capes, and the hundreds of other utterly authentic adornments he fashioned for our large cast. *The Leaf People* was blackballed from the Tony nomination process as surely as if it had been an obese and pimply freshman rushing the bastions of Sigma Chi. To this day I remain convinced that the most unworthy victim of that ostracism was Mr. Barcelo. His work on the show was absolutely inspired, and not to have accorded him so much as a Tony nomination was nothing short of grotesque.

Several excellent photographic studies of Amazonian cultures are in print. They should be freely consulted. Pay particular attention to hair styles.

Props: The weapons used by Amazonian Indians—bows, arrows, and (in northern Amazonia) blowpipes—are amazingly large, especially in view of the diminutive stature of the Indians themselves. Bows can be seven feet high, arrows five feet long. If a director feels this reads humorously onstage, feel free to shrink them accordingly. Great reverence is accorded to drums made from hollow tree trunks (dead souls are thought to abide within). Hoof rattles are common, as well as very long horns covered with bark. Whistles, pipes, reedy instruments all have ancient usage. But the most bizarre prop required is the hide of a human being with the head attached, and the head must look like whoever is playing Shaughnessy. It was used to chilling effect on Broadway, but frankly, I haven't a clue how it was fabricated.

Sets: Flexibility is the key here. Lots of dangling vines, trees, etc. The structures—be they *tapiri*, *tukul*, or *maloca*—are minimal and highly portable, preferably capable of being flown in. O'Horgan's production made wonderful use of vertical space by means of three levels of tiered shot cord over which Indians clambered as if the cords were vines or branches. But this feature is hardly essential to a production.

Lights: The full palette. Many acting areas are defined solely by light.

Sound: In connection with The Interpreters, I've mentioned the necessity of a careful aural balance throughout the house. See also my notes on the use of music. The cries of monkeys and birds (herons, toucans, macaws, wild turkeys, parrots, and a noisy little critter called the *pia* bird are all appropriate) have their place in *The Leaf People*, particularly when The Sound inadvertently fires the pistol. But too much of this stuff makes the show sound like "Sheena, Queen of the Jungle."

The trickiest sound effect is the Hovercraft. I recommend using the sound of a helicopter.

And so, enough. I hope these detailed production notes will in some way partially atone for the quite extraordinary demands my play makes.
Hyairsu she dohna ahlajahm.

                                                                      DENNIS J. REARDON

Notes on the Leaf Language

(Compiled from the diary of Theophilus Shaughnessy, recovered by prospectors in the employ of the Gulf Oil Corporation.)

The Leaf People have two words for 'raindrop' and three words for 'sun'. They have no words at all for: good, evil, hello, goodbye, please, thank you, if, then, time, or jungle. To date I have catalogued some 400 words, discounting specific flora-fauna nouns, built from a distinguishable sound pool of about 140. I'm sure there can't be 600 words in the entire lexicon, and I'm equally sure it has remained at substantially that level for generations. Leafish is a stabilized proto-language with virtually no cognates in any other tongue known to me.

This lack of cultural borrowing is consistent with the most characteristic Leafish trait: an unrelenting xenophobia. Their fear and hatred of strangers is intricately woven into their language. Consider something as fundamental to identity as the personal pronoun. In Leafish it declines as follows:

I	moh	we	toh
you	doh	you	doh
he, she	koh, loh	they	kahtahsh

Kahtahsh, obviously, is out of place. It turns out not to be a personal pronoun at all, though it is pressed into that function at times. It is more correctly a compound noun meaning literally 'Danger Men' and generally received as 'the Others'. It applies to the entire non-Leaf universe. Kahtahsh, along with toh, are the only true plurals in Leafish: 'They' and 'We' may be the most primordial Leafish dichotomy, and the instincts underlying that perception—if properly channeled—could prove to be their best hope for continued survival. At any rate, all other Leafish nouns take their number from context, like the English 'deer'.

The limitations on Leafish hospitality are also implicit in the words oota, ootoh, and hiwahtet. The Leafs use oota to mean 'guest', though its literal import is 'stray' in the sense of 'Sheep will stray.' 'Guests' are always unexpected—strays—and there are no salutations in Leafish. Furthermore, the distinction between guest and 'captive' is as close as oota and ootoh. (Many concepts which we perceive as antonyms are near homonyms in Leafish. For instance, 'life' and 'death' are differentiated only by a nasal: moor and noor.) But hiwahtet may be the most succinctly xenophobic word of all. It is translated as 'strange'. It means, literally, 'not Leaf'.

The 'Sun' Words

Much can be inferred concerning the Leaf religion by an examination of the three 'Sun' words: zhooyahdish, Hyahdeena Hyairsu, and deezh. No Sun word—even deezh, the most colloquial—is ever used flippantly. There can be no doubt that in the recent past the Sun was the chief Leaf god in a simple animistic pantheon. That pre-eminence, as we shall see, is being gradually usurped, but the Sun remains the holiest physical object to the Leaf People.

Zhooyahdish is the most ancient of the Sun words and is now used only in the most formal contexts. It provides a classic illustration of the Leafish use of composition as a word-building technique. It is formed from the adjective dish (dry), yahdish (big), zhoo (light), and zhoodish (holy): thus, 'holy big dry light'. One would presume that a rain forest people would grow to accept the wet gloom of their habitat with indifference; on a day-to-day basis the Leaf People have certainly made the necessary adaptations to their environment, and made them well. Nonetheless, the traditional worship of zhooyahdish suggests that the summum bonum of the Leafs is the absence of moisture and darkness; 'dry light'. This hypothesis is supported by the choice of political power tokens, the Leaf Robe worn by the leader and the Sound's Leaf Cape, both of which essentially serve as raincoats.

But the Leaf religion at this juncture seems to be in a fascinating state of flux. This is linguistically reflected by the current phasing out of zhooyahdish in favor of the more colloquial deezh and the more abstract Hyairsu. Hyahdeena Hyairsu means 'Eye of the Invisible' and is a religious/poetic honorific for Sun. However, implicit within the title is the conception of a deity vaster than zhooyahdish, a force that can not be perceived but whose power is visibly intimated by the Sun. And it is that more sophisticated intuition which the Leafs increasingly worship: Hyairsu, the Invisible. It is quite possible that this step beyond a God of Light presages a darker tribal vision and perhaps a more supplicatory religious posture.

Deezh, now the most common name for Sun, appears to have been formed by linking the dee in Hyahdeena Hyairsu with the zh sibilant beginning zhooyahdish. Though colloquial, the word deezh carries much weight. Indeed, like many Leafish words, its emotional and aural reverberations can hit the Leaf ear with an incantatory force. Not only does deezh envelope all the connotations of the other Sun words, still freshly implicit, but it evokes allied concepts such as Deesht (the incantatory word for 'Blood-Tribe'), heezh and neezh ('fire' and 'snake' respectively, both animist deities). A host of other words may also be linked to these religiously impregnated sounds.* Such aural word association with allied sounds is a fundamental characteristic of fluency in Leafish. Like a continuous and usually humorless punning, certain words bounce meaning into other words in what can become a striking chain reaction. A related technique by which this tiny lexicon attains a surprising richness can be observed in the Tohdoh-Kahndor word chain.

The Tohdoh-Kahndor Series

Precisely because the word pool is so small, the Leaf People can play with etymology as easily as our poets play with rhyme. A young pre-initiate boy is called tohdoh; his brother, tohmoh. When he has survived the rather grisly puberty rites, he is called tohndor, a word thought to be more in keeping with his new dignity within the tribe. When he becomes a father, tohndor phases into tahndor. And when he wins full recognition as a warrior (usually with his first enemy kill), the ubiquitous vocable indicating 'danger', kah, becomes part of his title; he is respectfully addressed as kahndor, warrior.

---

*To name a few: lahneesh (river); deezho (sunlight); sutreesh (flower); mahleezh (sand); leesh (happy); and possibly even reesh (head) and teesh (what).

Thus, a boy's role progression within the tribe's hierarchy is neatly mimicked by an easily grasped evolution of title. The effect of this is to lend great honor to the term kahndor, whereas the word tohdoh can be deliberately misapplied with wonderful insult value.

Leafish Grammar

Leafish grammar is so simple as to be non-existent. The Leafs recognize a past and a future tense, and they dispose of them with two simple particles. Ahn linked to a verb stem means Past. Rahn means Future.

Roh (much; many) functions as an all-purpose intensifier. Added to an adjective, the word becomes a comparative. Hence, hee (tall) and roh hee (taller). It is nearly impossible to form a superlative in Leafish. The construction roh hyeenish, implying 'best', is the only one that comes to mind, and it occurs rarely. There are cultural implications in this, I belive, having to do with a tribal psyche which discourages internal competition. It is of no great value to be best, but it is praiseworthy to do better.

Na is the genitive particle, used like the Spanish de in the formation of possessives. Shem is a highly flexible all-purpose affirmative, and tet is the equivalent general negation. In addition, tet plays a vital role in the vocabulary by forming antonyms. For instance, roo (see) and rootet (blind).

There is almost no inflection in Leafish, and when it does occur, it is always quite regular. Many words can be different parts of speech without altering in any way. This is particularly true of the verb-nouns such as moor: life; to live. Oomee, noor, tayhuah, roosh, klee, keent all come to mind immediately, and there are many others. It is all much less confusing than one might think.

In fact, the lack of inflection and the flexibility of the parts of speech combine with the inherent euphony of the language to produce an amazing vocal fluidity. The Leafs never grope for the right word or the correct construction. A thought delivered haltingly can only mean that the speaker does not truly wish to express it. And there is so little ambiguity of meaning that I have never heard a listener ask for a sentence to be repeated (other than to indicate simple incredulity).

Generally the sentence structure is subject-object-verb, but this rule is broken so often I have concluded that euphony alone is the major structural determinant. All the Leafs, even the children, seem to think in complete sentences, and the words invariably emerge in precisely the most pleasing phonetic sequence. In addition, the cadences of Leafish are so distinct and so regular that I am tempted to theorize that Leafish was at one time, at least in part, a tonal language.

The only aspect of the grammar that I found at all perplexing—and this only until I adjusted my responses—is the absence of a conditional tense. It is not precisely absent; it simply resides entirely in the mind of the listener. The speaker will use the future tense: Koo rahn doh noorkuleem: "When I kill you." That actually means "If I kill you" directly to the extent that you have it within your power to deter me from my stated intent.

Euphony

The Leaf People cherish the sound of the human voice. The major function of the Sound, the second most powerful member of the tribe, is to extract the full majesty of the words uttered by the Leader and to amplify them in all their glory to the rest of the tribe.

The sounds of Leafish are surpassingly euphonious. There is an abundance of long, broad, whooshing sibilants—soomlahsh, zhoodish, lohzh, etc. There is no F, Q, V, X, or W; no initial I; and essentially no U (though *oo* is common). The Leafs really get their mouths around their sounds; there is much greater movement in the lips, jaws, and tongues than tight-lipped Americans find comfortable.

Again, the tiny sound pool is transformed into an asset. Almost all the sounds are compatible when they bump against one another. Naturally occurring internal rhyme is so common that it goes unremarked. I have never heard a Leaf song or chant that consciously employed any structured rhyme scheme.

Curious Words

Buzzards, not surprisingly, are regarded as unsavory. The word for them, chohmoosh, means 'eat heart' or possibly 'rip out heart'. The buzzard is featured in many Leafish idioms using death imagery. The Leaf attitude toward fish is a bit more puzzling. The sound chum—the 'fish' word—is considered comic in a disdainful and repellant way. Many of their most pejorative words are built on the chum sound, including chumleet (fishbelly), the derogatory term for pale-skinned Others. Leet, besides meaning 'belly', echoes the more salacious meaning of the verb gahleet—namely, to fuck. Chumleet becomes, then, a dangerous de-humanization, an obscenely comic combination of sound which unquestionably renders 'Fishbellies' more readily killable. I personally do not enjoy hearing the Sound address me by that term.

Kahdek means literally 'danger teeth' and is an omnibus word referring to all creatures that kill or wound with teeth, fangs, or stings, be they insects, reptiles, or mammals—including Man himself. As such, it resembles the proto-Indo-European omnibus word for 'wild animals', ghwer.

Roosh (breath; to breathe) also means Fate, or a reasonable facsimile thereof. Thus, bahroosh ('begin to breath') means not only 'to be born' but to begin the unfolding of one's Fate. When one ceases to breathe, his Fate is perceived to have been disclosed.

The Leafs revere age, particularly in males. No doubt this is because aged males are rare. Wars kill off most men quite early. Women are usually taken alive and swapped around by the raiding warriors, eventually gaining acceptance in the tribe of their captors.

I have never heard the Leafs speak of the Moon, though I'm sure they sometimes must. I am also sure there is another word I have yet to hear. I surmise that it is pronounced chohtahsh, and it would mean 'eat man'; the word 'eat' itself is chohtohm, literally 'eat corpse'. At any rate, I am certain the Leaf People are at least occasionally cannibalistic. But game is plentiful. In addition, several neighboring tribes better versed in husbandry are made to pay tribute of livestock and fowl whenever the Leafs demand it. Consequently, cannibalism is probably confined to Power Acquisition, the belief common among primitive animists that an enemy's strength can be made part of one's own by eating him.

Prime Roots

Earlier, I mentioned the sound kah. It is what I call a Prime Root. Any discussion of them must necessarily be somewhat hypothetical since I do not pretend to fully understand these syllables. But I do know that they add yet another layer of emotional meaning to most Leaf words.

Leafish, as I have said, is a proto-language, an embryonic collection of roots, stems, and particles. Fully 88% of the words I've learned are one- and two-syllable words, striking evidence of the primitive level at which this language seems to have been frozen. Indeed, the only word having more than three syllables is ahseelahtil (jaguar) and that happens to be one of the few 'borrowed' words in Leafish. (A direct cognate exists in numerous Central and South American languages, going as far back as Mixtec.)

A high percentage of the two- and three-syllable Leafish words are compound words constructed from one syllable root words (e.g., 'untimely': bah-roosh-tet: 'begin-to breathe-not'). Many of these mono-syllabic roots are primary vocables. The Leaf People call them keetahss: man-sounds. From these Prime Roots, these amoebas of structured noise, languages are born. Within them, if we but had the ears to hear, is a perfect one-to-one correspondence among what is perceived, what is felt, and what noise is expelled. That noise is pure 'word', and that word speaks of our origins.

Kah is such a sound. Choh is another. And mool. And many others. The presence of any of these Prime Roots in a given word creates exactly the same response in every Leaf who hears it. It hits them viscerally, in some instances, subliminally in others, and they are hard put to make it understood to me. But again, a look at the lexicon helps. Here are the initial kah words:

> danger; blow-spit-shoot dart; danger teeth; flee; wither; devil; warning; fear; mystery; warrior; night; stars; the Others; and sharpen.

Whatever underlying terrors unite and animate the above concepts in the Leaf mind, those awesome feelings are embodied in the Prime Root kah, the syllable that begins the Leafish word for each of them. Kah, 'danger', is the closest Leafish approach to our word Evil.

The initial choh words: bite; kick; buzzard; rip out; devour. One may reasonably infer, I think, that the Leaf People do not derive much aesthetic enjoyment from the sound choh. Nor from mool, which means 'poison'. It happens that a word exists which combines each of these lurid Prime Roots. The word is moolkahchoh. It is rendered, predictably enough, as 'hideous, terrifying'. The word hits so powerfully on the Leaf ear that it can re-create the condition it is meant to verbally symbolize. So the Leaf People almost never say it.

There is no doubt in my mind that the mysterious and pervasive force of the Prime Roots imparts an intensity to Leafish that has dropped out of the 'civilized' langauges of the world. I believe Prime Roots represent the most fundamental level of communication. They are archetypal sounds. So many of them—pah, huah, gah, bah, tah, kah, lah, etc.—are based on the sound AH that I suspect it could be the first conscious noise Man ever uttered.

The Virtues of Leafish

Obviously a lexicon as small as Leafish cannot rival the great languages in subtlety and richness of expression, particularly in abstract discourse. But ambiguity and subtlety are of no value to the Leaf People, and they make do nicely without them. Emotion is valued, and they make an art both of expressing it and controlling it. For this, their language is a superb tool. Word for word, I know of no other tongue that impacts so much resonance into its vocabulary without sacrificing exactitude of meaning. To recapitulate the techniques by which Leafish achieves this:

(1) *Assimilation.* Many words usurp the connotations of near homonyms, immeasurably enriching the subject word (as in the case of deezh).

(2) *Innovative use of Composition.* Zhooyahdish is typical of the many forceful compound words formed by a striking synthesis of two or more separate concepts.

(3) *Lucid etymology.* Leafish has a type of verbal exoskeleton, an audible frame intuitively grasped by its speakers, and illustrated in the Tohdoh-Kahndor sequence.

(4) *Accuracy of perception.* By which I mean that words such as kahtahsh ('they; the Others; Danger Men') precisely reflect the Leaf environment as their common experience has revealed it to them. Such words both describe and subjectively re-affirm all the key Leaf values.

(5) *Fluidity of speech.* I have suggested that this quality is made possible both by the lack of inflection and the inherent euphony of the sounds. The euphony, in turn, is due to both the small sound pool and to the relative flexibility of the parts of speech.

(6) *Prime Roots.* These vocables achieve a degree of correspondence between pure sound and verbal meaning unmatched by other languages of my acquaintance.

If I knew nothing of these strange Indians but their language, I would still be fascinated by the Leaf People.

The Future of Leafish

Easily deduced. As the Fishbellies encroach upon the Leaf People, their language will experience a sudden influx of hitherto unimaginable concepts: soap, bullet, syphilis, Brazil, etc. They will enter upon a brief period of linguistic decadence as these alien sounds and ideas are transferred intact into the Leafish vocabulary.* Then, within no more than two generations, both the Leaf language and the Leaf culture will be extinct.

The process is as inevitable as a sneeze, and just as infectious. I myself have already unwittingly taught Yawahlapeetee the word 'airplane.'

List of Song Recordings

The Overture

Miles from Nowhere: Written and sung by Cat Stevens; Freshwater Music/ Irving Music, BMI; from *Tea for the Tillerman*, A&M SP-4280, 1970.

When I Paint My Masterpiece: Written and sung by Bob Dylan; Big Sky Music; *Bob Dylan's Greatest Hits, Volume II*, Columbia 31120, 1971 and 1972.

It's Only Rock 'n Roll: Written by Keith Richard and Mick Jagger, sung by The Rolling Stones; from *It's Only Rock 'N Roll*, Rolling Stones Records, CCC 7901; published Promopub, B.V. (ASCAP), 1974.

A La Mina No Voy (I Am Not Going to the Mine):   Traditional; sung by Teofilo Potes; from *Afro-Hispanic Music From Western Colombia and Ecuador*, Folkways FE 4376.

I Am a Pilgrim: Traditional, adapted by Merle Travis, sung by Nitty Gritty Dirt Band from *Will the Circle Be Unbroken*, United Artists 9801; Westpar Music Corp./BMI.

Enigma (instrumental):   Written by Efrain Orozco; from *Music of Colombia*, Folkways FW 6804.

*   End of Overture   *

Act One

Watching the River Flow: Written and sung by Bob Dylan; Big Sky Music; from *Bob Dylan's Greatest Hits, Vol. II*, Columbia 31120, 1971.

On the Amazon: (Fragment, app. 1:30 used) Written by Skip Battin and Kim Fowley; KYO Music/Badboy Music (BMI); from the New Riders of the Purple Sage's *Brujo*, Columbia PC 33145, 1974.

The Yellow Snake: Written by Robin Williamson, sung by The Incredible String Band; from *Wee Tam*, Elektra EKS-74036; Paradox Muxic (BMI) and Warner-Tamarlaine Publishing, Inc., 1969.

Someday Never Comes: (Fragment, 1:37 used) Written and sung by John Fogarty; from Creedence Clearwater Revival's *Mardi Gras*, Fantasy 9404; Primeval Ltd. and Greasy King Music Inc., 1972.

Out in the Woods: (Fragment, 1 minute used) Written and sung by Leon Russell; from *Carny*, Shelter SW-8911; Skyhill Publishing Co., 1972.

The following two numbers are played during Intermission:

All Along the Watchtower: Written and sung by Bob Dylan; use version from Bob Dylan/The Band's *Before the Flood*, Asylum AB-201; Dwarf Music, 1968.

The End of the World (instrumental):   Written by Dee-Kent, played by The Nitty Gritty Dirt Band featuring Vassar Clements; from *Will the Circle Be Unbroken*, United Artists 9801; BMI, publisher pending.

Act Two

If (Fragment, 1:25 used):   Written by Roger Waters; from Pink Floyd's *Atom Heart Mother*, Harvest Records S KAO-382; published TRO-Hampshire House/ Lupus Music Ltd. (ASCAP), 1971.

I Shall Be Released: Note: Sung live by actor, recording not used; Written by Bob Dylan, recorded version on *Bob Dylan's Greatest Hits, Vol. II*, Columbia KC 31120; Dwarf Music, 1967 and 1970.

Farther Along: Traditional, arrangement by Clarence White; sung by The Byrds from their *Farther Along*, Columbia KC 31050; Byrdland Publishing Co. (BMI), 1971.

Except where noted, all songs are played in their entirety. All songs used with permission. All rights reserved.

ntozake shange

for colored girls who have considered suicide/ when the rainbow is enuf

NTOZAKE SHANGE is also the author of *Betsey Brown* and three collections of poetry, *From Okra to Greens, Nappy Edges,* and *A Daughter's Geography,* as well as the novel, *Sassafrass, Cypress, and Indigo.* She has written for *Black Scholar, Yardbird Reader, Invisible City, Third World Woman, Time to Greez, Margins, Black Maria, West End* magazine, *Broadway Boogie, APR,* and *Shocks.* Her play, *A Photograph: A Still Life With Shadows/A Photograph: A Study in Cruelty* was produced by the Public Theatre in New York City in the winter of 1977. Along with Jessica Hagedorn and Thulani ("The Satin Sisters") she wrote and performed in *Where the Mississippi Meets the Amazon,* presented by Joseph Papp at the Public Theatre Cabaret. Her latest play, *Spell #7,* was presented at the Public Theatre in the summer of 1979.

For information regarding stock and amateur production rights, including all other rights, contact: Broadway Play Publishing, Inc., 357 West 20th Street, New York, NY 10011.

Original Production Notes

For Colored Girls Who Have Considered Suicide/When the Rainbow Is Enuf
was produced in New York by Joseph Papp and Woodie King, Jr., under
the direction of Oz Scott, at the Henry Street Settlement's New Federal
Theatre. It then opened at the New York Shakespeare Festival Public
Theatre, where it ran from June 1–August 29, 1976. It then ran at the
Booth Theatre on Broadway, from September 15, 1976 until July 16,
1978, with the following cast:

Lady in Brown	Janet League
Lady in Yellow	Aku Kadogo
Lady in Red	Trazana Beverley
Lady in Green	Paula Moss
Lady in Purple	Risë Collins
Lady in Blue	Laurie Carlos
Lady in Orange	ntozake shange

Scenery by Ming Cho Lee; lighting by Jennifer Tipton; costumes by
Judy Dearing; choreography by Paula Moss; music for *"I Found God in
Myself"* by Diana Wharton. Associate Producer, Bernard Gersten. A New
York Shakespeare Festival Production in association with the Henry
Street Settlement's New Federal Theatre.

(The stage is in darkness. Harsh music is heard as dim blue lights come up. One after another, seven women run onto the stage from each of the exits. They all freeze in postures of distress. The following spot picks up the LADY IN BROWN. *She comes to life and looks around at the other ladies. All of the others are still. She walks over to the* LADY IN RED *and calls to her. The* LADY IN RED *makes no response.)*

LADY IN BROWN: dark phrases of womanhood
of never havin been a girl
half-notes scattered
without rhythm/no tune
distraught laughter fallin
over a black girl's shoulder
it's funny/it's hysterical
the melody-less-ness of her dance

don't tell nobody don't tell a soul
she's dancin on beer cans & shingles

this must be the spook house
another song with no singers
lyrics/no voices
& interrupted solos
unseen performances

are we ghouls?
children of horror?
the joke?

don't tell nobody don't tell a soul
are we animals? have we gone crazy?

i can't hear anythin
but maddening screams
& the soft strains of death
& you promised me
you promised me . . .
somebody/anybody
sing a black girl's song
bring her out
to know herself
to know you
but sing her rhythms

carin/struggle/hard times
sing her song of life
she's been dead so long

---

closed in silence so long
she doesn't know the sound
of her own voice
her infinite beauty
she's half-notes scattered
without rhythm/no tune
sing her sighs
sing the song of her possibilities
sing a righteous gospel
the makin of a melody
let her be born
let her be born
& handled warmly.

LADY IN BROWN: i'm outside chicago

LADY IN YELLOW: i'm outside detroit

LADY IN PURPLE: i'm outside houston

LADY IN RED: i'm outside baltimore

LADY IN GREEN: i'm outside san francisco

LADY IN BLUE: i'm outside manhattan

LADY IN ORANGE: i'm outside st. louis

LADY IN BROWN: & this is for colored girls who have considered suicide
but moved to the ends of their own rainbows.

EVERYONE: mama's little baby likes shortnin, shortnin
mama's little baby likes shortnin bread
mama's little baby likes shortnin, shortnin,
mama's little baby likes shortnin bread

little sally walker, sittin in a saucer
rise, sally, rise, wipe your weeping eyes
an put your hands on your hips
an let your backbone slip
o, shake it to the east
o, shake it to the west
shake it to the one
that you like the best

LADY IN PURPLE: you're it

(As the LADY IN BROWN *tags each of the other ladies they freeze. When each one
has been tagged the* LADY IN BROWN *freezes. Immediately "Dancing in the Streets"
by Martha and the Vandellas is heard. All of the ladies start to dance. The* LADY IN
GREEN, *the* LADY IN BLUE, *and the* LADY IN YELLOW *do the pony, the big boss line,
the swim, and the nose dive. The other ladies dance in place.)*

LADY IN YELLOW: it was graduation nite & i waz the only virgin in
     the crowd
bobby mills martin jerome & sammy yates eddie jones & randi
all cousins
all the prettiest niggers in this factory town
carried me out wit em
in a deep black buick
smelling of thunderbird & ladies in heat
we rambled from camden to mount holly
laughin at the afternoon's speeches
& dangling our tassles from the rear view mirror
climbing different sorta project stairs
movin toward snappin beer cans &
GET IT GET IT THAT'S THE WAY TO DO IT MAMA
all mercer county graduated the same nite
     cosmetology secretarial pre-college
         autoshop & business
all us movin from mama to what ever waz out there

that nite we raced a big old truck from the barbeque stand
trying to tell him bout the party at jacqui's
where folks graduated last year waz waitin to hit it wid us
i got drunk & cdnt figure out
whose hand waz on my thigh/but it didn't matter
cuz these cousins martin eddie sammy jerome & bobby
waz my sweethearts alternately since the seventh grade
& everybody knew i always started crying if somebody actually
tried to take advantage of me
         at jacqui's

ulinda mason was stickin her mouth all out
while we tumbled out the buick
eddie jones waz her lickin stick
but i knew how to dance
         it got soo hot
vincent ramos puked all in the punch
& harly jumped all in tico's face
cuz he was leavin for the navy in the mornin
hadda kick ass so we'd all remember how bad he ·﹨.
seems like sheila & marguerite waz fraid
to get their hair turnin back
so they laid up against the wall
lookin almost sexy
didnt wanna sweat
but me & my fellas   we waz dancin

since 1963 i'd won all kinda contests
wid the cousins at the POLICE ATHLETIC LEAGUE DANCES
all mercer county knew
any kin to martin yates cd turn somersaults
fore smokey robinson cd get a woman excited

(The Dells singing "Stay" is heard.)
we danced   doin nasty ol tricks

(The LADY IN YELLOW *sings along with the Dells for a moment. The* LADY IN ORANGE
and the LADY IN BLUE *jump up and parody the* LADY IN YELLOW *and the Dells. The*
LADY IN YELLOW *stares at them. They sit down.)*

doin nasty ol tricks i'd been thinkin since may
cuz graduation nite had to be hot
& i waz the only virgin
so i hadda make like my hips waz into some business
that way everybody thot whoever was gettin it
was a older man cdnt run the streets wit youngsters
martin slipped his leg round my thigh
the dells bumped "stay"
up & down—up & down the new carver homes
WE WAZ GROWN
        WE WAZ FINALLY GROWN

ulinda all sudden went crazy
went over to eddie cursin & carryin on
tearing his skin wid her nails
the cousins tried to talk sense to her
tried to hold her arms

lissin bitch sammy went on
bobby whispered i shd go wit him
fore they go ta cuttin
fore the police arrived
we teetered silently thru the parkin lot
no un uhuh
we didn't know nothin bout no party
bobby started lookin at me
yeah
he started looking at me real strange
like i waz a woman or somethin/
started talkin real soft
in the backseat of that ol buick
WOW
by daybreak
i just cdnt stop grinnin.

(The Dells singing "Stay" comes in and all of the ladies except the LADY IN BLUE
join in and sing along.)

LADY IN BLUE: you gave it up in a buick?

LADY IN YELLOW: yeh, and honey, it was wonderful.

LADY IN GREEN: we used to do it all up in the dark
in the corners...

LADY IN BLUE: some niggah sweating all over you.

LADY IN RED: it was good!

LADY IN BLUE: i never did like to grind.

LADY IN YELLOW: what other kind of dances are there?

LADY IN BLUE: mambo, bomba, merengue

when i waz sixteen i ran off to the south bronx
cuz i waz gonna meet up wit willie colon
& dance all the time
          mamba bomba merengue

LADY IN YELLOW: do you speak spanish?

LADY IN BLUE: olà
my papa thot he was puerto rican & we wda been
cept we waz just reglar niggahs wit hints of spanish
so off i made it to this 36 hour marathon dance
con salsa con ricardo
'suggggggggggar' ray on southern blvd
next door to this fotografi place
jammed wit burial weddin & communion relics
next door to la real ideal genuine spanish barber
          up up up up up stairs & stairs & lotsa hallway
wit my colored new jersey self
didn't know what anybody waz saying
cept if dancin waz proof of origin
          i was jibarita herself that nite
& the next day
i kept smilin & right on steppin
if he cd lead i waz ready to dance
if he cdnt lead
i caught this attitude
          i'd seen rosa do
& wd not be bothered
i waz twirling hippin givin much quik feet
& being a mute cute colored puerto rican
til saturday afternoon when the disc-jockey say
'SORRY FOLKS WILLIE COLON AINT GONNA MAKE IT TODAY'
& alla my niggah temper came outta control
& i wdnt dance wit nobody
& i talked english loud

& i love you more than i waz mad
uh huh uh huh
more than more than
when i discovered archie shepp & subtle blues
doncha know i wore out the magic of juju
heroically resistin being possessed

ooooooooooooooh the sounds
sneakin in under age to slug's
to stare ata real 'artiste'
& every word outta imamu's mouth waz gospel
& if jesus cdnt play a horn like shepp
waznt no need for colored folks to bear no cross at all

& poem is my thank-you for music
& i love you more than poem
more than aureliano buendia loved macondo
more than hector lavoe loved himself
more than the lady loved gardenias
more than celia loves cuba or graciela loves el son
more than the flamingoes shoo-do-n-doo-wah love
     bein pretty
oyè négro
te amo mas que   te amo mas que
when you play
yr flute

EVERYONE: *(Very softly)* te amo mas que   te amo mas que

LADY IN RED: without any assistance or guidance from you
i have loved you assiduously for 8 months 2 wks & a day
i have been stood up four times
i've left 7 packages on yr doorstep
forty poems 2 plants & 3 handmade notecards i left
town so i cd send to you have been no help to me
on my job
you call at 3:00 in the mornin on weekdays
so i cd drive 27½ miles cross the bay before i go to work
charmin charmin
but you are of no assistance
i want you to know
this waz an experiment
to see how selfish i cd be

if i wd really carry on to snare a possible lover
if i waz capable of debasin my self for the love of another
if i cd stand not being wanted

when i wanted to be wanted
& i cannot
so
with no further assistance & no guidance from you
i am endin this affair

this note is attached to a plant
i've been waterin since the day i met you
you may water it
yr damn self

LADY IN ORANGE: i dont wanna write
in english or spanish
i wanna sing   make you dance
like the bata   dance   scream
twitch hips wit me cuz
i done forgot all abt words
aint got no definitions
i wanna whirl
        with you

(*Music starts*, "Che Che Cole" *by Willie Colon. Everyone starts to dance.*)
our whole body
wrapped like a ripe mango
ramblin whippin thru space
on the corner in the park
where the rug useta be
let willie colon take you out
swing your head
push your leg to the moon with me

i'm on the lower east side
in new york city
and i can't   i can't
talk witchu no more

LADY IN YELLOW: we gotta dance to keep from cryin

LADY IN BROWN: we gotta dance to keep from dyin

LADY IN RED: so come on

LADY IN BROWN: come on

LADY IN PURPLE: come on

LADY IN ORANGE: hold yr head like it was ruby sapphire
i'm a poet
who writes in english
come to share the worlds witchu

EVERYONE: come to share our worlds witchu

we come here to be dancin
    to be dancin
   to be dancin
  baya

(There is a sudden light change, all of the ladies react as if they had been struck in the face. The LADY IN GREEN *and the* LADY IN YELLOW *run out up left, the* LADY IN ORANGE *runs out the left volm, the* LADY IN BROWN *runs out up right.)*

LADY IN BLUE: a friend is hard to press charges against

LADY IN RED: if you know him
you must have wanted it

LADY IN PURPLE: a misunderstanding

LADY IN RED: you know
these things happen

LADY IN BLUE: are you sure
you didnt suggest

LADY IN PURPLE: had you been drinkin

LADY IN RED: a rapist is always to be a stranger
to be legitimate
someone you never saw
a man wit obvious problems

LADY IN PURPLE: pin-ups attached to the insides of his lapels

LADY IN BLUE: ticket stubs from porno flicks in his pocket

LADY IN PURPLE: a lil dick

LADY IN RED: or a strong mother

LADY IN BLUE: or just a brutal virgin

LADY IN RED: but if you've been seen in public wit him
danced one dance
kissed him good-bye lightly

LADY IN PURPLE: wit closed mouth

LADY IN BLUE: pressin charges will be as hard
as keepin yr legs closed
while five fools try to run a train on you

LADY IN RED: these men friends of ours
who smile nice
stay unemployed
and take us out to dinner

LADY IN PURPLE: lock the door behind you

LADY IN BLUE: wit fist in face
to fuck

LADY IN RED: who make elaborate mediterranean dinners
& let the art ensemble carry all ethical burdens
while they invite a coupla friends over to have you
are sufferin from latent rapist bravado
& we are left wit the scars

LADY IN BLUE: bein betrayed by men who know us

LADY IN PURPLE: & expect
like the stranger
we always thot waz comin

LADY IN BLUE: that we will submit

LADY IN PURPLE: we must have known

LADY IN RED: women relinquish all personal rights
in the presence of a man
who apparently cd be considered a rapist

LADY IN PURPLE: especially if he has been considered a friend

LADY IN BLUE: & is no less worthy of bein beat within an inch of his life
being publicly ridiculed
having two fists shoved up his ass

LADY IN RED: than the stranger
we always thot it wd be

LADY IN BLUE: who never showed up

LADY IN RED: cuz it turns out the nature of rape has changed

LADY IN BLUE: we can now meet them in circles we frequent for
companionship

LADY IN PURPLE: we see them at the coffeehouse

LADY IN BLUE: wit someone else we know

LADY IN RED: we cd even have em over for dinner
& get raped in our own houses
by invitation
a friend

(The lights change, and the ladies are all hit by an imaginary slap, the LADY IN RED
runs off up left.)

LADY IN BLUE: eyes

LADY IN PURPLE: mice

LADY IN BLUE: womb

LADY IN BLUE and LADY IN PURPLE: nobody

(The LADY IN PURPLE *exits up right.)*

LADY IN BLUE: tubes tables white washed windows
grime from age wiped over once

legs spread
anxious
eyes crawling up on me
eyes rolling in my thighs
metal horses gnawing my womb
dead mice fall from my mouth
i really didnt mean to
i really didnt think i cd
just one day off . . .
get offa me alla this blood
bones shattered like soft ice-cream cones

i cdnt have people
lookin at me
pregnant
i cdnt have my friends see this
dyin danglin between my legs
& i didnt say a thing
not a sigh
or a fast scream
to get
those eyes offa me
get them steel rods outta me
this hurts
this hurts me
& nobody came
cuz nobody knew
once i waz pregnant & shamed of myself.

(The LADY IN BLUE *exits stage left volm.)*

*(Soft deep music is heard, voices calling "Sechita" come from the wings and volms.
The* LADY IN PURPLE *enters from up right.)*

LADY IN PURPLE: once there were quadroon balls/elegance in st. louis/
laced
mulattoes/gambling down the mississippi/to
     memphis/new
orleans n okra crepes near the bayou/where the
     poor white trash
wd sing/moanin/strange/liquid tones/thru the
     swamps

(The LADY IN GREEN *enters from the right volm; she is Sechita and for the rest of
the poem dances out Sechita's life.)*

sechita had heard these things/she moved as if she'd
known them/the silver n high-toned laughin/

the violins n marble floors/sechita pushed the clingin
delta dust wit painted toes/the patch-work tent waz
poka-dotted/stale lights snatched at the shadows/
creole carnival waz playin natchez in ten minutes/
her splendid red garters/gin-stained n itchy on her
thigh/blk-diamond stockings darned wit yellow
threads/an ol starched taffeta can-can fell abundantly
orange/from her waist round the splinterin chair/
sechita/egyptian/goddess of creativity/2nd
millennium/threw her heavy hair in a coil over her
neck/sechita/goddess/the recordin of history/
spread crimson oil on her cheeks/waxed her
eyebrows/n unconsciously slugged the last hard
whiskey in the glass/the broken mirror she used to
decorate her face/made her forehead tilt backwards/
her cheeks appear sunken/her sassy chin only large
enuf/to keep her full lower lip/from growin into her
neck/sechita/had learned to make allowances for
the distortions/but the heavy dust of the delta/left a
tinge of grit n darkness/on every one of her dresses/
on her arms & her shoulders/sechita/waz anxious
to get back to st. louis/the dirt there didnt crawl
from the earth into yr soul/at least/in st. louis/the
grime waz store bought second-hand/here in
natchez/god seemed to be wipin his feet in her face/

one of the wrestlers had finally won tonite/the
mulatto/raul/was sposed to hold the boomin half-
caste/searin eagle/in a bear hug/8 counts/get
thrown unawares/fall out the ring/n then do searin
eagle in for good/sechita/cd hear redneck whoops n
slappin on the back/she gathered her sparsely
sequined skirts/tugged the waist cincher from under
her greyin slips/n made her face immobile/she made
her face like nefertiti/approaching her own tomb/
she suddenly threw/her leg full-force/thru the
canvas curtain/a deceptive glass stone/sparkled/
malignant on her ankle/her calf was tauntin in the
brazen carnie lights/the full moon/sechita/goddess/
of love/egypt/2nd millennium/performin the rites/
the conjurin of men/conjurin the spirit/in natchez
the mississippi spewed a heavy fume of barely movin
waters/sechita's legs slashed furiously thru the
cracker nite/& gold pieces hittin the makeshift
stage/her thighs/they were aimin coins tween her
thighs/sechita/egypt/goddess/harmony/kicked
viciously thru the nite/catchin stars between her toes.

(*The* LADY IN GREEN *exits into the stage left volm, the* LADY IN PURPLE *exits into up
stage left.*)

(The LADY IN BROWN *enters from up stage right.)*

LADY IN BROWN: de library waz right down from de trolly tracks
cross from de laundry-mat
thru de big shinin floors & granite pillars
ol st. louis is famous for
i found toussaint
but not til after months uv
cajun katie/pippi longstockin
christopher robin/eddie heyward & a pooh bear
in the children's room
only pioneer girls & magic rabbits
& big city white boys
i knew i waznt sposedta
but i ran inta the ADULT READING ROOM
    & came across

    TOUSSAINT

    my first blk man
(i never counted george washington carver
cuz i didnt like peanuts)
    still
TOUSSAINT waz a blk man a negro like my mama say
who refused to be a slave
& he spoke french
& didnt low no white man to tell him nothin
    not napolean
    not maximillien
    not robespierre

TOUSSAINT L'OUVERTURE
waz the beginnin uv reality for me
in the summer contest for
who colored child can read
15 books in three weeks
i wun & raved abt TOUSSAINT L'OUVERTURE
at the afternoon ceremony
waz disqualified
    cuz Toussaint
      belonged in the ADULT READING ROOM
        & i cried
& carried dead Toussaint home in the book
he waz dead & livin to me
cuz TOUSSAINT & them
they held the citadel gainst the french
wid the spirits of ol dead africans from outta the ground

TOUSSAINT led they army of zombies
walkin cannon ball shootin spirits to free Haiti
& they waznt slaves no more
      TOUSSAINT L'OUVERTURE
became my secret lover at the age of 8
i entertained him in my bedroom
widda flashlight under my covers
way inta the night/we discussed strategies
how to remove white girls from my hopscotch games
& etc.
TOUSSAINT
waz layin in bed wit me next to raggedy ann
the night i decided to run away from my
      integrated home
      integrated street
        integrated school
1955 waz not a good year for lil blk girls

Toussaint said 'lets go to haiti'
i said 'awright'
& packed some very important things in a brown paper bag
so i wdnt haveta come back
then Toussaint & i took the hodiamont streetcar
to the river
last stop
only 15¢
cuz there waznt nobody cd see Toussaint cept me
& we walked all down thru north st. louis
where the french settlers usedta live
in tiny brick houses all huddled together
wit barely missin windows & shingles uneven
wit colored kids playin & women on low porches
      sippin beer

i cd talk to Toussaint down by the river
like this waz where we waz gonna stow away
on a boat for new orleans
& catch a creole fishin-rig for port-au-prince
then we waz just gonna read & talk all the time
& eat fried bananas
      we waz just walking & skippin past ol
        drunk men
when dis ol young boy jumped out at me sayin
'HEY GIRL YA BETTAH COME OVAH HEAH N
      TALK TO ME'

well
i turned to TOUSSAINT (who waz furious)
& i shouted
'ya silly ol boy
ya bettah leave me alone
or TOUSSAINT'S gonna get yr ass'
de silly ol boy came round de corner laughin all in my face
'yellah gal
ya sure must be somebody to know my name so quick'
i waz disgusted
& wanted to get on to haiti
widout some tacky ol boy botherin me
still he kept standin there
kickin milk cartons & bits of brick
trying to get all in my business
        i mumbled to L'OUVERTURE 'what shd I do'
finally
i asked this silly ol boy
'WELL WHO ARE YOU?'
he say
'MY NAME IS TOUSSAINT JONES'
well
i looked right at him
those skidded out cordoroy pants
a striped teashirt wid holes in both elbows
a new scab over his left eye
& i said
        'what's yr name again'
he say
'i'm toussaint jones'
'wow
i am on my way to see
TOUSSAINT L'OUVERTURE in HAITI
are ya any kin to him
he dont take no stuff from no white folks
& they gotta country all they own
& there aint no slaves'
that silly ol boy squinted his face all up
'looka heah girl
i am TOUSSAINT JONES
& i'm right heah lookin at ya
& i dont take no stuff from no white folks
ya dont see none round heah do ya?'
& he sorta pushed out his chest

then he say
'come on   lets go on down to the docks
& look at the boats'
i waz real puzzled goin down to the docks
wit my paper bag & my books
i felt TOUSSAINT L'OUVERTURE sorta leave me
& i waz sad
til i realized
TOUSSAINT JONES waznt too different
from TOUSSAINT L'OUVERTURE
cept the ol one waz in haiti
& this one wid me speakin english & eatin apples
yeah.
toussaint jones waz awright wit me
no tellin what all spirits we cd move
down by the river
st. louis 1955   hey wait.

(The LADY IN BROWN *exits into the stage right volm.)*

(The LADY IN RED *enters from the stage left volm.)*

LADY IN RED: orange butterflies & aqua sequins
ensconsed tween slight bosoms
silk roses dartin from behind her ears
the passion flower of southwest los angeles
meandering down hoover street
past dark shuttered houses where
women from louisiana shelled peas
round 3:00 & sent their sons
whistlin to the store for fatback & black-eyed peas
she glittered in heat
& seemed to be lookin for rides
when she waznt & absolutely
eyed every man who waznt lame white or noddin out
she let her thigh slip from her skirt
crossin the street
she slowed to be examined
& she never looked back to smile
or ackrowledge a sincere 'hey mama'
or to meet the eyes of someone
purposely findin sometin to do in
her direction
          she was sullen
          & the rhinestones etching the corners of
             her mouth

      suggested tears
      fresh kisses that had done no good
she always wore her stomach out
lined with small iridescent feathers
the hairs round her navel seemed to dance
& she didnt let on
she knew
from behind her waist waz aching to be held
the pastel ivy drawn on her shoulders
to be brushed with lips & fingers
smellin of honey & jack daniels
      she waz hot
      a deliberate coquette
      who never did without
      what she wanted
& she wanted to be unforgettable
she wanted to be a memory
a wound   to every man
arragant enough to want her
      she waz the wrath
      of women in windows
         fingerin shades/ol lace curtains
           camoflagin despair &
             stretch marks
so she glittered honestly
delighted she waz desired
& allowed those especially
schemin/tactful suitors
to experience her body & spirit
tearin/so easily blendin with theirs/
& they were so happy
& lay on her lime sheets full & wet
from her tongue   she kissed
them reverently   even ankles
edges of beards ...

(The stage goes to darkness except for a special on the LADY IN RED, *who lies motionless on the floor; as the lights slowly fade up the* LADY IN RED *sits up.)*

at 4:30 AM
she rose
movin the arms & legs that trapped her
she sighed affirmin the sculptured man
& made herself a bath
of dark musk oil egyptian crystals
& florida water to remove his smell

to wash away the glitter
to watch the butterflies melt into
suds & the rhinestones fall beneath
her buttocks like smooth pebbles
in a missouri creek
layin in water
she became herself
ordinary
brown braided woman
with big legs & full lips
reglar
seriously intendin to finish her
night's work
she quickly walked to her guest
straddled on her pillows & began
        'you'll have to go now/i've
        a lot of work to do/& i cant
        with a man around/here are yr pants/
        there's coffee on the stove/it's been
        very nice/but i cant see you again/
        you got what you came for/didnt you'
& she smiled
he wd either mumble curses bout crazy bitches
or sit dumbfounded
while she repeated
        'i cdnt possibly wake up/with
        a strange man in my bed/why
        dont you go home'
she cda been slapped upside the head
or verbally challenged
but she never waz
& the ones who fell prey to the
dazzle of hips painted with
orange blossoms & magnolia scented wrists
had wanted no more
than to lay between her sparklin thighs
& had planned on leavin before dawn
& she had been so divine
devastatingly bizarre the way
her mouth fit round
& now she stood a
reglar colored girl
fulla the same malice
livid indifference as a sistah
worn from supportin a wd be hornplayer
or waitin by the window
        & they knew
        & left in a hurry

she wd gather her tinsel &
jewels from the tub
& laugh gayly or vengeful
she stored her silk roses by her bed
& when she finished writin
the account of her exploit in a diary
embroidered with lilies & moonstones
she placed the rose behind her ear
& cried herself to sleep.

(All the lights fade except for a special on the LADY IN RED; *the* LADY IN RED *exits into the stage left volm.)*

(The LADY IN BLUE *enters from up right.)*

LADY IN BLUE: i usedta live in the world
then i moved to HARLEM
& my universe is now six blocks

when i walked in the pacific
i imagined waters ancient from accra/tunis
cleansin me/feedin me
now my ankles are coated in grey filth
from the puddle neath the hydrant

my oceans were life
what waters i have here sit stagnant
circlin ol men's bodies
shit & broken lil whiskey bottles
left to make me bleed

i usedta live in the world
now i live in harlem & my universe is six blocks
a tunnel with a train
i can ride anywhere
remaining a stranger
    NO MAN YA CANT GO WIT ME/I DONT
    EVEN KNOW YOU/NO/I DONT WANNA
    KISS YOU/YOU AINT BUT 12 YEARS OLD/
    NO MAN/PLEASE PLEASE PLEASE LEAVE
    ME ALONE/TOMORROW/YEAH/NO/
    PLEASE/I CANT USE IT
    i cd stay alone
    a woman in the world
    then i moved to
HARLEM
i come in at dusk
stay close to the curb

(The LADY IN YELLOW *enters, she's waiting for a bus.)*

round midnite
praying wont no young man
think i'm pretty in a dark mornin

(The LADY IN PURPLE *enters, she's waiting for a bus.)*

wdnt be good
not good at all
to meet a tall short black brown young man fulla
      his power
in the dark
in my universe of six blocks
straight up brick walls
women hangin outta windows
like ol silk stockings
cats cryin/children gigglin/a tavern wit red curtains
bad smells/kissin ladies smiling & dirt
sidewalks spittin/men cursing/playin

(The LADY IN ORANGE *enters, she is being followed by a man, the* LADY IN BLUE
becomes that man.)

'I SPENT MORE MONEY YESTERDAY
THAN THE DAY BEFORE & ALL THAT'S
MORE N YOU NIGGAH EVER GOTTA
HOLD TO COME OVER HERE BITCH
CANT YA SEE THIS IS $5'

never mind sister
dont play him no mind
go go go go go go sister
do yr thing
never mind

i usedta live in the world
really be in the world
free & sweet talkin
good mornin & thank-you & nice day
uh huh
i cant now
i cant be nice to nobody
nice is such a rip-off
regular beauty & a smile in the street
is just a set-up

i usedta be in the world
a woman in the world
i hadda right to the world
then i moved to harlem
for the set-up
a universe

six blocks of cruelty
piled up on itself
a tunnel
closin

(The four ladies on stage freeze, count 4, then the LADIES IN BLUE, PURPLE, YELLOW, *and* ORANGE *move to their places for the next poem.)*

LADY IN PURPLE: three of us like a pyramid
three friends
one laugh
one music
one flowered shawl
knotted on each neck
we all saw him at the same time
& he saw us
i felt a quick thump in each one of us
didnt know what to do
we all wanted what waz comin our way
so we split
but he found one
& she loved him

the other two were tickled
& spurned his advances
when the one who loved him waz somewhere else
he wd come to her saying
yr friends love you very much
i have tried
& they keep askin where are you
she smiled
wonderin how long her friends
wd hold out
he waz what they were lookin for
he bided his time
he waited til romance waned
the three of us made up stories
bout usedta & cda been nice
the season waz dry
no men
no quickies
not one dance or eyes unrelentin
one day after another
cept for the one who loved him
he appeared irregularly
expectin graciousness no matter what

she cut fresh strawberries
her friends callt less frequently
went on hunts for passin fancies
she cdnt figure out what waz happenin
then the rose
she left by his pillow
she found on her friends desk
& there was nothing to say
she said
i wanna tell you
he's been after me
all the time
says he's free & can explain
what's happenin wit you
is nothing to me
& i dont wanna hurt you
but you know i need someone now
& you know
how wonderful he is
her friend cdnt speak or cry
they hugged & went to where he waz
wit another woman
he said good-bye to one
tol the other he wd call
he smiled a lot

she held her head on her lap
the lap of her sisters soakin up tears
ach understandin how much love stood between them
how much love between them
love between them
love like sisters

(Sharp music is heard, each LADY *dances as if catching a disease from the* LADY
next to her, suddenly they all freeze.)

LADY IN ORANGE: ever since i realized there was something callt
a colored girl an evil woman a bitch or a nag
i been tryin not to be that & leave bitterness
in somebody else's cup/come to somebody to love me
without deep & nasty smellin scald from lye or bein
left screamin in a street fulla lunatics/whisperin
slut bitch bitch niggah/get outta here wit alla that/
i didn't have any of that for you/i brought you what
joy i found & i found joy/honest fingers round my
face/with dead musicians on 78's from cuba/or live

musicians on five dollar lp's from chicago/where i
have never been/& i love willie colon & arsenio
rodriquez/especially cuz i can make the music loud
enuf/so there is no me but dance/& when i can
dance like that/there's nothin cd hurt me/but i get
tired & i haveta come offa the floor & then there's
that woman who hurt you/who you left/three or
four times/& just went back/after you put my heart
in the bottom of yr shoe/you just walked back to
where you hurt/& i didn't have nothin/so i went to
where somebody had somethin for me/but he waznt
you/& i waz on the way back from her house in
the bottom of yr shoe/so this is not a love poem/
cuz there are only memorial albums available/& even
charlie mingus wanted desperately to be a pimp/
& i wont be able to see eddie palmieri for months/
so this is a requium for myself/cuz i have died in a
real way/not wid aqua coffins & du-wop cadillacs/
i used to joke abt when i waz messin round/but a
real dead lovin is here for you now/cuz i dont know
anymore/how to avoid my own face wet wit my
tears/cuz i had convinced myself colored girls had no
right to sorrow/& i lived & loved that way & kept
sorrow on the curb/allegedly for you/but i know i did
it for myself/
i cdnt stand it
i cdnt stand being sorry & colored at the same time
it's so redundant in the modern world

LADY IN PURPLE: i lived wit myths & music waz my ol man & i cd
dance a dance outta time/a dance wit no partners/
take my ills & keep right on steppin/linger in
non-english speakin arms so there waz no possibility
of understandin
& you YOU
came sayin i am the niggah/i am the baddest
muthafuckah out there/
i said yes/this is who i am waitin for
& to come wit you/i hadta bring everythin
the dance & the terror
the dead musicians & the hope
& those scars i had hidden wit smiles & good fuckin
lay open
& i dont know i dont know any more tricks

i am really colored & really sad sometimes & you hurt
me more than i ever danced outta/into oblivion isnt far
enuf to get outta this/i am ready to die like a lily in the
desert/& i cdnt let you in on it cuz i didnt know/here
is what i have/poems/big thighs/lil tits/& so much
love/will you take it from me this one time/please
this is for you/arsenio's tres cleared the way & makes
me pure again/please please/this is for you i want
you to love me/let me love you/i dont wanna dance
wit ghosts/snuggle lovers i made up in my
drunkenness/lemme love you just like i am/a colored
girl/i'm finally bein real/no longer symmetrical &
impervious to pain

LADY IN BLUE: we deal wit emotion too much
so why dont we go on ahead & be white then/
& make everythin dry & abstract wit no rhythm & no
reelin for sheer sensual pleasure/yes let's go on & be
white/we're right in the middle of it/no use holdin
out/holdin onto ourselves/lets think our way outta
feelin/lets abstract ourselves some families & maybe
maybe tonight/i'll find a way to make myself come
witout you/no fingers or other objects just thot which
isnt spiritual evolution cuz its empty & godliness is
plenty is ripe & fertile/thinkin wont do me a bit of
good tonight/i need to be loved/& havent the audacity
to say
where are you/& dont know who to say it to

LADY IN YELLOW: i've lost it
touch wit reality/i dont know who's doing it
i thot i waz but i waz so stupid i waz able to be hurt
& that's not real/not anymore/i shd be immune/if
i'm still alive & that's what i waz discussin/how i am
still alive & my dependency on other livin beins for
love i survive on intimacy & tomorrow/that's all i've
got goin & the music waz like smack & you knew abt
that & still refused my dance waz not enuf/& it waz
all i had but bein alive & bein a woman & being
colored is a metaphysical dilemma/i havent conquered
yet/do you see the point my spirit is too ancient to
understand the separation of soul & gender/my love
is too delicate to have thrown back on my face

(The LADIES in RED, GREEN, and BROWN enter quietly; in the background all of the *ladies except the* LADY IN YELLOW *are frozen; the* LADY IN YELLOW *looks at them, walks by them, touches them; they do not move.)*

LADY IN YELLOW: my love is too delicate to have thrown back on my face

(The LADY IN YELLOW *starts to exit into the stage right volm. Just as she gets to the volm, the* LADY IN BROWN *comes to life.)*

LADY IN BROWN: my love is too beautiful to have thrown back on my face

LADY IN PURPLE: my love is too sanctified to have thrown back on my face

LADY IN BLUE: my love is too magic to have thrown back on my face

LADY IN ORANGE: my love is too saturday nite to have thrown back on my face

LADY IN RED: my love is too complicated to have thrown back on my face

LADY IN GREEN: my love is too music to have thrown back on my face

EVERYONE: music

MUSIC:

(The LADY IN GREEN then breaks into a dance, the other ladies follow her lead and soon they are all dancing and chanting together.)

LADY IN GREEN: yank dankka dank dank

EVERYONE: music

LADY IN GREEN: yank dankka dank dank

EVERYONE: music

LADY IN GREEN: yank dankka dank dank

EVERYONE: *(But started by the* LADY IN YELLOW*)* delicate
delicate
delicate

EVERYONE: *(But started by the* LADY IN BROWN*)* and beautiful
and beautiful
and beautiful

EVERYONE: *(But started by the* LADY IN PURPLE*)* oh sanctified
oh sanctified
oh sanctified

EVERYONE: *(But started by the* LADY IN BLUE*)* magic
magic
magic

EVERYONE: *(But started by the* LADY IN ORANGE*)* and saturday nite
and saturday nite

and saturday nite

EVERYONE: *(But started by the* LADY IN RED*)* and complicated
and complicated
and complicated
and complicated
and complicated
and complicated
and complicated
and complicated

(The dance reaches a climax and all of the LADIES *fall out tired, but full of life and togetherness.)*

LADY IN GREEN: somebody almost walked off wid alla my stuff
not my poems or a dance i gave up in the street
but somebody almost walked off wid alla my stuff
like a kleptomaniac workin hard & forgettin while
stealin
this is mine/this aint yr stuff/
now why dont you put me back & let me hang out in
my own self
somebody almost walked off wid alla my stuff
& didnt care enuf to send a note home sayin
i waz late for my solo conversation
or two sizes too small for my own tacky skirts
what can anybody do wit somethin of no value on a
open market/did you getta dime for my things/hey
man/where are you goin wid alla my stuff/this is a
woman's trip & i need my stuff/to ohh & ahh abt/
daddy/i gotta mainline number from my own shit/
now wontchu put me back/& let me play this duet/wit
this silver ring in my nose/honest to god/somebody
almost run off wit alla my stuff/& i didnt bring anythin
but the kick & sway of it the perfect ass for my man &
none of it is theirs this is mine/ntozake 'her own
things'/that's my name/now give me my stuff/i see
ya hidin my laugh/& how i sit wif my legs open
sometimes/to give my crotch some sunlight/& there
goes my love my toes my chewed up finger nails/
niggah/wif the curls in yr hair/mr. louisiana hot link/
i want my stuff back/my rhythms & my voice/open
my mouth/& let me talk ya outta/throwin my shit
in the sewar/this is some delicate leg & whimsical
kiss/i gotta have to give to my choice/without you
runnin off wit alla my shit/now you cant have me

less i give me away/& i waz doin all that/til ya run
off on a good thing/who is this you left me wit/
some simple bitch widda bad attitude/i wants my
things/i want my arm wit the hot iron scar/& my
leg wit the flea bite/i want my calloused feet & quik
language back in my mouth/fried plantains/
pineapple pear juice/sun-ra & joseph & jules/i want
my own things/how i lived them/& give me my
memories/how i waz when i waz there/you cant
have them or do nothin wit them/stealin my shit
from me/dont make it yrs/makes it stolen/somebody
almost run off wit alla my stuff/& i waz standin
there/lookin at myself/the whole time & it waznt
a spirit took my stuff/waz a man whose ego walked
round like Rodan's shadow/waz a man faster n my
innocence/waz a lover/i made too much room for/
almost run off wit alla my stuff/& i didnt know i'd
give it up so quick/& the one running wit it/dont
know he got it/& i'm shouting this is mine/& he dont
know he got it/my stuff is the anonymous ripped off
treasure of the year/did you know somebody almost
got away with me/me in a plastic bag under their
arm/me danglin on a string of personal carelessness/
i'm spattered wit mud & city rain/& no i didnt get
a chance to take a douche/hey man/this is not your
perogative/i gotta have me in my pocket/to get
round like a good woman shd/& make the poem in
the pot or the chicken in the dance/what i got to do/
i gotta have my stuff to do it to/why dont ya find
yr own things/& leave this package of me for my
destiny/what ya got to get from me/i'll give it to ya/
yeh/i'll give it to ya/round 5:00 in the winter/
when the sky is blue-red/& Dew City is gettin
pressed/if it's really my stuff/ya gotta give it to me/
if ya really want it/i'm the only one/can handle it

LADY IN BLUE: that niggah will be back tomorrow, sayin 'i'm sorry'

LADY IN YELLOW: get this, last week my old man came in saying, 'i don't
know how she got yr number baby, i'm sorry.'

LADY IN BROWN: no this one is it, 'o baby, ya know i waz high, i'm sorry'

LADY IN PURPLE: 'i'm only human, and inadequacy is what makes us
human, & if we was perfect we wdnt have nothin to
strive for, so you might as well go on and forgive
me pretty baby, cause i'm sorry'

LADY IN GREEN: 'shut up bitch, i told you i waz sorry'

LADY IN ORANGE: no this one is it, 'i do ya like i do ya cause i thot ya could take it, now i'm sorry'

LADY IN RED: 'now i know that ya know i love ya, but i aint ever gonna love ya like ya want me to love ya, i'm sorry'

LADY IN BLUE: one thing i dont need
is any more apologies
i got sorry greetin me at my front door
you can keep yrs
i dont know what to do wit em
they dont open doors
or bring the sun back
they dont make me happy
or get a morning paper
didnt nobody stop using my tears to wash cars
cuz a sorry

i am simply tired
of collectin
    i didnt know
    i was so important to you'
i'm gonna haveta throw some away
i cant get to the clothes in my closet
for alla the sorries
i'm gonna tack a sign to my door
leave a message by the phone
    'if you called
    to say yr sorry
    call somebody
    else
    i dont use em anymore'
i let sorry/didnt meanta/& how cd i know abt that
take a walk down a dark & musty street in brooklyn
i'm gonna do exactly what i want to
& i wont be sorry for none of it
letta sorry soothe yr soul/i'm gonna soothe mine

you were always inconsistent
doin somethin & then bein sorry
beatin my heart to death
talkin bout you sorry
well
i will not call
i'm not going to be nice

i will raise my voice
& scream & holler
& break things & race the engine
& tell all yr secrets bout yrself to yr face
& i will list in detail everyone of my wonderful lovers
& their ways
i will play oliver lake
loud
& i wont be sorry for none of it

i loved you on purpose
i was open on purpose
i still crave vulnerability & close talk
& i'm not even sorry bout you bein sorry
you can carry all the guilt & grime ya wanna
just dont give it to me
i cant use another sorry
next time
you should admit
you're mean/low-down/triflin/& no count straight out
steada bein sorry alla the time
enjoy bein yrself

LADY IN RED: there waz no air/the sheets made ripples under his
body like crumpled paper napkins in a summer park/
& lil specks of somethin from between his toes or the
biscuits from the day before ran in the sweat that
tucked the sheet into his limbs like he waz an ol
frozen bundle of chicken/& he'd get up to make
coffee, drink wine, drink water/he wished one of his
friends who knew where he waz wd come by with
some blow or some shit/anythin/there waz no air/
he'd see the spotlights in the alleyways downstairs
movin in the air/cross his wall over his face/& get
under the covers & wait for an all clear or til he cd
hear traffic again/

there waznt nothin wrong with him/there waznt
nothin wrong with him/he kept tellin crystal/any
niggah wanna kill vietnamese children more n stay
home & raise his own is sicker than a rabid dog/that's
how their thing had been goin since he got back/
crystal just got inta sayin whatta fool niggah beau waz
& always had been/didnt he go all over uptown sayin
the child waznt his/waz some no counts bastard/&
any ol city police cd come & get him if they wanted/

cuz as soon as the blood type & shit waz together/
everybody wd know that crystal waz a no good lyin
whore/and this after she'd been his girl since she waz
thirteen/when he caught her on the stairway/

he came home crazy as hell/he tried to get veterans
benefits to go to school & they kept right on puttin
him in remedial classes/he cdnt read wortha damn/so
beau cused the teachers of holdin him back & got
himself a gypsy cab to drive/but his cab kept breakin
down/& the cops was always messin wit him/plus not
gettin much bread/

& crystal went & got pregnant again/beau almost beat
her to death when she tol him/she still gotta scar
under her right tit where he cut her up/still crystal
went right on & had the baby/so now beau willie had
two children/a little girl/naomi kenya & a boy/
kwame beau willie brown/& there waz no air/
how in the hell did he get in this mess anyway/
somebody went & tol crystal that beau waz spendin
alla his money on the bartendin bitch down at the
merry-go-round cafe/beau sat straight up in the bed/
wrapped up in the sheets lookin like john the baptist
or a huge baby wit stubble & nuts/now he hadta get
alla that shit outta crysal's mind/so she wd let him
come home/crystal had gone & got a court order
saying beau willie brown had no access to his
children/if he showed his face he waz subject to
arrest/shit/she'd been in his ass to marry her since
she waz 14 years old & here when she 22/she wanna
throw him out cuz he say he'll marry her/she burst
out laughin/hollerin whatchu wanna marry me for
now/so i can support yr ass/or come sit wit ya when
they lock yr behind up/cause they gonna come for
ya/ya goddamn lunatic/they gonna come/& i'm not
gonna have a thing to do wit it/o no i wdnt marry yr
pitiful black ass for nothin & she went on to bed/

the next day beau willie came in blasted & got ta
swingin chairs at crystal/who cdnt figure out what the
hell he waz doin/til he got ta shoutin bout how she
waz gonna marry him/& get some more veterans
benefits/& he cd stop drivin them crazy spics round/
while they tryin to kill him for $15/beau waz sweatin
terrible/beatin on crystal/& he cdnt do no more with

the table n chairs/so he went to get the high chair/&
lil kwame waz in it/& beau waz beatin crystal with
the high chair & her son/& some notion got inta him
to stop/and he run out/

crystal most died/that's why the police wdnt low
beau near where she lived/& she'd been tellin the kids
their daddy tried to kill her & kwame/& he just
wanted to marry her/that's what/he wanted to marry
her/& have a family/but the bitch waz crazy/beau
willie waz sittin in this hotel in his drawers drinkin
coffee & wine in the heat of the day spillin shit all over
hisself/laughin/bout how he waz gonna get crystal to
take him back/& let him be a man in the house/&
she wdnt even have to go to work no more/he got
dressed all up in his ivory shirt & checkered pants to
go see crystal & get this mess all cleared up/he
knocked on the door to crystal's rooms/& she didnt
answer/he beat on the door & crystal & naomi started
cryin/beau gotta shoutin again how he wanted to
marry her/& waz she always gonna be a whore/or did
she wanna husband/& crystal just kept on screamin
for him to leave us alone/just leave us alone/so beau
broke the door down/crystal held the children in
fronta her/she picked kwame off the floor/in her
arms/& she held naomi by her shoulders/& kept on
sayin/beau willie brown/get outta here/the police is
gonna come for ya/ya fool/get outta here/do you
want the children to see you act the fool again/you
want kwame to brain damage from you throwin him
round/niggah/get outta here/get out & dont show yr
ass again or i'll kill ya/i swear i'll kill ya/he reached
for naomi/crystal grabbed the lil girl & stared at beau
willie like he waz a leper or somethin/dont you touch
my children/muthafucker/or i'll kill you/

beau willie jumped back all humble & apologetic/i'm
sorry/i dont wanna hurt em/i just wanna hold em &
get on my way/i dont wanna cuz you no more
trouble/i wanted to marry you & give ya things
what you gonna give/a broken jaw/niggah get outta
here/he ignored crystal's outburst & sat down motionin
for naomi to come to him/she smiled back at her
daddy/crystal felt naomi givin in & held her tighter/
naomi/pushed away & ran to her daddy/cryin/daddy,

daddy come back daddy/come back/but be nice to
mommy/cause mommy loves you/and ya gotta be
nice/he sat her on his knee/& played with her ribbons
& they counted fingers & toes/every so often he
looked over to crystal holdin kwame/like a statue/&
he'd say/see crystal/i can be a good father/now let
me see my son/& she didnt move/& he coaxed her &
he coaxed her/tol her she waz still a hot lil ol thing &
pretty & strong/didnt she get right up after that lil ol
fight they had & go back to work/beau willie oozed
kindness & crystal who had known so lil/let beau
hold kwame/

as soon as crystal let the baby outta her arms/beau
jumped up a laughin & a gigglin/a hootin & a
hollerin/awright bitch/awright bitch/you gonna
marry me/you gonna marry me . . .
i aint gonna marry ya/i aint ever gonna marry ya/for
nothing/you gonna be in the jail/you gonna be under
the jail for this/now gimme my kids/ya give me
back my kids/

he kicked the screen outta the window/& held the
kids offa the sill/you gonna marry me/yeh, i'll marry
ya/anything/but bring the children back in the
house/he looked from where the kids were hangin
from the fifth story/at alla the people screamin at
him/& he started sweatin again/say to alla the
neighbors/you gonna marry me/

i stood by beau in the window/with naomi reachin for
me/& kwame screamin mommy mommy from the
fifth story/but i cd only whisper/& he dropped em

LADY IN RED: i waz missin somethin

LADY IN PURPLE: somethin so important

LADY IN ORANGE: somethin promised

LADY IN BLUE: a layin on of hands

LADY IN GREEN: fingers near my forehead

LADY IN YELLOW: strong

LADY IN GREEN: cool

LADY IN ORANGE: movin

LADY IN PURPLE: makin me whole

LADY IN ORANGE: sense

LADY IN GREEN: pure

LADY IN BLUE: all the gods comin into me
layin me open to myself

LADY IN RED: i waz missin somethin

LADY IN GREEN: somethin promised

LADY IN ORANGE: somethin free

LADY IN PURPLE: a layin on of hands

LADY IN BLUE: i know bout/layin on bodies/layin outta man
bringin him alla my fleshy self & some of my pleasure
bein taken full eager wet like i get sometimes
i waz missin somethin

LADY IN PURPLE: a layin on of hands

LADY IN BLUE: not a man

LADY IN YELLOW: layin on

LADY IN PURPLE: not my mama/holdin me tight/sayin
i'm always gonna be her girl
not a layin on of bosom & womb
a layin on of hands
the holiness of myself released

LADY IN RED: i sat up one nite walkin a boardin house
screamin/cryin/the ghost of another woman
who waz missin what i waz missin
i wanted to jump up outta my bones
& be done wit myself
leave me alone
& go on in the wind
it waz too much
i fell into a numbness
til the only tree i cd see
took me up in her branches
held me in the breeze
made me dawn dew

that chill at daybreak
the sun wrapped me up swingin rose light everywhere
the sky laid over me like a million men

i waz cold/i waz burnin up/a child
& endlessly weavin garments for the moon
wit my tears

i found god in myself
& i loved her/i loved her fiercely

(All of the LADIES *repeat to themselves softly the lines* 'i found god in myself & i
loved her.' *It soon becomes a song of joy, started by the* LADY IN BLUE. *The* LADIES
sing first to each other, then gradually to the audience. After the song peaks the
LADIES *enter into a closed tight circle.)*

LADY IN BROWN: & this is for colored girls who have considered
suicide/but are movin to the ends of their own
rainbows